THE MUSIC PROFESSION IN BRITAIN
SINCE THE EIGHTEENTH CENTURY

The Music Profession in Britain since the Eighteenth Century.

A Social History

CYRIL EHRLICH

CLARENDON PRESS · OXFORD

1985

Oxford University Press, Walton Street, Oxford OX2 6DP
Oxford New York Toronto
Delhi Bombay Calcutta Madras Karachi
Kuala Lumpur Singapore Hong Kong Tokyo
Nairobi Dar es Salaam Cape Town
Melbourne Auckland
and associated companies in
Beirut Berlin Ibadan Nicosia

Oxford is a trade mark of Oxford University Press

Published in the United States
by Oxford University Press, New York

British Library Cataloguing in Publication Data
Ehrlich, Cyril
The music profession in Britain since the
eighteenth century : a social history.
1. Musicians—Social aspects—Great Britain
I. Title
305.9'78   ML3795
ISBN 0–19–822665–9

Printed in Great Britain by
Biddles Ltd,
Guildford and King's Lynn

For three musicians,
    Ruth, Paul, and Robert

Acknowledgements

GRATEFUL acknowledgement is due to the Social Science Research Council for a grant in aid of research. I am indebted for encouragement and advice to Professor Nicholas Temperley, Professor William Weber, and my colleague Ken Brown. For help in illustrating this book I am grateful to the National Portrait Gallery, the Mary Evans Picture Library, and the BBC Hulton Picture Library. Staff at Belfast Public Library, Birmingham Public Library, the British Library, Glasgow University Library, Liverpool Public Library, the Pendlebury Library, and The Queen's University Library have rendered much service. Louise Porter has provided expert secretarial assistance. Finally I must express my appreciation for frequent stimulus and tactful criticism to Andrew Roberts.

Contents

Illustrations

I

Before the Flood

GOLDSMITH. The greatest musical performers have but small emoluments. Giardini, I am told, does not get above seven hundred a year.

JOHNSON. That is indeed but little for a man to get, who does best that which so many endeavour to do. There is nothing, I think, in which the power of art is shown so much as in playing on the fiddle. In all other things we can do something at first. Any man will forge a bar of iron, if you give him a hammer; not so well as a smith, but tolerably. A man will saw a piece of wood, and make a box, though a clumsy one; but give him a fiddle and a fiddlestick, and he can do nothing.

Numbers and problems

In the absence of an official census we can only guess at the number of professional musicians in late-eighteenth-century Britain: on the eve of the great expansion there were probably no more than 2,000. Two attempts were made to list them. In 1763 a 'Nobleman and Gentleman's True Guide to the Masters and Professors of the Liberal and Polite Arts and Sciences' included them because 'a knowledge of music contributes one part of polite education', and gave ninety-five names of musicians living in or near London. The compiler claimed to know of others, who had been omitted because they were no longer practising, or for want of an address.[1] Thirty years later J. Doane published a more comprehensive directory, and promised further instalments, which never appeared. He lists 1,333 'composers and professors of music', including a 'number of amateurs', sellers of instruments and music, copyists, and paper-rulers, and claims to be withholding several hundred additional names until their addresses are received. Taking 'every care to avoid offence to the Profession' he eschews 'anything which might be construed into a judgement' of ability, but apologizes for introducing 'so many Amateurs and Performers of inferior note'. The occupation's notorious mobility also presented difficulties, for he admits to including several musicians who have recently gone abroad, to Italy or such other places as the new theatre in Philadelphia. In addition to each person's instrument and address Doane tries to indicate his status, by noting membership of societies and principal engagements.[2]

A glance through these directories raises several questions of method. How should we attempt to count and describe a profession which embraced extremes of fame and obscurity, genius and mediocrity, mobility and quiescence? Doane lists Dr Joseph Haydn of 18 Pulteney Street, composer and pianist, appearing at the Opera, Salomon's, and the Professional Concerts; and Henry Beaumont, member of the Royal Society of Musicians, playing horn at the Westminster Abbey Concerts. Is the latter the same Henry Beaumont who, as we know from other sources, earned 5s. a day as a violinist at Covent Garden and died in 1791, leaving a widow and three sons in poverty which was temporarily relieved by the RSM's allowance of £8 funeral expenses and £4. 17s. 6d. a month?[3] Some professional musicians have left no record of their lives and work, and for many the most basic information—country and dates of birth and death, social origins, training, engagements, and income—is unavailable or unreliable. Even the careers of successful men have frequently been obscured by subsequent indifference. Dr William Parsons (1746?–1817) who became Master of the King's Music in 1786, was knighted in 1795 'more on the score of his merits than the merit of his scores', and is one of the few musicians to appear in the *Dictionary of National Biography*, has left scant record of his first *forty years*. He was a chorister at Westminster Abbey and failed to get an engagement at Covent Garden, so 'betook himself to Italy for the improvement of his voice and method', returning to a presumably successful career as singing teacher and magistrate.[4] None of this evidence is much use for social analysis.

Contemporary newspapers were recklessly careless in reporting names and places. Thus the solo violinist who appeared at Salomon's concerts in March and April 1795, is variously described as Madame Gillburg, Guilberg, and Guillberg, native of Sweden and Germany.[5] Unreliable, unrepresentative data which have been further obscured by centuries of neglect or carelessness, are inadequate material for an elaborate survey which, if it were undertaken, would imply greater statistical accuracy than the available facts will bear. The problems are familiar and formidable:

In any historical group, it is likely that almost everything will be known about some members of it, and almost nothing at all about others; certain items will be lacking for some, and different items will be lacking for others. If the unknowns bulk very large, and if, with the seriously incompletes, they form a substantial majority of the whole, generalizations based on statistical averages become very shaky indeed, if not altogether impossible.[6]

Lawrence Stone's warning applies precisely to our material, but it appears in an essay which encourages the writing of collective biography. This book implies a similarly cautious optimism. Instead of abandoning the exercise as premature until more work has been done on individual cases, we shall try to give a general portrait of the profession while observing a few elementary safeguards. It is a commonplace, for example, that fame or notoriety leave more trace than mundane working lives. Veneration for genius and appetite for gossip should therefore not be allowed to dominate what is intended to be a representative survey of the group. Similarly, formal or institutional training, which enormously increased during the nineteenth century, is generally better documented than family tradition and self-education, though arguably less important. There are many other pitfalls. Surviving records, for example, tend to distort a musician's social origins: innocently because high birth is better documented, or deliberately to exaggerate either blue-blooded ancestry or childhood poverty overcome by subsequent achievement. Moreover the participants and their agents often encouraged such mythology because social mobility was an essential aspect of the successful career.

Demand

By far the greatest number of mid-eighteenth-century musicians, perhaps some 1,500, were based in London. Apart from the university cities, no provincial centre, except Dublin, Bath, and, for a brief period, Edinburgh, could provide regular employment for more than a score of full-time practitioners; and even their complements never exceeded fifty. The 'Cities and liberties of London and Westminster, the boroughs of Southwark and parts adjacent'[7] comprised the largest, fastest-growing and most prosperous urban centre in Europe, with twice the population of Paris, thrice that of Vienna. It therefore offered more market opportunities, as distinct from patronage, than anywhere else, and acted as a magnet to musicians throughout Europe.

It is useful to distinguish between patronage and the market as sources of the musician's livelihood. Under the former system he was subject to a patron's whim, his bargaining power tempered by immobility and the disciplines of a closely-knit social system which might offer paternalistic benevolence, but exact dire penalties for intransigence.[8] The gradual commercialization of music allowed him to escape into an open society, but imposed new and unfamiliar risks. He lost old forms of security and the privilege of making music for a small, intimate and, perhaps, cultivated circle. He gained a measure of freedom and access to diverse and potentially remunerative, if less discriminating, audiences and pupils. The change is symbolized by Haydn's removal in 1791 from Esterhazy to Salomon's London concerts: 'It is doubtful whether a musician ever made a more abrupt transition from the past to the present.'[9] The image is potent, depicting genius at a precise time and place of fundamental change; but, like most symbols, it also distorts the untidiness of history, implying that English musical life, in contrast to conditions elsewhere, had already made a complete and irrevocable break with the past.

Direct and indirect support from aristocratic patrons continued to be important throughout the eighteenth century, not least to singers and instrumentalists of the first rank who sought access to remunerative performance and teaching.[10] The most remarkable example was John Brydges, first Duke of Chandos and eminent war profiteer, whose musical establishment at Cannons, near Edgware, numbered twenty-four in 1719. Handel was its cynosure; Pepusch its director between 1712 and 1732, with a quarterly salary of twenty-five pounds, room, board (including a seat at the Chaplain's table), and extra cash for writing music and repairing instruments. Humbler talents could procure a pittance and occasional lessons. George Monroe, who later became organist at St Peter's, Cornhill, and harpsichordist at Goodman Fields Theatre, came to Cannons as a page, showed musical promise, was taught by Pepusch and Handel, and employed as a servant and keyboard player at £7. 10s. 0d. a quarter. Other servant musicians included a trumpeter who had deserted from the army, and a boy treble who degenerated into a 'scoundrel butler'. One Ghiraldo (Gherardo or Ghirardo), 'one of my Musick', was selected by Brydges to accompany Lord Carnarvon on his foreign travels as a body servant who 'shaves very well and hath an excellent hand on the violin, and all necessary languages'. The quarterly wages of such men ranged from £5 to £12. 10s. 0d., the latter paid to an oboist, Kytch, whose later destitution was to have significant results.[11] Cannons has been described as 'a first class private music school',[12] even as 'an academy of music, with Handel and Pepusch turning young pages into musicians'.[13] In practice its contribution to the training of professional musicians was negligible. Patronage probably declined after 1770, perhaps because aristocrats became less willing to devote years of study to an instrument, and because the extension of city night-life 'made concertgoing seem rather a tame way of spending the evening'.[14]

Eighteenth-century England witnessed an expansion in the music market, though we should be cautious about its extent until we have quantitative evidence. J. H. Plumb has described the nation's 'cultural poverty' before 1700, without newspapers, public libraries, provincial theatres, picture galleries, or museums. There were virtually no public concerts and very little music was published. Within a century, argues Plumb, all this was transformed by the purchasing power of a 'culture-hungry consumer society'.[15] The growth of publishing, which did not necessarily imply much employment of professional musicians, is more easily quantified than concert life: more notices of concerts may simply reflect an increase in reporting. Sales of printed music expanded enormously after the establishment of Walsh and Hare in 1695, until there were more than 400 publishers in London. In Scotland the six which were active before 1740 were joined by sixty new firms by 1800.[16]

Concert life began to grow. Much ink has been spent in tracing its origins. Again we have symbolic events: December 1672, when John Banister 'opened an obscure room in a publick house in White fryars; filled it with tables and seats, and made a side box with curtaines for the musick. 1 shilling a piece, call for what you please, pay the reckoning, and *Welcome gentlemen*. Here came most of the shack [vulgar] performers in towne, and much company to hear; and divers musicall curiositys were presented.'[17] These 'beginnings of musik in publick in England' are variously described as 'a landmark in the social history of the art'[18] and a fundamental realignment 'from performances where the musician relied for remuneration on the generosity of his listeners, to those where the audience was only admitted if it paid beforehand'.[19] Historians have also drawn upon Hawkins's account of Tom Britton, the 'Musical Small Coal man' whose concerts between 1678 and 1714 employed Pepusch, and were visited by Handel and 'the young, the gay, and the fair of all ranks, including the highest order of nobility'. Britton's 'club', says Hawkins, was 'the first meeting of the kind, and the undoubted parent of some of the most celebrated concerts in London'.[20]

For our purposes it is less important to trace origins and subsequent development in concerts, theatre, and diverse entertainments than to understand that they enlarged the market for musicians. It was a slow, cumulative expansion in employment opportunities, ranging from fairly stable jobs in theatres and subscription concerts to a few days at a provincial festival, occasional professional 'stiffening' of amateur groups, or the band at Marylebone Gardens in 1738, which was 'selected . . . from the Opera and the Theatres to play, from six to ten, eighteen of the best concertos overtures and airs'.[21] Covent Garden employed nineteen orchestral players in 1760, plus a harpsichordist and copyist.[22] After its restoration in 1775 the King's Theatre in the Haymarket engaged up to twenty singers and an orchestra of at least twenty-four instrumentalists, sometimes far more. A popular singer might give thirty performances there, and an instrumentalist play for up to seventy evenings during the season, which lasted from September to the middle of May. There were several concert series, private engagements, and 'benefits' for leading performers. Fashionable artists could pursue a profitable line in teaching, though much of this also had to be squeezed into the season when 'society' was in town. Hence the frenzied activity of Dr Burney, scribbling at his History *en route* to another pupil, fitting a Countess in at seven in the morning, twice a week, because his day was completely filled after eight.[23] Musicians with less talent, or poorer connections, could also find occasional pupils. Even the fiddlers who accompanied strolling companies of actors 'eked out a living by giving lessons in the towns where they played'.[24]

'An Itch of Music'

How did the supply of musicians keep pace with increasing demand? A distinction must be made between Englishmen and foreigners. The latter flowed in from readily available pools of talent, responding quickly to new opportunities in London and personal, economic or political disincentives at home. The flow of English talent was much slower, not merely because audiences were prejudiced in favour of foreigners, as was certainly the case, but because the available pool was very small and could not quickly be replenished. There were practical and social constraints upon entry to the profession. Few people, particularly outside the larger towns, were exposed to enough music to awaken interest and latent talent. Even fewer were ever likely to experience a performance of sufficient eloquence to inspire devotion and commitment. Members of a musician's family might have access to instruments, tuition, and an appropriate environment, both within the family and through professional contacts; outsiders rarely had such opportunities. Instruments were scarce and costly. Square pianos became increasingly common by the 1790s, but at prices upwards of £20 they were far beyond most people's means. A musician's willingness to give lessons might be dampened by any suggestion that his pupil could become a competitor, particularly in places where the market appeared to be small and unlikely to expand. Thus William Gardiner recalled the Leicester of his youth (*c.*1785) when there were only two harpsichord teachers 'who both refused to give me lessons, supposing that I was intended for the musical profession. I was thus left to struggle on as well as I could.'[25] Most parents who could afford instruments and lessons were unlikely to encourage their offspring to confuse a minor social accomplishment with a potential career. If musicians were no longer commonly regarded as 'toys to prick up wenches withal',[26] their image was still predominantly raffish, their prospects too insecure to allow more than dilettante interest.

There can be few more spectacular examples of parental opposition than Ann Ford (1737–1824). Amateur only in the sense that she did not ultimately depend upon music for her livelihood, she also illustrates the unromantic theme that talent is not always dependent upon low birth. Her father was a legal dignitary, one uncle the Queen's physician, another Attorney-General of Jamaica. But her fashionable performances on the viola de gamba and musical glasses (for which she published an instruction pamphlet) and songs to her own guitar accompaniment were evidently highly accomplished. Her subscription concerts took place in the teeth of parental disapproval, sufficiently determined to muster Bow Street Runners around the theatre: dispersed by an aristocratic supporter's threat to summon a detachment of guards. She married the abrasive and litigious Philip Thicknesse, patron of Gainsborough who painted her gloriously, and outlived her husband by thirty-five years, publishing music and several books. Her professional status was once attested by no less authority than the French revolutionary government: widowed and imprisoned while travelling, she was released under a 1794 decree which allowed the liberation of anyone who could provide unequivocal evidence of ability to earn a living.

Parental opposition seldom escalated to Ford-like warfare, but it was usually formidable. Charles (1757–1834) and Samuel Wesley (1766–1837) both displayed precocious gifts and were discouraged by their father with such deterrents as the rejection of appointments to the Chapel Royal and the imposition of a 'thorough classical education'. Both were eventually allowed to enter the profession, despite the continuing disapproval of their uncle John and his Methodist entourage. Samuel later regretted his father's weakening resolve, which had allowed him to join a 'trivial and degrading business to any man of spirit or of any abilities'.[27]

Traditional means of entry to the profession were formal, by apprenticeship, or informal, mainly through the family; and often a mixture of both. Charles Burney is a familiar example, beginning as assistant to his half-brother James, an organist in Shrewsbury who apparently taught him little but imposed the useful drudgery of tuning harpsichords and copying music. He also studied the violin and French with Matteis, son of the famous virtuoso; but his formal indenture, in 1744 at the age of eighteen, was to Thomas Arne, who took him off to London. Again he received little direct instruction, but transcribed his master's music for Drury Lane and Vauxhall Gardens, coached singers, played the violin or viola and passed earnings back to the rapacious Arne. From his thoroughly professional training and servitude he was rescued, on payment of £300 to cancel his articles, by Fulke Grenville, gentleman and connoisseur, who escorted him to higher society. Half a century later John Field's training was similar in many respects, although his background, talent, and ultimate success were of quite a different order. Taught by his father, a Dublin theatre violinist, and grandfather, an organist, his début as a child prodigy was followed by removal to London and apprenticeship for 100 gns. to Clementi.

Ill-used and ill-clothed, but well-taught, he was still deputizing for his master, and handing over fees, after the end of his seven years indenture. Escape came only after a stunning début in St Petersburg and his establishment there as a fashionable piano virtuoso and teacher.[28]

Information about the system of apprenticeship is diffuse and inconclusive. Woodfill argues that seven years was still the minimum term during the seventeenth century, but finds no specific evidence of training procedures.[29] Material for the next century is also scanty, but career guides provide some indication of current opportunities and prejudices. 'A General Description . . . by which Parents . . . may, with greater Ease and Certainty, make choice of trades', published in 1747, attempts to distinguish between music sellers and musicians. The latter are said to practise 'a Science not a Trade, and the Youths they train up are called Pupils, to learn which they do not serve apprenticeships but either attend the different Masters or are attended by them . . . and when they become properly qualified, many of them fall into good places by which they are handsomely supported'. The duties of music-sellers are 'light but ingenious' and 'the shopkeeping part is genteel'. Apprenticeship normally cost about twenty pounds, and an additional three hundred pounds were required to set up a 'middling music shop'.[30]

Campbell's *London Tradesman*, published in the same year, is more realistic and censorious:

The Masters of Musick Shops are supposed to understand Musick and Composition, but few of them do more than mouth the names of the most noted Masters, which they have learned by Rote, and can scarce hum a tune in proper time, but if they new [*sic*] a little more before they set up the Trade, both of the Theory and Practice of Music, they would have a better chance to thrive. If they take Apprentices it is only to keep Shop, not to learn them any thing relating to Musick.

Voicing common sentiments, Campbell urges parents to dissuade their offspring from a dilettante interest in music:

if a Youth is not resolved to turn Musician entirely or has not an independent Fortune I would have him avoid any improvement in singing. If he is obliged to follow any Business that requires Application, this Amusement certainly takes him off his Business, exposes him to Company and Temptation to which he would otherwise have been a stranger . . . a Tradesman who could sing a good song, or play upon any Instrument, seldom or never prospered in his Business.

Campbell's prejudice against the profession, as distinct from mere enjoyment, of music appears to be based upon patriotic sentiment rather than fear of unemployment:

If a Parent cannot make his son a Gentleman, and finds that he has got an Itch of Music, it is much the best way to allot him entirely to that Study. The present general Taste of Music in the Gentry may find him better Bread than what perhaps the Art deserves. The Gardens in the Summer Time employ a great Number of Hands, where they are allowed a Guinea a Week and upwards according to their merit. The Opera, the Play-Houses, Masquerades, Ridottoes, and the several Music-Clubs, employ them in the Winter. But I cannot help thinking that any other Mechanical Trade is much more useful to society than the whole Tribe of Singers and Scrapers; and should think it more respectable to bring up my son a Blacksmith (who was said to be the Father of Music) than find him Apprentice to the best Master of Music in England. This I know must be reckoned an unfashionable Declaration in this Musical Age; but I love my country so well, that I hate everything that administers to Luxury and Effeminacy.[31]

Another guide to careers, Joseph Collyer's *The parent's and guardian's directory and the youth's guide in the choice of a profession or trade*, published in 1761, warns against apprenticeship, and wisely stresses the importance of starting young:

The youth who is to obtain a living by teaching music, or by being a performer, ought undoubtedly to have the natural qualifications necessary to the art; a very delicate ear, and light slender fingers; and these qualifications should be early improved by a good master, at a time when the joints of the fingers are most pliable, and acquire a natural facility in the performance. The youth in learning this science, is not to be put apprentice, but to attend different masters at the expense of his friends, till he has acquired great skill, both in the theory and practice; after which he may be employed as a Composer of Music; he may teach gentlemen and ladies to sing or play on Musical Instruments; may become organist to a church or gain a living by playing at one of the Theatres, Vauxhall, etc.

Music-selling, by contrast, was best approached, Collyer advised, through an apprenticeship, costing about £20, and £400 or £500 to set up 'a handsome shop'.[32]

There were no music colleges, though several were envisaged, with varying degrees of practicality. An early project was Daniel Defoe's 1728 'Proposal to prevent the expensive Importation of Foreign Musicians, etc., by forming an Academy of our own'. It was to be atttached to Christ's Hospital, presumably because of that institution's resemblance to the *conservatori* or *ospedali* of Naples and Venice. Three masters should be employed for four hours a day and paid 'handsome salaries' of £100 a year. Pupils would attend for seven or eight years, and then be bound as apprentices, to 'make them thorough Masters, before they launch out into the World: for one great hindrance to many Performers is that they begin to teach too soon, and obstruct their

Genius.' Their 'operas, consorts or otherwise' would help to defray expenses, to such effect that the total cost of maintaining sixty students need only be £300 for ten years 'instead of £1500 per annum, the price of one *Italian Singer*'. It was, as Brian Trowell has remarked, a 'sane and on the whole very practicable scheme'.[33] In 1762 John Potter published a scheme which Trowell justly dismisses as pretentious and imprecise. It does however embody two ideas which future institutions were to neglect, with dire results. Pupils, Potter argued, should start young, at least two years before the usual time in other professions: if they proved to have no talent then time would not have been lost. Supply must be rigorously controlled: 'Particular care must be taken . . . that the present musicians are no way injured either in reputation or interest, by suffering any of the pupils to deprive them of their present advantages or possessions; but when vacancies happen at churches or in the bands at the play-houses, or any other public places, then these pupils should have a right to be presented.'[34] Potter thus rather lamely evades the crucial problem of how to control supply, except by what modern planners would call 'natural wastage'.

Twelve years later came a project which, unlike Defoe's and Potter's, was devised by experienced musicians, and came close to being put into effect. In 1774 Charles Burney and Felice de Giardini (the eminent violinist whose income had been discussed by Goldsmith and Johnson) presented a 'Sketch of a Plan for a Public Music School' to the governors of the Foundling Hospital. As in Defoe's project, the school was intended to be attached to a charitable institution, for Burney had been much impressed by the *conservatori* on his Italian tour in 1770, and Giardini, of course, was intimately acquainted with that system. They proposed to supervise staff, contribute compositions and assist at public performances (a task already performed by Giardini, who was also a governor of the Hospital) for salaries of £200 a year. Four assistant masters should each be paid £50, and supplies of instruments and books cost another £200 in the first year. There were to be two departments, teaching girls singing and boys composition and various instruments. Those with inadequate musical talent could learn to transcribe, tune, and repair. Pupils would first be recruited from the Hospital and, later, if necessary, from charity schools and workhouses which would contribute to their upkeep. In due course the school might also take paying pupils. The primary aim was to train native musicians to replace foreigners.[35] 'In England', as Fanny Burney declaimed, with inimitable pomp,

where more splendid rewards await the favourite votaries of musical excellence than in any other spot on the globe, there was no establishment of any sort for forming such artists as might satisfy the real connoisseur in music; and save English talent from the mortification, and the British purse from the depredations, of seeking a constant annual supply of genius and merit from foreign shores. An institution, therefore, of this character seemed wanting to the state, for national economy; and to the people, for national encouragement.[36]

The Hospital's governors were apparently delighted with the scheme, for the prestige it would bring and, surprisingly, because they regarded it as a potential source of funds. But, for reasons that remain obscure, it was eventually turned down.

Families

Family tradition has always contributed largely to the supply of musicians. As Francis Galton remarks, 'the inheritance of musical taste is notorious and undeniable';[37] but in most cases nurture was more important than nature. In eighteenth-century England the family was a mainstay, particularly in the occupation's lower reaches, for apprenticeship was expensive, and unable to meet new demands; and alternative means of training, apart from private lessons which catered primarily for amateurs, had not yet evolved. The typical family of musicians engaged in activities which were humdrum and little noticed. We therefore have scant records: few lineages; usually only a shared name, with the occasional individual emerging momentarily from obscurity. The Abingtons, some of whom achieved a measure of distinction, do not appear in modern reference books and may therefore be rescued from oblivion to serve as an example. Three were listed by Mortimer in 1763: Joseph (*fl.* 1710, d. 1774) was a violinist in the King's Music, had 'benefits' at the Greyhound Tavern, Strand in 1710–11 and at Hickford's in 1720 and 1722; played at the Foundling Hospital 'Messiah' performances in 1754 and 1758 (for ten shillings), and was a founding governor of the Royal Society of Musicians. Joseph Abington junior (*fl.* 1763) who played trumpet and harpsichord, was probably his son. Leonard (*fl.* 1763, d 1767) who is listed as a violinist, trumpeter, singer, and composer, was responsible for a number of slight pastoral ditties which were published 'as sung at Marylebone Gardens'. Probably he played there too. William (*fl.* 1774–94) was a composer and 'instrumentalist'. James (*fl.* 1752, d. 1806) attained a little notoriety. We know that he was a singer and King's trumpeter who performed a 'concerto' at Hampstead Long Room in August 1752. We can guess that he was a competent vocal coach, for one of his pupils, Frances Barton, whom he married in 1759, was already appearing at Drury lane and subsequently became a celebrated actress. In her social climb from the street-singing urchin known as 'Nosegay Fan' to arbiter of ladies fashion, Fanny Abington parted from James and paid him a regular allowance 'upon condition that he forbore to approach her'.[38] Mrs Abington's contract at Drury Lane in 1781 was for 18 gns. a week, a benefit, and £500 a year for her wardrobe. It was sufficient for a lady to say 'Mrs Abington wore this' to 'stop the mouth of fathers and husbands'.[39]

Although a balanced collective portrait must avoid undue concentration upon outstanding talent and success, it would be tedious to enumerate too many family sagas of modest competence. One more example may help to illustrate common patterns. James Blake Adams (b.*c.*1749 *fl.* 1794) may have been related to John (*fl.* 1739), an original subscriber to the Royal Society of Musicians. He played the cello at the Westminster Abbey Handel commemorations in 1784 and in the Ancient Music season of 1787–88 (for a £4. 10s. 0d. fee). He also played the organ and violin, and published a few compositions and an elementary treatise which earned him a place in Grove's *Dictionary of Music and Musicians*. James (born *c.* 1771) was probably his son, playing the violin and cello, the latter at Ancient Music Concerts, and organ at Brompton and Hampstead churches. John (*fl.* 1794) played the organ or horn at the Cecilian Society and Surrey Chapel Society. George (1777–1810) was allegedly proficient on violin, viola, cello, horn and trumpet; taught the piano and harp, joined the RSM in 1798. In 1814 his orphaned son applied to the Society for £5 to assist his passage to the East Indies as a steward. Thomas (1785–1858) was more successful, studying under Busby, the prolific musical journalist, playing the organ in Lambeth and Deptford, and consolidating his career by marrying the daughter of a Bank of England official.

Even Jewish families could make a living as musicians, at a time when they were virtually excluded from most occupations and could not be apprenticed to Christian masters.[40] We have considerable, if sometimes conflicting, information about one Jewish family of musicians, the progeny of John Abraham (possibly a musician) and Esther Lyon, sister of Meyer Lyon, a singer professionally known as Michael Leoni.[41] Six daughters were singers, including Harriet (*c.*1758–*c.*1822) a protégé of Arne, who became a fashionable performer at exclusive concerts and a successful composer of ballads; Theodisia (*c.*1765–*c.*1834) a splendid contralto; and Eliza (*c.*1772–*c.*1830) who also played the piano. Three sons were instrumentalists. Charles (*fl.* 1794) played the cello at the Academy of Ancient Music concerts, Handel Celebrations, and the opera house. William (*fl.* 1794) played the violin and viola at the Academy concerts. David (1775–1837) was articled to a Mr Griffiths *c.*1785 and elected to the Royal Society of Musicians in 1799 on the recommendation of the leader of the Ranelagh band. He played the violin and viola, and sometimes sang, changed his name to Bramah, was paralysed in 1827, and frequently received sick relief from the RSM.

There remains to be considered one problematical but most illustrious son. John Braham was born in London in 1774 or 1777, and became one of the most celebrated tenors in the history of the English stage. Neither *Grove* nor the *Dictionary of National Biography* connects him to the Abraham family, but Boase firmly describes him as 'son of John Abraham of Goodman's Fields, London, a German Jew', an opinion which is endorsed by the most exhaustive of modern authorities.[42] Braham sang at the Great Synagogue in Duke's Place and was trained by Leoni (his uncle) who introduced him as a boy soprano at Covent Garden in 1787. After his voice broke and Leoni had fled bankruptcy to Jamaica, he was generously assisted by the prominent financier Abraham Goldsmid, whose social circle included Pitt, Nelson, Salomon, and Haydn. He taught piano for a time while his voice settled, continued vocal studies in Bath and was launched upon a long and prodigiously successful career. The Duke of Sussex was godfather to one of his sons; a daughter became Countess Waldegrave, the social and political hostess; an illegitimate son by Nancy Storace became a minor canon of Canterbury. It is said that as a child Braham sold pencils in East End streets. Certainly he and the rest of the Abraham family experienced the deprivations and abuse of ghetto existence, until their talent brought escape and lifted Braham and Harriet into high society.

Women

We have already encountered several female musicians. Although music was one of the few occupations open to women, apart from domestic service, their numbers were still small by comparison with a later period when they outnumbered men in the profession. To what extent were they dependent upon family tradition? A comparison can be made with the visual arts. According to Germaine Greer

The single most striking fact about the women who made names for themselves as painters before the nineteenth century is that almost all of them were related to better-known male painters, while the proportion of male painters who were *not* related to other painters is nearly as high as the proportion of women who were. The reason might be obvious, but it is also highly significant; for a woman in whose family circle painting was not practised there was no possibility of access to training, except in very unusual circumstances.[43]

Although we are concerned with all musicians, not only those of repute, and cannot be so confident about precise numbers and proportions, it is tempting to borrow this argument. Unfortunately the family backgrounds and career lines of female musicians cannot be reduced to simple assertions. First there were the singing actresses, some of whom earned the highest fees in the profession. Many of them, including the most distinguished, came from musician families. The great soprano Elizabeth Billington (1765/8?–1818) was the daughter of well-known musicians and was taught singing by J. C. Bach and piano by J. S. Schroeter. Nancy Storace (1765–1817), Mozart's first Susanna, was the daughter of an Italian double-bass player and agent or 'fixer'.[44] But some successful singers emerged from far less privileged backgrounds. Anne Catley (1745–89) whose 'extraordinary power of voice and articulation' was recalled by Parke as comparable to Sontag's, was the daughter of a coachman and a washerwoman.[45] Miss Brown (Mrs Cargill c.1756–84) whose achievements included a sensational 'Messiah' in Calcutta and a benefit which netted 12,000 rupees, was the daughter of a coal merchant, whose disapproval extended to abducting her twice and attempting to ship her to America.[46]

A second group of women, more modest in every sense, and therefore ill-documented, was probably small at this stage, but destined to become the largest category of professional musicians. They were a diverse group. Probably the largest element might be described as 'daughter-musicians' who supplemented the family income by teaching and, in some cases, occasional playing. Miss Hoffman, listed by Doane as 'Soprano, Pianoforte, Organ and Harp', lived at 214 Oxford Street with John Andrew Hoffman ('Trumpet, Violin, Viola, Organ') and Master John ('Pianoforte'). Miss May Hudson ('Canto, Organ') was a church organist and sang in the chorus at the 1784 Westminster Abbey 'Messiah'.[47] Robert Hudson ('Organ, Principal Tenor'), member of the Chapel Royal, St Paul's Choir, and the Abbey chorus, was presumably her father or brother, listed at the same address. Miss Burton, organist at Piercey Chapel, Rathbone Place, was probably related (as daughter?) to the celebrated harpsichordist and organist John Burton. These examples among many illustrate a general tendency; but what are we to make of the apparently unattached Miss Bonwick ('soprano, organ')? Was she a precursor of that vast army of spinster music teachers who, despite their unmusical backgrounds, later came to turn knowledge acquired as part of a genteel education to remunerative account?

Women were apparently not yet employed as rank-and-file orchestral players, but a few were beginning to appear as soloists. Madame Deleval and Anne Marie Krumpholz played the harp, and Mme Geutherot the violin at several of Haydn's London concerts. The newly fashionable piano began to offer a profitable line in performance and teaching, later to become endemic, exemplified by the career of Jane Mary Guest (later Mrs Miles, c.1765–after 1814). Daughter of a tailor in Bath, she made her début as a child prodigy, allegedly 6 years old, studied with Rauzzini and J. C. Bach, and attracted court patronage. She played frequently in

London, Bath, and Bristol Hot Wells, published simple sonatas, and taught such pupils as Mrs Thrale and Princess Charlotte.

A final category of female musicians who have received pious scholarly attention are the 'composers': a recent compilation discovers forty-two operating in eighteenth-century Britain. Since published work is the sole criterion, their activities are easily documented. Assessment is more equivocal. The list includes such ladies as George II's wife Caroline, whose 'sacred composition, "Church Call", is still played today before church parades in some army units';[48] and Georgiana Cavendish, Duchess of Devonshire and creator of 'I have a Silent Sorrow Here'.[49] Ann Ford appears, ironically in a feminist book, as Miss [sic] Thicknesse.[50] There are numerous ballad-mongers who would merit attention here if it were likely that their products had been a source of income. One possible contender appears to have ended her productive years in America: Mary Pownall (Mrs Wrighten in England) who penned 'Advice to the Ladies of Boston' and 'died of shock eight days after the elopement of her daughter with a pantomimist'.[51] Mrs Jordan was, of course, a very celebrated actress, Reynolds's favourite, but appears here as composer of the 'Blue Bells of Scotland'.

Perhaps the most significant fact about women professionals in a period of extraordinary risks and opportunities is the diversity of experience, between individuals and sometimes within a single lifetime. Some achieved considerable fame, affluence, and social elevation. Most were less fortunate, even the talented, and several offer sad testimony to the precariousness of the musician's life. Charlotte Brent (*c*.1735–1802) was articled, like several girls, as a pupil to Arne, and became his mistress for a while. After a sensational début as Polly at Covent Garden in 1759 she was soon established as England's leading soprano. In 1766 she married Thomas Pinto, a moderately successful violinist with financial problems, who took her to Dublin in 1770, by which time her career was virtually finished. She died in poverty.

The Davies sisters, daughters of an obscure Irish flautist, are a remarkable example of clogs to clogs in one generation. Cecilia (1757–1836) was acclaimed as prima donna in Italy, where she was known as 'L'Inglesia'; and welcomed at court in Vienna, where she taught the Empress Maria Theresa's daughters (later Queens of France, Spain, and Naples). Marianne Davies (1744–1816) played the flute and harpsichord as a child, but became famous as an exponent of the glass harmonica, which had recently been perfected by Benjamin Franklin, whose niece she claimed to be. During the late 1760s and 1770s the girls toured the continent with their parents, much assisted by letters of introduction acquired through Catholic circles in London. All extolled their virtuosity and virtue, some were written by J. C. Bach to his brothers and to various patrons in Italy. In Milan's 'most respectable inn' they were visited by Leopold Mozart (who recalled earlier acquaintance in a letter to his wife).[52] And so the environment of distinction continues: Burney described Cecilia's 'powers of execution' as 'unrivalled by those of any other singer that had been heard (by 1773) in England'.[53] Yet, a decade later, Lord Mount-Edgcumbe found them 'unengaged and poor' in Florence, where the English residents arranged a benefit concert to send the sisters home. Cecilia made a few more brave oratorio and concert appearances in 1787 and 1791, but Marianne's 'nerves had been shattered by playing so much on an instrument of so peculiar a nature',[54] and she never performed again after 1784. By 1797 they were reduced to teaching lady amateur singers in London, and failed to build a successful practice. Cecilia lived on to a penurious old age, maintained by a £25 pension secured with difficulty from the National Benevolent Fund, a small donation from the Royal Society of Musicians, and gifts from friends.

A talented girl could most effectively escape to prosperous security by means of a 'good' marriage. Thus Cecilia Maria Barthelemon (1770–*fl.* 1827) allowed an auspicious career to fade into calm domesticity, although she continued to write music, publishing six sonatas (one dedicated to Haydn) and some vocal works. Her musical background and education were impeccable. François, her father, was a leading violinist and successful composer, established in London since 1764. Her mother, Polly, was an accomplished singer, one of the gifted Young family who had been apprenticed to Arne, her brother-in-law.[55] Cecilia studied the piano with Schroeter, performed with her parents, and regularly met the best musicians in London. She received a legacy from Mrs Arne and married the son of John Henslow, Navy Commissioner.

Foreigners

If music was one of the very few occupations open to women, it was certainly the only one dominated by foreigners. Immigrant musicians had been familiar for centuries, not merely as exotic temporary visitors, but as long term or permanent residents. The court had been hospitable since Elizabethan days. In 1590 nineteen out of twenty-nine members of the Queen's Musick were aliens, and during the seventeenth century sons and grandsons of immigrants continued to predominate. By the late eighteenth century few foreign names appeared in the court establishment. In 1775 it was made up as follows: Dr William Boyce, drawing an annual stipend of £200 as Master; C. Weidemann as conductor (£100); E. Toms and John Beard (£100 each) as Serj. Trumpeter and Vocal Performer in Ordinary; and a band of twenty-five (£40 each) among whom only one, Scola, had a foreign name.[56] But the anglicizing of the

King's Music indicates less a diminution in the general prevalence of foreign musicians than in the relative size and importance of royal patronage. The court ceased to be a focal point of musical life. At one time it had attracted the best musicians with superior conditions of pay, security, access to fine instruments and artistic stimulus. Henceforth it was to provide little more than a minor source of direct income, and potentially remunerative social contacts for concert engagements and lessons.

Foreigners were present at every growth point of the new music market. In 1710 the orchestra at the Queen's Theatre was observed to be 'all foreigners'.[57] In 1727 Quantz visited what was now the King's Theatre to hear a band, under Handel's direction, and led by Castrucci (Hogarth's 'Enraged musician'); consisting of Italians, Germans, and a couple of Englishmen.[58] A distribution map of Italian composers between 1675 and 1750 shows eighty-three resident in London, only exceeded by the 112 in Vienna; Paris had fifty.[59] The influx accelerated after 1750. Germany was an important recruiting ground for instrumentalists: literally so in the case of military bandsmen, for several regiments brought them back from the Seven Years War.[60] The great astronomer William Herschel first came to England as an oboist in the Hanoverian Guards in 1753, returned in 1757, failed to make a living copying music in London, and joined a Yorkshire militia band. After 1790 refugees came from France, most of them returning as soon as possible. There were even some black musicians, mainly in military bands following the Janissary fashion, although one, Bridgetower, was a distinguished violinist, and the less familiar Ignatius Sancho was a published composer.[61]

Far the largest contingent came from Italy which, with four professional training centres in Naples and four in Venice, all financed by the State, and a network of theatres, was uniquely responsive to new demands. Italian dominance was frequently denigrated as an expensive fad, indulged by idlers who

> Join fashion's circle when my lady doats
> on the soft warblings of Italian throats.[62]

The allegedly exorbitant fees of Italian singers had long been a target, although the market's recognition of rewards due to unique talent was sometimes endorsed in print. Thus when Nicolini's 800 gn. contract was terminated in 1712 Addison, no opera fanatic, complained in the *Spectator* at the loss of 'the greatest performer in dramatic music that is now living, or that perhaps ever appeared on a stage'. Foreigners were attacked equally for remaining to dominate and for absconding with their ill-gotten gains. 'The greatest part of the foreign musicians who visited London remain there', said Archenholz in 1789, 'for as that great city is actually a PERU to them, they do not choose to deprive themselves of the lucrative monopoly which they there enjoy, in regard to their own profession'.[63] Wendeborn observed in 1791 that 'many foreign singers, fidlers [sic] and dancers are extravagantly paid; and if they are the least frugal, they are enabled to return to their own country where they may live in affluence, enriched by English money.'[64] W. T. Parke, leading oboist and garrulous diarist, retails what was doubtless common gossip among English orchestral players, reserving special venom for the castrati: 'That Italian singers receive in this country enormous sums for their exertions is well known; and that they expend very little of it in England is equally notorious.'[65] Farinelli returned to build 'a temple on his domain, and dedicated it to English folly'. Pacchiarotti retired to Italy in 1784, it was said, with £20,000; Marchesi left, after three seasons, allegedly with £10,000.[66] Nepotism, surely unremarkable in these circles, was also a potent source of grievance. The oboist Guillaume Catalani, 'not an exotic plant, but a weed of the Italian soil' was found a place whenever his illustrious sister sang.[67]

Such animadversions are easily countered. Family connections were a normal source of engagements, common to foreigners and natives alike. If singers were peripatetic this was the inevitable pattern of their working lives, imposed by theatre economics and repertory. If they tried to take their earnings home it was, as they frequently protested, to retreat from a climate which ruined their voices, and from the highest living costs in Europe. It was the instrumentalists, Italian and German, and a few French, who tended to stay, and their dominating positions were usually the result of superior training and musicianship, not mere fashion. High fees were confined to a few singers: until Paganini no instrumentalist attracted large enough audiences to achieve the status and emoluments of a star. Many foreigners were poorly paid. George Smart, who played the violin and viola as a youth in Haydn's 1794 concerts for half a guinea, later recalled the foreign players employed by Salomon at 'very low salaries' who wore their great coats at rehearsals 'in order to save their other coats for the performances'.[68] Even Haydn, whose total assets before arriving in London were '500 Gulden in cash and a little house in Eisenstadt: not a very good balance for the most famous composer alive', was gratified to receive a guinea for a lesson. How is such a sum to be assessed: a fortnight's wage for the contemporary English labourer, riches to a Croatian peasant, negligible to the master's aristocratic pupil?

Fees must also be reckoned against the probable vicissitudes of an individual's career. Income was highly seasonal and subject to fluctuations in the economy, changes in fashion, and political events.[69] Always there was the nagging dread of illness or failing technique. Even Wendeborn, whose rosy view of the musician's life has already been noted, acknowledged some of its uncertainties:

I have heared of some receiving a guinea, or half a guinea for a lesson, who now, perhaps, must be content with five shillings. Nay, those that had acquired a kind of celebrity, kept their carriages to wait on their scholars, as is the case in these days with some hairdressers who are in high vogue. Musicians of note are frequently called to private concerts of the rich, where they received four or more guineas for a few hours playing . . . (but) . . . this kind of liberality is at present somewhat lessened.[70]

Musicians worked in a cutthroat market-place, open to anyone and unprotected by trade unions, professional associations, watertight contracts, experienced and reliable agents, or generally accepted codes of conduct.[71] It was common for gentlemen visiting London for the season to attempt to renege on their daughters' tuition fees. It was possible for unscrupulous entrepreneurs to manœuvre a composer into losing hundreds of pounds from an opera which brought them thousands.[72] Harsh circumstances nurtured those symptoms of 'envy and jealousy' which contemporaries were already beginning to perceive as 'the besetting sin of musicians'. It was inevitably exacerbated by the latent antagonism which found expression in Dibdin's 'ballad':

> *Io sono moosic maestro jose come de St. Fiorenza*
> Vid my friend who always made a rule
> To spend the english guinea,
> and laugh at Jacky Bull.[73]

In such conditions it was essential to make hay intensively and selfishly in brief periods of sunshine. Finally we must remember that most contemporary comment concerns a small élite of fashionable musicians, including the floating population of eminent foreigners. Many less talented or favoured practitioners faced similar risks with fewer opportunities to build up reserves against an uncertain future. Even the élite were sometimes hard put to it to keep up appearances, always an essential part of the musician's style of life, and expensive in an age when good clothes were luxuries, costly enough to figure prominently in an ordinary man's estate.

The provinces

From the individual musician's point of view the provinces offered limited opportunities of employment, perhaps a few hundred rather tenuous jobs. Concerts were rare and mainly amateur, sometimes requiring poorly-paid support by a few professionals. Thus during the 1780s Chichester's enthusiasts would meet privately every Friday

evening to play concertos by Corelli, Geminiani, and Handel, the
concerto grosso style being ideal for amateur groups. Once a month during
the winter they would give a public concert, engaging a leader from
Portsmouth and a couple of horns from the Sussex band.[74] Leicester's
subscription concerts began in 1785 with an orchestra consisting of the
vicar and his son, seven other amateurs, and 'the five professors of
music' drawn from two families, who were paid 2s. 6d. a night. The 15s.
subscription was equivalent to only 7d. a concert, with programmes
similar to Chichester's, but still covered expenses adequately.[75] Even
small towns, notably in prosperous East Anglia and Suffolk, made
similar arrangements, though some were less advanced. 'Hull was the
most unmusical place I ever visited (*c.*1790). I attended a concert given
by Mons. Aldy [Alday, a refugee from France] the celebrated violinist.
Scarcely more than half a dozen persons were present, and so few
professors resided in the place that a violoncello performer could not be
found to accompany him; this part was wretchedly performed by a man
upon the bassoon'.[76] No doubt when the actor-manager Tate Wilkinson
described Hull as 'The Dublin of England' he was recalling conviviality
rather than music.[77]

Few of these activities offered immediate prospects, but a fundamental
transformation had begun, both in the pattern of demand for musicians
and in their potential supply. Opportunities expanded with the growth of
towns and their citizen's aspirations. In 1700 Norwich was the second
largest town in England, its population of 30,000 barely 4 per cent of
London's. Only six other towns had 10,000 people, including Bristol,
York, and Yarmouth. A century later Norwich had grown to 37,000 but
fallen to eighth place, dwarfed by Manchester (84,000) and Liverpool
(78,000). The fundamental shift in people and resources which these
figures represent was obviously significant for musicians, and will be
examined in later chapters. At this stage we are concerned less with
locational change than with the general evolution of the music market.
By 1800 there were forty-three towns with populations over 10,000. As
they grew, some of their citizens 'put on London airs', purchasing some
accoutrements of metropolitan pleasures, including music.[78] It was done
with varying degrees of intensity and sophistication, but always with
increasing opportunities for performers and teachers. Meanwhile a no
less significant change was taking place within the profession. During
the seventeenth century professional music-making outside London had
been still largely in the hands of the town waits. They were few in
number: three waits were usual in all but the smallest towns, and even
the largest rarely had more than five. But their interests were well
protected: at least half a dozen towns granted them outright monopolies
of paid performance, and in many more they enjoyed effective immunity

from competition.[79] In 1672, for example, a worsted weaver 'leaving his trade and turning fiddler' was 'complained of by the waits for encroaching on their privileges'. He was ordered to 'betake himself to his trade, and if after Michaelmas he shall not forbear to leave his lazy and idle course of life he is to be proceeded against'.[80] An independent musician could find employment only where there were no waits, or in a few towns large enough to require more music than they could supply. By the 1740s the balance had shifted rapidly and irredeemably in favour of independent musicians, as demand and mobility increased and old regulations eroded. The process can be illustrated with a few examples, chosen not to survey provincial music-making but to illustrate changing patterns of employment.

In the early years of the eighteenth century waits were still patrolling Norwich four nights a week in November and December, and turning out for such celebrations as Gunpowder Plot Day. In 1711 they were equipped with new cloaks to accompany their silver chains and badges, and were now playing bassoons and French horns in place of the obsolete sackbuts and cornetts. But increasingly they had to face competition from independent musicians, both visiting and, increasingly, resident.[81] Norwich had long been the leading provincial town. It was now becoming an important centre for recreation, fashion, and display. Distant enough to be independent of London and the new centres of conspicuous consumption at Bath and Tunbridge Wells, and thus offering some protection to local musicians, it could nevertheless attract patrons and pupils from much of Norfolk and Suffolk.[82] A music society was established in 1724, arranging weekly concerts at inns and the rooms of dancing-masters. Probably the performers at first were amateurs, stiffened by a few professionals. Certainly by the 1740s foreign musicians, with fashionable drawing power, began to make regular visits from London during the slack summer months. In 1746 a Venetian violinist, Antonio Pizzolato, was appointed as leader and offered lessons, prudently requiring his pupils to commit themselves for at least a year. The building of a theatre (which employed seven or eight musicians), assembly rooms and pleasure gardens consolidated this process.[83] Individual waits doubtless found occasional employment on the periphery of this burgeoning market, but their institution, and the protection it once offered, succumbed to competition and became a quaint anachronism. Still functioning at civic banquets in the 1770s, the waits were finally discarded as a costly excrescence in 1789.

Meanwhile independent Norwich musicians waxed in number, if not fortune. The wealthiest parish paid its organist £20 a year in 1717, £25 in 1780. The theatre orchestra's director never earned more than 30s. a week. Such incomes were supplemented by teaching, again ousting the

waits, up to fifteen miles out of town—a day's ride. The leading half
dozen musicians could expect an annual benefit concert, preferably
arranged during Assize or Sessions week, which could bring publicity
and perhaps a profit 'upwards of £20'. Trading, tuning and repairing
instruments were common alternative or additional sources of income.
James Hook (1746–1827) who was later to achieve wealth and eminence
in London as an organist, teacher (making £600 a year from school
pupils), and prolific composer of light music, began his career by thus
piecing together a modest living. The physically handicapped son of a
cutler who died when he was eleven, Hook was an infant prodigy taught
mainly by the cathedral organist, and perhaps by Burney. At the age of
17 he was advertising lessons in guitar, harpsichord, violin, and flute,
and a willingness to tune, copy, transpose, and compose music for voice
or instruments. Within a year he had left for London, and Edward
Beckwith, assistant organist at the cathedral, was attempting to attract
his former pupils. Presumably the lucrative procedure of selling a
'practice' had not yet begun in Norwich.

Several towns with divergent economic and social structures followed
a similar course of musical development. Yarmouth lost its five waits and
gained a musical society and several professionals, including a German
violinist and harpsichordist, J. C. Mantel.[84] Leeds, with a rapidly
growing population which reached 53,000 in 1800, engaged a new
organist in 1757, more energetic than his long-established predecessor,
who began to organize annual benefit concerts, with visiting provincial
soloists. William Herschel, abandoning military music, turned up as a
violinist in 1763 and stayed for three years, teaching and playing at
concerts and private music parties. By 1768 subscription concerts were
being held weekly, and an obsession which was to persist through the
next century began with eighteen consecutive performances of the
'Messiah', every other Friday.[85] It is a commonplace that this habit
penetrated deep into the roots of Northern industrial society. In 1788
Dibdin noted 'the facility with which the common people join together
throughout the greatest part of Yorkshire and Lancashire in every
species of choral music . . . Children lisp "For unto us a child is born"
and cloth makers, as they sweat under their loads in the cloth-hall, roar
out "For his yoke is easy and his burden is light".'[86] Here are the origins
of a great choral tradition which surfaced a generation later; an amateur
tradition, to be sure, but inextricably linked with the commercialization
of music and, therefore, the employment of professional musicians.
Meanwhile in Leeds, as in other industrial cities, there was a steady
increase in their numbers. Some visitors brought diversity. In September
1779 Signora Rossi arrived from Vienna to perform 'most surprising
Feats on the Stiff Rope, also Capers and Elevations with great Dexterity,

Decency, and Elegance'. She played 'on the Violin on the Rope in six different positions, quite new and agreeable' and 'a Solo on the German Flute and a Sonata on the Italian Salterio, a very sweet musical instrument'.[87]

In the West Midlands the locus of employment shifted from Lichfield to Birmingham. Johnson, Garrick, and Erasmus Darwin had established the former city's cultural eminence, and serious music was well provided by the cathedral's musicians, including John Saville, vicar choral and an esteemed Handelian tenor. Music became 'an abiding passion' among the literati, and the inauguration, in 1742, of an annual Cecilia concert was of more than local interest.[88] But by the second half of the century Birmingham was beginning to enjoy a more varied, if less discriminating musical life. Church musicians were again prominent, including Jeremiah Clarke, organist at St Philip's from 1765 until 1803. Described as 'the town's first fully qualified professional musician, in the modern sense of the word' (a claim which begs many questions) Clarke, who later became organist at Worcester Cathedral, also played the harpsichord and taught the violin. Other church musicians pieced a living together from diverse activities: postmaster, concert promoter, music publisher, composer for the theatre. Increasing demand gradually extended the market and allowed more musicians to specialize: the Hotel Subscription Dancing Assemblies; concerts by the Dilettanti Musical Society under Clarke; and ultimately triennial festivals, beginning in 1768, with a local newspaper's hymn to the new spirit of civic pride:

> In other towns, while oratorios please,
> Shall we in gloomy silence spend our days?
> Nor taste of those enjoyments that impart
> Melodious sounds to captivate the heart?[89]

Two cities lay outside these common forms of provincial musical development: Bath and Dublin both acquired musical establishments of some size and prominence, which declined after 1800. Beau Nash's arrangements in 1704 for the entertainment of visitors to Bath included half a dozen musicians, each paid 1 gn. a week. Later, seven instrumentalists were engaged to play mornings in the Pump Room and evenings in the Assembly Rooms for 2 gns. In 1750 Bath probably had a settled population of over 10,000, and could entertain 12,000 or more visitors during the season. By 1801 the population was 33,000 and 147 coaches arrived from London each week. When Herschel was appointed organist at the Octagon Chapel in 1766 the seasonal influx provided numerous opportunities, which could be extended towards Salisbury, Winchester, and Bristol. In addition to playing the violin in the established band, to which he could send a deputy if otherwise engaged, there were lessons, private concerts, and benefits. His teaching practice was built up with an energy and social adroitness rivalling that of Burney in London. At first he was prepared to undertake three day journeys once a fortnight, covering seventy miles on horseback to play and teach in noble houses during the summer months when business was slack in Bath. By 1774 he was giving up to eight private lessons a day during the high season. His circle of pupils was so extensive and fashionable that the Marchioness of Lothian organized twenty private concerts to display their talents, accompanied by a professional quartet. Amateurs and professionals frequently played together. Goldsmith noted in 1762 that 'persons of rank and fortune who can perform are admitted into the orchestra'.[90]

Herschel's principal rival for pre-eminence in this society was Thomas Linley (1733–95) whose claims were strengthened by the talents and beauty of his 'nest of Linnets'.[91] Eight of the twelve Linley children were good musicians, but two were quite extraordinary. Elizabeth (1754–92) was an immensely successful soprano whose admirers included George III, ogling 'as much as he dares to do in so holy a place as an oratorio, and at so devout a service as Alexander's Feast'.[92] Father and daughter also gave a five-hour command performance for which Thomas received £100 in immediate cash. After a spectacular elopement Elizabeth married Sheridan and ended her professional career because her husband wished it so.[93] Thomas Linley junior (1756–78) shared more than a birth-year with Mozart. In 1770 they met in Florence and played duets 'not as boys, but as men' wrote Leopold, and swore eternal friendship.[94] Thomas studied violin with Nardini and composed so much and so well that he might have filled the gap in significant English music between Purcell and Elgar: nineteen of his twenty violin concertos perished in a Drury Lane fire. He died in a boating accident, aged 22.[95]

The rivalry between Herschel and Linley senior culminated in a notorious row which, to the advantage of future historians, was well documented by a tattling press which catered to a readership uncommonly diverted by gossip about musicians. The ostensible causes of battle, an absurd story of misplaced music stands and wounded self esteem, are less significant than its illumination of social and economic conditions among the forty or so musicians then working in Bath. It provides more evidence of precariousness, envy, and jealousy; and proof of the key role played by benefit concerts which Linley expected to monopolize, with Elizabeth as an exclusive attraction. Successful exploitation of such occasions 'on a provincial concert platform might well mean the difference between modest affluence and real poverty'.[96]

A monopolist's power is limited, of course, by his ability to keep out competitors. Bath musicians were protected by distance from London, sufficient to preserve their catchment area but close enough to allow such eminent soloists as Fischer, the oboist, to visit overnight. Since the Bath and London seasons roughly coincided, a musician had to make his base in one place or the other. Linley's increasing commitments at Drury Lane forced him to resign from directing the New Assembly Rooms band. He was inevitably succeeded by Herschel, until 1782, when the royal grant of a £200 annual salary finally enabled the latter to quit music for astronomy. His successor was Rauzzini, for whom Mozart had written *Exsultate Jubilate*. Enough has been said to indicate the size and excellence of Bath's musical establishment; but its days were numbered by the end of the eighteenth century, since it was fundamentally dependent upon temporary fashion. When Haydn stayed with Rauzzini in 1794 he was shrewdly aware of the city's limitations: 'All the inhabitants live of this influx without which the city would be very poor: there are very few merchants and almost no trade, and everything is very dear'.[97] Trade would improve, but not music, though the number of musicians working in Bath increased during the nineteenth century. An 1819 directory lists thirty-six, including traders; by 1826 the total had risen to fifty-eight. But there are no distinguished names, and far more teachers than performers.[98] Bath was becoming 'sedate and dull', its musical establishment narrowly provincial.[99]

In Dublin the Lord Lieutenant's orchestra and the theatre provided basic employment for a colony of musicians who supplemented their income with concerts and lessons in the usual fashion. The quantity of music-making is impressive: during the 1749/50 season there were more than thirty oratorio performances, fifty operas or musical plays, and much instrumental music.[100] But apart from its eighteenth-century prominence followed by decline Dublin had little in common with Norwich, and even less with any major centre of music. The general level was mediocre and provincial, despite occasional, sometimes extended, visits by notable musicians, such as the much celebrated *première* of 'Messiah' in 1742. Professional activity was constrained by geographical and social isolation. An unpleasant journey of several days separated Dublin from London; and the common tendency of colonial societies to caricature metropolitan institutions and manners created an uncongenial climate for musicians. Thus Lord Mornington's Musical Academy was inaugurated in 1757 with the firm rule that 'No public mercenary performer, professor or teacher of music shall ever be admitted into any rank of the Academy on any account whatsoever'.[101]

Eighteenth-century Edinburgh offered even fewer opportunities for ambitious musicians. Its concert life grew slowly for sixty years, flourished for twenty, and then collapsed. At the beginning of the century perhaps a dozen 'downtrodden, underpaid' unfortunates could scrape a living from 'teaching untalented upper class children'.[102] Improvement was largely due to the Edinburgh Musical Society whose fashionable Friday night concerts began to attract some good musicians with direct payments, benefits, and access to remunerative teaching. The former increased from a *total* of nine guineas in 1727 to £641. 18s. 6d. in 1776, the year of Adam Smith's *Wealth of Nations*;[103] the latter can be illustrated by the example of Nicola Pasquali (c.1718–57). Arriving from Dublin in 1752 he remained 'for 6 or 8 months without any Scholler but no sooner did he appear in the Musical room than he had every hour Employed and continued so till his dying day'.[104] The Society's 'brief, but glorious period of power' began with the opening of St Cecilia's Hall in 1762, reflecting aristocratic support which was not sustained. Few immigrant musicians stayed in Scotland, and native Scots had no chance of adequate training. Only music *publishers* were really successful: 'artists in big business and legal intrigue with music as a sideline'.[105]

Representative organizations

Despite increasing demands for its services, the widely acclaimed skills of leading practitioners, and a growing perception of vulnerability, the music profession lacked sufficient coherence to form protective associations. In this it was typically Georgian: as yet 'few occupations were anxious to elevate themselves into formally chartered liberal professions',[106] and a trade union was inconceivable. We should however take note of three institutions which represented respectively the old decayed order and attempts to grapple with the new. The Worshipful Company of Musicians, which had seen better days and was to enjoy a happy revival in the twentieth century, was by now a scandalous anachronism. An expansion of its membership from thirty-one in 1739 to 264 in 1794, which apparently conflicts with this view, has been euphemistically described as 'unselective'.[107] More bluntly the Company had temporarily lost sight of its eponymous function. Hawkins and Burney competed to denigrate its activities, their accounts doubtless laced with snobbery. The former deplored an institution by which 'the only one of the liberal sciences that conferred the degree of Doctor, was itself degraded, and put upon a footing with the lowest of the mechanical arts; and under the protection of their charter the honourable fraternity of musicians of the city of London derive the sole and exclusive privilege of fiddling and trumpeting to the mayor and aldermen, and of scrambling for the fragments of a city feast'.[108] Burney was outraged by its neglect of music and musicians, and even more scornful:

this company has ever been held in derision by real professors, who have regarded it as an institution as foreign to the cultivation and prosperity of good Music, as the train-bands to the art of war. Indeed, the only uses that have hitherto been made of this charter seem the affording to aliens an easy and cheap expedient of acquiring the freedom of the city, and enabling them to pursue some more profitable and respectable trade than that of fidling [*sic*]; as well as empowering the company to keep out of processions and city-feasts every street and country-dance player of superior abilities, to those who have the honour of being styled the *waits of the corporation.*[109]

The Company's official historian valiantly defends it against these 'malicious distortions of the facts' which lead to the 'inescapable deduction' that it had become 'essentially a non-musical body'. Yet he concludes that it had indeed 'ceased to take a serious interest in the Art or Science to which it was dedicated': out of 700 admitted to the Roll of Freedom between 1743 and 1769 only 19 were musicians. In 1794 two out of 264 'Liverymen' and fourteen out of 342 in the 'Yeomanry' are listed as musicians or musical instrument makers.[110] Encroachment by non-musicans was accompanied by failure to prevent 'outsiders' from performing in the City. In 1763 the Company had prosecuted someone for employing non-freemen to play at the Lord Mayor's Banquet, but no official action was taken after a similar complaint in 1801. Like the waits it was obsolete, the practices of a medieval guild proving impotent and irrelevant to the needs of an open profession. Haydn made a private note of the City's musical standards when he attended a Lord Mayor's lunch for about 1,200 people on 5 November 1791. After excellent food and drink there was dancing to 'a wretched dance band, the entire orchestra consisting only of two violins and a violoncello', and an alternative room where 'the music was a little better, because there was a drum in the band which drowned the misery of the violins'. In the great hall 'the band was larger and more bearable' in so far as it could be heard above the drunken 'yelling songs . . . and terrific roars of "Hurrey" '.[111]

More appropriate to the age was the Society of Musicians, which received its Royal Charter in 1790. Established in 1738 as a 'Fund for the Support of Decayed Musicians or their Families' it was allegedly inspired by an incident which illustrates a recurring theme of this book: the hazards of the musician's existence in modern society.[112] Apparently three London instrumentalists, Festing, Weidemann, and Vincent, standing outside the Orange Coffee House in the Haymarket, recognized two destitute boys as the orphaned sons of a formerly successful colleague. Jean Christian Kytch was a Dutchman who had come to England in 1709 and rapidly established himself as a leading player of the recorder, oboe, and bassoon.[113] He became a protégé of the Duke of Chandos, playing in Pepusch's band, and performed frequently at

Hickford's Room and the King's Theatre, including music written for him by Handel. His precipitous downfall, like that of many subsequent unfortunates, has been variously attributed to improvidence, and the vicissitudes of the concert and opera seasons: 1737/8 was a particularly bad year. In any case the experience was sufficiently alarming to persuade musicians of the need for mutual aid. A 'Declaration of Trust' received 226 signatures, including Handel, Arne, Boyce, Pepusch, and Sammartini. By 1755 the 441 subscribers included virtually all of London's leading musicians, and there were 210 honorary members drawn from the 'cream of society'. Fashionable patronage was obviously important for raising funds, both directly and by stimulating attendance at such benefit concerts as the first London performance of 'Messiah' in 1743 and the 'Grand Musical Festival' of 1784 which alone netted £6,000 for the Society. There were also gifts, Handel's legacy of £1,000 being far the most generous, and annual subscriptions, raised from 10s. to 1 gn. by 1794.[114]

Calls upon the fund amply document the casualties among men whose fluctuating incomes failed to provide adequate protection against sickness and age. As the scope of the problem became apparent, benefits had to be administered with increasing caution. The original intention had been that 'no Person or his Family shall receive any Benefit from this Fund, who has not been a Professor of Musick, and also a Subscriber to this Charity, at least one year'. A qualified claimant would receive medical aid, and his widow funeral benefit and a maximum weekly allowance of 7s. unless she remarried. After 1752 membership was allowed only to one who had 'served a legal Apprenticeship to the Profession, or studied and practised Musick for a livelihood, at least for the space of seven Years'. Among later rules there was a reduction of grants to members with personal savings exceeding £20, and an unequivocal restriction of aims:

That the true intent for which this Society was founded may not be misunderstood, it is hereby declared that the allowance is not to be considered as an annuity for every widow, but only for those who are in real want; and that the Members must understand that it was established for the relief of the aged and infirm, and not those whose only plea is want of business, and it is impossible for the Fund to answer the numerous demands which would infallibly take place, if that were allowed.[115]

In addition to restricting benefits to full-time professionals, the Society effectively excluded provincial musicians, who retorted with the protest that they were entitled to 'some relief from that fund which their labour helped to accumulate'.[116] But the problem was fundamental, for specialization depends upon the extent of the market, and men outside

London, even less likely to secure a steady income from music than their metropolitan colleagues, were frequently semi-professionals. Charles Dibdin, always querulous and eager to spot trickery, understood this when he admitted that 'the effort to procure relief for country musicians is however, as extravagantly absurd as it is nobly liberal', though he attacked 'paltry haggling bargains' and insinuated malfeasance: the profits of the Abbey festivities were, he alleged, sifted like flour, and some 'stuck by the way'. The controversy reached a crisis when George Smart, a music-seller and double-bass player, was refused membership on a technicality: he had reported four children when his wife was pregnant with a fifth. Along with Dr Edward Miller, Doncaster organist and pamphleteer in the provincial musicians' cause, Smart formed a rival friendly society, the New Musical Fund in 1786, which accepted provincial members even if they were only part-time musicians.[117]

Smart's son will guide us to the next chapter. We have already met him as a youthful member of Salomon's orchestra. We shall meet him again as the very model of a successful musician in early Victorian England: an achievement which required not merely musical talent but an ability to manipulate the new system. For if precariousness was henceforth to be the keynote of professional life, then good musicianship was an insufficient guarantee against its risks, and a friendly society could offer only temporary and peripheral benefits. Success required new skills.

II

Making a Living

You don't perhaps know that I have already some time been thinking of leaving off professing Musick and the first opportunity that offers I shall really do so. It is very well, in your way, when one has a fixed Salary, but to take so much for a Concert, so much for teaching, and so much for a Benefit is what I do not like at all, and rather than go on in that way I would take any opportunity of leaving off Musick; not that I intend to forget it, for it should always be my chief study tho' I had another employment. But Musick ought not to be treated in that mercenary footing.

(Herschel to his brother, 12 April 1761)[1]

Success in music, at least until the modern age of meretricious 'hype', has commonly been ascribed to talent, training, perseverance, luck, and, in some circles, sobriety. Failures are assumed to be those whose 'itch for music' is unmatched by ability, though a few who do not fulfil expectations may be allowed to have encountered or invited ill fortune by keeping bad company. A vignette by Hawkins expresses the latter sentiment with typical acuteness and pungency: John James, a celebrated organist of the 1730s, whose style was 'learned' and 'sublime', was so lacking in self-interest as to 'prefer the company and conversation of the lowest of mankind to that of the most celebrated of his own profession. To the wonder of all that knew him, his love of an art that has a general tendency to improve the mind had not the least influence on his manners, which were to so great a degree sordid and brutal, that his associates were butchers and bailiffs, and his recreations dog-fighting and bull-baiting.' Affecting the character of 'a blackguard, he indulged an inclination to spiritous liquors of the coarsest kind, such as are the ordinary means of ebriety in the lowest of the people; and this kind of intemperance he would indulge even while attending his duty at church'. He died in 1745, leaving a few songs and popular voluntaries. His funeral 'was attended by great numbers of the musical profession, and was celebrated by the performance of a dead march composed by himself. He left behind him a son, baptized by the name of Handel, who now rows a sculler on the Thames'.[2]

Such behaviour may have been incongruous for a church musician, though it was by no means unique: 'rogue organists' were known to desert instrument and wife.[3] Elsewhere in the profession, excessive drinking and raffish behaviour were common enough. The memoirs of Francis Fleming (alias Timothy Ginnadrake), who led the Pump Room Band at Bath for many years until his dismissal in 1767, relate a rake's progress of loutish pranks, drunken bouts, and vituperation against foreign rivals; riotous journeys in dubious company, and a crazily haphazard marriage.[4] For all its hibernian extravagance, the book portrays a style of life which was familiar among theatre and concert musicians. It helped to create an image of the profession which later generations, becoming obsessed with the quest for respectability, were determined to overcome.

Paths to success

What forms did vocational aspiration and achievement take during the transitional period from rakishness to sobriety? It may be futile to seek consistent patterns. Certainly there was no abrupt break with the past: old styles of life and work persisted. It would also be anachronistic to anticipate modern stereotypes of 'professionalism', in the sense of an institutionalized pride of calling and allegiance to idealized codes of practice: even the medical profession had barely begun to move in that direction. Nor can one discern generally acknowledged forms of training, technical accomplishment, promotion, and hierarchy, for music was long to remain a profession singularly lacking firm career lines of accreditation and advancement. Among the better musicians there was, no doubt, a sense of vocation and dedication to the art; but Herschel's objections to his way of making a living probably expressed what many felt. The need to piece together an income from diverse sources imposed a sense of vulnerability which tended to encourage mercenary behaviour, and the increasing influence of market forces required attitudes and skills more common among tradesmen than artists. If fees were tempting one might relax musical standards, take on more work than could adequately be performed, or send deputies to less remunerative functions. For those bourgeois ambitions there was also the matter of social aptitude and adjustment, which Herschel does not discuss, perhaps because it came easily to him. Few occupations offered so many opportunities to cross frontiers of wealth and class which were closed to most people: entering rich households to play and teach, sometimes mingling with the company or even achieving a degree of intimacy with one's betters. In most cases the crossing was temporary and constrained, to be followed by a return from mansion to garret, the expensive uniform carefully put away for the next engagement. But for many musicians it provided incentives, and for some opportunities, of more permanent social elevation. Such emigrations were hazardous, for few places are less familiar or welcoming than those occupied by an elevated social group, eager to identify and exclude intruders. Success, whether achieved within the profession or by marrying money, required more than musical talents: sensitivity to niceties of social behaviour and confidence to brazen out solecisms, an eye for the main chance, and careful bookkeeping. The latter skill was particularly important.

In a famous passage Max Weber notes a fundamental characteristic of individualistic capitalism: 'that it is rationalised on the basis of rigorous calculation, directed with foresight and caution towards the economic success which is sought in sharp contrast to the hand to mouth existence of the peasant, and to the privileged traditionalism of the guild craftsman and the adventurer's capitalism, oriented to the exploitation of political opportunities and irrational speculation'.[5] In nineteenth-century Britain musicians were forced to abandon 'privileged traditionalism' without always escaping the consequences of 'irrational speculation' by impresarios. Many retained peasant-like time horizons, preferring cash in hand and immediate expenditure to 'foresight and caution'. But for men whose income was intermittent and diverse, 'rigorous calculation' was a *sine qua non* of success.

The lives of three musicians will serve to illustrate these characteristics and experiences. Only one was an infant prodigy, perhaps a genius, but all three rose from humble circumstances to become pillars of early Victorian society. They enjoyed long profitable careers, spanning a period of fundamental economic and social change, during which music itself was transformed by the creation of the Classic-Romantic style, when much of today's standard repertory was created. They differed markedly in the extent to which they attempted to master the new music, but each proved adept at new social skills.

Three success stories

The claim of R. J. S. Stevens (1757–1837) to a place in musical history is based on a few glees, and his appointment in 1801 to the then undistinguished Gresham professorship, which required nothing but a few public lectures. But his manuscript diaries, account book and 'recollections' are a realistic guide to an industrious life which offered opportunities of social, as distinct from artistic, advancement.[6] His father was a clothier and self-taught flautist who actively encouraged his son to enter the profession. Starting as a chorister at St Paul's at the age of seven, Stevens was apprenticed in 1768 for seven years to William Savage, Master of the Boys. For this his father agreed to pay a 'trifling' £10 a year, in lieu of the customary premium. With several other apprentices he lived with his master who agreed to instruct him 'in the Science of Musick in general and particularly in the several Arts and Methods of singing and playing or performing on the Harpsichord and in all things incident thereto' and to provide 'good and sufficient Meat, Drink and Lodging (except in case of sickness or accidents happening to the same Richard Stevens)'. This form of training was probably already inadequate preparation for anything except the organ-loft and elementary teaching, though it was enlivened by opportunities to meet and hear important musicians in London. Certainly his upbringing insisted upon habits of caution and frugality. His father wrote to the 16-year-old boy, remonstrating against high costs of laundry and clothes: 'Your opportunity is by far greater than mine ever was, but you have more Idle ways of Expending.' Such admonitions were taken to heart, as were experiences of meanness and avarice. One month's work as deputy to the organist at the Charterhouse was rewarded with half a crown, which Savage ordered him to return to the 'mean devil': but the boy had already spent it.

In 1775 his apprenticeship ended, and Savage said 'You are now out of your time; and you must henceforward endeavour to get your living. I give you Five Guineas to begin the World with: I hope that you will be industrious and successful: I meant to give you Twenty Guineas, but find I cannot afford that sum.' Stevens 'thanked him sincerely for all his kindness . . . shook hands and parted'. Returning to live with his father he began to piece together an income, singing at glee clubs, including the Anacreontic Society, taking over one of Savage's pupils, a 'Jewess, Serra', and applying for organist jobs. His audition for an Ely appointment, whose present incumbent had taken to the bottle, was a 'perfect service' but failed because the inebriate was given another chance. Instead, Stevens obtained a Goldberg-like position as personal musician to Sir Thomas Robinson, ex-governor of Barbados, amateur architect, and spendthrift director of Ranelagh Gardens. Stevens was supposed to live in and play at dinner, Sunday service, occasionally during the day, and after the old man had retired to bed. Abhorring this 'species of servitude' he was paid off with 8 gns. for six weeks work, which he considered 'very handsome'. Having a 'smattering of the violin' he went to the leading player, Barthemelon, for weekly lessons at a cost of 5s. 3d., but had to give up after twelve because his teacher had fled from debt. Finding other violin teachers 'superficial' he abandoned his attempt at self-improvement, though his violin once earned him half a guinea playing at a 'Crown and Anchor' benefit concert.

Through Barthemelon he secured an engagement to sing at two concerts for Arne. After repeated attempts to extract his fee of two guineas from that 'strange, improvident, imprudent, extravagant mortal'

he finally confronted him and 'made a present' of it. Other contacts were
to prove more remunerative. In 1779 when he was teaching four young
ladies at a Dulwich school (4 gns. each per annum) a chance meeting
opened new opportunities. After playing the spinet and singing to a Mrs
Harvey he was engaged to teach her natural daughter, Miss Thurlow,
whose father was the Lord Chancellor, a formidable patron. There were
difficulties at first. The young teacher discovered that 'the elementary
part of most sciences is perplexing to most minds' and, 'too eager' in his
instruction of Miss Thurlow, reduced her to tears and her mother to 'a
violent passion'. Ordered from the house—'my daughter shall not be made
miserable by you, nor any of your *nasty musick*', he 'walked out very
quietly . . . surprised at the vulgarity' but was soon reinstated. Another
pupil was daughter of a prosperous upholsterer and cabinet-maker who,
after six months of lessons without paying a penny, made 'a violent
scene' when presented with the bill and threw money on the floor, in
front of 'twenty working women'. Thus Stevens learned the duties of a
music master, to such effect that he was soon able to build up an
extensive practice. He was helped in this by several organist appointments with small stipends but useful prestige, at St Michael's Cornhill
(£40 a year), Inner Temple (£25) on Lord Thurlow's recommendation,
and the Charterhouse (approximately £60). Thurlow raised his fee (the
correct procedure: one waited, one did not ask) from 5s. 3d. to 7s. and
later 10s. 6d. a lesson. He also supported Stevens's private concerts,
similar to Herschel's in Bath, for doting relatives by select pupils, with
the assistance of 'an admirable instrumental band' which, in 1790,
included such leading professionals as Lindley and Cramer. There were
other contacts with the profession: a setting of 'Who is Sylvia?' was sung
in a Covent Garden production of *Two Gentlemen of Verona*, and he sold
the copyright of *Sacred Music* (selections from the most esteemed
composers) for 100 gns.

But the main source of Stevens's income was elementary teaching of
keyboard and voice at schools for young ladies. The incessant, but
remunerative drudgery is meticulously recorded in his diary: a typical
week in November 1802 began with three Sunday services, proceeded
to assorted 'privates', singing pupils, and a Gresham lecture on 'Hebrew
Music' (the chair brought him £100 a year), and culminated in three
eleven-hour days at a school which paid him £596. 11s. 9d. that year. In
December 1803 he was adding military training to this appalling timetable, having joined the Volunteers in anticipation of Napoleon's
invasion. Eleven hours of teaching was common, thirteen possible
'though not well'. In 1806 his income was a little over £800 and he gave
£70 to charity, but the year was 'quite barren in composition. I could not
bring my mind to attempt it.' It has been suggested that his

unproductiveness and apparently declining interest in music during this period were due to 'amatory sufferings'—he had been rejected by a former pupil, Anna Jeffery, whom he was to marry a decade later.[7] There are more mundane explanations: making a 'respectable' living left little time for music; artistic creation required leisure and intellectual stimulus beyond the resources of a girls' school. In the circumstances it is less surprising that his taste remained narrow and conservative than that he retained any appetite for music. His working life aptly confirms Herschel's apprehension, quoted at the beginning of this chapter, and illustrates the complaint, by one of Stevens's contemporaries, that an English musician 'must toil to his knowledge and his acquisitions through a routine as common as the drudgery of any mechanical trade'.[8] Such drudgery would continue to be the common experience of apparently successful musicians. Thus Walter MacFarren, professor of piano at the Royal Academy of Music from 1846 until 1903 (*sic*), organist at Harrow, composer and prolific editor of standard classics, spent two days a week between 1852 and 1862 at a 'seminary for young ladies', teaching piano and singing to four pupils an hour from 9 a.m. till 7 p.m., his account never fully paid.[9]

Stevens's progress was further advanced when another highly placed friend secured him the post of music master at Christ's Hospital (£40 a year), his rival 'a man of genius and ability but by no means a gentleman in behaviour'. The risks of failure were brought home when an old colleague called on a begging visit: a former apprentice of Pepusch and deputy organist at the Charterhouse, now 'aged, feeble and poor', he was grateful for half a guinea. In 1810, aged 53, Stevens finally married Anna, who was now 42, and began to relax. She brought him £8,000 and an additional settlement of £6,000 invested at 3 per cent, but only on condition that he resigned most of his appointments, retaining only the Charterhouse organ and Gresham chair. His expenditure doubled that year. The marriage was long and happy; there was even a son, and Stevens maintained a gentlemanly interest in music, preferably old music, into ripe old age.

The potential talents of William Crotch (1775–1847) were less equivocal. His biography is readily accessible and need not be recapitulated here, but the unpublished papers reveal something of the environment in which a musician of brilliant promise had to make his way in England.[10] He was an entirely self-taught infant prodigy, son of a carpenter and a grasping, empty-headed mother who began to tour him mercilessly when he was three. The family's sole contribution to his education was to provide a home-made organ, which stimulated his initial interest; teach the names of the notes (long after he had begun to tour); and procure 'a very absurd' fiddle which prevented him acquiring a proper technique. Having astonished countless audiences with his tricks, charmed the Royal family, and moved Dr Burney to present a report to the Royal Society, he received a rude shock on arriving 'at an age when children who had received instruction played better'. Later he was to recall these wasted, distorting years with benevolent indulgence: 'I heard my mother perpetually advised to place me under some good musician, but if she duly appreciated such counsel (and no wonder if she did not) she had not the means of following it. I blame no one. I see not what else could have been done for me.'

When his education was taken in hand it was by men with firm ideas about the status of musicians and the learning appropriate to a higher calling. His patron, the Rev. A. C. Schomberg, tutor of Magdalen College, wrote to the seven-year-old: 'Unless it be your highest ambition to become an organist in a country town, to teach ladies at thirty shillings a quarter, and a guinea extra for riding a hack around the neighbourhood, with a profitable engagement at two genteel boarding schools. I say unless this be your highest ambition something must be learned besides the gamut and the fingerboard.' Bored by Latin, Greek, and Italian, in preparation for the University and Church—'I could learn nothing. I could teach myself anything' —he had to find his own musical education, albeit in convivial and learned company. At the age of eleven he became assistant to the septuagenarian professor of music at Cambridge, playing services daily, and six, sometimes seven times on Sundays, presiding at concerts, and assimilating a large repertoire. Cambridge did its best for him, offering musical stimulus and generous friends, but it could not compensate for the boy's lack of rigorous training in the art and technique of music, the gamut and keyboard so despised by his learned mentors.

His subsequent career was successful, within the narrow and parochial confines of English academic appointments, occasional concerts, and a small output of compositions for which even devotees can find only mild praise. This failure to fulfil early promise has been attributed by his hagiographer to 'the harsh musical environment in England' which apparently refers primarily to his countrymen's 'indifference to music from any mere Englishman', although allowance is made for his lack of adequate professional instruction.[11] The argument is too fragmentary to be convincing, and there are opposing views. Fétis, for example, considered that Crotch's reputation as 'the most learned of the English musicians' was 'no great compliment to English musical science', resting solely on 'an obscure work in which the facts are ill-classed, the views of art superficial, and of reasoning not a particle'. His name was 'not known beyond the limits of his native country' his career 'an instance of the little dependence that can be placed on precocity of talent'.[12]

But the fact remains that Crotch continued to generate intellectual and artistic energy throughout a long working life, which was thinly spread over a wide range of activities. In this respect he is a more significant and more tragic figure than Stevens, despite their similar worldly success. He acquired the Chair of music at Oxford at the age of 21, and became the first principal of the Royal Academy of Music in 1823. His teaching, more extensive and varied than Stevens's, was also more remunerative: 15*s.* a quarter for professional pupils, and one guinea for amateurs. It probably absorbed too much time, without degenerating into the drudgery practised by Stevens, but we cannot be sure of this. If the society in which he moved provided inadequate stimulus to his talent, he did at least maintain contact with live music and musicians although, like Stevens, he eschewed the theatre. Occasionally he could command high fees: for presiding over the music at an Oxford academic ceremony in July 1810, when Braham and Catalani were among the performers, he received £542. He was also capable of insisting upon professional standards. At a St Paul's concert in May 1815 he found 'the performers different at the performance to what they were at the rehearsal' and resigned. This early brush with the deputy system is a good point at which to leave him, although his last public appearance, as organist at a Handel festival, was in 1834. His estate included a fine library and property valued at £18,000.

Both Stevens and Crotch learned how to climb social ladders, but neither established himself with the zest and assurance of Sir George Smart (1776–1867) whose beginnings were equally obscure, though he did have the advantage of a musician father. Moreover the punctiliousness which enabled him to become a leader of English musical society also ensured thorough documentation of his career. There is a published version of these copious papers which has been dismissed, with some justification, as negligible.[13] Certainly the original manuscripts are more useful for our purposes because they chart his social climb, the costs and benefits of each step, with great candour.[14] They also provide fresh insights into the education of a musician in a period before that process became newly institutionalized. 'Professional' has come to mean many things. In Smart's youth a professional man was recognized by his demeanour and apparently expert knowledge. But what kind of expertise was appropriate to a musician, and where was it to be sought? Clearly not at university where, as Crotch discovered, only classics and mathematics were taken seriously and education was strictly non-vocational. Nor in apprenticeship, which, except perhaps for church musicians and rare cases like Field's attachment to Clementi, was degenerating into a repository of obsolescent skills.

The most fascinating aspect of Smart's career, apart from his adroit manipulation of the social and economic environment, is his systematic acquisition of expertise, of a new kind and breadth: for Smart became England's first orchestral conductor. The term requires care. It is misleading to describe him as 'the authoritative exponent of the works of Haydn, Mozart and Beethoven'[15] because this implies standards of orchestral discipline and interpretation which were unknown to London for at least another generation. When a pianist played Chopin's first concerto, with its easy orchestral part, at a Philharmonic Society concert in 1844, a critic noted that he was 'fettered by the discordant beatings of no less than three different individuals, viz.—Sir George Smart, who wielded the baton—Mr Loder, the leader of the evening—and Mr T. Cooke, *not* the leader of the evening. These gentlemen were all beating different times.'[16] But this was late in Smart's career. He had been an innovator. Ten years earlier he was reported at a Westminster Abbey festival 'not playing himself, but beating time with a baton. This method has long been pursued abroad, but was not introduced into this country till very lately.'[17]

Smart was probably not particularly skilled in any single branch of music. Playing second violin or viola in Salomon's concerts required little technique, even by the modest standards of the period, which he acquired in a few lessons from Garaboldi, a double-bass player. The well-known incident of his instruction in timpani from Haydn, 'very elementary' in his own words, simply means that he was shown how to hit a drum. His alleged prowess as a keyboard-player is not attested by substantial appearances as a solo pianist, but he had lessons on the new instrument from J. B. Cramer, which he later ascribed to his father's good judgement. As an organist he gained some esteem, but his playing excluded the use of pedals, long after such abstention ceased to be professionally acceptable. His compositions were unimportant but, unlike Stevens, for whom much contemporary music was too 'boisterous', he was not confined to the organ-loft, glee club, and schoolroom. The most perceptive account attributes his status as a conductor to 'his social position, administrative ability, punctilious accuracy, and thorough knowledge of performing traditions'.[18] One might question the latter claim which Smart derived, as a Handelian, from his experience as Joah Bates's assistant, turning pages and correcting parts for that direct link with the master. Performing tradition is an elusive concept, at least for times before the gramophone began to provide incontestable evidence. 'Social position' is the keynote, but it had to be acquired.

Smart began as a chorister at the Chapel Royal, leaving in 1791 to work as an organist at St James's Chapel, Hampstead. At home, in the music shop, he taught the piano, handing the fees to his father in payment for board, lodging, and clothes, but receiving 2s. 6d. a lesson for teaching his brother and sister. He also assisted Dr Arnold, with a salary, at Westminster Abbey, where on Sundays the organ-loft was 'crowded with talented professors'.[19] In addition to the fiddle lessons and jobs already described he sang bass in the Italian Opera House chorus for Gluck's 'Alceste' and Handel's 'Acis' in 1795. Non-musical acomplishments were also cultivated: he becomes a mason, takes French and Italian lessons, receives his Freedom at Grocer's Hall (which certainly does not mean that he became a grocer),[20] joins the Volunteers, like Stevens, but is promoted to Sergeant, then Lieutenant (the uniform cost £12. 10s. 0d.). Income is procured from various sources, and carefully noted. Arnold secures his first school pupils, after audition by a deaf 'expert' who is hoodwinked by spectacular sight-reading, and £2. 8s. 0d. a week for 'presiding at the harpsichord' for a summer season of opera. He sells the copyright of a piano 'lesson' to his father for £20, and records a profit of £48. 10s. 0d. on 'books, pianoforte, flute, etc. sold to Captain F.' By 1801 he is well established: in addition to London appointments he makes 'professional visits' to Bristol, Bath, and Trowbridge and spends part of the summer working in such places as Hastings, Dover, and Maidstone. So frequent are his out-of-town journeys that he has to take furnished lodgings in Hornsey for 1 gn. a month; but they enable him to purchase the lease of a Portland Street house for £850, with the assistance of a £300 loan from John Broadwood, who also gives him a grand piano.

Smart's education continues with seven lessons in chemistry, and a visit to France, accompanied by father and brother, at a cost of £55, including purchases of music. He notices that musicians at the opera in Paris 'are on a yearly salary, they play three times a week all the year around and are allowed a pension for life when too old to sing or play. This is proper, for after a man has contributed the prime of his life to the amusement of the public it is but right that they should contribute to his comfort when he is no longer able to earn for himself.' In England a musician must cultivate his own garden, and keep careful accounts. Smart steadily amasses capital, income, clientele, and entourage. In 1804 his 'Aeolus Frigate Contredanse' has 'a large sale and handsome profit': the frigate attended the Royal yacht and his piece was 'danced by the Royal ladies'. He keeps a horse and chaise and, in 1806, returns his 'Income Paper' (for tax) at £300 a year plus £55 for the house. His social contacts include leaders of music and society: Mrs Billington and the Storaces; dinner at Lady Hamilton's with Lord Nelson present. He conducts a concert for the Middlesex Hospital under the patronage of the Prince of Wales, and organizes functions for such ladies as the

Countess of Charleville. He sells some glees for £42 and is presented with £20 for assisting at a Billington-Braham benefit, noting a dishonest ticket official: 'they were satisfied with the receipts but I was not'. His business acumen leads him to make a sensible arrangement to halve fees with his apprentice assistant, for school pupils whom he cannot himself attend, thus avoiding the drudgery of a Stevens or sharp practice of an Arne. In 1812 master and assistant each made over £120 by this device. Meanwhile the Duke of Sussex has become a friend: with expensive tastes—it costs £20. 17s. 6d. to dine him—but of inestimable worth as patron and guide.

The year 1811 was a watershed. Conducting in Dublin (his assistant taught during his absence), Smart was knighted by the Lord Lieutenant. This was the most costly and, presumably, profitable, of his social outlays: nearly £200, including £51. 10s. 8d. to the Lord-Lieutenant's household and £4. 12s. 3d. for registering his coat of arms. He could now fry succulent fish: a quartet party at the Marchioness of Douglas, with Weichsel (Mrs Billington's violinist brother) and the cellist Lindley, the hostess playing a violin part on the piano under his 'superintendence'; a concert and fête at the Earl of Shrewsbury's, Bryanston Square, 'a most magnificent affair—ripe grapes were strung up in passages to the rooms' (£18. 8s. 6d.). The first of many oratorio seasons began at Drury Lane and, in 1816, visits to Liverpool and Manchester with the singer Miss Goodall who, according to Sainsbury, was 'remarkable for a sweet and elegant style, for the purity of her public manner, and her goodness in private life'[21] (terms for both £145; expenses £52. 17s. 6d.). Not all concerts were so profitable: four at the Dublin Rotunda, entailing an absence of ten weeks, brought only £24. 7s. 0d. after paying all expenses. But the general trend, social, financial, and musical, is steadily upwards. In 1821 he performs at three Royal concerts and converses amiably with the King, who congratulates him on the sort of response 'which will carry you through every Court in Europe'. In August 1825 he meets Weber in Coblenz (the composer was later to die in his London house), accompanying the Covent Garden manager to discuss 'Oberon';[22] and then visits Beethoven in Vienna to get advice on tempi and hear the new quartet, op. 132.[23] In the following year he signs a three year contract at Covent Garden which guarantees a minimum annual income of £1,000. He had also been appointed organist at the Chapel Royal: dining at the same cookshop he used to frequent when deputy to Arnold he noted that appetite and humility were unchanged, but the 1s. dinner was now 1s. 2d.

Social position did not debar discreet trade. Between 1832 and 1861 Smart lists commissions totalling £1,092. 17s. 7d. from Broadwood, Chappell and Erard for recommending pianos, and 8s. 9d. from Novello for a copy of Hawkins's History. There are also intriguing niceties of court etiquette to be mastered: he introduces the pianist Mrs Anderson, who 'declines payment' for playing at Kensington Palace, and then recommends her as teacher to Princess (later Queen) Victoria. Ultimately the Queen settles a pension of £100 on Mrs Anderson, with Smart as trustee. Fees might be supplemented by 'Royal Munificence', on which the Master of the Queen's Music would seek Smart's advice. His responses to such requests merit attention because reliable information on musicians' fees was, like the 'trade' price of pianos, customarily obscured by coy reticence.[24] For an 1825 concert Signor Velluti asked the highest 'professional terms' (£13. 10s. 0d.) and Smart suggested that he should receive £42. Last of the great Italian castrati, Velluti was arousing controversial interest as the first of his species to be heard in London since 1800, and had scarcity value. Mme Cardori, like several other leading singers, asked 10 gns. and was to be paid 15 gns. A celebrated Cherubino, she had been appearing with Velluti in a Meyerbeer opera at Drury Lane. Prominent instrumentalists, including Lindley and Dragonetti, were to receive 8 gns. instead of their customary 5 gns. Smart's normal five guineas was to be doubled, and the same arrangement was made for Thomas Attwood. The latter, who had studied composition with Mozart, was a favourite at Court, described in 1800 as one who 'in addition to musical science . . . possesses the well cultivated understanding of a *gentleman*'.[25]

For the Duke of Sussex's concert at Kensington Palace on 28 July 1830, Mrs Anderson, Attwood, and Smart respectfully declined payment. Others received 3, 4, and 5 gns. These occasions usually made few musical demands upon the artists: a couple of arias or drawing room pieces would normally suffice. There was a distinction between dinner parties, for which a common fee was 3 gns., and (private) concerts for which 5 gns. was asked. At St James's Palace on 28 May 1836 the concert began at 9.35 and ended two hours later. It consisted of arias and ensembles by Rossini, Bellini, and Balfe (who took part); madrigals, and variations for violin and piano by Czerny. The total cost was £157. 10s. 0d. Smart presided at the piano and paid the musicians at his house. He also organized the royal Entertainment at the Guildhall for Lord Mayor's Day, a notable feat of management, accounting, and discretion. On 9 November 1837 there were forty-nine performers. Two singers were paid 5 gns. and nine received 3 gns. Rank and file instrumentalists got 1 gn. and principals two, except for the clarinettist who earned 3 gns. The latter player was Thomas Willman, master of the Grenadiers' band and principal at the Opera. Skilled clarinettists were evidently still rare and expensive. Smart received an inscribed 'cadeau' for arranging everything, even the allocation of wine to the performers: twenty-nine bottles were drunk, twenty-eight tickets returned.

Towards the end of his life Smart summed up his work with typical statistical precision.[26] Between 1798 and 1858 he had conducted 1,494 concerts, taught approximately 110 professional students, some 550 school and 602 private pupils. It was indeed a 'blameless and unsullied life', as Sullivan wrote to Lady Smart,[27] and one of such prodigious energy and self-improvement as to qualify for a place in the Samuel Smiles pantheon. It was an extraordinary achievement for the son of a musician shopkeeper to become an eminent Victorian, enjoying the freedom of Dublin and Norwich, and presiding over Philharmonic Society concerts, to which a tradesman was admitted only on assurance that he never served behind the counter.[28] Much of Smart's success was directly attributable to commercial acumen: 'A more rigid and methodical man of business I never met', wrote the experienced singer Henry Phillips, with warm approval.[29] Even more remarkable is the fact that he achieved eminence without leaving the music profession. It is instructive to compare his career with that of an illustrious predecessor. Charles Burney's 'chief ambition and achievement was to be accepted as a man of letters'. Half way through his career Burney sought, quite self-consciously and without precedent, to transcend the social limitations of his profession, and was 'duly rewarded with an equally unprecedented welcome into the most distinguished intellectual and social circles of his time'.[30] We cannot be sure that the man who became Weber's champion and Beethoven's acquaintance, 'Sir Smart', won equivalent acceptance. Certainly the intellectual and social status of musicians continued to be questioned in England long after his death. In 1868, when the eminent conductor Costa's candidacy for the Athenaeum club was blackballed, it was said that Smart had been elected, not as a musician, but as a knight.[31] Musicians remained below the salt, but Smart's example was significant, for what scope could there be in a profession whose ablest members sought approval by leaving it?

Mid-century appraisals

'What shall we do with Music?' asked the Revd. Peter Maurice DD of New College, Oxford, in 1856.[32] Since his pamphlet appeared, under that title, in the form of a letter addressed to the Earl of Derby, Chancellor of the University, its message is obscured by donnish verbiage and tedious parades of learning. But Maurice was a sympathetic observer who desired improvement, so his snobbery is the more illuminating. The great barrier to music's advancement is 'the disrespect it meets with from that very class which ought to be best able to appreciate its desserts. A Musician, let him be ever so talented and exemplary in moral conduct, ranks scarcely above an ordinary artizan; and nobody seems competent to award him his proper place.' Skill, dedication, and musicianship are insufficient to please, for 'a man that is all Music is no better than a mere sportsman, or any other enthusiast'. Given 'a proper educational training' musicians 'would be as sensitively alive to all the requirements and most delicate adjustments of social etiquette as they, unquestionably, are well versed in all the harmonic etiquette of the orchestral beau monde'. There need then be 'no discussion as to the accidents of their position in the circle, or their place of reception and entertainment. No misgivings as to whether the small drawing-room, the lower library, or servants' hall, might be appropriated for their accommodation.' The learned writer has no exact prescription for betterment, though he is gratified by the spread of education. The number of Oxford music graduates has increased from seven, between 1800 and 1830, to thirty-four plus five doctorates in the years since. In no other country is music so honoured, by degrees conferred at Oxford, Cambridge, Dublin, and by the Archbishop of Canterbury. Such increased study of 'the Science' indicates that the status in music will soon 'bear comparison with its most palmy days in England'. The presence of instruments in Oxford colleges, including 125 pianos and 30 concertinas, which some undergraduates can play but do not 'lest it should interfere with other studies', is further evidence that 'music is taking the lead'. This is a 'marvellous change' since the 1820s, when hardly a college had a piano. Yet the performance of academic exercises is 'a burlesque, an academic sham' which 'shows us either as utterly destitute of discernment or stupidly indifferent of everything else, except our Latin and Greek'. Outside the university there has been so great an increase in the provision and desire for musical education that future schoolmasters will require appropriate qualifications. And so Maurice ifs and buts his way through a rambling discourse, always concerned for the elevation of music and musicians, always convinced that it can be achieved only by academic education and examinations: a quintessentially mid-Victorian belief.

More down to earth, but pursuing similar themes, is a contemporary, much consulted, book on the choice of a profession.[33] Of all professions, wrote Byerly Thomson, its lawyer compiler in 1857, music is the 'most undefined and vague'. Law, medicine, and the church assign 'a certain position in the social scale', but a musician may be 'an itinerant fiddler, and of the lowest grade of society; or a man of the highest attainments, moving in the most exclusive circles, and occupying an exalted position in the literary world'. Note that, as with Burney and Crotch, it is the literary, not the musical world which must be appeased. The reason for so 'undefined' a status is that 'music is altogether unprotected. Its portals are open to all who choose to enter'.[34] The remedy lay in close adherence to formal training and certification, to which Thomas devotes respectful attention, quoting Maurice, and listing the regulations of Universities and the Royal Academy of Music. He also makes a brave attempt to classify the profession 'without impropriety' in three categories, theoretical, practical, and critical. Composers can expect to earn practically nothing, as such. While a 'respectable London professor of the pianoforte will make from £400 to £800', several must realize by teaching alone at least £2,000. Leading vocalists notoriously earn 'enormous sums'. London parochial organists get an average of £50, 'cathedrals about £150 and sometimes a house'. Such appointments also give 'a certain position, and are calculated to afford an advantageous introduction'. Cultural levels vary considerably. Successful singers and instrumentalists must practise so incessantly that 'all else in the way of education, literary or musical, is but too frequently sacrificed'. But some have not allowed music to 'monopolise so much of their time as to necessitate the total neglect of every other kind of mental culture'. Indeed many 'occupy a good position in society and have received a liberal general education'. The profession 'offers ample scope for the exercise of the highest *literary* attainments' (my italics).[35] The message for parents is clear: music is still, as it was a century before,[36] a possible career to contemplate; but if a mastery of notes might prove remunerative, competence with letters was socially indispensable.

Professionals

Vocational aspiration and achievement could take a quite different form, in which art and cash outweighed the desire for social elevation. Many performers could thus be categorized as professional musicians, in the simple sense which distinguishes them from pedants, dilettanti and amateurs; teaching a few pupils, perhaps, but essentially dependent upon the practice of music for their livelihood. One group whose lives continued to follow eighteenth-century patterns were the star singers, whose drawing power ensured high fees. Before giving some examples, we must sound a note of caution. Many *public* statements about fees and incomes must be treated with suspicion. Long before the onset of punitive taxation and the black economy, which obscure such information today, musicians and their employers had good reasons for concealment. Fear of invidious and divisive comparisons; a desire (particularly by impresarios) to impress or deprecate; bouts of reticence or recklessness: all led to conspiracies of silence, or confident pronouncements which had little basis in reality. The general lack of widely publicized, reliable information, itself an indication that the market for musicians was 'imperfect', ensured the continuance of disparities between the payment of individuals for similar services. Private accounts not intended for public scrutiny are, of course, an ideal source; but such records are scarce and sporadic. A notable exception is the splendid archive of the Philharmonic Society which contains information, over a long period, about payments to conductors, soloists, and orchestral players; but these were usually lower than the prevailing market rate. Whether through loyalty to the Society, or a desire for the prestige, and therefore ultimate profit, to be derived from association with its activities, musicians were usually persuaded to give their services cheaply. One should therefore avoid facile generalizations about levels of remuneration. Rigid insistence upon 'hard' data, however, would be the statistical equivalent of teetotalism, an arid pursuit. Common sense suggests modest indulgence, and careful reference to the source.

Angelica Catalani (1780–1849) is said to have received £5,250 in 1808, plus the proceeds from two benefits, for a season of seven months, two performances a week. According to Gardiner her formal knowledge of music was negligible, and she played the piano with one finger, but she could sing 'louder than any female had done before.' Her pearl necklace was dismissed as 'noting, only 270 guinea; you come to see my fine necklace, sixteen tousand guinea; my tiara and earing, four tousand guinea; de all twenty tousand guinea'.[37] Stamina and quick returns were crucial to the success of such a career. Eliza Salmon (1787–1849) was capable of travelling 400 miles in a week, before railways facilitated such journeys, singing every night. In 1820 Spohr paid her £20 for a single aria, placed near the concert's end because she had another engagement, six miles away, on the same evening.[38] By 1825 her voice was finished, and she died in poverty. Malibran, who was described by Lamartine as the 'Saint Cecilia of the nineteenth century', was paid £2,000 for fifteen performances at the Drury Lane Theatre in 1833.[39] For nineteen nights in 1835 her employer claims that she received £2,375, each week's payment on Monday morning, in advance. Seven extra performances brought her a total of £3,463. 16s. 3d. for twenty-six performances, and the impresario presented her with a bracelet and ring of diamonds and rubies. She refused £10,000 for a year in America, and died in Manchester at the age of twenty-eight.[40] 'Benefits' could procure substantial extra income. Beginning in the late seventeenth century as a special managerial concession to exceptional performers, they degenerated into a complex, widely abused, system which was subject to endless disputes, particularly about dates: managers preferred them early, performers late in the season.[41] By the 1830s the device of a 'nominal benefit', as in Malibran's 1835 contract, ensured the star's drawing power while management kept the cash.

Until Paganini transformed the public's concept of instrumental virtuosity and its rewards, no instrumentalist could command such sums. Spohr was paid £262. 10s. 0d. for leading the Philharmonic

Society's orchestra during the 1820 season,[42] and gave lessons for 1 gn.: forty-five minutes, with fifteen minutes allowed for travelling time. Presumably he needed the money since most of his pupils had 'neither talent nor industry, and took lessons only in order to be able to say they were pupils of Spohr'.[43] Even the most eminent pianists were similarly placed. In 1823 Moscheles was offered 10 gns. by the Philharmonic Society, but reminded that 'no other resident piano player has hitherto received any remuneration for his performance'.[44] Piecing together a satisfactory income from incessant teaching and playing was a 'steeple-chase' which he was later glad to abandon.[45] The thirteen-year-old Liszt received an unprecedented £100 in 1824 for two Manchester concerts, during which he was upstaged by an infant harpist.[46] Three years later he was offered an engagement by the Philharmonic 'provided his terms do not exceed ten guineas'.[47]

Paganini's unprecedented earning power and alleged avarice were discussed as widely as his pact with the devil and fondness for women. Pecuniary estimates include the *Harmonicon's* 'authentic figures' for fifteen concerts at the King's Theatre in 1831. Ticket prices were doubled, and total receipts were said to be £9,000. The manager, Laporte, allegedly took £4,142, out of which he was supposed to pay the orchestra, two of whom took legal action to recover their dues.[48] A modern estimate suggests £10,000 for eighteen London concerts.[49] Such earnings excited patriotic remonstrance (because money was taken out of the country) and radical sentiment. In Dublin his £500 fee was denounced as 'a sum that would rescue at least eighty Irish farms from the miseries of hunger during the whole of the ensuing winter'.[50] Stamina was, again, an indispensible attribute. Despite his miserable state of health, Paganini's 1831 tour extended, outside London, to forty-nine provincial concerts, twenty-three in Scotland, and twenty-two in Ireland. Like Smart, from whom he differed in every other respect, he was 'a shrewd patient accumulator [who] never failed to maintain an astounding grasp of his financial interests'.[51] Listing his concerts for March 1831 to 1832, he declared 'If I had made such a tour in England ten or twelve years ago, I should have taken in at least £60,000'.[52] His belated entry into the lucrative international market has been attributed to the need 'to prove that he was more than a technical wizard'.[53] It surely also had something to do with the evolution of that market. By the 1830s it was far wider, and more easily exploited than ever in the past, particularly in Britain. That process would attain unimagined dimensions with the railway age and the opening up of American opportunities.

Meanwhile a group of instrumentalists was establishing patterns of life and work which were to survive almost intact to the present day. These were the London based freelance orchestral players, whose versatility, and ability to read practically any music at sight, made a virtue of necessity in a society where scratch ensembles were the norm. Since none of them were diarists or men of letters, though one wrote an entertaining memoir,[54] their working lives are not easily documented: Dragonetti, wrote Phillips, 'never penned an *entire* letter in his life'.[55] Their names survive because of repeated public appearances, occasional reminiscences, and, in at least one case, accomplishment still acknowledged by leading players today. A representative list of men—and it is noteworthy that all were men—active during the early decades of the nineteenth century, must include the following names: the violinists Franz Cramer, George Griesbach, Mori, Charles Weichsell, and Yankiewicz; Lindley, an excellent cellist, and his inseparable companion for fifty-two years, the great double-bass virtuoso Dragonetti: 'giants they were in talent, such as had never existed before';[56] the flautists Ashe and Nicholson, and the oboist Parke; the Mahon brothers and Willman, clarinettists; the horn-playing Petrides brothers, and trumpeter Thomas Harper. They shared certain characteristics. Their living depended almost exclusively upon their instrumental skills. As far as we can tell, investment, marriage, or trade made no significant contribution to their income. According to Phillips, Mori occasionally bought and sold songs, but more as a gambler than as a man of business.[57] Dragonetti was an exception, though the form of his investment is illuminating: two houses in Leicester Square, pictures and instruments. In his will he bequeathed fiddles to members of the opera orchestra, including a Stradivarius and an Amati; he also left a Gasparo di Salo double-bass to St Mark's, Venice.[58] Generally, however, thrift and bookkeeping were not customary in this group, although a craftsman's insistence on a fair price for the job was common enough. Several of them wrote tutors and study pieces for their instruments, but none pretended to be serious composers. Harper was 'Inspector of musical instruments for the East India Company' but this can hardly have absorbed much of his time. Even teaching was a subsidiary activity: some might take a few, usually professional, pupils, but none attempted to build up an extensive teaching practice. All specialized in a single or related instruments: e.g. violin and viola, though even here specialization became increasingly common. This was a significant change from earlier practice, becoming practically universal among professional players as the century progressed. Thus John and William Mahon, whose activities are difficult to disentangle, played violin, viola, oboe, and clarinet for the greater part of their careers, but their successor, Willman, performed only on instruments of the clarinet family.

Growing specialization reflected both economic and musical change: only a large market could provide sufficient employment for a specialist;

only highly skilled specialists could perform the increasingly difficult music placed before them. Even Dragonetti was taxed by his part in Beethoven's ninth symphony. In correspondence with the Philharmonic Society, notably lacking in the obsequiousness which pervades letters from many of his contemporaries, he agrees to accept 10 gns. for the night, and play the 'solos in Beethoven's new symphony but . . . had I seen it before I sent in my terms I would have asked double. I must be paid likewise 5 guineas for each trial [rehearsal] of Beethoven's symphony'.[59]

These musicians were inevitably based in London, playing in the opera, Ancient Concert, Philharmonic Society, oratorios, and any public or private concert which could afford their fees. The orchestra at the King's Theatre *c*.1817, for example, was described as a 'strong phalanx of instrumental talent' and included Weichsl [*sic*] as leader, Lindley, Dragonetti, Willman, and the Petrides brothers.[60] Their names were sufficiently familiar to figure in announcements of provincial concerts. Thus a Bristol Festival in October 1821 proudly listed Cramer, Griesbach, Lindley, Ashe, Willman, Mahon, and the Petrides in its advertisement.[61] Only Yankiewicz left London permanently, to settle first in Liverpool and later Edinburgh. Despite his excellence as a violinist it may have been lack of sufficient employment which led him to venture into music publishing and selling in the former city. Not for another generation would even this major provincial centre provide adequate opportunities for a first-class player. Until railways came to revolutionize the speed, cost, and reliability of transport, distance from London was a formidable obstacle. In 1819, writing from Edinburgh, Yankiewicz had to ask 100 guineas for two dates with the Philharmonic Society, arguing that this would merely cover his expenses.[62]

One final characteristic of the group requires some emphasis. All came from strong musical backgrounds, mostly musicians' families, and had been expertly taught since childhood. It therefore follows that most of them were foreigners: the exceptions almost invariably had a significant measure of training by foreigners. Ashe was born in Lisburn, N. Ireland, but travelled widely as a child, and was first flute at the Brussels opera before the age of 20.[63] Lindley began violin lessons with his father when six years old, cello when nine, and was taken over at the age of 16 by Cervetto, the outstanding cellist of his day.[64] The Mahon brothers and Parke lacked foreign training, but both were immersed in music from childhood. The former belonged to an extraordinary Irish family of musicians (Mrs Salmon was a relation); the latter began flute with his brother at the age of 10, and oboe a year later.

Their fees were generally modest, as can be deduced from a bassoonist's letter to the Philharmonic Society in 1822, demanding the same payments as at the Harmonic and Mme Catalani's concerts—£1. 11s. 6d. for rehearsals, and £2. 12s. 6d. for each concert. He insisted that this request was 'not unreasonable, for I assure you that very frequently I am scarcely able to walk home after very laborious rehearsals, for which I have hitherto received one guinea'.[65] The tone of that letter, incidentally, is unrepresentative of the orchestral player's approach to his employer in this period. Compare the unctuousness of the young William Cramer, accepting, in 1834, 'the Honour you have conferred upon me, in offering me an engagement to play the Violin at your most distinguished concerts. I have to return you, respectfully, my most sincere thanks and hope, by a strict observance to my duties in the Orchestra and a desire to rise in the Profession, to render myself worthy of the distinguished situation you have so graciously appointed me to. I have the honour to remain, Gentlemen, your most Obliged, Humble, Servant'.[66]

The Society began by paying only wind instrumentalists, but soon had to remunerate most of its orchestra.[67] In 1821 front desk strings received £52. 10s. 0d. for ten rehearsals and eight concerts; principal woodwinds £27. 6s 6d. and brass £20. 9s. 6d. In 1824 principal winds received 2 gns. for one rehearsal and performance, but three guineas if they must 'come forward for a solo performance'. Garcia sang three nights at 10 gns. each, but a second trumpet received £1. 11s. 6d. Dragonetti was offered 50 gns. for the 1827 season, with the privilege of cutting rehearsals 'except when anything new may be performed'. F. Cramer accepted the same terms in 1831 'as one of the leaders', without leave from rehearsals.[68]

The opera orchestra was a more substantial source of income, but evidence is fragmentary. When Dragonetti first came to England in 1794 to play in the King's Theatre, he was engaged at an annual salary of £250 plus a benefit. This was probably equivalent to £5 a night for the season's sixty performances. London fees generally ranged from 3 to 5 gns., with occasional gifts or 'royal munificence'. Provincial festivals paid similarly. At Norwich in 1824 the principal instrumentalists received 25 gns. for eight to ten concerts. In 1827 Oxford paid Dragonetti £33. 12s. 0d. and Willman £21 for three days.

Freelance incomes are notoriously difficult to assess, but we may hazard a guess that Dragonetti, at the peak of his earning capacity, made about £1,000 a year: roughly equivalent to a modestly capable physician. Fashionable lawyers and doctors could extract ten times this sum. The Lord Chancellor's fees in 1810 amounted to £22,730. Other leading instrumentalists possibly pieced together £500 in a busy year. Willman allegedly never earned more than £300.[69] The Petrides brothers 'by frugality and good conduct ... acquired a modest competency' and retired home in 1824. According to the same authority, their successors, 'after long service in our best orchestras' became dependent upon RSM pensions, and 'no other wind instrumentalists acquired an independence by orchestral employment in London'.[70] Like Smart he remarks upon the contrast with Paris, where opera musicians had a retirement pension.

It is probable that, despite their excellent musicianship, the London professionals earned less than Smart, Crotch, or Stevens. Equally significant was the widening social gap between the two breeds. Even if one acccepts the unproven proposition that successful musicians in eighteenth-century England had enjoyed high economic and low social status,[71] the early-nineteenth-century instrumentalists did no more than continue that tradition. They neither achieved, nor perhaps did they seek, embourgeoisement. They ranked, as the learned Dr Maurice had remarked, 'scarcely above an ordinary artizan'. Yet the emerging shape of the new industrial society entailed a class structure in which the status of occupations was clearly defined. Where was the profession of music to fit?

III

The Growth of Demand

Assize balls, musical festivals and horticultural shows are well enough for the rich, but some rich people stand in greater need of a work day than a holiday. After all I think it may be safely asserted that we have no real holidays in England . . . We are rather too fond of the dark side of things.

Household Words (1853)

A little of what you fancy does you good.

Marie Lloyd

Numbers and problems

The most basic fact about professional musicians in nineteenth-century Britain is the huge increase in their numbers, accelerating rapidly after 1870 and finishing soon after 1930 (see Table I). It was an expansion which far outstripped the rapid growth of the country's population: the latter almost doubled during this period, while the number of musicians increased sevenfold. In 1840 approximately 7,000 musicians were at work among some 27m. people; by 1930 there were about 50,000 musicians in a population (England, Wales, Scotland, and both parts of Ireland) of nearly 50m. people. Before exploring further statistics it is worth noting that nineteenth-century evidence enables us to count more accurately than was possible for an earlier period. The official censuses give information about occupations which can be supplemented by directories, both town and professional, and by the various reports and surveys produced by a society which became increasingly concerned with measurement. Whereas our estimate of 2,000 musicians in late eighteenth-century Britain was merely an informed guess, we can be increasingly confident about later figures. But although it is better than for previous centuries, the evidence is not always sufficiently reliable or comprehensive for our purposes. Thus at various times musicians were grouped in the census as 'musicians and organists', 'musicians, not teachers', 'musicians and music masters', 'musicians, music masters and singers': categories which defy uniform reclassification. It is particularly unfortunate that whereas 'music teachers' and 'musicians' are recorded separately before 1881 and after 1911, they are amalgamated during the intervening period, which was a time of significant change. Similar problems arise when interpreting information culled from directories which are never comprehensive but list only those individuals who chose, and usually paid, to be listed. There can be no doubt, for example, that in 1910 there were at least 1,017 violinists (including violists), 245 cellists, and 179 clarinettists in London, for we have their names and addresses (see Table IV). But such figures represent only *minimum* totals of musicians who were presumably fairly active, and probably full-time. They obviously exclude players who were unable or unwilling to be listed: in addition to the impecunious, lethargic, and indifferent full-time musicians, there were many part-timers who were anxious to conceal their 'moonlighting' from employers and tax-collectors. An aggregate of directory statistics will therefore invariably be less than the comparable census figure which, in turn, does not account for every individual who may, on occasion, have earned money from music while reporting a different occupation to the enumerator. Some occupations required musical skills as an additional qualification. Lunatic asylums, for example, commonly advertised as follows: '*Gloucester County Asylum*. Assistant Carpenter wanted. Wages £30 per annum, with board, lodging, and washing. Must be a Musician and be able to play at sight'.[1] 'County Asylum, Whittingham, Preston. WANTED, Tall, Strong, Active Girls, to train as ASYLUM NURSES. Wages to commence at £18 a year, with board, lodging, washing, and dresses. Preference to those capable of singing in the choir'.[2]

Accurate statistics are therefore elusive, and it is sometimes impossible to be precise about the timing and size of specific changes. Such vital transitions as the move from amateur to professional, and from part-time to full-time employment (or back) may defy counting, even if the general trend is clear. The problems are similar to those encountered today when attempting to measure the 'black economy'. Nevertheless several trends are readily discernible, in addition to the conspicuous evidence of massive expansion. London continued to be the dominant market, but the location of provincial employment shifted to the industrial midlands and north. A 1900 directory lists names of 318 musicians in Liverpool, 315 in Manchester, and 273 in Birmingham (see Table III); but Norwich, once a major provincial centre, has only 40, including the cathedral choir of 8 lay clerks and 14 choristers. While most towns retained or attracted an increasing number of performing musicians, the overwhelming majority of the 'profession' were now teachers in a new and limited sense: 'professors', as they were termed in the directories and often described themselves, with little or no experience of public performance. The largest group taught elementary piano, and perhaps the 'rudiments' of music, privately at home. In London there was probably a more even balance between performers and teachers: a 1900 directory distinguishes between 2,533 'orchestral instrumentalists' and 4,823 'professors of the pianoforte, organ, singing, etc.' Another discernible pattern by 1900 is that in most industrial cities there appears to be a fairly consistent ratio of musicians to population: from one to two per thousand inhabitants. Since the directories give every town's population before listing its musicians this relationship was evidently considered to be relevant by those concerned, and may, in a highly mobile society, have influenced decisions about where to live and work, particularly among teachers.

Another fact to emerge from the statistics is that music became a female occupation, to such an extent that women eventually outnumbered men. A precise turning-point is obscured by the change in census classification already described, but the general trend is quite clear. The 1851 census for England and Wales reported more male than female music teachers: approximately 2,800 and 2,300 respectively. By 1861 women had overtaken men: 3,100 and 2,400. Teachers were not separately classified again until 1921, by which time the women greatly outnumbered men: 16,400 and 4,900. Returning to the 1861 census for numbers of musicians, as distinct from teachers, we find far more men than women: 7,800 and 600. By 1921 males still predominated, but less substantially: 15,600 and 6,900. Finally if we combine the figures for 'musicians' and 'teachers', as we have to for most of the period, women overtook men during the first decade of the twentieth century, and retained a slight lead until the 1930s. It is evident that music-teaching became pre-eminently a female occupation by the 1850s, while music-making remained a masculine preserve (an absolute monopoly in certain branches) which was subject to increasing challenge as the century progressed (see Table I).

Further statistics are available in the Appendix, but enough have been quoted to indicate that there were fundamental changes in the size, structure, and location of the profession after 1840. Why did this happen? It cannot be explained in purely musical terms: an autonomous change in the 'musicality' of British society. Apart from the inherent implausibility of such a thesis, it would collapse in the face of events after 1930 when the profession was forced to contract violently. There is no evidence to suggest that the nation was then becoming *less* 'musical'; rather the contrary. Since we are concerned with the expansion, and subsequent contraction, of a market for people's services, it follows that we should seek explanations in market forces. Some of the social and economic factors which shaped patterns of demand and supply were already perceptible by the late eighteenth century, but fifty years later they were far more powerful, met less resistance, and were augmented by potent new influences. One fact remained unaltered: until the coming of recording and broadcasting any increase in the demand for music was immediately translated into a demand for musicians because there was no means by which their 'productivity' (output per unit of input) could be increased, except by playing in larger halls or theatres: a limited procedure before the invention of the microphone. Demand for the services of musicians, like that for domestic servants or corner shopkeepers, was therefore likely to increase *at least* proportionately to the growth of population.[3] Many additional factors, as will be seen, reinforced this virtually inevitable upward trend.

It will also be appreciated that the demand for music is not autonomous and therefore cannot in reality be separated from supply. In the simplest sense supply creates a demand: the taste for music is both slaked and stimulated by its availability. But in addition the demand for particular kinds of music can be manipulated by procedures long familiar: 'the puff direct, the puff preliminary, the puff collateral, the puff collusive, and the puff oblique, or puff by implication'. Nineteenth-century impresarios practised such activities with new intensity and inventiveness. The most remarkable instance was P. T. Barnum's promotion of Jenny Lind, in America, creating vociferous audiences, and earning $176,675 for the 'Swedish Nightingale' and $535,486 (gross) for himself, from ninety-five concerts in ten months.[4] To compare with present values one would have to multiply those figures at least by ten. No English entrepreneur matched that exploit, though Colonel Mapleson ran it close on both sides of the Atlantic.

The manipulation of markets sometimes addressed intrinsically musical requirements, such as the need to attract and educate audiences towards 'better' music, but it also exploited social aspirations, among which none were more significant than emulation and respectability. Illustrating these processses raises problems of historical exposition. Since any specific musical event displays both supply and demand at work, its selection as an example of one or other is often arbitrary, but necessary to avoid irksome repetition. The rest of this chapter will be concerned with the demand for musicians; the following two chapters will consider their supply. All will chronicle musical events and institutions.

Mass entertainment

The expanding demand for professional musicians derived, in large measure, from an efflorescence of commercial entertainment.[5] As increasing numbers of people acquired higher incomes and more leisure there was a massive expansion in their effective demand (desire backed by the ability to pay) for goods and services beyond the basic necessities of life, accelerating during the 1870s, when the prices of those necessities steadily fell, leaving more cash for luxuries. Moreover the new purchasing power was concentrated in several ways which eased its identification and exploitation. Relentless urban growth was a crucial factor. Whereas in 1800 only London had a population over 100,000, by the 1890s there were twenty-three towns of that size, and 70 per cent of the people lived in cities. A transport revolution, beginning with trains and steamships in the 1840s, and continuing with trams in most large towns by the 1870s, lowered costs, established timetables, increased speed, and reliability, and thus greatly extended the catchment area for performers and audiences. A simple example is the Crystal Palace and South London Junction Railway, which opened in 1865 as 'an approach to a turnstile'.[6] Another is the prospectus for a typical provincial 'Grand Opera House' of the 1890s which tempted investors by stressing the site's proximity to a railway station and 'tramway cars . . . from all parts of the city'.[7]

There was an enormous increase in country-wide and even international touring. In 1867 a self-styled 'enterprising impresario' remarked that 'public amusements have been affected to an extraordinary degree by the great change brought about by railroads'. Thirty years earlier a concert party of six would require two travelling carriages, or have to endure the expense and discomfort of the post-chaise. Now singers or whole productions could play Manchester and London within the same week. Touring had once been 'practically a monopoly' because capital and knowledge were scarce. Now it was becoming competitive, thanks to Bradshaw's timetable and agents, 'country correspondents'.[8] In 1865 Mapleson began a series of provincial opera tours and, in the following year, took two parties of singers to 120 concerts in seventy towns in sixty successive days, combining both companies for opera in Edinburgh and Glasgow.[9] By 1872 he could boast of giving '48 concerts in 48 cities in 48 days'.[10] In 1878 he led a company of 140 to America, and then proceeded to move 'costumes, properties, and even singers . . . to and fro across the ocean in accordance with my New York and London requirements'.[11] Daily communication by telegraph and even a trans-Atlantic commuting ballet master became part of this enterprise. By 1893 a Dramatic and Musical Directory was suggesting four alternative itineraries for visiting 30 provincial towns, including Dublin, Belfast, Aberdeen, and Plymouth, 'booked as close as possible', giving third-class rail fares at a total cost of less than £8 for each tour. Eighty-nine towns containing at least one theatre were placed in four categories, according to size, not the 'quality' of their potential audiences: Hull and Glasgow were among the fourteen 'first class' towns; Bournemouth and

Torquay in the 'fourth class'.[12] By 1900 there were 142 special trains every Sunday in England and Wales to transport touring companies of actors and musicians.

The growth of seaside resorts, again dependent upon railways, was important, not only because it assembled large audiences in a few weeks of concentrated spending, but because the season coincided with the musician's traditionally slack summer. Resort employment was not new: in addition to the spas musicians had long been accustomed to visiting Brighton and a few similar places. Parke describes a fortnight in Margate in August 1803, in the company of other London players 'whose principal object was sea bathing', though they assisted Braham at the 'little theatre which held about £60'.[13] Even small halls could be remunerative in fashionable resorts during the high season. According to Kuhe a Brighton impresario in August 1847 was able to pay Jenny Lind £500 for a single concert, plus the fees of supporting artistes, and make a net profit of £500 from a capacity audience of 600. Seats were priced from 1 to 3 gns.[14] Late Victorian activities were on quite a different, generally more demotic, scale. The 1871 census already listed forty-eight seaside resorts, with small resident populations but large seasonal influxes: Blackpool had only 6,000 residents but was entertaining 600,000 visitors in the season.

Subsequent development was very rapid and embraced all classes, the extent and form of organized entertainment depending upon the 'social tone' of each resort. Musicians were employed everywhere, in minstrel and pierrot shows, diverse theatrical entertainments, and instrumental ensembles which ranged in a size and quality, from genteel tea-time groups and exotically uniformed 'Viennese' or 'Hungarian' bands (their cockney and Mancunian accents suitably muted), to the proto-symphony orchestras developed with dedicated industry by Bantock at New Brighton, Clifford at Harrogate, and Godfrey at Bournemouth.[15] A visitor to the Isle of Man in 1889 noticed more than eighty musicians at work in the three main places of entertainment. A hall which accommodated nearly 2,000 dancers employed 'an excellent orchestral band' of twenty-six players. Another employed twenty-five, including 'many experienced members of Hallé's and de Jong's Manchester bands'. The newly-erected Castle Mona Palace, seating 5,000, was used for music hall during the week, accompanied by a thirty-piece band, and for oratorios on Sundays.[16] If seaside holidays provided a few months' employment for musicians, it may not be too fanciful to suggest that they also helped to stimulate the demand for music throughout the year. Much as cheap foreign travel encouraged a later generation to seek wine and 'exotic' food at home, the tawdry or subdued delights of Victorian holidays stimulated the demand for music and dancing throughout the year.

An attempt to calculate the size of the entertainment industry in 1892 estimated that 530 English towns possessed 1,300 places of amusement, accommodating more than 1m. people, 'representing' some £6m. capital, employing 350,000 workers directly and many more indirectly. The total was made up of 200 theatres, 160 music halls, and 950 halls, 'galleries', and gardens of various kinds. Put forward as 'a fair and laboriously made estimate', the apparent precision of this statement may have been designed to impress a Parliamentary Committee, but it probably did not exaggerate the industry's size. The estimated (minimum) labour force of 350,000 was about one-quarter of the numbers then employed in the textile industry, and double those engaged in public administration.[17]

Apart from drinking, fornication, and sport, the most popular form of entertainment in the second half of the nineteenth century was the music-hall. After 1854 licences were issued liberally, and by the mid-1860s music-halls greatly outnumbered theatres in many cities. The precise demarcation continued to be a matter of acrimonious dispute and government intervention for the rest of the century. Theatre proprietors attempted, with diminishing success, to establish 'an absolute distinction between the theatre and the music-hall, that the theatre is the representative of cultured dramatic feeling, and that the music-hall is a place where you primarily go to drink and smoke, and where there happens to be a performance as well'.[18] In their proclamations of respectability and 'cultured feeling' the music-hall proprietors were inclined to boast that orchestras played a leading role. Since the examples given in 1892 were bands of fifteen players at the 'Metropolitan' and twelve apiece at the 'Cambridge' and 'Oxford', all London halls, it can reasonably be assumed that the typical provincial music-hall probably employed between five and ten players. But the industry was growing to such an extent as to offer unprecedented opportunities for fairly regular employment for much of the year. Developed from singing saloons by publican entrepreneurs and, after the 1862 limited liability legislation, by large companies, the music-halls became a prototype of modern 'show business'. The Alhambra, which opened in 1860, drawing a nightly audience of 3,500 from Londoners and a mounting influx of tourists, was followed by Morton's 'Oxford', the first purpose-built music-hall, with elaborate stage facilities and 1,200 seats, including fixed stalls in place of the traditional tables and chairs. By the mid-1860s there were more than thirty large halls in London, with average capitalization of £10,000 and seating capacity of 1,500. A further 200 to 300 small halls survived precariously in a highly competitive market, with seats at 6d. or less. There were at least 300 provincial halls, mainly small and shabby, but a few in the large industrial towns began to rival London in size of audience and lavishness of entertainment.[19] Indeed the final phase in the modernization of music-hall and its transformation into 'Variety' came from the provinces, when Edward Moss and Oswald Stoll consolidated their empire of 'Empires' and moved into London.[20]

Social historians have interpreted these developments in various ways. For some it is a story of degeneration, from genuine, spontaneous, working-class entertainment, to an industry 'produced entirely by professionals who realised immense profits'. Others have explored its political connotations and, a theme to which we shall return, its contribution to 'rational recreation'.[21] For the moment we are merely concerned with its effects on employment. Musicians had always worked in theatres, and continued to do so on an increasing scale as more theatres were built and some provided more elaborate shows, partly as a result of competition from the music halls. In 1895 an article on music in the legitimate theatre complained that bands were too small: even at 'Arms and the Man', where the author might have insisted on higher standards, 'a few violins, a flute or so, and a tinny piano' made a 'scratchy din'. Managers and audiences, it argued, were ignorant and uninterested; only gallery and pit arrived in time to hear the overture, and interval music was intended merely to provide background for the conversation of teetotallers who stayed in the house between acts. Yet even this critical account admits that most 'middling' theatres employed about twelve musicians, while several were more generous. St James's Theatre had sixteen good players and at Irving's theatre, the 'Lyceum', there was an orchestra of thirty, with extra instrumentalists for special occasions.[22] Meanwhile the music halls provided additional employment which was continuously reinforced and extended by each new development: matinées and twice-nightly performances; elaborate tableaux and ballets; the copyrighting of 'hit' songs which were identified with 'star' singers; and the establishment of large orchestras in prestige theatres. At the 'Empire', for example, opening in 1884, the variety programme included spectacular ballets which culminated in Wenzel's 'The Press' (1898), danced by Adeline Genée and scored for an orchestra of sixty players, led by John Barbirolli's father, Lorenzo. Its rival theatre in Leicester Square, the 'Alhambra', by now had a band of fifty playing under Georges Jacobi, who composed more than sixty ballets. Musical comedies and musical plays, by such composers as Sydney Jones and Leslie Stuart, which were hugely successful on a national and, for a time, international scale, created further jobs: particularly in London where most of the largest theatres and touring companies were based.[23]

Theatre and music-hall had become nation-wide phenomena. One result of this proliferation of work-places, with broadly similar, usually miserable, working conditions, was the creation of a sufficiently stable and homogeneous labour force to encourage the formation of trade unions: not, perhaps, for the first time, but henceforth clearly identifiable and durable.[24] We have estimates of its size in 1911 because the census of that year included some detailed figures. Approximately 3,700 musicians, predominantly male, were listed as working in the theatres and music halls of England and Wales. Another 460 were already finding jobs in 'picture theatres', a group which would soon rapidly expand, as the 'silent' cinemas became a major source of employment, uniquely continuous throughout the year. These official figures are certainly underestimates, for reasons already explained. In the same year the Amalgamated Musicians' Union had 6,180 members, mostly working in theatres and music-halls. The London Orchestral Association represented another 1,000 instrumentalists who were predominantly theatre musicians.

Concerts and the shilling public

Concert life began to widen its audience before 1850. William Weber has calculated a threefold increase in the number of London concerts between the mid-1820s and mid-1840s, keeping pace approximately with the growth of population.[25] One need not entirely accept his arguments about the social structure of musical taste and the concert-going public to acknowledge the increasing influence of middle-class demand. The Concerts of Ancient Music, founded in 1776, faltered and eventually died in 1848 because of their exclusiveness, conservative repertory, and amateurish standards. They were described in 1837 as 'most pertinaciously exclusive of any other persons than of such as had the privilege of belonging to the "upper ten thousand"'. Outsiders could sometimes get in 'but only to be wearied to death with the unceasing round of dull conformity'.[26] Performances were 'directed' by the odd duke or archbishop. The Philharmonic Society was established in 1813 with the intention of imposing professional standards and autonomy, and appealing to a middle-class audience. Initially restricting its audience to subscribers, in 1841 it took the important step of selling tickets to the general public. Despite good intentions and distinguished musical associations however, it too 'developed the inertia that feeds on social success', allegedly becoming, for a time, 'a worthless vessel manned with decrepit mariners, and o'erloaded with useless ballast'.[27] One of the principal mariners was Sir George Smart. Temporarily more seaworthy was the New Philharmonic Society, launched in 1852 by the music publisher Beale, and sunk in 1879. Although it was a strictly commercial venture it provided Berlioz with an orchestra which he claimed, in a private letter, 'at times surpassed all that I have ever heard in verve, delicacy and power': strong testimony to the potential quality, given adequate direction, of London's freelance players.[28] Tickets for the New Philharmonic Society were cheaper than their rivals', priced from 2s. 6d. to 10s. 6d. (Philharmonic tickets cost 1 gn.)

Meanwhile the man who did most to democratize and vitalize London's concert life was seizing the 'one shilling public' with flamboyance which concealed a wider musicianship than many of his detractors could discern or admit. It was Jullien, with thirty-six Christian names, and a jewelled baton on a silver salver for Beethoven, who 'directed the attention of the multitude to the classical composers . . . broke down the barriers and let in the crowd'.[29] A typical concert, at the Theatre Royal, Preston, in 1848, included the 'Zampa' overture, selections from 'Elijah' and 'Sonnambula', quadrilles, Beethoven's Symphony in F (presumably No. 6, possibly excerpts), and a 'Comic Polka—Three Blind Mice'. Tickets were priced from 1s. to 2s. 6d.[30] If, at times, he was slow to pay (disgruntled horn-players, threatening to strike, are reported by Berlioz),[31] Jullien provided considerable employment for musicians and drew the crowds: his 1845 *concerts monstres* at the Royal Zoological Gardens, which entertained audiences of many thousands, featured a number from Bellini's *Puritani* arranged for cornets, trumpets, trombones, ophicleides, and serpents, twenty of each. In 1851 his 'Great Exhibition Quadrilles' were performed by 207 players.[32] Quite apart from such freakish events, the size of the typical symphony orchestra increased considerably after 1850. Salomon had mustered forty players for Haydn: twenty-eight strings (16 violins, 4 violas, 4 cellos, and 4 double-basses), ten winds, timpani, and piano. By 1900 performance of contemporary music, by Richard Strauss for example, required, and the public generally expected, an orchestra of at least 100 instrumentalists, dominated by a magisterial, interpretative conductor. Reorchestration for economy, sometimes involving gross distortions of the score, was a common practice, particularly with touring and provincial orchestras; but wherever possible promoters were expected to field as large and loud a band as possible, and make them all play, even in Bach or Mozart.

The general pattern of London's concert life was becoming established by the 1860s, leading the country in a modernizing process which encountered pockets of resistance for many years. It was wholly professional, amateurs no longer playing along, less still pretending to 'direct' the proceedings. This transformation, with obvious implications for costs, was both cause and result of rising standards and a more difficult repertory, and was later reinforced by trade union pressures. Concerts were increasingly profit-seeking ventures, without obligatory fund-raising for charity to attract patronage. While private concerts and subscription series continued to flourish, tickets for public concerts and the opera were sold to anyone who cared to buy, though sartorial conventions and snobbery imposed social constraints even on metropolitan audiences. The number of events increased to such an extent that by the 1890s newspapers, which were also proliferating, complained that their critics could not be expected to 'cover' them all. In June 1893 the *Daily News* and the *Saturday Review* separately estimated that there were about fifty concerts a week during the season. Among various attempts to attract and educate the new public, both satisfying and creating demand for good music through attractive programmes and cheap tickets, two were particularly successful. At the 2,000 seat St James's Hall, built in 1858 by two music publishers, the Monday or Saturday 'Pops' offered diverse vocal and instrumental music, often by leading artists, for forty years. In a South London suburb the Crystal Palace company was more ambitious, covering the costs of a full symphony orchestra by filling a vast arena with cheap seats. Organized by George Grove and conducted by August Manns, these Saturday concerts 'formed the backbone of orchestral musical culture in England' between 1855 and 1901.[33]

Attempts to quench the 'thirst for orchestral music' were hampered by the lack of an adequate hall. 'London clamors in vain', complained Shaw in 1889, 'for a West-end concert-room capable of accommodating on every Saturday afternoon enough people at a shilling a head to support an orchestra 200 strong. It not only clamors, but gives repeated proofs of the sincerity of its demand and the readiness of its shillings'.[34] Shaw blamed the stupidity of entrepreneurs who would finish the Channel tunnel and carpet the Northwest Passage before providing an escape from St James's Hall where economics dictated that the orchestra be too small or the prices too high. The Albert Hall was no answer: an 'irretrievable blunder' in size, acoustics and location, declared the economist W. S. Jevons, expressing a common view. 'How strange it is that those whose purpose was the elevation of the public taste, the taste surely of the masses, should have placed their instrument of elevation as far as possible from the masses they were to elevate'.[35] Although some promenade concerts were held at Covent Garden, the real need was only met in 1893, by the superb Queen's Hall.

In the industrial midlands and North a large potential market was opened up by the railways, which greatly facilitied the organization of concerts by visiting soloists, small groups, and occasional events by larger forces. Musical directories began to list provincial concert rooms, their rents and seating capacities: £2 to £5 a night for halls seating 500 to 1,000 people. But to cover the costs and risk of regular orchestral concerts required a sustained effort, to build up audiences for whom concert-going might become a normal pursuit rather than a rare experience. Only Manchester and, to a lesser extent, Liverpool made substantial progress in this direction. Both had prosperous middle-class communities and large halls with excellent acoustics, in an age when architects understood such matters. Liverpool's Philharmonic opened in 1849, and was later described by Richter as the finest concert-room in Europe. Manchester's Free Trade Hall which opened in 1856 was generally acknowledged as better than any in London until the Queen's Hall was built. Both Lancashire towns had sizeable German communities with an inherent taste for music, which formed a nucleus of regular concert-goers, but there was also an element of commercial enterprise and municipal pride. Hallé was first invited to Manchester by a businessman who assured him 'on behalf of many devoted lovers of music, that Manchester was quite ripe *to be taken in hand*, and that they thought me the fittest man to stir the dormant taste for the art'.[36] He began modestly enough, supported by lady pupils and audiences drawn mainly from the 'German colony'. His first chamber concerts in 1848 had sixty-seven subscribers, a list which was trebled within a year. An initial venture into Liverpool secured an audience of eleven, including four reporters.[37] He also played Beethoven's Emperor concerto with the orchestra of the Gentlemen's Concerts Society, an experience which tempted him to abandon Manchester, after recent familiarity with orchestral standards in Paris.[38] But the Society was wealthy, proud of its four decades of existence and, far from seeking wider audiences, maintained a three-year waiting list for subscribers. It also sought to improve standards, a task which Hallé accepted on condition that he be allowed to weed out the orchestra and allow a wider public into at least some of the concerts, which hitherto had been full-dress and 'clandestine' affairs, with even the programmes a jealously guarded secret.

A major step towards Manchester's general public came in 1857 when a committee organizing an Arts Treasures Exhibition deemed it 'expedient to enhance the general attraction of the Exhibition' by a daily performance of music. 'Tenders were received from several eminent professors. The offer of Mr Charles Hallé was accepted . . .' Some 1,500,000 people attended the exhibition, and Hallé noted that many thousands heard a symphony for the first time, their appreciation growing as the weeks passed. Rather than disband his newly enlarged orchestra after the exhibition closed, he moved into the Free Trade Hall and gave thirty weekly public concerts; tickets at 1s. and 2s. 6d., the audience gradually increasing until, by the end of the first season, he had made 30d. profit. Reducing the series to twenty concerts and opening a subscription list, which was not socially exclusive, he demonstrated by 1860 that 'high class orchestral music had taken hold of the public'.[39] The *Musical World* commented that 'Mr Charles Hallé's Manchester concerts are becoming the vogue with all classes, from the rich merchant and manufacturer to the middle-class tradesmen and bourgeois ... to the respectable and thrifty, albeit humbler, artisans'.[40]

Liverpool is only thirty-five miles from Manchester, and communications were excellent by the 1850s, so its concert life was inevitably influenced by Hallé's activities. Perhaps this helps to explain why it developed more slowly, less professionally, and was apparently more constrained by class rigidities. The Philharmonic Society segregated its audience rigidly, allowing public access only to the gallery, much of it standing. The prevailing tone of exclusiveness is conveyed by a pompously obscure rule, frequently reiterated in programmes, which remained in force until 1909:

No Gentleman above twenty-one years of age residing or carrying on business in Liverpool or within ten miles thereof, and not being an Officer of the Army or Navy, or Minister of Religion, is admissible to the Boxes or Stalls at the Philharmonic Society's concerts unless he be a Proprietor, or member of the family residing at the house of a Proprietor, or has his name upon the list of Gentlemen having the *Entree* exhibited in the Corridors. Resident Gentlemen who are not Proprietors can acquire the right of Purchasing Tickets or of making use of Proprietors' Tickets during the season on payment of a Entrance Fee of 10s. 6d.[41].

The orchestra was initially made up of amateurs, local professionals, and 'metropolitan talent' commuting in cheap, efficient trains. Increasing opportunities of employment induced musicians to settle in the district. At the opening festival seventy-five of the ninety-six instrumentalists were Londoners, mostly from Covent Garden and Her Majesty's Theatre.[42] Some were induced to settle. In December 1849 the principal clarinet at Drury Lane wrote to say that Hallé, 'having found fault with some of the instrumentalists' in Manchester was trying to recruit men from London, and had offered him £43 a year. He asked for a similar sum from Liverpool, and a 'promise to push me forward for all other concerts'.[43] Amateurs were gradually weeded out, an 1851 rule excluding them from front desks. Local musicians were willing, at first, to accept inferior positions. In 1850, for example, a double-bass player accepted the second desk, while insisting that he was as 'capable of doing the business as is anyone out of London'.[44] Gradually, however, the Philharmonic was drawn exclusively from Manchester and Liverpool musicians; a process doubtless hastened by Costa's refusal to give leave to his players during the opera season, as one of them complained to the Society.[45]

Two amateur groups were also increasingly reinforced by professionals. The Societa Armonica, despite its use of the Mechanics' Institute Hall, insisted upon its audience wearing full evening dress. In the 1890s it was described by the conductor Eugene Goossens II as a 'staid and very earnest group of socialites, shipping magnates and professional men and women'.[46] The People's Orchestral Society was founded in 1884, conducted, and largely financed, by Alfred Rodewald, a cotton-broker and excellent musician, in collaboration with the social worker Father Nugent. Originally an amateur orchestra, giving Sunday concerts for predominantly working-class audiences, it was soon reorganized as the Liverpool Orchestral Society, recruiting professional players and extending its repertory to include modern works as large and difficult as Strauss's 'Tod and Verklärung'. Six years after Rodewald's death in 1903 the orchestra collapsed through lack of financial support. Clearly it had been largely dependent upon an individual's patronage, rather than on public demand.[47]

The most ambitious attempt to tap and educate a large Merseyside audience happened at New Brighton, a cheap ferry trip from Liverpool, where, during the 1890s, holiday facilities modelled on Blackpool were being developed. The Tower management appointed a musical director to conduct a band which was intended to provide military and dance music for five or six hours a day. The post was filled by Granville Bantock, a young composer, unemployed after provincial tours with George Edward's Gaiety company in such newly popular musical comedies as 'The Gaiety Girl' and 'Gentlemen Joe'. Once installed, Bantock met his employers' needs profitably and, since the music required was easily read at sight, used rehearsal time to prepare a more demanding repertory: a visitor was astonished to hear him working at the 'Tristan' prelude. Augmenting his band of wind and percussion with predominantly amateur string players to an orchestra of about 100, Bantock began to give afternoon concerts, in addition to the evening dance music. These were popular, both in the sense that entrance was cheap, and that repertory was substantial but not too adventurous. Gallery tickets were free to people who had paid sixpence to enter the Tower grounds; seats cost an extra 6*d*. A typical 'serious' concert in June 1898 consisted of the *Egmont* overture, Tchaikovsky *Elegy*, 'Jupiter' Symphony, *Siegfried Idyll*, and Liszt's *Second Hungarian Rhapsody*. A year later, apparently disdaining the sugaring of pills, Bantock was presenting undiluted programmes of English contemporary music, by Corder, Cowan, Elgar, Parry, Stanford, and Wallace, often conducted by the composers. Losing his sole supporter on the board of management, and probably alienating the popular audience, Bantock had to abandon his venture, and left New Brighton in 1900.[48]

The most sustained and successful attempt to build an audience for good music in a seaside resort was at Bournemouth. In 1893 Dan Godfrey, heir to a great family tradition of military music, was appointed by the corporation to provide a band of thirty, with uniforms and music, for £95 a week. The wind band played on the pier, and a sufficient number were 'double handed' to form a string orchestra which performed in the Winter Gardens. Some 5,000 people paid 3*d*. a head to attend the first concert, which included Schubert's 'Rosamunde' music and a selection from 'The Gondoliers'.[49] In the following year Godfrey became resident conductor of the country's first permanent municipal orchestra; musicians were retained through the winter, and 'classical' concerts given every Tuesday afternoon. By March 1897 there had been 100 symphony concerts, including substantial works in each programme, and even a performance of the Schubert 'Great' C major Symphony under Manns. Between 1893 and 1914 the net loss to the corporation was £5,443, although profits were made in some years.[50] For less than £300 a year it had acquired a cultural asset of inestimable value which also brought external economies of some relevance to the commercial prosperity of a seaside town. The orchestra was, as Godfrey later remarked, 'a good commercial proposition, indirectly if not directly'.[51]

A few other resorts made brief excursions into 'municipal music', and there was even talk of it, usually coached in utopian rhetoric, in less salubrious towns.[52] In 1913 Glasgow corporation paid £500 to the Scottish Orchestra for four concerts to 'popularise music among the workers'. Tickets were priced at 3*d*., 6*d*., and 1*s*.[53] The most ambitious propagandist for municipal music was W. M. Ingall, who proposed the creation of 228 orchestras in 48 years, to be financed by a special orchestral rate. The Queen's private secretary regretted that 'Her Majesty is unable to offer any opinion upon the subject'.[54] In general, municipal initiatives contributed little to the nation's musical development, or to the employment of musicians.

Time, rational recreation, and social emulation

Throughout the nineteenth century the demand for music and musicians was stimulated by two powerful undercurrents of social change: the reordering of time between work and leisure, and the cult of 'rational recreation'. The former is conceptually elusive, although its stimulus to the demand for professional entertainment, including music, is easily perceived; the latter has often excited comment, usually in the form of scornful distaste for Victorian humbug, but its precise effects on the market are more obscure. Time was reordered by the industrial revolution, and eventually by legislation. The factory system imposed regular working hours in place of traditionally haphazard alterations of diligence and idleness.[55] As the new 'discipline of the clock' was assimilated throughout society a working week of fifty to sixty hours was widely adopted after the Ten Hour Act of 1847, Saturday half holidays were generally established by the 1870s, and 'Sweet Saturday Night' became *the* time for a spree. Thus leisure and increased spending power were concentrated, for the first time as a mass market, into specific periods, a focus which was intensified in Britain by acute Sabbatarianism: the majority of consumers therefore converged for evening and Saturday afternoon entertainment. This formal allocation of time made inroads into former habits of spontaneous music making, as practised by handloom weavers for example, who were notoriously prone to assert their 'leisure preference' whenever the mood took them. Thus the extensive musical activities of the Larks of Dean were only possible, as a contemporary recalled, because 'so long as the fabric got done, in time for due delivery and their money earned, they could do pretty much how they liked'.[56] Factory discipline destroyed that freedom, but it also enabled people to finish work regularly, and eventually early, enough to attend organised rehearsals and performances, a vital fact for the burgeoning choral and brass band movements.

'Rational recreation' was regarded by many Victorians as a highly desirable concomitant of the new leisure. The civilizing of industrial society, or its 'social control', was to be achieved by a two-pronged attack: the suppression of barbarous traditionally popular pastimes, and their replacement, in the phrase of an eminent factory master of the 1830s, by 'endless sources of rational amusement'.[57] Both contemporaries and later historians have disagreed about the effectiveness and significance of these policies and attitudes, some tending to sentimentalize the alleged values of a hypostatized pre-industrial popular culture—folk song and dance, cockfighting and drink—and deplore the constraints of Victorian priggishness; others asserting or assuming the innate superiority of imposed values.[58] If the assault on traditional amusements was frequently a thin-lipped, and sometimes two-faced, attempt to quench pleasure and enforce discipline and subservience, it also contained genuine elements of altruism: a desire to educate and improve. These sentiments gained increasing force as commercialized entertainment expanded and, inevitably, sought to exploit lowest common denominators of taste. The cultural relativism of our own time, which denies or ignores a hierarchy of taste; its populist and commercial attacks on high culture, and strange use of the word 'élitist' as a term of opprobrium: all are so far removed from the cultural self-confidence of reformers, from Matthew Arnold to John Reith, that objective appraisal is now extraordinarily difficult. Fortunately our present theme requires only brief recognition of the movement and, more immediately, some discussion of its likely effects on the demand for professional musicians.

Many reformers were anxious to recruit music as a powerful ally in the war against undesirable pleasures, old and new. An 1835 advertisement for the Preston Vocal and Instrumental Society was typical in offering 'a rational and pleasing source of evening recreation, apart from the seductive influence of the tavern'.[59] In the first number of *Household Words* (1850) Dickens proclaimed and welcomed the fact that 'classical music has of late years been gradually descending from the higher to the humbler classes', and praised the ironmasters, Strutt of Derby and Crawshay of Merthyr, for their bands, which provided 'a rational and refined amusement for classes whose leisure time would otherwise probably have been less creditably spent than in learning or listening to music'.[60] W. S. Jevons, assessing 'Methods of Social Reform' in 1878, vigorously advocated the promotion of music as certainly 'the best means of popular recreation'. Returning from a visit to Norway and Sweden and Denmark he was appalled by 'the contrast between the poor gentleman peasants of Scandinavia, and the rich, rowdy, drunken artisans of England'. The root cause, he argued, was cultural deprivation: a dearth of facilities for civilized amusement, and 'the low state of musical education among the masses' which rendered them 'helpless . . . when seeking recreation'.[61] Belief in the improving qualities of music found its most ardent exponent in the Revd. H. R. Haweis, whose widely-read 'Music and Morals' exudes dotty piety and enthusiasm. He believed that certain kinds of melody were intrinsically capable of inducing wholesome thoughts, and his desire to establish music's credentials even leads him to an elaborate defence of the musician's inherent morality. Most musicians, he was convinced, were embodiments of virtue, except for 'a large number of very low-class foreigners, with foreign habits and very foreign morals [who] have unhappily taken up their abode in England'. Many great composers were 'examples not only of steady and indefatigable workers, but also of high-minded moral and even religious men'.[62]

If few people shared Haweis's convictions as to the explicit moral force of music and musicians, there was widespread adherence to two interconnected beliefs: that, given an appropriately genteel setting, music was a 'highly respectablising activity', and that it could and should be morally uplifting. These beliefs were related in turn to patterns of social emulation. In most societies a major driving force can be variously described as ambition, emulation, or embourgeoisement. Thus a distinguished historian of France attaches great importance to 'the ambitions of ordinary men'.[63] That social emulation was not peculiar to the nineteenth century can be adduced from today's displayed, but unread, encyclopaedias and uniformly bound classics, or from the advertisements in English Sunday supplements, and the *New Yorker*. Victorian symbols, if outwardly different, performed similar functions. In a society which was profoundly conscious of class yet offered chances of social mobility, it was necessary for the ambitious to recognize and exhibit appropriate symbols of aspiration and achievement. Some of the most potent badges were pinned to music, particularly in respectable settings: ownership of a piano;[64] music lessons for daughters; attendance at the oratorio, the quintessentially Victorian socio-musical event; membership of a concert society, preferably exclusive like all good clubs; appearance at the theatre or ball, suitably clad and preferably bejewelled. Newspaper reports, particularly in the provinces where such signals are more easily transmitted and read, reflected social priorities as much as aesthetic innocence, when they devoted less space to music and performer than to the 'respectability' and 'eminence' of the audience. Of course many people continued to seek music for simple reasons of conviviality and enjoyment, and some through devotion to the art, but the trappings of social emulation steadily underpinned the expanding demand for music and musicians. The demand for these trappings affected the employment of musicians with varying intensity. Oratorios and pianos were most important because most ubiquitous.

It is a commonplace that Victorian attitudes towards music were usually suffused with, and frequently suffocated by, postures of religion and morality. Their most intense manifestation was the oratorio, attendance at which was a tribal rite, demonstrating piety and respectability; a form of religious observance at which applause was an irreverence and the audience made up for lack of musicality by its submission to orthodoxy. The English, noted a German visitor, 'esteem in oratorio music a bit of divine service'.[65] Discussing a performance at the People's Palace of Gounod's miserable, and highly profitable *Redemption*, Shaw wrote 'I understand that various members of the industrial classes of Mile End pretended to enjoy it, which shows how the hypocrisy of culture, like other cast-off fashions, finds its last asylum among the poor'.[66] Shaw was describing, in 1889, as on so many other hilarious occasions, a prevailing pharisaism which could mount Saint-Saëns's *Samson et Delilah* as a sacred oratorio, or banish *La Traviata* from the theatre to the dank sobriety of Exeter Hall. The cultural effects of oratorio on musical genre, style, and taste is a familiar theme.[67] Its economic effect was to provide a regular and devout audience, and therefore employment for musicians, throughout the land, particularly at the great provincial festivals. Choirs were predominantly amateur, but orchestras were recruited from local musicians, increasingly professional, usually reinforced by a few London or Manchester instrumentalists; and many singers built their careers on the *Messiah* and Mendelssohn circuit.

In contrast to the increasingly modern connotations of metropolitan concert life—anonymous ticket-buying audiences, professional performers, and profit-seeking entrepreneurs—the provincial oratorio tended to perpetuate traditional extra-musical associations. Funds were raised for charity, and there was an associated emphasis upon named patrons to lend prestige and guarantee cash. In 'their desire for respectability the middle class made it their duty to be present'.[68] The fact that choirs were amateur both lowered costs and added relations and friends to the paying audience. A typical event was the first Glasgow Musical Festival in January 1860, belated because Calvinism had delayed the acceptance of sacred music, fighting a long campaign before the first Scottish performance of *Messiah* in 1844. The 1860 prospectus, which listed four pages of patrons, admitted that until recently performances of a single oratorio had been unprofitable in the city. Now improvement in the public taste allowed a festival which would provide not merely a 'Grand Musical Demonstration' but also a source of funds for 'The most important charities'. In addition to the inevitable 'Messiah' and 'Elijah', there would be 'Gideon' by Charles Horsley (who also wrote 'David', and 'Joseph'), and a ragbag concert. Clara Novello was among the soloists, and a band of fifty-six included Blagrove and Carrodus from London.[69] The choir was 400 strong. The initiation and continuance of such events was often closely associated with municipal development and pride. Leeds, for example, began its series of festivals in 1858 to celebrate the new town hall and outbid Bradford. Its burghers demonstrated their wealth by buying 'the biggest town hall, the best artists, the best composers and a massive orchestra, with chorus and orchestra provided by themselves'.[70] Approximately £5,000 was paid to the performers and the profit of £2,000 went to the General Infirmary. The orchestra 'comprised the most celebrated performers of the Metropolis, with whom were associated a few local artists of repute in the West Riding'.[71] The chorus became justly famous, not least because it was 'one of the few forms of cultural expression over which Anglican, Methodist and dissenter did not fall out'.[72]

Teachers

Government expenditure on education had little effect on the demand for professional musicians during the nineteenth century. By far the largest item—it was estimated at £100,000 a year in 1878—arose from the practice, instituted in 1874, of granting schools 1s. per head if inspectors reported that singing was 'part of the ordinary course of instruction'.[73] A later modification allowed 6d. for singing 'by ear' and 1s. 'at sight': teaching by rote instead of by note had been attacked by Hullah as 'a sham'. Further details would lead us into the tortuous history of tonic sol-fa.[74] The essential point for our purpose is that few of the teachers, or even the inspectors, could reasonably be described as professional musicians. Some contemporaries deplored the contrast between public expenditure on this scheme and the paltry, precarious sums allotted for professional training; £500 to the Royal Academy of Music and £250 to the Irish Academy. An anonymous correspondent to *The Times* expressed the opposing view, which was to prevail for at least the next fifty years: 'Musical talent and the higher development of musical art may be safely left to look after themselves'; more important was the 'wholesome pleasure' and moral improvement to be procured from elementary singing.[75]

It was in the private sector that the vast majority of music teachers found employment. Most built up a circle of pupils from scratch, but 'practices' could be purchased, as in medicine. They got cheaper as competition increased. In 1845 Walter MacFarren went to Southampton, on the recommendation of Sterndale Bennett, 'with a view to purchasing the connection there of a professor who had recently died. For three weeks I took up his teaching and his parish organ, but when I ascertained the prohibitive terms on which I was to retain the deceased musician's *clientele*, I "threw up the sponge" and returned to London and the Royal Academy of Music'.[76] Buyers and sellers advertised in the *Musical Times*: 'A Gentleman is desirous of treating for the purchase of an established teaching connection in the provinces. A fashionable watering place with an organist's appointment preferred'.[77] 'Wanted: married Music Master to attend Ladies School in the country. May probably be appointed organist in parish, and may obtain other teaching. Payment for school £100 a year. House rent and coals cheap. Frome'.[78] By the 1880s advertisements frequently linked music teaching, selling, and piano tuning:

MUSIC BUSINESS and TEACHING CONNECTION for SALE, together or separately, as a going concern, in a large town in South-west Lancashire. Capital hiring, tuning, and counter trade; easily managed. Net profits £550 per annum. Price, including complete stock, fixtures, goodwill, etc. £1,400.[79]

DISPOSAL—Old-established MUSIC BUSINESS at Seaside, North Wales, Steady Hiring trade, yielding upwards of £160 per annum. Good tuning connection. Opening for efficient Teacher. Rent (house and shop), £40. Price merely nominal.[80]

Since self-employed teachers were the largest single category of professional musicians by the end of the century, and the majority taught only elementary piano, the demand for such teachers was clearly of paramount importance. Its roots had less to do with inherent musical needs than with social emulation, a pattern which was set by the 1840s and immortalized by Thackeray's Miss Wirt. That 'most invaluable person' who 'had lived in the very highest society' was no 'rosebud but she had been near it'. The Ponto sisters entertain the family circle with polkas, as played at Devonshire House, displaying a brilliant touch and, on that already 'somewhat exploded instrument', the harp, a fine arm. Miss Wirt, their governess and Squirtz's favourite pupil, takes over a stunning performance of 'Gettin' Up Stairs'. It had been the favourite of her previous employer, the dear Duchess, and she had taught it to the Ladies Barbara and Jane. While hearing the latter's rendition the dear Lord Castletoddy first fell in love with Lady Jane. He was only an Irish peer, with no more than £15,000 a year, but Miss Wirt had persuaded Jane to have him. Mr Snob was suitably impressed by her status and authority, for he had been accustomed to seeing governesses bullied.[81] A generation later the market for pianos and piano lessons was moving down the social scale, but purchasers continued to gaze upwards. In 1871 Haweis guessed that there were some 400,000 pianos and 1m. pianists in the British Isles. Forty years later there were probably between 2m. and 4m. pianos in British homes, one for every ten to twenty people. The evolution of piano mania has been explained in another book, and the evidence need not be repeated here.[82] Essential items of respectable furniture, pianos were not all played, but the same process of social emulation which influenced their purchase prompted the desire for lessons. Access to a piano could be an incentive to play it simply for enjoyment and enlightenment, for no other instrument gives access to so wide a literature. But the extent of piano-teaching, and its precipitous decline after the 1920s, cannot be explained in purely musical terms. While demand manifested itself throughout society, a particularly important new group of consumers were the rapidly expanding white-collar workers—schoolteachers, clerks, commercial travellers, and low-level managers, earning salaries between £150 and £300—who were able and eager to purchase improvement and culture for their children. Massive undiscriminating demand for cheap lessons was probably the greatest single stimulus to the employment of musicians, of a sort, in late Victorian and Edwardian society.

Among the upper classes the demand for music teachers was severely limited by sexual codes of behaviour. If pupils at all levels of society were predominantly female, music was virtually forbidden to boys of 'good family', particularly if they betrayed signs of talent or serious interest. Sir Frederick Ouseley's Oxford Mus.B. degree was taken in 1850 against the dean of Christ Church's advice that 'it was utterly derogatory for a man in his social position to entertain such an idea'.[83] E. H. F. Fellowes was too well-born to be allowed to take up Joachim's extraordinary offer of violin lessons. His uncles, who took pride in their classical scholarship, were so alarmed at his mother's proposal to take him to a Handel festival that they withdrew the proffered tickets. For such people classics and mathematics were the 'exclusive subjects for a gentleman's education' and flirtations with music were regarded 'with indignation and bewilderment'.[84] Sometimes the general disapproval was tempered by idiosyncratic prejudice: Fuller Maitland was brought up to believe, in the early 1870s, that 'it was not considered right for a boy to play the piano' but he was allowed to sing and play the violin.[85] All three of these men had some music in their family background, but were subjected to the crippling constraints appropriate to their caste. The vast majority of gentlemen, of course, were born and bred away from music, their immunity reinforced by preparatory and public school. Even Fellowes, who was given an Amati violin by his parents (price £100 with a Tourte bow in 1879; they would cost at least 200 times that sum today) was forced to abandon music in term time, practising only during the holidays.

For most of the nineteenth century the majority of public schools effectively suppressed any manifestations of latent musicality among their pupils, and certainly did not employ musicians on their staff. A few new schools began to engage organist choir masters before 1850, and Uppingham, whose headmaster was tone deaf but believed in 'the refining and elevating influence of music', appointed a good German music teacher in 1865. At Harrow John Farmer began to teach the piano unofficially in 1862, and was later recognized as a member of staff, before moving on to Balliol in 1885.[86] When Joseph Barnby became precentor at Eton in 1865 he found no music and was astonished 'that these young patricians had by no means the natural ability that was to be found in the lower strata of life'. His estimate was that scarcely 30 per cent had the 'faintest notion of sound' against at least 70 per cent among the lower orders.[87] Despite these animadversions, couched to appease petty bourgeois prejudice at a meeting of the Incorporated Society of Musicians, music was enlarging its influence in the public schools by the 1890s. Several were permitting boys in junior forms to have lessons during school periods, 'a great advance', according to one of the teachers, which considerably increased the numbers learning instruments.[88] A 1904 list names seventy-three public school chapels, each employing at least one musician, usually an FRCO or graduate.[89] Far larger numbers, of course, were working in equivalent girls' schools, where a display of musical accomplishment was almost *de rigueur*. In some the activities were more ambitious, notably among members of the Girls' Public Day School Trust. At Streatham Hill High School, Stewart Macpherson was experimenting with 'musical appreciation'.

Patronage

What was the role of 'patronage' in the expansion of 'demand'? Both terms are ambiguous, and sometimes used interchangeably. It is useful to distinguish at least four types of patronage: 'personal', with the patron as direct employer; 'official', which often implies a measure of ideology and authoritarianism; 'open market'; and 'subvention', in which public and private patrons underwrite costs.[90] No one system is necessarily exclusive of others, though official patronage in Nazi Germany and Soviet Russia has sought that ideal. Nevertheless in most societies, over long periods of time, specific types of patronage can be seen to predominate.[91] Thus it is obvious that music in Britain was mainly influenced by the 'open market' during the nineteenth century and first thirty years of the twentieth century, with 'subvention' playing a significant role thereafter. Despite the munificence of a few individuals, and the largesse bestowed by society hostesses upon visiting celebrities, personal patronage was neither sufficiently extensive, nor educated and consistent enough, to make much difference to emerging forms of music-making and therefore of musicians' employment. The overall pattern of demand determines the quantity of music supplied, but it also influences its form and quality; and much will depend upon the attitudes and interests of society's leaders, which, in Britain, were generally ignorant, and ranged from indifference to hostility. After Albert's death, as citizens of a liberal democracy were at liberty to observe, nothing could be expected from the court. 'Had the life of this prince been spared', wrote Ella in 1878, 'the arts in England would have had an advocate to plead successfully on behalf of their institutions'.[92] The widow Queen's attitude towards musicians was noted by Clara Schumann, with some asperity;[93] and later the court's artistic proclivities descended to the overt philistinism of George V. With few exceptions the nation's leaders followed suit: neither music nor musicians were taken seriously.

In some areas the effect was direct and self-evident. Attempts to create a first-class national conservatory, for example, in which the Prince Consort had a vital and informed interest, were dissipated after his death. More generally the implications of royal and official indifferences were indirect but insidious. The lack of a sustained commitment to opera, in the age of Verdi and Wagner, was, as many commentators have pointed out, the most crippling weakness in British musical life. The London season was short, irregular, and dominated by arbitrary fashion; while provincial events were confined, at best, to scratch performances by impoverished touring companies. The 'Grand Opera' houses designed by Frank Matcham had barely nodding acquaintance with opera. The absence of permanent symphony orchestras is another example of the system's inherent weakness. No orchestra offered full-time employment, and even the best musicians spent much of their time sight-reading, and playing far below their capabilities. Although the Hallé came closer to permanency and adequate rehearsals than any London orchestra before 1930, it too was incapable of offering players year-long contracts. In London the main concert halls held a total audience of only 13,000, and were closed to music for substantial parts of the year. Novello's Albert Hall concerts and Chappell's 'Pops' were losing custom by the 1890s, and there were other signs that the demand for serious music was falling.[94] In 1909 several observers, including the young Havergal Brian, reported a 'crisis', in which there were few opportunities for British composers, too many orchestras, and a proliferation of concerts which reflected 'the enthusiasm of musicians rather than the craving of the people'.[95] Enthusiasts for 'musical appreciation', like Macpherson and Scholes, sought to correct this imbalance by educating listeners.[96]

A sociologist has depicted the symphony orchestra in ninetenth-century England as an alien organisation seeking assimilation into an unfriendly environment;[97] but the implied contrast with continental practice is misleading, and the nature of inhospitality requires more explicit identification. Even in those countries whose cultural climate was more welcoming, few orchestral musicians could make a living from symphony concerts, though some orchestras, in Leipzig, Berlin, and Amsterdam, for example, were supported by public or private subsidies. It was employment in theatres which gave most of them their main working experience and source of income; and it was in the great network of civic opera houses that they, and not least their conductors, learned their craft. British players were similarly dependent upon the theatre; but in place of discriminating, or at least interested, continental audiences and managements, and a repertory which seldom sank below the level of Lortzing, the British working environment placed music low in its scale of priorities. It is remarkable that throughout the long debate about working conditions,[98] neither management, workers' represent-atives, nor officials displayed much genuine concern for the quality of music being performed.

Opportunities for solo work and chamber music were similarly constrained. Foreign instrumentalists were generally preferred, allegedly through prejudice but, at least in part, because English performers were caught in a vicious circle of inexperience and neglect. This cultural impoverishment affected both the demand for and the supply of talented native musicians. Reduced to dependence upon ballad concerts, tea-time music, the oratorio circuit, musical comedy, and the accompaniment of music-hall artists, they had few opportunities of advancement.

Conductors faced a dispiriting round of hack-work, relieved by occasional stabs at the serious repertory with under-rehearsed, scratch orchestras whose personnel played musical chairs at the behest of the deputy system. Some, like Landon Ronald (1873–1938) and Henry Wood (1869–1944), achieved a level of proficiency. Only one, Thomas Beecham, was comparable to the greatest of his foreign contemporaries, and it is notable that he was not dependent upon the open market, putting far more cash into music than he ever took from it.

The existence of these limitations has been obscured by talk of an English 'renaissance',[99] and loyal resistance to the taunt of 'Das Land ohne Musik':[100] arguments which cannot be resolved by the identification of a solitary great composer and the counting of musical events and musicians. An anecdote of the bassoonist Archie Camden may tell us something about the levels of taste and understanding which underlay England's demand for music before 1914. Along with other first-class instrumentalists, he would spend the summer months at Buxton or Eastbourne, earning a few pounds in a scratch band. It was their favourite pastime to play movements from Beethoven symphonies, attributing their composition, in turn, to individual members of the band, who would solemnly acknowledge the audience's applause.[101]

IV

Supply and Training

The exorbitant rewards of players, opera-singers, opera-dancers, etc., are founded upon those two principles: the rarity and beauty of the talents, and the discredit of employing them in this manner . . . Should the public opinion or prejudice ever alter with regard to such occupations, their pecuniary recompense would quickly diminish. More people would apply to them, and the competition would quickly reduce the price of their labour. Such talents, though far from being common, are by no means so rare as is imagined. Many people possess them in great perfection, who disdain to make use of them; and many more are capable of acquiring them, if anything could be made honourably by them.

Adam Smith, 1776

He had been a very indifferent musical amateur in his better days; and when he fell with his brother, resorted for support to playing a clarionet as dirty as himself in a small theatre orchestra.

Dickens, *Little Dorrit*

How can we account for the huge and unprecedented expansion in the number of musicians during the nineteenth century? In an open market the *potential* supply of musicians is always highly 'elastic', responding to new opportunities. In practice the speed of response will depend upon three factors: the size and extent of incentives, economic, social, and aesthetic; the efficiency of communications, which signal job opportunities and enable musicians to take them up; and the availability of talent. The first two were transformed, as already described. The third is more difficult to categorize than Adam Smith's simplistic account would suggest. Immunized by a surfeit of hyperbole, and made cautious by an austere musicology which tends to underrate the creativity of performing artists, our generation is loath to accept those gradations from 'exceptional talent' to 'genius' which were once a commonplace of music criticism. Yet accounts like Kuhe's description of Patti's debut in 1861 ('no case of merely exceptional talent; we were face to face with phenomenal genius')[1] or personal experience of such irreplaceable artists as Callas or Furtwängler, prompt the belief that such gradations do indeed exist, and that 'genius' with its attendant 'drawing power', is exceptionally rare and can always name its price. For the general run of musical competence, however, no such limitation of supply and monopoly price need long apply.

To a degree unmatched by other skilled occupations there are, in music, few natural barriers of age, physique, sex, or language. Children can learn to play most instruments from an early age (indeed in most cases it is necessary that they do so) and, if sufficiently gifted and properly taught, they can soon reach a standard unattainable by experienced but mediocre adults. 'There is no career', remarked Galton, 'in which eminence is achieved so early in life.'[2] Despite ancient prejudices about their alleged physical inadequacies, women can play any instrument as well as men. It might be thought that actors, apart from obvious limitations of repertory, enjoy a similarly open access to work; but even that most 'open' of professions denies entry to foreigners unless they have mastered the appropriate language, dialect, or accent. Music imposes no constraints of this kind, except in rare and special cases. Foreigners can gain employment immediately on arrival in a new country, and may even be preferred. Entry to the profession is also greatly facilitated by the ease with which amateur musicians can move to part-time and then full-time professional employment and, if necessary, back. A final bridge to entry is the inexperience or ignorance of the public, except, perhaps, when listening to singers, whose qualities are more easily or naturally assessed. It is important to remember that, until recently, when recording and broadcasting began to widen circles of experience and raise standards of discernment, mediocrity and incompetence easily won acceptance, and meretriciousness acclaim, outside a few sophisticated centres.

Most of these conditions, which ease the potential supply of musicians, apply with even greater force to music teachers. Children in musician families have traditionally instructed their siblings, and young students have assisted their masters, or helped pay for lessons by teaching others, if not prevented from doing so. Women have won readier access to pupils than to platforms; and foreign teachers, when not actually preferred, have never been much hampered by linguistic difficulties. Finally a general public which is sufficiently naïve to welcome mediocre performers will also provide employment for mediocre teachers, its ignorance reinforced by indifference to any but the most superficial results (a diploma, or performance of a simple piece), and by the fact that few pupils are likely to progress to a stage where they tax the teacher's resources too obviously. Therefore the only serious constraints upon people who wish to enter the profession are access to instruments and tuition, and some aptitude. Society may also, by its disapproval, impose additional barriers: that 'discredit' of employment which Smith considered a major reason for 'exorbitant rewards' and has frequently led respectable parents to discourage their children from becoming musicians.

In practice, as we have seen, these economic and social disincentives were once very powerful, and were reinforced by institutional restrictions on entry to the profession. Instruments and tuition were scarce and expensive. Apart from their own children, and perhaps an apprentice or two, musicians' pupils were usually the daughters of affluent men who were not destined to compete with their masters, though some might marry them. Interlopers were kept out, originally by formal guild regulations and, long after these had broken down, by informal means of guarding the 'mysteries' of the craft. All this effectively limited entry in such closed, immobile societies as eighteenth-century France, and even continued to restrict the flow of native musicians into the freer and more rapidly expanding market of pre-industrial England, though immigrants, the 'surplus products' of continental Europe, found ready employment. The traditional procedures of apprenticeship survived particularly, but not solely, for the training of church musicians. The Bradford organist A. T. Akeroyd (*b.*1862), for example, who was later active in the Incorporated Society of Musicians, described himself as 'the articled pupil of F. C. Atkinson, ARCM'.[3] Edward Williams's indentures are reproduced *verbatim* (see Appendix) because of their intrinsic interest and because his son, J. B. Williams, was later to create the Musicians' Union. Edward, who became a theatre musician, was apprenticed in 1860 at the age of 17. The archaic legal jargon of his articles binds him for four years to his master in conditions of absolute subservience, and give the latter half-share in his earnings.

As the demand for musicians increased it was unlikely that many young musicians would submit to such constraints when alternative modes of entry became available. Within a few decades the determinants of supply were utterly transformed. Old barriers, which had become increasingly ineffectual, or irrelevant, finally crumbled; and new attempts to control supply, by forming professional associations and trade unions, were yet to come. Instruments, sheet music, and tuition, became cheaper and more accessible. The flow of musicians seeking employment rapidly increased and, after 1870, became a torrent, which continued to be channelled into jobs so long as demand remained buoyant. By the twentieth century music was still a labour-intensive activity, dependent upon cheap labour. As we have already remarked, outstanding talent never ceased to be rare: the huge fees commanded by a Patti or Melba were based upon absolute scarcity, and skilful manipulation of demand. There were also occasional shortages of competent players of some instruments, but such temporary scarcities could soon be removed by tapping a world market. Generally performers, and particularly teachers, became abundant, manning an industry which had not yet explored ways of saving labour, and had little incentive to do so.

The newly positive determinants of supply, as distinct from the erosion of old constraints, were only slowly beginning to take effect before 1870. The costs of instruments, notably pianos, books and sheet music, remained high in relation to the general level of incomes. Teaching was becoming cheaper and more widely accessible, both socially and geographically: a slow, but relentlessly cumulative process, since even students took pupils, and many took short cuts: 'musical education is so expensive' wrote John Ella in 1869, 'that most must dispense with instruction while still half educated'.[4] But the most important innovation was less significant in immediately quantitative terms than in the precedents it set for the future. The country's first national conservatory opened in 1823. Its early history would not merit detailed examination if we were solely concerned with the numbers or distinction of its students. But its first four decades of penury raised questions and set precedents of fundamental importance for the future of the profession, culminating in an extensive inquiry of crucial importance to an understanding of mid-Victorian attitudes towards music, its practitioners, and their education. Since historians have hitherto either ignored these matters or reduced them to Panglossian simplicities, they demand at least an interim scrutiny appropriate to their importance.

The Royal Academy of Music

Between 1823, when it first attempted to raise funds, and 1866, when the Society of Arts investigated its activities,[5] the RAM suffered a meagre and precarious existence. Most of its troubles stemmed from poverty, but grandiloquent and muddled aspirations, incompetence, and petty rivalries all played their part. Its direct contribution to the supply of professional musicians during this period was limited in quantity and quality. About 1,300 passed through its doors, perhaps 7 per cent of the total number working in Britain during the 1860s, and few achieved much distinction. A list of former students, attached to the Society's report, proudly names seventy-six 'established professors', but all were provincial teachers of modest attainment. Nor did it have much impact upon the supply of players. The *Athenaeum* published 'facts and figures furnished by an orchestral artist' to challenge claims made on behalf of the Academy that 'our orchestras have been mainly fed from that source', and concluded that 'the number of competent instrumental solo players who have been turned out during the last thirty years is some half a score'.[6] Since Henry Chorley, the *Athenaeum's* music critic, was probably the most vociferous of the Academy's many opponents, the statistics may be suspected of bias. But they were never challenged; not even by MacFarren, who never missed an opportunity to defend his Alma Mater and ridicule Chorley.[7] We therefore reproduce the figures, in tabular form. Most players worked in more than one of the named

Orchestral players in the main London orchestras, 1866

	Total players	English players	ex-RAM	Principals ex-RAM
Royal Italian Opera	87	71	17	4*
Her Majesty's Theatre	80+	40	6	0
Philharmonic Society	c.70		15	4†
Musical Society	85	69	17	6
New Philharmonic Society	97	73	16	5

* viola, double-bass, trumpet, horn.
† violin, viola, cello, bassoon.

orchestras, so their numbers cannot be totalled, but the table probably gives a fair representation of the Academy's contribution to the supply of orchestral musicians during the first three decades of its existence. Its poor record was further diminished by total neglect of many indispensible intruments. As the *Athenaeum* pointed out, Costa's opera orchestra, probably the best in London, included not a single performer on harp, flute, oboe, clarinet, bassoon, or trombone, from the Academy.

Since previous schemes had either been purely conjectural, or had come to nothing,[8] the launching of a national conservatory was something of an achievement. Only a few months earlier T. F. Walmisley, an organist and glee composer, had called a meeting of the Philharmonic Society with a similar purpose, and gained the support of several prominent members of London's musical society including Henry Bishop, Charles Neate (who gave the English première of Beethoven's 'Emperor' concerto), and Vincent Novello. But the 'foundation was diverted into the hands of noble amateurs',[9] initiating a conflict with professional musicians which was to dog the Academy's fortunes for at least half a century. The amateurs were led by Lord Burghersh (later Westmoreland), a dilettante 'composer': doubts were expressed about his authorship of two operas and a mass.[10] Without relevant experience or knowledge, he was supported by a committee of similarly qualified aristocrats. They proposed to create an institution where 'musical students might have the highest possible education, and should be fitted for the art they followed, without having to seek in continental institutions an education which hitherto has been impossible at home'.[11] Its subsequent history, at least until the 1880s, was a sequence of rebuffs to these aspirations.

The staff, as announced in the *Morning Post*, was to have included Clementi and a number of those 'specialist' professionals described in Chapter III: Dragonetti, Griesbach, Mori, and Willman. In practice, however, most teaching was done by 'obscure natives' rather than 'eminent foreigners', in the words of an official historian of the Academy.[12] Lack of funds was doubtless the prime, though not the sole, reason for so many undistinguished appointments. First-class instrumentalists would have contributed a measure of practical experience and competence to the training of British professionals. Moreover they could have fitted teaching responsibilities into working lives which, before the railway age, were busy but not yet excessively mobile. It soon became apparent, however, that the Academy could not afford to insist upon high standards among its staff or, even more sadly, its students. The public's response to appeals for funds was feeble, the Government's assistance derisory. Hoping for £150,000 the Committee secured only £5,000 in donations and £500 in subscriptions. The latter included 100 gns. from George IV, signifying, as the distinguished Belgian musicologist Fétis tartly remarked, 'that the King has taken it under his protection without offering it any succour'.[13] By March 1824 there was already a deficiency of £1,600, and attempts to balance the books began to destroy the Academy's alleged purpose and function. Fees, which had originally been fixed at 10 gns. for promising 'foundation students' and 20 gns. for the rest, were raised to an undiscriminating and prohibitive £40. Teachers were forced to give up three month's pay. Henceforth they were usually paid well below prevailing market rates, and often late. By the 1840s most of them were getting 3s. 6d. an hour, though a few were able to insist on 5s. Nobody received a regular stipend. 'Sub-professors', barely trained pupil-teachers who received no payment, were widely employed.[14]

Even if funds had been ample, the appointment of staff to a national conservatory would have required more knowledge and tact than the committee could muster. Many of those musicians who were not appointed would be likely to resent the prestige and privileges, real or imagined, accorded to those who were, and some would nurse grudges, which there was ample opportunity to vent. Foreigners would inevitably arouse chauvinistic antagonism, yet their exclusion would have greatly increased the difficulty of recruiting adequate teachers, particularly if strong links were to be forged with the opera house, the heartland of contemporary secular music and principal workplace of the best players and singers. These inescapable difficulties were exacerbated by the committee's unique blend of ineptitude and arrogance, and by middle-class resentment of its dominance by fashionable aristocrats, who were presumed to be always 'ready to receive any foreign pretender'.[15]

It was unfortunate, in these circumstances, that hostage was given to fortune by the appointment of Nicholas Charles Bochsa, not only as professor of harp, but as general secretary. Bochsa was a good, versatile musician, whose 'method' and composition for the harp 'immensely expanded its technical and expressive range'.[16] He was also a condemned forger and, allegedly, a bigamist. The 'monstrous absurdity' of his appointment was first attacked on the ground that a Secretary should have better command of English,[17] but criticism soon degenerated into scurrilous abuse of the Academy for allowing a 'French Felon' into England, and reducing the country to a 'common sewer—the receptacle of all the filth and corruption of Europe'. Open letters were addressed to the Archbishop of York, a patron, from a parent who wished to send his children to the Academy but feared the influence of a 'foreign convict who . . . obtains his daily bread by shuffling and swindling'.[18] Widespread scandal-mongering, of which the quoted passages are but a taste, must have damaged the Academy's image, and therefore its ability to attract funds and good teachers. Its immediate effect was to remove a key member of staff who, whatever his moral failings, had planned a co-ordinated curriculum (soon to disintegrate) and demonstrated a 'remarkable talent for organisation and the greatest facility in musical arrangement'[19]—MacFarren's opinion is corroborated by Henry Phillips, who describes a 'wonderful feat' of rapid arrangement which astonished his fellow musicians.[20] It was an invaluable skill where student orchestras had to be formed from diverse and incomplete instrumental resources. Although Bochsa had the monarch's personal support, which secured him the musical directorship at the King's Theatre when vituperation was rampant, he was forced to resign from the Academy in 1827.

There were no other professors of comparable experience and specialist skills. Crotch, the first principal, was long past his best; too eccentric and inexperienced in the practical world of music to carry weight, impose coherent programmes of study, and defend his staff against the committee. He too was forced to resign in 1831 by the guardians of morality. His sin was to reward the playing of a lady student, 'as an old gentleman might', with a chaste kiss.[21] Cipriani Potter, who took over as principal, was a composer and pianist who gave the English premières of several Beethoven and Mozart concertos. His limited musicianship was once demonstrated by his unwillingness to transpose an accompaniment at sight—a task immediately performed by the 13-year-old Liszt.[22] He also lacked appropriate qualifications for the 'orchestral studies' which he had inherited from Bochsa. Lindley was one of the few successful instrumentalists to take pupils, including Charles Lucas, who was later to succeed him in the Opera orchestra, and eventually become principal of the Academy. In 1829 Fétis noted the absence of a coherent school of violin-playing, considering the existing professors 'incapable of forming good pupils'. He was more impressed by the piano-teaching of Moscheles, Potter, and Mrs Anderson, but this would not long survive.[23] In general neither vocal nor instrumental standards were established with enough consistency and permanence to prevent an inexorable slide into mediocrity.

The Academy's deficiencies as a national institution for the training of professional musicians soon became apparent when contemporaries compared it with the conservatories of Paris, and later Leipzig. At the *Conservatoire*, which opened in 1795, officially approved texts ensured uniform, and frequently excellent, standards of teaching under the direction of a senior authority. Thus Louis Adam, who taught Kalkbrenner, one of the first piano virtuosos, published in 1798 *Méthode ou principe générale du doigte pour le Forte Pianoforte*. A large volume, containing verbal direction, 150 pages of exercises, and a 'dictionary of passages', 359 excerpts from Haydn, Mozart, Clementi, and others, it was clearly intended to train serious pianists:[24] a significant distinction for an instrument which, more than any other, was taken up by amateurs. Similarly violin instruction at the *Conservatoire* was firmly based on the *Méthode* by Baillot, Rode, and Kreutzer (1803) and later on Baillot's *L'Art de violin* (1834) 'perhaps the most influential violin treatise of the nineteenth century'.[25] J. B. Arban (1825–89), professor of cornet, published a classic *Méthode* in 1864 which later became the 'bible' of English brass band players.[26] Standards were vigorously maintained by an elaborate system of competitions and examinations. Precise age limits were prescribed for various levels of study, and a carefully planned, highly centralized system of education was underpinned by the celebrated compulsory course in solfège, to which students could be admitted at the age of nine. The institution was directed, at least after 1822, when Cherubini took over, by a musician of universally acknowledged eminence. It differed from the Academy and later British conservatories in two other important respects: attractiveness to foreign students, despite attempts to exclude them, and a preponderance of men. Throughout the nineteenth century the responsible Minister was subjected to political pressure against the admission of foreigners. In 1822 he insisted that only rare exceptions were allowed to a general exclusion. By the 1880s ninety foreigners were enrolled out of a total of 630 students. There were particular objections to their prominence in string classes which, since they trained orchestral players as well as soloists, were thought to represent a potential threat to local employment. The award of cello prizes to foreigners three times out of four was also cause for remonstrance. Henceforth, it was decided, no more than two foreigners would be allowed in any class. There were always more men than women students, in stark contrast to English practice, and with significant implications for the balance between professional and dilettante.[27] In 1822 the ratio was 193:124; in 1892 394:278.

The Leipzig Conservatory, established in 1843, also rapidly began to 'act as a proving ground and licensing agent for the new "profession" of music'.[28] Although it differed from Paris in several respects, avoiding contests and prizes, and actively encouraging the enrolment of foreign students, its insistence upon a unified curriculum and high standards was even more rigorous. Most of its staff were successful, practising musicians, who were expected to continue an active career. Mendelssohn was the first director. The piano faculty, which attracted most attention, also included Schumann for a brief period, Moscheles, and Plaidy, who taught von Bülow. Moscheles's appointment proves that cash was not the sole determinant in recruiting distinguished staff. Gladly abandoning a brilliant career in London for a modest salary at Leipzig, he realized his 'dream of emancipation from professional slavery; in the Conservatory I am engaged 16 hours per week, at home I have only eight private lessons to give; what is that after the daily steeplechase in London?' He was therefore willing to sacrifice the 'material comforts' of London for an 'art atmosphere'.[29]

The RAM could offer no similar incentives to compensate for paltry remuneration. Individual teachers went their separate ways and were denied even a semblance of corporate identity or coherent purpose, since there was no board of professors. The institution was administered autocratically by a committee of amateurs who meddled at every level. It was even possible for Burghersh to stop the student orchestra from practising a Haydn symphony in order to play his own 'Magnificat'.[30] Courses of study inevitably failed to impose uniform standards or achieve balance between the various parts of an anarchic syllabus. In the early years when pupils were boarders, aged between ten and fourteen, much time was devoted to religious and moral instruction, with obsessively strict separation of the sexes. It must be admitted that a similar concern was active at the *Conservatoire*, leading to a famous confrontation between its director and Berlioz. But his criticism of that institution's shortcomings inhabits a different world from London: a plea for minor reforms to an acknowledged centre of excellence.[31] Musical training was absurdly limited at the Academy: 'two lessons of 18 minutes each in duration per week—about the time (not quite) afforded by masters to the little Misses in the commonest boarding schools' was a contemporary verdict. It came, not from one of many snipers in the profession, but from R. M. Bacon, who had prepared the Academy's first prospectus, and had frequently been consulted by its Directors. Practice sessions were a communal bedlam. A visitor during the early 1830s found twenty pianos producing an 'incessant jangle' in a single room, and diverse adjacent instruments contributing to the general din.[32] The procedure was similar to the 'dutch concert' which Burney had observed at the Naples *conservatorio*[33] in 1770, a fact which was sometimes adduced in its defence: 'Laugh not at this', MacFarren warned a later generation of students, 'it was supposed that such habit would serve to concentrate the attention of the students on their work, and would make not only their work more earnest, but refine their ears, and make musical perception the quicker'.[34] Such excuses for a foolish system, which were frequently reiterated, failed to notice that Burney had been scathing in its condemnation:

This method of jumbling them all together may be convenient for the house and may teach the boys to stand fire, by obliging them to attend their own parts with firmness whatever else may be going forward at the same time. It may likewise give them force, in obliging them to play loud in order to hear themselves, for nothing but noise can pervade noise, but in the midst of such jargon and continued dissonance it is wholly impossible to acquire taste, expression or delicacy—there can be no polish or finishing given to their performance and that seems to account for the slovenliness and coarseness remarkable in their public exhibitions, and for the total want of taste, neatness and expression in these young peformers till they have acquired it elsewhere.[35]

The need to go elsewhere was one factor in the destruction of the Academy's claim to the status of a national conservatory. Henry Blagrove (1811–72), for example, who was a pupil in 1823, and became one of the few nineteenth-century British violinists to achieve more than a modest competence, studied privately with Spagnoletti, and later with Spohr in Germany.[36] Nor were such studies merely a final polish to firmly-based technique. The problem was particularly acute for instrumentalists who, unlike many singers, must acquire their basic skills when young: only first-class experienced players could lay such foundations in their pupils. But the poverty which prevented the Academy from recruiting such teachers also led to the lowering of entry standards, and this was arguably even more pernicious; for talented students can often educate themselves and each other, but to flood a college with untalented and unambitious young people is to condemn it to mediocrity. 'It would be melancholy', wrote Burghersh, 'when such vast sums are spent on foreign artists, to see such an establishment destroyed for want of a petty sum of a few hundred pounds'.[37] He was wrong in two ways: success would have required more than a few hundred pounds; failure involved not the literal destruction of the institution, but its bare survival, though the abandonment of its original high purpose. Instead of closing down, as was mooted in 1827,[38] the Academy survived 'by admission of a mob of students whose sole qualification seems to have been the ability to pay for their instruction'.[39]

An additional cost of survival was submission, by staff and students, to the arbitrary authority of men whose background rendered them quite incapable of understanding the economic realities of the musician's life. Two seemingly trivial incidents of the 1840s will serve to illustrate this unbridgeable gulf. An ex-student was asked to play the clarinet without fee at the Academy concert. His obsequious letter to Burghersh explained that 'after years in ardent and expensive study for a professorship in a science which is to be our only support' he was still dependent 'solely on casual favour', and therefore hoped that 'a remuneration for our time under these present slender circumstances will not be deemed improper'. The noble lord's crushing reply described the toil of raising £40,856 which 'has placed you in the situation of respectability and profit which you now occupy'.[40] Shortly afterwards another student was expelled for his connection with 'strolling players', and allowing his name to appear on a provincial playbill as 'of the Royal Academy of Music'.[41] Unquestioning loyalty and penurious respectability were the essential virtues.

In 1853, while Burghersh was safely abroad, the committee at last decided to consult its staff, who recommended that 'whatever pains for the gathering of revenue might be taken by aristocratic legislators, the technical management should be left to the care of practical musicians'. Their main suggestion, which was immediately adopted, was to cease boarding, since the Academy's duty was 'to teach music' rather than concern itself with 'the moral or the literary education' of students and their 'domestic necessities'.[42] One detects the relish with which MacFarren reports events in which he had taken part; resulting in the victory, temporary at first, but soon to be consolidated, of professional musicians against autocratic amateurs. He returns to the theme, describing the ultimate triumph and subsequently businesslike administration of the victors: 'musicians who administer a school as the duty of their lives' replacing 'lovers of music who open schools for their amusement'. The theme so concerned him that, thirty years after the event, he chose to discuss it with great frankness, in an 'inaugural address' to students. It articulated prejudices which were destined to permeate British musical institutions thenceforth, expressing tension or open conflict between musicians, proud of a constantly proclaimed, often narrowly conceived, 'professionalism', and those whom they deemed amateurs. Inherited from an understandable resentment of eighteenth-century-style aristocratic *hauteur*, and the condescension of literary dilletanti, it soured relationships with a later and different breed of men: administrators, journalists, critics, anyone who inhabited the world of music, but could be denied the imprimatur of 'professional musician', conferred by formal examinations. MacFarren's conception of a professional school was far removed from R. M. Bacon's original high-falutin aspirations for a national academy, treating music as 'a liberal art which requires the aid and support of a liberal education', its inmates 'trained to elegant pursuits and attainments'.[43] But in asserting professional autonomy MacFarren also embraced parochial, sometimes philistine attitudes, which were to have far reaching consequences.

The abolition of boarding, which was precipitated by a student riot over stinking fish,[44] had one practical implication. By raising the age of entry the Academy abdicated responsibility for that preparatory training which string players, at least, require if they are to acquire a sound technique. An intrinsically sensible measure of economy thus threatened to be yet another step towards mediocrity. But this was a minor defect in a rapidly worsening situation. The victory of the professionals was described as only temporary because Burghersh returned to England in 1856, dismissed the professorial board, and ruled 'despotically' (again in MacFarren's words), until his death in 1859. By then the Academy's finances were still precarious, despite various attempts to raise funds, and its morale was at a low ebb. In thirty-seven years it had attracted approximately £55,000 in subscriptions and donations, little more than one third of its original target, and had received nearly £96,000 in fees. Expenditure had amounted to £59,000 in payments to teachers, and £86,000 on 'upkeep'.[45] There followed a series of negotiations for Government assistance, of tedious complexity and sparse result. In 1864 Gladstone, as Chancellor of the Exchequer, allowed a grant of £500, which Disraeli refused to increase three years later, informing Parliament that 'the results of the institution were not in fact of a satisfactory character'. The Government then decided to cease subsidizing 'a central and quasi-independent association', in order to 'establish a system of musical instruction under the direct control of some Department of Government'.[46] The committee tried once more to resign its charter, but was prevented from doing so on the grounds that it would be illegal without the staff's approval. Again the Academy was 'saved' and taken over by a new committee representing its teachers. In 1868 Gladstone, back in office, enabled it to flounder on by reinstating the annual grant of £500. But opinion was growing that only the creation of a new institution could meet the nation's needs, though few could agree about defining those needs. Meanwhile the question was illuminated and the desire for reform invigorated by a substantial investigation and quasi-official wide-ranging report.

Training Musicians in the 1860s

It is a commonplace that Victorian Britain periodically indulged in bouts of self-appraisal, accumulating information in voluminous reports which stimulated public debate as a prelude to the formation of policy. The most familiar and complete manifestations of this tendency were the great Royal Commissions of the social reform movement, but there were numerous more modest exercises, and even musical education was expected to submit to the treatment. In 1865 the Society for the Encouragement of Arts, Manufactures and Commerce appointed a Committee to enquire into the state of musical education at home and abroad. Had he lived, Prince Albert would doubtless have presided, and might well have pushed matters to a firmer conclusion. But in the event the committee's most prominent member was Henry Cole, hero of the Great Exhibition, who was preparing the ground for the 1870 Education Act, and attempting to make South Kensington a popular cultural centre.[47] Cole was the principal exponent, after Albert's death, of belief in the arts as crucial to the nation's economic prosperity and moral progress: all this was highly relevant to the future of the RAM. The Committee's report merits careful study for several reasons. It is relatively inaccessible and has been neglected by historians. The RAM's crisis, which was its primary, but not sole concern, is of more than passing interest, since it derived from weaknesses which were to persist in the subsequent history of English musical education. The Committee's terms of reference were very wide and were liberally interpreted, allowing witnesses of diverse experience, accomplishment, and opinion to expatiate on musical training, secular and ecclesiastical, at home and abroad, providing information which is generally not available elsewhere. It is therefore an indispensable document, and was so regarded by contemporaries. Yet no historian has given it serious attention. Indeed it may even have fallen victim to a conspiracy of silence. Walter MacFarren, for example, never mentions it in his immensely detailed, and otherwise undiscriminating, autobiography. Corder, without discussing its contents, ridicules it as a 'plan to accommodate as many civil servants as possible' in 'a sort of gallery of bygone celebrities, like Madame Tussaud's'.[48] This is a travesty, not merely because it ignores substantial documentation, but because, in truth, far from attempting to impose a bureaucratic straitjacket, the report was obsessively open-minded and therefore failed to provide firm guide-lines for future policy.

It was inevitable that such an investigation would give prominence to the Academy's weakness, not merely by providing a platform for hostile outsiders, but in the testimony of its own staff, who were frank, if not always consistent. Even the principal, Charles Lucas, admitted that there were currently only three violin students and that the orchestra was 'very deficient' in wind instruments, but argued, with more loyalty than sense, that pupils got 'a better musical education here than they do in the conservatories of the Continent'.[49] The fee of £33 was indeed more than they could afford, and total costs for students from the country amounted to £100 a year. Standards had fallen and 'we have been obliged to take in almost anybody', The library was insignificant; a few students used the British museum, but could not borrow scores. Otto Goldschmidt, professor of piano, with personal experience of Leipzig and some acquaintance with procedures at Paris, Vienna, Dresden, and Stockholm, deplored teaching procedures at the Academy which were chaotically uncoordinated and, by implication, incompetent: 'a teacher ought to be able to play for his pupils all the music that he puts before them'. Too many professors, all poorly paid and without hierarchy, tried to impart a dozen different styles of piano playing, with no regular testing except for the annual examination. Students entered too late and ill-prepared because, outside the cathedral towns, adequate musical instruction was practically unobtainable (an interesting comment on the decision to cease boarding). Asked if he would like the institution to be 'confined to persons intending to pursue music as a profession' Goldschmidt assented but complained that, under present conditions, it could 'hardly afford to reject students for want of qualifications', and that the aim should be to produce, not a few 'conspicuous talents' but many 'well instructed and competent musicians'.

Sir George Clark, chairman of the Academy's management committee, confirmed that although it had no desire to educate amateurs it was admitting 'anybody who can pay'. Vociferous criticism came from Henry Chorley, the irascible *Athenaeum* critic and knowledgeable opera-goer. detecting 'radical defects' everywhere he argued that inadequate payment had ensured an incompetent staff, including five unproven pianists, three unknown professors of composition, and six singing teachers who had never sung in public. A government grant should never have been allowed and should certainly not be renewed. A fresh start should be made with an entirely new institution, adequately financed at, say, £10,000 a year. With so many first-class musicians in London, it would be possible to provide good cheap musical education, but there must be some appreciation of market conditions: 'Any competent musician is sure of remunerative occupation in this country', and with less waiting and intriguing for press support than was the practice in France, Germany, and Italy. Languages should be properly taught to aspiring singers. Above all it was essential to appoint a principal of stature, the equal of Cherubini (director of the Paris *Conservatoire* from 1822 until 1842), who would require a salary of £1,500 and inducements to compose in his spare time. Answering a question which implied that he had exaggerated the Academy's shortcomings, he agreed that ex-students were playing in the opera and Philharmonic orchestras, but added, 'there has not been one command-ing English artist, vocal or instrumental, turned out of the Academy during the last twenty-five years; as I, who have to give an account of London music from week to week, feel very vexatiously'.

Two luminaries of the Society of Arts, Peter Le Neve Foster, its Secretary, and Henry Cole, expressed similar opinions, more kindly. Foster described the superior facilities and standards of the Brussels *Conservatoire*, which gave a thorough professional training, and did not welcome amateurs. Cole argued that it was the duty of a civilised government not to waste musical talent. Music did not stand 'on the usual principles of political economy', and there were, in any case, several precedents for Government support without undue interference, including the Universities of Oxford and Cambridge, and the Royal Society. Without explicitly advocating the abandonment of the RAM, he felt bound to say that there was 'little life in it'. An academy should train its students 'primarily to sing and play in public; secondarily to teach' (a fundamental point, clearly implying that current practice reversed these priorities).

A spirited, if somewhat muddled, defence came from G. A. MacFarren. The Academy, he argued, had 'lived down the opposition of the musical profession'. Its many successful graduates, particularly provincial teachers, whom he evidently rated more highly than did Goldschmidt, had established for it a reputation which any new foundation would take many years to equal. There was admittedly room for improvement: greater professional autonomy; the use of English(!) as a basis for singing instruction; a wider range of instrumental instruction; more church and operatic music, the latter only if singers did not raise moral objections. All this would require more finance. Neither a library nor a museum of musical instruments, both suggested by the committee, were required. Chorley, who was recalled for further information, considered that MacFarren's testimony confirmed his 'conviction that the whole establishment is in such a thoroughly rotten state that there is no possible patching of it up'. The dogfight between the two men was continued in the *Athenaeum* and an appendix of the report.

The next witness was the eminent conductor Michael Costa, generally acknowledged to have raised orchestral standards at the Opera and Philharmonic to unprecedented levels of excellence, which were prevented from equalling the best in Europe only by insufficient time for rehearsal. A strict disciplinarian, Costa had greatly improved the morale and status of his players: 'if he could not raise their salaries, he at any rate continued to raise their artistic worth in the estimation of those whom they served'.[50] Few musicians would have acknowledged Costa as one of the 'greatest men in their profession of modern times',[51] but none could gainsay the relevance and weight of his opinion. Generally he corroborated Cole's testimony. England had abundant talent but gave it no encouragement. The excellent Opera orchestra, which he had trained 'with absolute power' since 1837, consisted predominantly of Englishmen, some of them ex-Academy students. But this did not disprove the need for a new institution, since they had come to him ill-prepared and uneducated: 'I know and am sorry to say that some of the finest orchestral players can scarcely write their own names'. He agreed with MacFarren that a chapel was required, and a theatre obligatory. A 'literature master' might repair the prevailing illiteracy, and the director would have to be a distinguished musician.

Similar views were expressed by a very different kind of musician. Henry Leslie[52] was a prominent choral conductor, a leading advocate of amateur music, and had been principal of the short-lived 'National College of Music', a privately endowed establishment of pretentious intention and negligible achievement. The establishment of a national conservatory, he considered, would enable 'students to become something more than teachers'. Artistic quality had long been falling because they were poorly educated and had to take jobs prematurely. He agreed with Costa that a uniformly high standard must be imposed but, curiously, did not wish amateurs to be excluded, observing that 'many men walk the wards and attend lectures without any intention of becoming surgeons'. Another college principal who did nothing to conceal his antagonism was Henry Wylde, conductor-entrepreneur (he had been acrimoniously associated with Berlioz during the 1853 New Philharmonic concerts), Gresham professor, and director of the London Academy of Music. The 'decadence and inutility' of the RAM, he claimed, had not been ameliorated by the Government's 'liberal' grant of £500 (no irony was intended). Its mediocrity represented 'an absolute stumbling block in the path of musical progress'. Musicians needed a fine education and opportunities to hear great performances. Special training was required but it could not be organized on a large scale. Public money would be better spent, Wylde concluded, on a national opera and a system for displaying and encouraging native talent.

One of the most distinguished musicians to appear before the Committee was far less dogmatic about past deficiencies and future remedies, though he too can hardly be regarded as an unprejudiced witness. Sterndale Bennet[53] had studied at the Academy between 1826 and 1836, earned respect as a pianist and conductor, and shown sufficient promise as a composer to impress Mendelssohn and Schumann. The subsequent fading of his genius may be attributed to its intrinsic limitations or to an environment which gave it no stimulus. By 1865 he was professor of music at Cambridge, submerged by extensive teaching commitments, and about to become principal of the Academy. In these circumstances his views were peculiarly significant, and modestly expressed. Admitting that present conditions were unsatisfactory, he wished to reform rather than supplant, for 'an institution, whatever may be its present state, cannot have existed for forty years without having established some ground'. He wished to reintroduce boarding, cut staff to a few active professors, establish a theatre, library, and museum of instruments, and keep the Academy small and restricted solely to intending musicians. These proposals, apart from the reintroduction of boarding, were supported by Ernst, a reputable pianist and editor of music who had taught at the Academy for six years. His tally of students had fallen from nine to one, and he did not seek more because even the highest permitted fee was far too low. But he implies that fees are less important than social status. In Vienna they were rarely higher than 6s. a lesson; in Central Germany commonly 4s. But in Vienna, as holder of the Order of Franz Joseph, he could attend Court. The RAM should have a Government Grant of £10,000 and a Director with a salary of £1,000 and 'a social position which has hitherto been quite unknown among musical people in this country'. The number of professors could well be cut by two thirds, since most of them merely sought 'a nice title to print on a visiting card': some thirty piano pupils were taught by twenty-one 'professors'. Instead, one principal professor should be appointed for each instrument, responsible to the Director. The Academy could thus be transformed, but reform must not be 'too delicate'.

John Hullah, who was soon to become government inspector of music, brought wide experience and forthright opinions to broaden the debate.[54] A prominent advocate of all forms of musical education, he regarded a museum of musical instruments, and library, as self-evident needs. The British Museum, thought by some to provide adequate library facilities, was indeed 'rich in curiosities ... but the average student does not want curiosities'. Where could he study a Haydn symphony, even one of the few currently in print? Hullah had been briefly at the Academy thirty years before, and knew 'nothing, save by hearsay' of its existing state. He was convinced that it had improved the quality of piano-teaching, which he regarded as, inevitably, the principal occupation of the English musician. This was a remarkable comment from the leading exponent of tonic sol-fa. Even more interesting is that an expert on amateur music should distinguish it so clearly from the professional's needs. The 'great-desideratum' for a national academy, he argued, was its power to *reject* pupils: in places of *general* education something could be done for the dullest pupil; but in a place of *special* training, 'the art and the individual are equally wronged'. But then he retreats from the exclusive implications of that perception, and argues that entry need not be restricted to prospective 'performers or professors'. He would admit 'the public', but 'take care they did not impede the real business of the institution', the training of professionals. His indications of how this might be achieved are contradictory and unconvincing: 'At first there might be a great risk of idle people in search of a sensation—people who did not care to learn anything, but who wanted amusement'. They could be made to pay highly for their amusement, 'but I do not think any payment would compensate for the nuisance caused by their presence'. The RAM was 'very ill indeed—moribund, perhaps, but not dead yet'.

Clearly Hullah was unable to reconcile fundamental inconsistencies which he was too intelligent to muff and too honest to conceal. This dilemma was to pervade English musical colleges for many years to come: without adequate funds it was impossible to impose rigorous professional standards, even if those standards could be satisfactorily defined, a complex problem, to which we shall return. Meanwhile Hullah wished to discuss another delicate matter. The English, he opined, were a musical people; but whereas in other countries the finest aptitude and taste were to be found among the aristocracy, in England 'precisely the reverse is the case . . . the difficulties of teaching music in schools of the higher classes are enormously greater than in those of the lower'. The extent of musical ignorance and ineptitude among the English upper class, including its womenfolk, was due, he believed, not to 'physical inability', but to lack of cultivation since the middle of the seventeenth century. Which great officer of church or state kept, or even occasionally engaged an orchestra? Who among his friends would listen if he did? People of rank attended the opera, but that was 'a social affair, which has little to do with music itself'. Upper-class Englishmen were even inclined to 'proclaim their ignorance of music as though expecting admiration' (a trait, incidentally, which was to survive into the twentieth century, in pronouncements, for example, by politicians, the judiciary, and even at college high tables). He was not sanguine of Parliamentary support: the spirit which had nearly stamped out music in the seventeenth century was not yet dead, and any proposal to assist theatres 'would be met by a howl of indignation'. Nevertheless it might be possible to procure Government funds, if there were evidence of sufficient public support, as with the training college for schoolmasters (a significant comparison). That support would have to be created, rather than revived, and, Hullah concluded, it would therefore be best to suspend the present RAM.

Finally the Committee turned to two groups of professional musicians whose work apparently set them apart, with precisely defined vocations, but for whose training a national academy might bear some responsibility. Both church and military musicians had their own training institutions and traditions; both seemingly required specific skills and offered specific avenues of employment. But neither existed in total isolation from the general body of musicians, becoming increasingly significant as competitors for jobs and leaders of professional advancement. Several witnesses discussed the training of church musicians, interpreting their brief liberally, and illuminating a broad social and educational context. Information about the education of choristers was provided by James Turle, who had been organist at Westminster Abbey since 1831. The sixteen boy choristers came to the Abbey at the age of 7 or 8, received between eight and thirteen guineas a year, and an education of the 'National School kind' which was 'necessarily most imperfect . . . only suited to an inferior class'. When their voices broke, at 14 to 16, it was a 'peculiar hardship' that they were cast out and left to shift for themselves. Magdalen College, Oxford, behaved more responsibly, giving its choristers a good classical education, with prospects of a scholarship to the University: professional men were thus 'induced to send their sons'.

These matters were explored at greater length in an appendix to the Committee's report which lists the replies of Deans and Chapters to a letter seeking their interest in free scholarships to the RAM for choristers. Durham, Oxford, York, and Canterbury approved; Exeter did not. The response from Ely was enlightening. Most of its boys were reported to be the sons of musicians who earned a slender living as lay clerks or 'vicars' in the choir. They learned the rudiments of music at home, received some vocal training and, when their voices broke, could often 'play chants and psalms respectably in the parish church'. This was 'a serious evil' complained W. E. Dickson, the Precentor and Choir Master. Poor parents would keep a child at home for his 'paltry earnings' as a local organist. The 'ill-trained and half educated' boy then had no chance of 'shaking off the innumerable faults which are inevitable under such circumstances, and can never rise beyond the lowest rank in his profession'. Even when parents could afford to pay the cathedral organist for regular lessons, the result was 'seldom satisfactory', for the pupil 'very commonly acquired the mannerisms and peculiarities of a master who has himself resided long enough in a provincial city to have become indisposed to adopt modern methods of study'. Scholarships to the Academy might offer such boys precisely the advantages which were now attainable, 'sound and intelligent instruction in the theory and practice of the musical art, together with freedom from the influences of local and provincial traditions and habits'. But a new department would be required to train chapel masters who must live in, separated from distraction by young women, and aiming at 'the highest rank in their profession'. Their education should be free and dependent upon 'competitive examination only'.

Sir Frederick Arthur Gore Ouseley, professor of music at Oxford who, incidentally, left an estate of over £54,000 when he died in 1899, and presumably understood the social hierarchy, agreed that 'good chorister boys should be encouraged to become good musicians . . . and so gain a livelihood', an end for which the present available means were 'miserably inadequate'. A few years later he was to return to this theme in a notable essay. 'The position of a cathedral boy', he then argued, had been 'very much degraded'. Selected from the lowest reaches of society, they were 'badly schooled, badly cared for in morals and religion, snubbed, despised, slighted and eventually sent forth into the world with no adequate provision for their maintenance, and no such acquirements as might enable them to rise in life by their own efforts'.[55] Another respondent to the Committee's letter, the organist at St George's Chapel, Windsor, was either more complacent or less sanguine of the alternative prospects at the Academy: 'articled pupils under me (or any other cathedral organist) have better opportunities for church music than at the RAM'.

The need to appoint a distinguished principal, which several witnesses had stressed, was raised again, but in terms which reflected a perceived distinction between social eminence and professional competence. The Revd. J. M. Capes, MA (Oxon.), composer of *The Druid*, a tragic opera, had written to the *Pall Mall Gazette*, extolling what he regarded as the social elevation of music in England. His opinions were deemed sufficiently important to merit an appendix to the Committee's report. The trend, he argued, could readily be discerned. It was now common to hear cultivated men *complain* that they had not been taught music. Oxford boasted a baronet as professor (Ouseley), and Edinburgh a baronet's brother (Herbert Oakeley). But society failed to educate future performers and teachers adequately, expecting them to assume positions equivalent to a 'journeyman pianoforte maker or printer'. Musical children were often encouraged by working class parents, simply because they could set up as 'professors' cheaply and quickly. Therefore the principal of a national academy should be an educated *non*-musician with administrative ability, a gentleman of course, like Dr Arnold. Questioned by the Committee, Cape reiterated his formula: the ideal director should be a 'sound musician' but 'not one who gains his living by music as a profession'.

Inevitably this opinion prompted a crushing reply from MacFarren. Musicians were no more illiterate than other artists, though he allowed that wide literary and scientific study were 'incompatible with sound musicianship'. The essential point, however, was that a principal could only gain the confidence of musicians and the public if he had 'passed through all the vicissitudes'. Arnold had succeeded by moral influence and modernizing the public school curriculum, but this was only possible because he knew his subject. The RAM's weaknesses were 'totally due to the non-professional element in its constitution'. Society's 'crying evil' was 'this widely spread system of amateurism, which invests with dignities gentlemen who fill them with self inflation, instead of sterling ability and who are placed in their positions from regard to their social standing, instead of to their technical competency'. The 'present deplorable state of our national church music, at which all musicians groan' was due to its control by non-musicians. Imagine 'a physician at the head of a military college', or 'a soldier to direct the studies of painters!'

It was clear to the Committee that soldiers were directing the studies of their own musicians with considerable success. The Military School of Music at Kneller Hall had opened in 1857. Its staff consisted of nine 'permanent' and four 'occasional' professors, and a schoolmaster who provided one hour a day of general education. Several of the teachers were outstanding instrumentalists, such as the clarinettist Henry Lazarus, and Alfred Phasey, later described as the man who 'practically invented the euphonium'.[56] An average of about seventy students, usually not below 15 years of age, were admitted each year. Few of them had any previous musical training, and we know from another source that some were very unpromising, because regiments were 'not as yet taking Kneller Hall very seriously'.[57] Yet the school was so efficient that approximately half returned to their regiments as bandsmen after two years training. A smaller group, later to be categorized as 'students' in contrast to the boy 'pupils' were 'band sergeants training to be bandmasters'.[58] Cheap tickets and train fares were awarded to diligent students, to encourage them to attend concerts and the opera: 900 were issued in one year, and many more individuals went at their own expense. 'The opportunity of hearing good music is not one of the least advantages gained by the pupils of Kneller Hall', remarked the

Committee: a civilized comment which it would be anachronistic to dismiss as a truism in 1865. The institution's statistics were presented in admirable detail (see Table) but the Committee could not be aware of their potential significance for the future supply of professional musicians, military and civilian. British military music had long been dominated by foreigners.[59] An 1862 list of bandmasters includes forty-five out of 110 with such names as Faccioli, Hagermeyer, Kalozdy, Koelbel, and Riemeri, though it also, notably, contains two Godfreys. By 1900 a list of 192 bandmasters consists predominantly of English names.[60] The first graduates of Kneller Hall were the vanguard of this anglicization. Without Government assistance for another decade, and despite, or perhaps because of, its narrowly conceived purpose, the Military School of Music was already indicating that it would become the most successful of nineteenth-century British music colleges. In due course it would produce many of the country's finest wind and percussion players. Clearly it required no assistance from a moribund Academy in 1866, despite the Committee's solicitude and presumptuous talk of 'certificating' bandmasters.

Students at Kneller Hall, 1857–1864

	Admitted	Knew little or nothing of music	Practical musicians	Left as Bandmasters	Bandsmen
1857/8	147	114	33	5	29
1858/9	79	71	8	4	41
1859/60	59	37	22	9	29
1860/62	83	61	22	7	38
1862/3	79	52	27	11	59
1863/4	145	94	51	27	75
Totals	592	429	163	63	271
	158 remaining under instruction.				

Despite its rich legacy of information and opinion, the Report was inconclusive, and produced no immediate practical results. Its liberal documentation of conflicting viewpoints doubtless made its recommendations unpersuasive. Acquiescing without enthusiasm in the continuation of the Academy, it suggested increased Government support, some free scholarships, and new accommodation at South Kensington. 'The old coat is to be patched', complained the *Athenaeum*,[61] and this, in all its threadbare inadequacy, was soon confirmed. Charles Lucas retired as principal, to be succeeded not by Costa, as had been rumoured (an appointment which would have shifted training towards instrumentalists, rather than teachers), but by Sterndale Bennett. Application for an annual grant of £2,000 was rejected, and the half promise of new accommodation was forgotten, so discourteously as to move him to public remonstrance.[62] In 1868, with sixty-six pupils, a reinstated grant of £500 and 'salary list' reduced from £660 to £160 the Royal Academy of Music was reduced to penury 'training young women for music teachers'.[63] The Government's intentions were focussed elsewhere. It wanted a system of 'cheap musical instruction', claimed Bennet at a public meeting. Mr Cole would become 'music master to the nation', he quipped, presiding at 'the National Cemetery of Arts and Sciences' in South Kensington; perhaps students could be assembled in Hyde Park and taught by electric telegraph.[64]

Cheap instruction was indeed appropriate to the spirit of the age, for it was during the 1860s that the broader context of education, already meagre, had been further degraded by 'payment by results'. Many poorer countries had established systems of universal compulsory education long before the British subdued their distrust of national authority and their religious antagonisms sufficiently to allow a modicum of literacy.[65] Between 1833 and 1851 the provision of elementary education approximately doubled, to serve about one in eight of the population. In 1862 Lowe's Revised Code imposed a grimly utilitarian pattern, cut expenditure from £840,000 to £705,000 in two years, and lowered the status of school teachers.[66] In these circumstances there were scant public funds for music training, but the problem was not solely financial. Cheap elementary education was the lowest of three layers of provision, deemed appropriate to the three classes of society. In 1861 the Clarendon Commission applied the new criteria of entrepreneurial efficiency and Arnoldian character-moulding to the upper-class public schools. In 1864 the Taunton Commission classified middle-class secondary schools in a further tripartite subdivision, by class, according to the fees, leaving age, and potential careers of their boys. These attempts to force education into straitjackets of social class only survived a couple of decades, but they represent 'the mid-Victorian high water mark of the entrepreneurial ideal in formal education'.[67]

It was a singularly inappropriate social environment for the articulation of sensible national policies for training musicians. As the Society of Arts *Report* amply demonstrated, neither their vocational needs nor their social position could be defined with any measure of agreement. The latter question provoked agonized debate as musicians attempted to establish their status as 'professionals', a theme to which we shall return in Chapter VI. Their vocational needs were most easily defined in relation to specific job requirements, which accounts in some measure for the comparatively rapid progress of Kneller Hall; but few groups of musicians could be so clearly categorized. The Royal Academy of Music added further confusion by its failure, enforced by poverty and inept administration, to discriminate between the education of professional and amateur students, or between those who aspired to become practising musicians and those who might, at most, be elementary teachers. The profession itself was not yet capable of providing firm guidance through this morass. Lacking indigenous traditions of excellence and a leader of universally acknowledged distinction, a Mendelssohn or Cherubini, it was prey to every whim of Government and public, informed or ignorant, indulgent or repressive.

Before 1870 few professional musicians were affected by the Academy's vicissitudes or the ensuing debate. Over ninety per cent of them had learned their craft elsewhere: through apprenticeship, family connections, private lessons at home or abroad, or simply by 'picking up' an instrument. Their ranks included the advance columns of a vast army of piano teachers, and many instrumentalists who, like Dickens's dirty 'clarionettist', drifted between indifferent amateurism and penurious employment. After 1870, as the market grew at an accelerated pace, music colleges increased in size and number. Some had government support, but all were subjected to similar pressures to those which had all but overwhelmed their precursor. Henceforth they would have a greater influence on supply, both directly through their own students, and indirectly by means of a proliferating examination system which they would attempt to control.

V

The Flood

Except among the richer classes almost everyone who studies music ends by teaching music to someone else. Such is his fate whatever may have been his ambition.[1]

J. H. Mapleson, 1888

The musical profession is perilously easy to enter, for the simple reason that it does not require the investment of a large capital.[2]

Henry Fisher, 1888

The supply of musicians increased throughout the nineteenth century, but there was a significant change of pace after 1870: if their numbers are plotted on a graph, its slope is steeper during the 1870s and 1880s. The same pattern emerges if we chart the number of musicians per head of the population, or even of the urban population, both of which were also increasing rapidly: the *proportion* of musicians in society, and particularly in urban society, was growing at an accelerating pace.[3] This apparently smooth and easy response to a rapidly increasing demand was made possible by the cumulative influence of those 'positive determinants' which were briefly mentioned in the last chapter. To an unprecedented degree, the tools of the musician's trade and facilities for his instruction became cheap and accessible, ceasing to be effective barriers to recruitment.

Cheap tools

Free trade made a substantial contribution to the distribution of cheaper instruments. As late as 1853 the import duties on 'fancy articles', costly to collect, generating little revenue, encouraging smuggling, and generally raising costs and dampening trade, were applied with bureaucratic punctiliousness to musical instruments:

Musical-boxes, small, not exceeding four inches in length, the air, 3*d*.: large, the air, 8*d*.: overtures, or extra accompaniments, the air, 2*s*. 6*d*.; pianofortes, horizontal grand, each, £3: upright or square, each, £2; musical harmoniums or seraphines, and not exceeding three stops, each, 12*s*.: four stops, and not exceeding seven stops, each, £1 4*s*.: eight stops, and not exceeding eleven stops, each £1 10s.: exceeding eleven stops, each £2; musical instruments, not otherwise enumerated or described, for every £100 value, £10; accordians, commonly called Chinese, the 100 notes, 1s.; other sorts, including flutinas and common German square concertinas, the 100 notes, 5s.; concertinas of octagon form, not common German, each, 4s.; brass instruments, all sorts, the pound, 9d.[4]

These absurdities were swept away by the removal of protective tariffs, notably in the 1860 Cobden—Chevalier Treaty with France. Henceforth a highly competitive international market enabled the price of musical instruments to be driven down by cheap labour and large-scale production. In 1854 the cheapest flutes available from Rudall, Rose and Carte cost £3, and clarinets were priced at £4 to £12. By 1883 an esteemed French manufacturer offered flutes at retail prices ranging from 32s. to 6 gns., oboes at £6, clarinets £2. 14s. 0d., bassoons at £15, trumpets at £5. Low grade and second-hand instruments were much cheaper, though technical improvements had rendered many of the latter obsolete.[5] Violins were incredibly cheap. A contributor to the first edition of Grove's *Dictionary* reported that 'trade fiddles' from Mittenwald, Markneukirchen, and Mirecourt, which accounted for perhaps 90 per cent of the world's supply, could be bought 'for fabulously low sums'. The main distributor, Thibouville Lamy, supplied a detailed estimate of production costs, including 5d. for wood, 6d. for labour, 1s. 1d. for machine-cutting and shaping, 10d. for varnish, and 15 per cent profit, the instrument wholesaling at 4s. 6d.! Yet such a violin 'if carefully set up', could 'be made to discourse very tolerable music'. Instruments of better quality, costing from £1 to £2. 10s. 0d., were 'now sold all over the world'. Fine violins, predominantly French, were priced between £5 and £15; and cellos from £9 to £27; a Stradivarius or Guarnerius would fetch between £200 and £500.[6] Similarly low prices persisted into the twentieth century. In 1904 a 'soundly constructed' violin from the leading dealer, Hill, cost 1 gn., a bow 5s., and a properly lined wooden case 6s.[7] The relationship between cheap instruments and a glut of performers was noted by the great teacher Leopold Auer (1845–1930) whose pupils included Heifetz:

The parents of young children, or those who are in charge of their early training, so often fail to realize the seriousness of their act when they light-heartedly decide that a child shall have a musical career and forthwith select the instrument which is to bring him fame and wealth. In the case of the poor, or those of slender means, the violin, as a rule, is the instrument favoured because it may be bought so cheaply.[8]

Today, when good instruments cost many thousands of pounds, the idea that violinists should once have been encouraged by their cheapness is barely credible.

It was the piano, however, which became by far the most popular instrument. The transformation of its manufacture and marketing, which followed a widespread adoption of Steinway's technological innovations, has been explained elsewhere.[9] The essential point, for our present purpose, is that cheap, reliable pianos became generally available in Britain during the 1880s *for the first time*, satisfying a pent-up demand which was based upon increasing purchasing power, musical needs, and social emulation: possession symbolized respectability, achievement, and status. Accessibility was widened, not merely by lower prices, but by the 'three-year system' of hire purchase, and by the durability of these newly designed instruments, many of which continue to give service today. Discarded pianos were rarely destroyed, but entered a lively second-hand market and, ultimately, a humbler milieu. By the early years of the twentieth century sales of new pianos per head in Britain were at least three times higher than in 1850, and ownership of playable instruments had extended to at least one for every twenty people, perhaps one in ten. There is abundant contemporary evidence to confirm the prevalence of 'piano mania'.

So wide a dispersal of musical instruments, throughout society, was unprecedented, and its effects upon the potential supply of musicians can hardly be exaggerated, particularly if we consider the piano's unique educational qualities. Unlike most other instruments it lent itself readily to self-improvement, a cardinal Victorian virtue, widely espoused and practised. Whereas most instruments responded to a novice with discouraging noise, or no sound at all, the piano sang at first touch, encouraging persistence, by elementary instruction or even by untutored experiment: many people learned to play acceptably 'by ear'. It was an ideal beginner's instrument, not only for those who continued to be pianists, but for many who later turned to other instruments. Archie Camden, to quote a distinguished example, started on the piano, got his first professional engagement at the age of 9 (5s. for playing a Chopin polonaise) and continued to play seriously, only taking up the bassoon because a scholarship was available.[10] It is customary to applaud the social and educational benefits which flowed from the spread of pianos: the conviviality of family parlour music; the 'household orchestra' which gave access, before the age of radio and gramophone, to the literature of western music, by sight-reading, alone or 'quatre mains', from copies which were cheap, or could even be borrowed from the public library. Here we are concerned with a narrower focus. The piano was a recruiting agent, more effective than teachers and conservatories, for an army of musicians, at every level of attainment, who sought employment in pubs, music halls, cinemas, and, above all, as teachers.

There was a huge increase in the supply of printed music during the nineteenth century.[11] Annual production in Britain increased at least fifty, perhaps 100 times; but prices did not fall markedly until after 1870. The high costs of music were maintained by obsolete technology, restrictive practices in the printing unions, inadequate protection of copyright, and a general acceptance of high profit margins and low turnover in the trade. Additional burdens upon the consumer were imposed by the 'taxes on knowledge': excise duty on paper, stamp duty, and advertisement tax. The 1842 Copyright Act reduced risks to some extent; taxes on knowledge were repealed by 1861, and the production and distribution of music gradually became more competitive and efficient, a process which owed much to the entrepreneurial flair of Alfred Novello.[12] Production also became far more diversified, and geared to specific requirements, including a vast range of instructional music. Cheap editions from Peters of Leipzig began to appear during the 1870s. Expansion and 'product differentiation' is indicated, for example, by successive Novello catalogues between 1858 and 1913, with prices steadily reduced, and a subscription library introduced in 1871. The general fall in prices can be illustrated by the cost of a piano score of Handel's *Messiah*; 21s. during the 1830s, 1s. fifty years later. Sixpenny editions of sheet music became common, and prices were further reduced by widespread discounting and extensive 'piracy'.

This revolution in production and distribution brought unalloyed benefits to consumers, but for producers the effects were more equivocal. The main source of a composer's income shifted from lump sums of cash to royalty payments on sales. The system was pioneered by John Boosey, as a device to spread risks between publishers and composer, and became far more common in Britain than in other European countries, where *performing* rights were the rule. In Britain the Performing Right Society was not established until 1914. By then commercial exploitation of the music market was moving away from sheet music towards the gramophone.[13]

How did composers fare in this expanding, precarious, unstable market-place? Confident answers would require more information and research than is at present accessible, and a few generalizations must suffice. Some gained handsome rewards. Gounod received £4,000 for his 'Sacred trilogy' *Redemption*, once considered a great masterpiece, and he allegedly made a total of £168,000 from British copyrights. Dvořák received £1,750 for the English rights to four choral works. Stainer, whose lachrymose four-square *Crucifixion* has sold 1,250,000 copies since its publication in 1887, collected royalties at 2d. a time.[14] Sullivan's 'maligned masterpiece',[15] *The Lost Chord*, sold 500,000 copies between 1877 and 1902. Popular 'hits' would commonly sell 200,000 copies. In 1898 Boer War fever boosted sales of 'Soldiers of the Queen' to 238,000. It was ironical, however, that some of the most popular composers earned little because they were prime targets for piracy. Within a week of publication, pirated copies could be got on to the streets for as little as 2*d*., and the law offered no protection. In 1905 Leslie Stuart earned only a few pounds from such enormously popular songs as 'Lily of Laguna' and 'Soldiers of the Queen'.[16] In 1906 piracy was at last defeated by a legal reform which allowed summary procedures.[17] It was to reappear seventy years later, when the law again proved unable to defend musicians against the depredations of new technology.

Cheap instruction

Equipped with cheap instruments and music, aspiring musicians were wooed by an ever-expanding army of importunate teachers, pleading for their custom. Its size is indicated by statistics drawn from the Census (Tables I and II) and from trade directories (Tables III and IV), all of which understate the true dimensions. The Census excludes part-timers: such as the gilder and piano-tuner who, in 1863, offered piano, violin, and dancing at 6*d*. a lesson;[18] the Kilbirnie tailor who did 'a good deal of business in the fiddling way, teaching and playing at dances';[19] and thousands of others, who rarely advertised their activities, but relied upon local connections. Nor does the Census distinguish between musicians and music teachers during the crucial years of expansion, 1871–1911. But any such distinction would be arbitrary, since most musicians teach for at least part of their working lives. Occasional lessons by visiting musicians had long been common, and were particularly valuable where local teaching was unavailable or inadequate. Two friends of Havergal Brian's youth, for example, got spasmodic lessons from orchestral players in the touring Carl Rosa Opera Company. Both became professionals, one as principal clarinet in the Hallé orchestra.[20] Players migrating to new places in order to take up jobs in theatres and music-halls were always eager to supplement their meagre wages by teaching. Archibald Milligan, who changed his name to Carl Volti, describes the process in Glasgow, but remarks that competition with established local teachers was inevitably limited to daytime, when few pupils were free.[21] Moonlighting clerks and other part-timers, however, were anxious to teach in the evenings. An informal shift system was evolving, widely noted by contemporaries, but missed by the statisticians.

It is reasonable to assume that the great majority of female musicians enumerated in the census were wholly or primarily teachers, rather than performers, as classification up to 1861 and after 1911 indicates, and abundant other evidence confirms. Indeed there can be no doubt that women, who in 1851 were still a minority, came to dominate music teaching in Britain, as in the United States at about the same time, with effects to be discussed in due course. The rapid growth of music as one of the few respectable occupations open to women, outside domestic service and seemingly less demeaning, is illustrated in Table I: more than threefold between 1851 and 1881. At a time when many middle-class women, consigned to lives of leisured dependence, genteel spinsterhood or widowhood, were seeking a measure of remunerative but respectable independence, music was an obvious outlet because relevant skills, acquired as a desirable feminine 'accomplishment', could be turned to professional use. Increasing numbers of less privileged girls, seeing a way of putting the family piano to profitable work, sought pupils with, perhaps, a diploma to enhance their earning power. Such ease of entry was not, of course, confined to women. A guide to the profession, published in 1888, depicts a young man who 'spends a little money in the purchase of sheet music, invests in a brass plate—and lo! he is a professor. How easily it is done, and what an amount of life-long misery has been the consequence of this fatal facility!'[22] An unreliable £2 a week and ultimate bankruptcy were the predicted result.

A similar picture emerges from the trade directories, which published names, addresses, and instruments, of musicians wishing to be listed, in great detail after 1890.[23] Throughout the country, particularly in expanding urban centres, the number of resident musicians (and music traders), most of whom were teachers, rapidly increased: a trebling was common between 1890 and 1910 (Table III). Every town entry included the size of its population, indicating the scope for more recruitment. In 1900 the number per thousand of the local population varied from approximately two, in Glasgow, to six in Manchester. Even small towns contained several music teachers: Andover, with a population of 6,000, listed five; Ayr (25,000) nineteen. London was, of course, *sui generis* (Table IV). Its teachers increased from nearly 2,000 in 1890 to some 5,000 in 1910; instrumentalists, not including pianists, rose from about 600 to 2,700, many giving lessons. These directory entries greatly understate the actual number of teachers because they contain only those wishing to be listed. An entry was no guarantee of competence but, since it implied a measure of activity, it does indicate the intensity of competition in each district. The number of people offering music lessons, most of them self-employed women, probably trebled between 1870 and 1914, and may have quadrupled.

One of the most curious features of English musical life was a proliferation of 'conservatories', which Table VI illustrates, without attempting to be comprehensive. By 1900 the directories listed thirty-three 'colleges of music' in London, and few provincial towns lacked an 'academy' or 'conservatoire': Liverpool had seven. Their profusion and variety is bewildering at first glance, for they appear to have little in common except poverty of resource and, with a few exceptions, haziness of purpose. The two traits were linked, for inadequacy precluded too narrow a definition of function. Many were merely family businesses or loose associations of teachers dignified by a label; sometimes staffed by competent musicians, but rarely pretending to offer professional training. Some were more ambitious: justifiably, like the excellent, Germanic, Manchester College;[24] vaingloriously, like many; or even with deliberate intention to defraud, like the notorious Victoria College, which sold its diplomas (see p. 191). Some, like the Huddersfield College of Music, claimed to provide both 'complete training for the profession and for recreative studies'.[25] Others, like the Metropolitan Academy of Music boasted of size (2,378 students) and credentials (31 LRAM, 12 ARCM, 28 ATCL and LTCL).[26] A few secured a measure of official recognition, or even a pittance, and claimed national status, with or without a Royal Charter.

It would be convenient (and would have caused less confusion to contemporaries) if distinctions between these various institutions were clear-cut, the 'national' conservatories associated exclusively with higher standards and responsibility for professional training. Unfortunately the system was latticed with ill-defined frontiers. The expanding group of 'national' institutions was subject to pressures, largely economic, similar to those which had afflicted the Royal Academy of Music since its inception, and similarly erosive of standards. A new complication was the vast network of external examinations and diplomas which grew in response to an insatiable demand for certification. Meanwhile 'private' colleges provided some of the best and worst training on offer. Moreover, to add to the confusion, many teachers held plural appointments, straddling the public and private sectors. Thus Tobias Matthay (1858–1945), whose pupils included Myra Hess and Harriet Cohen, taught at the RAM from 1876 to 1920, founded his own piano school in 1900, and established several provincial colleges under his name, which employed local teachers.[27] Albert Sammons (1886–1957), the only Englishman of his generation to become a prominent violinist, was a 'professor' at two institutions which emphasized their links with concert life: the 'Practical School of Music', giving 'practical musical tuition by artistes who are actually appearing before the public at the present time',[28] and the 'College of Violinists Ltd.', which assured its pupils that 'violinists are examined by violinists'.[29] His predecessor as England's leading violinist, John Carrodus (1836–95), taught at the National Training School (precursor of the Royal College of Music) and, along with Coleridge Taylor, at the 'Croydon Conservatoire of

Music' (established in 1883) which, 'by bringing first class musicians outside the great centre' was said to have done 'much to remove the stigma attached to local teaching'.[30]

Clearly excellence was not confined to the 'national' conservatories; indeed, at least until 1914, it might more confidently be sought outside them. Thus Mathilde Verne (1865–1936), a pupil of Clara Schumann who taught Harold Samuel and Solomon, ran a private school in Brighton with her sister Adela, also a distinguished pianist. To understand the evolution of this anarchic proliferation we must take up the story from the last chapter, where we left the Royal Academy, shaken but not quite demolished by the Society of Arts *Report*, and the Government contemplating a new, cheap institution.

National Conservatories

The National Training School, which Sterndale Bennett had lampooned (p. 98), lasted five years before handing its assets to the Royal College of Music in 1882. The School was headed, somewhat reluctantly, by Sullivan, who was also a professor at the RAM. Its senior staff consisted of Stainer, Pauer, Visetti, a singing teacher at various colleges, and Carrodus. Its avowed purpose of giving free professional training to talented students, with scholarships raised by public subscription, was soon abandoned because of inadequate funds. Hoping to establish at least 100 regionally based scholarships of £40 a year, it secured a maximum of ninety-three in 1880, and was then forced to take paying pupils. It would be pleasant to confirm a prevalent belief that the one outstanding scholar, Eugene d'Albert from Newcastle, owed something to his training at the School.[31] Certainly it gave him a platform, with performances of concertos at the Popular Concerts, the Crystal Palace, and Philharmonic, and of student compositions, at the age of sixteen. Subsequently he became one of Liszt's favourite protégés, a magnificent pianist and notable composer. But he had been given a thorough grounding in composition before entering the School, and later his frequent expressions of Anglophobia include a pointed denial that he had learned anything useful in London: Sullivan's lessons had been perfunctory and 'had I remained there much longer, I should have gone to utter ruin'. Fuller Maitland, who was close to these events, reports that the School's deficiencies probably influenced d'Albert's decision to abandon his English nationality.[32] By 1878 attempts to amalgamate the School and RAM had come to nothing, despite Royal support, because the Academy refused to be 'absorbed or smothered', as Corder notes with lip-smacking approval: 'education was moving apace; there was ample room for two music schools in London'.[33] Most accounts of these peculiar events are similarly complacent. Colles and Cruft, for example, simply assert without evidence, that 'there was room for both' and 'each needed the other'.[34] Yet, as Scholes remarks, it is bewildering to contemplate a society which 'seemed to be so indifferent to the welfare of the old-established Academy, and so enthusiastic at the idea of bringing into existence a new institution'.[35] Doubtless neglecting the old and welcoming the new made good sense in the light of the Royal Society of Arts report; but in that case why did a country which had manifestly failed to provide adequate resources for one national conservatory proceed to establish another?

The launching of the Royal College of Music in 1883 was reminiscent, in several respects, of the RAM's debut sixty years earlier. There was a similar disposition to invoke official support which was not forthcoming; a similar desire for education on the cheap, cloaked in grandiloquent prose—'charming piffle, but piffle none the less', as Stanford described Gladstone's contribution to the debate.[36] At numerous public meetings, scions of the establishment voiced the need to establish a truly national conservatory, of international standing, 'with greater scope, a wider basis, and a more authoritative position', which 'should be assisted by the public and be recognised and subsidised by the State'.[37] *The Times* applauded a remarkable demonstration of *'carrière ouverte aux talents'*: scholarships were awarded to a mill girl and sons of a blacksmith and a farm labourer.[38] Edith Oldham's mother was probably not alone in fearing that her daughter would be 'deteriorated' by such company.[39] But financial support proved sufficiently inadequate to allay these anxieties. Public assistance amounted to £110,000: an improvement on past efforts but, as the *Musical Times* complained, it was only equivalent 'to about one third of a farthing per head of the population . . . by no means munificent or encouraging'.[40] Yet it was the result of a campaign, organized with such assiduity by George Grove the College's director, that *Punch* was moved to print a whole page of spoof advertisements for the new institution.[41] The Government provided no cash, but enhanced the status of the profession by bestowing knighthoods upon Sullivan, MacFarrren, and Grove.

Before charting subsequent developments at the College and its rivals, it is necessary to consider one of the fundamental problems which confronts such institutions in a free, unplanned economy: the enormous difficulty of adjusting their output of graduates to changing demands. It arises from two separate groups of factors; those affecting every skilled occupation, and those peculiar to music. There is a common belief, all the more insidious because it is rarely made explicit, that education and training are somehow linked to the market, responding to its signals by expanding or contracting the supply of specific skills. But a long-term change in demand, as distinct from short-term fluctuations, reflects fundamental shifts in technology and taste. The former can be illustrated by the briefly flourishing demand for musicians in cinemas, which collapsed for ever in 1929 with the coming of talkies; the latter by the decline of piano lessons as piano-playing ceased to be a widely desired social accomplishment. It is implicitly assumed that training facilities will respond to such changes, producing sufficient and suitable people. In the long run this generally does happen, with reasonable ease, when the movement is upwards: more musicians appear in response to rising demand, although there may be temporary shortages of specific skills. The way down, when demand falls, is more hazardous, and can entail much human distress, both because existing practitioners are trapped in a disintegrating market, and because new aspirants continue to be pumped into the system: by institutions with a vested interest in continuity and, ironically, by individuals forced to intensify the glut which harms them. These long term inflexibilities are common, in some measure, to most forms of vocational training and higher education. In music they are acute, not least because musicians, unlike other skilled people, tend to take pupils when they need cash, even if they are not primarily teachers.

The difficulties of providing appropriate levels and types of professional training are exacerbated by another group of factors peculiar to music. Potential composers, performers, teachers, amateur and professional, cannot be rigorously separated from the outset. This is a problem which scarcely exists outside the arts, and is intensified for musicians by the paramount need to start young. Engineering and medical schools, to point a modern contrast, can recruit a comparatively homogeneous group of students with unequivocal commitment to their chosen profession. The age, talent, aspirations, tenacity, and ultimate vocations of music students are likely to be far more diverse. Even today very few institutions in free societies can, like the Juilliard School and Curtis Institute in the USA, pursue a determined policy of ruthless excellence and professionalism. Few also can afford to employ only first-class musicians to pass on their skills and experience. Their fees are high, and an itinerant life usually precludes frequent and regular attendance. A plausible resolution of these intrinsic difficulties is to make a virtue of necessity by claiming to train 'all round musicians', allegedly capable of adapting to changing market requirements. Unfortunately few such people acquire a sufficient level of any specific skill to gain and retain remunerative employment as practising musicians. Most become teachers.

The limited achievements of England's national conservatories before 1914 were therefore not mere reflections of Victorian parsimony and philistinism, destined for substantial improvement as society became more generous towards the arts. But poor and unstable finances certainly imposed an additional, crushing, burden, preventing them from employing, as teachers, enough successful musicians to bring high standards and prestige. Nor could they offer sufficient cash, training, and experience to talented but impecunious students, or afford to exclude those who were untalented, ill-prepared, and poorly-motivated, but prepared to pay. Yet, paradoxically, as Stanford remarked, the total allocation of scholarships was generous;[42] and the Royal College was therefore, at this stage, a successful recruiting agency. It trawled the country for potential musicians and educated them cheaply. Most were women; the overwhelming majority became teachers. The pattern of future developments was indicated by the first allocation of scholarships. There were 1,588 applicants from as far afield as Armagh, Dublin, Edinburgh, and Jersey,[43] who were reduced by preliminary local examinations to 480. Of these 'finalists' 49 per cent were aspiring pianists and 28 per cent singers; 70 per cent were women. The final awards of scholarships and *proxime accessit* were allocated as shown in the Table.

RCM Scholarships competition 1883

	Finalists		Scholarships		Proxime accessit	
	Female	Male	Female	Male	Female	Male
Piano	185	49	14	3	12	3
Singing	124	13	9	4	8	1
Composition	8	22	0	6		
Violin	16	35	1	7	2	0
Organ	1	20	0	1		
Violoncello	0	3	0	2		
Clarinet	0	1	0	1		
Oboe	0	1	0	0		
Flute	0	1	0	1		
Harp	1	0	1	0		
Total	335	145	25	25	22	4

The College made several attempts to impose professional standards. Sir Julius Benedict had insisted that training should be neither too cheap nor too brief, and that students should be admitted only if they undertook to complete their courses: seemingly anodyne principles, yet so unprecedented that Stanford attributed to them, 'albeit not carried out in their entirety, the success of the Royal College'.[44] The most rigorous conditions were imposed by Jenny Lind, before she agreed to accept the responsibility of teaching the 'genuine Italian method of singing'. She insisted on taking only 'foundation' (i.e. scholarship) students, selected 'in open competition and qualified by talent', reserving the right to 'veto the unqualified and untalented'. Another professor should be appointed to teach paying pupils. Each student must see her for at least two hours a week, and also take classes in sol-fa, piano, harmony, at least one language, deportment, etc., for a minimum of three years, preferably four or five.[45] Stanford describes her auditions for the 1883 scholarships: she 'sang from her seat a series of amazing roulades and cadenzas which the trembling young women had to imitate as best they could, divided between anxiety for themselves and astonishment at the Chopin-like passages which came so easily out of the throat of an elderly lady at the table. Some of them made surprisingly good attempts at the ordeal'.[46] Jenny Lind retired after only three years, but if no other teacher could afford to be so demanding, there were some who brought comparable practical and cosmopolitan experience; including George Henschel, who was briefly her successor, and Stanford, who taught several composers of the 'English musical renaissance'.[47]

One measure of the College's professionalism was its ability to fit training to specific job requirements. Inevitably this was easiest for organists and wind players, and practically impossible for pianists who, if they missed the concert platform, as practically all English-trained pianists did during the nineteenth century, could expect little, *qua* pianists, until the silent cinema created a large but short-lived demand for their services. Sir Walter Parratt was conspicuously successful in 'placing' his organ pupils, and there was a similarly healthy vocational bias in the wind departments. A striking example occurred during the early career of Dan Godfrey. Entering the College in 1885 for violin and piano, he took clarinet lessons privately from a Guardsman, with an eye to a military career, in the family tradition. But he was soon allowed to make the clarinet his principal study *within* the College, under the great player Henry Lazarus, who also taught at Kneller Hall.[48]

Two of the first scholarships were for flute and clarinet and, in order to strengthen the student orchestra, more were offered three years later in flute, oboe, clarinet, bassoon, and horn. By 1914 Stanford could boast that eleven of the twenty-six wind players in the Philharmonic Orchestra were ex-pupils, pointing the moral: 'in this department the players who have been educated at the College have seldom or never been stranded in after life'.[49] Supply had been nicely timed to the market's immediate needs. The conductor Wilhelm Ganz, for example, described his difficulties in keeping the New Philharmonic Orchestra together for rehearsals during the early 1880s. At midday players would move to Covent Garden and his rehearsal would finish with only half the orchestra: 'In those days wind and brass instrumentalists were very scarce, and I was obliged to share them'.[50] That scarcity lasted no more than a generation. By 1886 Kneller Hall was producing twenty bandmasters and eighty bandsmen each year. They would serve six or twelve years, often playing in the civilian market, and then frequently leave for 'more remunerative employment in theatres or concert rooms'.[51] A glut of wind players was thus eventually inevitable; but until that time the instrumentalists from the College found it comparatively easy to secure appointments.

An institution which attracted so many female students was bound to influence their position in the profession. There was a potential demand for violinists, who, unlike individual wind instrumentalists, made up a substantial proportion of most ensembles. To enter that market, however, women had to conquer social prejudice, as well as their instrument. It therefore took several decades before the RCM ladies made their mark (see Ch. VII), but good foundations were laid from the start. The appointment of Ysaye and Joachim as examiners indicated a serious attempt to impose high standards. Competent teachers were more elusive, primarily because of inadequate salaries, but also because, as others had discovered, there were peculiar occupational hazards attached to the education of young ladies. In 1893 the principal violin teacher was found demonstrating his affection for a student and sacked with a promptitude which must set a record for such encounters. Windows were inserted into the doors of teaching rooms, and a teacher installed whose Spanish reserve was deemed more appropriate than the passion of his English predecessor.[52] Since Fernandez Arbos was a pupil of Vieuxtemps and Joachim, standards of violin-playing at the College continued to rise.[53]

Although the finest talents still had to go to the Continent for intensive training, there can be little doubt that, against all odds, the College began to establish competent levels of professional musicianship among its better students. Their first concert consisted of reputable works, including a Haydn quartet; and in 1885 they essayed Wagner's demanding *Siegfried Idyll*, to the annoyance of Joachim, their visiting examiner. There were even student performances of opera: two acts of *Figaro* at the Empire Theatre. So much was to be expected from an institution led by a great Victorian who, as Shaw remarked in a splendid panegyric, was a 'true musician: that is, the man the professors call "no musician"'.[54]

But even Grove could not transform the values of a society whose demands for musicians were utilitarian and culturally impoverished. Stanford perceived the problem in these terms, and the point was taken, a generation later, by H. C. Colles; both in words which deserve close reading. Stanford argued that it had been a fundamental mistake to proliferate scholarships and neglect opera, producing 'shoals of artists the majority of whom find, when they have completed their pupilage, that they have no outlet for their talents'. England 'began at the wrong end. If the great effort made in 1881–82 had been towards founding a National Opera . . . men and women of gift and grit, but of small means, would have pinched themselves to qualify for it here as they do elsewhere'. An 'epidemic' of scholarships had resulted in the profession's overcrowding, and increasing domination by women, because men are 'obliged to take to professions which pay or promise a career, and to shun those which do not'. English musical institutions were becoming ladies' schools, the men 'confined to departments for which there is a market and a demand, the orchestra and the organ loft' (hence Stanford's approval of wind teaching, to which we have already referred). So far had supply outrun demand that, in 'the philanthropic desire to provide for the taught, the teachers are forgotten; and the great bulk of these have to give casual lessons wherever they can, at almost starvation wages . . . The taught in their turn exchange the certain emoluments of their scholarships for the uncertain pickings of the teacher. The larger the number of teachers the smaller the pickings'.[55]

H. C. Colles, writing with a wisdom of longer hindsight, but before the devastation of the 1930s, quoted Stanford with approval, and reached similar conclusions in a wider context: 'it would certainly have been well if the "Mayors and distinguished representatives of religious and educational bodies", called together by the Prince for the founding of the College, had been reminded that if they made young people take up a musical career, the responsibility for finding employment for them in after-life would be theirs'. If they had been required to pay adequate salaries to properly-trained musicians, these dignitaries might well have 'declined to co-operate, and the Prince's educational movement would have gone no further'. In practice 'composers, pianists, organists, singers, and orchestral players were, and still are, turned out in large numbers to earn their living by teaching others, by playing in theatre bands, restaurants, and later in cinemas, by anything but those higher forms of art for which they have been trained, often at the public expense'. Colles avoided 'the economic side of the situation' but concluded that 'the consequence to artistic perspective was that by first generating power and then neglecting to use it, the English people still remained at the end of the century what they had been before the revival began, interested amateurs of music'.[56]

In addition to a grandiloquent requirement to promote 'the cultivation of music as an Art throughout our dominions', the College's Royal Charter proclaimed two objectives: the advancement of music through 'a central working and examining body charged with the duty of providing musical instruction of the highest class, and of rewarding with academical degrees and certificates of proficiency and otherwise persons *whether educated or not at the College*'; and 'the promotion and supervision of such musical instruction *in schools and elsewhere*' (my italics).[57] At the first ARCM examinations in 1886, only five of the ten successful candidates were College pupils. Thereafter the College's main function was to train teachers within its walls, and attempt to supervise and validate their activities outside. This was how Grove envisaged his task, in line with society's effective requirements, as measured by the sort of jobs which were available, primarily in teaching.[58] The same was broadly true of the other 'national' colleges, at least until the 1960s, though there were considerable variations in the extent of their extra-mural activities. The contrary view has often been put forward. One authority believes that 'the colleges of music were largely created during the nineteenth century with a view to training performers, and to a more limited extent teachers'.[59] Another even asserts that they were 'formed for the specific purpose of training performers at a time when instrumental and vocal technique was rapidly advancing beyond the scope of the talented amateur and musical general practitioner'.[60] There is no evidence that this was ever a serious aspiration, at least after the Academy's initial disappointments. In any case intention is less important than achievement, and there can be little doubt that only a small proportion of students were destined to earn their living as professional performers. Meaningful figures are elusive. In 1896 it was suggested that 'orchestral pupils' included 150 at the Academy, 102 at the College, 664 at the Guildhall, and forty at Goldsmith's Company Institute,[61] but as an estimate of professional involvement this was far too high. Although the RCM was forced, by lack of funds, to abandon its original desire to restrict entry to holders of scholarships, it remained small. After ten years there were sixty-one scholars and 249 paying students. By 1900 the total had risen to approximately 400, and there it stayed until the war, with a high proportion of amateurs and potential teachers. Similar conditions prevailed at the Academy.

The Guildhall School of Music was established in 1880 by the Corporation of London, with annual subventions, not exceeding £350, to balance staffing costs against student fees. Enrolments grew prodigiously: 900 in 1882, 2,500 in 1887, 3,600 in 1896. But for thirty years it was intended for amateurs, typically girls from middle-class families who 'went for piano and singing lessons and had no professional ambitions' which, of course, did not prevent many from taking pupils.[62] Some of the first generation of students had professional careers, notably the musical comedy conductor Herman Finck, and singer Ethel

Cadman. But the GSM's essentially amateur orientation did not change until Landon Ronald was appointed as principal in 1910, at the age of 37. It was an unorthodox appointment, for Ronald was an active professional. Son of Henry Russell, the popular singer and composer, he had worked as accompanist and coach at Covent Garden, toured as Melba's accompanist, conducted the newly formed London Symphony Orchestra and other good orchestras abroad, opera in London and the provinces, and much musical comedy. Elgar dedicated *Falstaff* to him, and he was one of the first conductors to do serious work in the recording studio, accompanying such soloists as Kreisler, Backhaus, and Cortot.

Accepting the post only on condition that he be allowed to continue an active conducting career, Ronald deliberately attempted to import 'show business' to the conservatory, arriving each day, impeccably dressed, in a chauffeur-driven Rolls Royce. He was also an excellent, forceful administrator. Openly derisive of 'the old-fashioned views hitherto in vogue in our musical academies' and their fatal ability to 'turn out hundreds of third-rate pianists', he began by establishing a clear distinction between amateur and professional students at the Guildhall, although the latter remained a minority group. A fixed curriculum was introduced, with systematic training, language classes, a unified orchestra, and some outstanding teachers, including Lionel Tertis. In its first year under the new regime, 100 students enrolled for the professional course; concentrating upon 'light opera', which reflected market requirements. Such liveliness was bound to stir up controversy. There was the 'German piano scandal', inspired by an English manufacturer's resentment of foreign competition, which gave Ronald an opportunity to attack jingoist parochialism.[63] More serious was the defeat he suffered at the hands of outraged mothers determined not to allow their daughters to sell programmes at Hammerstein's new opera house: a scheme which would have greatly enhanced their musical education, at no cost, but apparently endangered their virtue. A contemporary pointed the moral: 'In England we have made music too genteel. With our bourgeois academies and respectable students, and general atmosphere of chaperoned mediocrity, we deliberately encourage music as an accomplishment for the weaker brethren'.[64]

There was a similar expert, if less flamboyant, sense of purpose at Manchester's College of Music which was established in 1893. Hallé was its first principal and professor of piano. Brodsky, who took over in 1895, had taught in Moscow and played the 'unplayable' Tchaikovsky violin concerto in Vienna under Richter. The great conductor, who settled in Manchester a few years later, had no official connection with the college, but was its constant benefactor. The Hallé orchestra provided teachers, opportunities to attend rehearsals and acquire standards, and jobs for such talented students as Archie Camden. Richter had provided the cash to train an English player of the German bassoon for his orchestra: a perfect example of specific vocational training. Senior staff at the College were appointed only after determined recruitment among leading musicians of the day. Diplomas, which were awarded after three years of study, required adequate readings of such works as the last three sonatas of Beethoven, Chopin's Studies and B minor Sonata from aspiring performers, and an easier, but respectable, repertory from candidates for the teachers' diploma. After ten years 650 students had attended the College, 105 taking diplomas and a dozen securing positions in the Hallé. Until the war approximately 160 students enrolled each year, women in a substantial but not overwhelming majority. Petition for a Royal Charter was refused, after opposition from the RAM and RCM on grounds of allegedly inadequate financial guarantees to ensure permanence.[65] In 1921 it was granted, on condition that non-students should not be examined and awarded diplomas: significant exclusion from an activity which else-where had reached grotesque proportions.

Certificates and diplomas

The testing and certification of external students was a uniquely British enterprise, with imperial outposts. Local examinations in 'theory and composition' were organised in 1866 by the Society of Arts and the tonic sol-fa movement, abandoned after a decade, and then resumed, with the addition of 'practical' examinations in piano, organ, harmonium, violin, and singing. For reasons which remain obscure these examinations never became popular, and were rapidly overtaken by the activities of Trinity College, London. According to the latter's spokesman the Society of Arts had confined its attentions to mechanics' institutes and working men's clubs, failing to 'touch the enormous field presented by the high schools and boarding schools for upper and middle class pupils'.[66] The potential market was indeed huge, though at a lower social level than was implied; and TCL exploited it with great energy and skill. The enterprise began modestly enough, in 1872, as the Church Choral Society of London and College of Choral Music, with the intention of improving church music. In this capacity it contributed to the reforming movement which raised choral standards during the 1870s.[67] With Gore Ouseley as president, it devised schemes for testing choir masters in the teaching and history of music, sight reading and choir management. After the first examination in 1874, four choral fellowships and two senior fellowships were awarded, the latter to candidates who were already B.Mus. graduates of Cambridge and Oxford respectively.

Incorporated as Trinity College in the following year, it turned to a wider, secular market, claiming to believe that musical education 'to be sound, must move hand in hand with general culture'.[68] Thus it insisted that diploma candidates should pass a matriculation examination. Over one thousand candidates were examined in 'theory' at fifty local centres in 1877. A year later the examinations were thrown open to women (an indication of secularization), and in 1878 practical tests of piano-playing and singing were introduced. Local examination centres, described as 'institutions enrolled in union with the College', were the focal points of rapid expansion: subject to approval by the College's academic board, any three people could set one up by signing the prescribed form. By 1882 there were 193 centres in England and Wales, 16 in Scotland, 9 in Ireland, 3 in British Islands, 3 in South Africa, and 1 apiece in Brisbane, Sydney, Calcutta, Naini Tal, Colombo, Rangoon, and Port of Spain.[69] By 1885 nearly 30,000 people had been examined and 5,000 were sitting every year. A debt of £4,000 in 1881, equivalent to a year's income, was liquidated by 1885, and income had risen to over £6,000.

The prime agent of this expansion was the Revd. H. G. Bonavia Hunt, a collector of degrees, diplomas, and fellowships: Mus.B. (Oxon), Mus.B. and Mus.D. (Dublin), FRSE, FRAS, FLS, FGS, LTCL, etc. Born in Malta and failing to qualify as as lawyer, he had intended to take an arts degree, but switched to theology and music. He then became a 'great advocate for raising the general culture of musicians and consequently their social status'. As Warden of TCL he organized the first fifty examination centres 'single handed in a few months'.[70] To him, more than to any man, is due, perhaps, the bizarre Victorian conception of a professional musician's career as a ceaseless quest for paper qualifications. The refusal of the Society of Professional Musicians to accept his application for membership in 1883 was probably unfair, but ironically appropriate.[71]

Operations were extended to Canada in 1887, and in 1895 'practical' examinations were held in Canada, Australia, New Zealand and South Africa, proudly 'bearing upon Imperial Unity'.[72] For this purpose examiners were dispatched from London, and the College *Academic Gazette* reported tales of derring-do: a missionary's wife rode five days horseback with her daughter to the Grahamstown centre. Dr Charles Vincent, examiner and prolific composer of oratorios, cantatas, instrumental pieces and text books, was granted audience with President Kruger of the Transvaal. 'Britain is a musical country', exulted the *Gazette,* so it is 'no matter of surprise that, notably in Australia and the Cape, the aspiring musician looks London-wards for a patent of his fitness as an executant or theorist'.[73] Between 1881 and 1895 over

10,000 colonial candidates were tested. Examiners later visited the
United States, Latin America, Palestine, India, and Japan. By 1913
Trinity College was dealing with about 28,000 students a year, and had
examined more than 500,000 since its inception. Publishing was an
important subsidiary. By 1897 100,000 copies of the *Junior Text Book of
Musical Knowledge* had been marketed, and 17,000 copies of local
examination papers were sold every year.

An overwhelming majority of examinees were girls learning the piano:
the typical 'centre' was a 'ladies college'. Occasional remonstrance at this
unbalance had little effect. As early as 1885 the Dean assured students
that 'the greatness of a music nation depended entirely upon the
number of its best orchestras' and urged them to 'earnestly consider
that point as a duty to society, to the nation, and to art' by giving
'attention to orchestral instruments'.[74] To anyone who might be moved
by these noble sentiments the College offered scant assistance, although
it insisted that examinations were not its sole *raison d'être*, and took pride
in offering 'the cheapest high class instruction in London', less than £3 a
term per course, a 'thorough training for professionals or amateurs
without leaving our shores . . . by teachers of recognised weight'.[75] In
practice the number of students directly taught was never more than a
tiny proportion of those examined, and the resources available for their
training were meagre. In 1913, when 28,000 sat examinations, only 400
were attending classes in London, many of them 'destined for the
profession'.[76] Choice of instrument was very limited, and the small staff
mostly nondescript, though Joseph Holbrooke and Albert Ketèlby (born
Vodorinski; composer of 'In a Monastery Garden' and 'In a Persian
Market') were among the piano teachers.

The Director of Studies and 'School of Pianoforte Technique' after
1905 was G. E. Bambridge, FRAM, etc. Born in 1842, and a student at
the Royal Academy during the 1860s, he joined TCL in 1881 and
became a widely travelled examiner. A laudatory obituary in the
Academic Gazette emphasizes his lifelong regret at not making the
Army his career, but gives no indication of any musical accomplishment.[77]
Another worthy was E.H. Turpin (1835–1907), who came to Trinity in
1874 and succeeded Hunt as Warden in 1892. A church organist at the
age of 15, he gave a recital at the 1851 Great Exhibition, became Hon.
Secretary of the College of Organists in 1875, receiving its fellowship,
and a Mus.D. from the Archbishop of Canterbury in 1889. Although he
inevitably wrote music, most of it unpublished, much of his time was
devoted to journalism, as editor of the *Musical Standard*, *Musical News*,
and the *Academic Gazette*. A sample of his style is an explanation of the
'universal desire to be examined'. This arose because 'an increased
strain upon any source of power brings with it the necessity of daily

testing the strength of the power to be employed. Thus the advancing musical tastes of the age ... have brought additional work and strain upon our artistic life'. Central examinations were therefore necessary 'for testing for attainments of the professional musician' and local examinations 'for testing and encouraging music students'.[78] In practice the distinction was not so clear. As the *Musical Times* explained, 'touting for examinees' encouraged holders of certificates, however elementary, to 'set up, not as learners, but as teachers'.[79]

Teaching diplomas, which were introduced in 1882, were highly marketable, some 700 candidates presenting themselves every year by the early twentieth century. The College laid great emphasis on the status of its diplomas as professional qualifications. A typical advertisement lists 'The Professional Diploma of A.Mus. TCL, The Professional Diploma of L.Mus. TCL, Professional Diplomas in pianoforte, organ solo, singing, violin, etc.' and an award of 'Certificated Pianist'.[80] Some 2,000 of the latter were at large by 1910.[81] The 'full professional course' cost £9 per term. Examinations were open to anyone, but candidates for the Licentiateship had to possess an A.Mus, TCL, an FRCO, or be graduates of a British University. Amidst all this testing and certificating there were occasional musical interludes. In January 1895 a student concert at the People's Palace in East London included a Mendelssohn quartet, and Ketèlby played two of his piano sketches. Sir Richard Webster MP, President of the College, 'spoke a few manly, characteristic words' asserting his 'faith in the innate good taste of East End audiences'.[82] Even more characteristic, one suspects, was the reaction of local secretaries to the suggestion that 'playing, in public or semi public' was an 'essential part of a performer's education'. But, they expostulated, 'some candidates were shocked even at the idea of playing before their father'.[83] Application for a Royal Charter was refused in 1917, after opposition by the RAM and RCM. In this, if in little else, Trinity College resembled the Manchester College of Music.

Meanwhile the Royal schools of music had formed their own examining board, with an unprecedented gesture of mutual goodwill and co-operation, eased by the arrival of Alexander Mackenzie as principal of the Academy in 1888. The Associated Board's first examinations were held two years later at forty-six local centres in Britain, attracting 1,141 candidates. Simpler 'local school' grades were then introduced, and the number of examinees rose to 10,000 in 1903, 20,000 in 1910, and 25,000 by 1913. Nearly all, never less than 80 per cent in these years, were elementary pianists. Approximately eight to 10 per cent were examined in 'theory', and never more than 7 per cent in string playing. Singers were a small, and other instrumentalists a negligible, proportion. Over 90 per cent of the candidates were girls, and a similar proportion of their teachers were women, mostly without formal qualifications, though their numbers were rising. (One sample analysis suggests that they increased from 30 per cent to 40 per cent between 1900 and 1914.)[84]

'Whether the extraordinary desire on the part of mankind, and especially of womankind, to be examined is on the whole in the best interests of the Art may be a moot point for discussion, but that this apparently irresistible stream of tendency should be directed into proper channels is beyond doubt', commented the *Musical Times*.[85] Some contemporaries were less charitable. Sir Frederick Bridge, who, curiously enough, was chairman of Trinity College, suggested that many musicians 'might as well put the whole alphabet after their names, and leave the admiring reader to sort the letters according to fancy'.[86] J. F. Runciman, the *Saturday Review*'s acerbic critic, was more explicit: 'in England the teaching profession is enormously overstocked, and in the race to gain pupils the teachers have eagerly sought certificates both for themselves and for their pupils. If A has twenty certificates, even if they are worthless certificates, he will appear, in the eyes of the stupid English bourgeois, a much greater man than B who has none, though he may be a much more competent musician and teacher'.[87]

The attempt to direct diploma-hunting into 'proper channels' was necessary, for reasons to be explored in our next chapter. But the 'moot point', discreetly skipped by the *Musical Times* and brutally exposed by Runciman, was far more significant. Perhaps only a minority of candidates for Trinity College and Associated Board examinations intended to enter the profession, But their aggregate number was so large, and their general level of accomplishment so low and narrowly focused, that most of them had no prospects but to swell the ranks of private piano teachers. Moreover the 40,000 or so British candidates every year were, in a very limited sense, an élite, whose certificates were not fraudulent, and whose studies were at least subjected to a modicum of scrutiny. With something between 2m. and 4m. pianos in Britain,[88] there were many more children taking unregulated lessons, some of whom would also eventually seek pupils. A cumulative, seemingly inexorable process threatened to flood the profession.

VI

Gentlemen

To be a member of the Incorporated Society of Musicians would (if all our leading players joined) be a guarantee that one was a thorough musician and a gentleman, and as such would be able to command respectable fees and a recognized status.

The British Musician, June 1896.

A view of the profession

In 1888 Dr Henry Fisher published a lengthy book, some 360 pages, entitled *The Musical Profession*, which was probably the first of its kind. At no point does he explicitly define his terms of reference, but there are abundant clues, including his own career.[1] Born in Blackpool in 1845, he was apprenticed to a Manchester music-seller, assistant to a Darlington music 'professor', and largely self-taught. Graduating Mus.B. in 1876 and Mus.D. 1878 at Cambridge, he settled in Blackpool as an organist and teacher of singing, piano, and harmony. Like most music graduates at that time, he never attended a university. In common with many lower-middle-class autodidacts, he collected diverse credentials, though his addiction was mild by contemporary standards: in addition to his music degrees he boasted a fellowship of the Geological Society. He had written two cantatas, a romance for viola, and text books on theory and tuning. In his latest book he took some pride in painstaking research; drawing much of his material from replies to a questionnaire which he had addressed to 'a multitude of competent teachers' drawn from 'all ranks of the musical profession' throughout the British Isles. Unfortunately the names of his informants are withheld, but readers are assured that, if published, they would provide 'ample warranty for the thoroughly representative character of this work'.[2] A useful source of information and opinion, it is also a revealing, if largely implicit, guide to the preoccupations of men who saw themselves as 'the profession'.

Fisher's elaborate discussion of amateur musicians is particularly illuminating. First among them is the 'accomplished musican'. Intelligent and cultivated, a skilled executant and good, but uncarping listener who is 'considerate for the faults of others',[3] he will frequently have passed examinations, even for a degree (in music), indicative of his all-round culture. He will certainly not 'seek out some obscure institution' with simple examinations and worthless diplomas. He might even earn money as an organist, though most of it would likely be spent on the choir. Such a paragon would surely be welcomed by professionals as 'our equal, or peradventure, as our superior'. A second type of amateur is less knowledgeable and talented. Frequently wealthy and generous, he supports music as others do a pack of hounds, racing stable, or yacht. His value to the musical world should not be denigrated by cynicism about the social prestige attending his activities, for that could be achieved more cheaply and effectively in other spheres. A third type is far more common: the 'incompetent amateur' who poses as an expert, ludicrously at concerts, dangerously if he exerts influence in church or chapel. Finally there is a group generally loathed by the profession, but more deserving of pity, mingled with contempt: best represented by 'the poor clerk' who tries to eke out his meagre income with an organ appointment and a few cheap pupils. He deserves sympathy for it is just such pupils who are most 'exacting, unreasonable, and dictatorial', demanding an unrelieved diet of the 'The Maiden's Prayer' and 'Silvery Waves'.[4]

The author then seeks his respondents' opinions about these various types of amateur. Is their competition injurious? How much teaching per week merits their recognition as professionals? Are their appointments mostly 'beneath the notice of a prosperous professional man'?[5] Are wealthy amateurs generous in their patronage? The reported answers suggest an improbable equanimity. One goes so far as to suggest that teaching by incompetent amateurs creates a demand for competent, professional lessons; a belief with which Fisher concurs. It is acknowledged that a few amateurs secure unmerited appointments, even in cathedrals, receiving stipends of £80 to £150; and that some patrons are motivated by self-aggrandizement, particularly 'when Royalty can be gratified'.[6] Others will drive a close bargain with musicians, yet pay lavishly for pictures (there was no love lost between the two artistic professions). But many examples are cited of generous patronage: to endow a child's musical training, an organ, or the payment of instrumentalists for local concerts. The general relationship between amateur and professional is depicted, with few exceptions, as remarkably equable.

Throughout the book it is assumed that 'professional musician' means music *teacher*. This is implicit in the lengthy treatment given to examinations, diplomas, degrees, 'business and legal matters', commercial travellers (should one purchase from them or from local music dealers? short teaching pieces should never cost more than sixpence a page), and that pedagogic shibboleth, 'the art of teaching'. Truly memorable, however, is Fisher's discussion of concerts. Given the self-evident premiss that they are financially 'a delusion and a snare',[7] he asks if they have 'any indirect value to a professional man?' A necessary but expensive advertisement is the best that can be said for them, and discussion then turns to the terms on which vocalists and instrumentalists may be hired: essentially from the viewpoint of prospective employers. One opinion is that performers cost 'far, far above their commercial value'; another that market rates are, happily, falling; yet another confesses ignorance because 'they are generally engaged and paid by secretaries'.[8] Concerts are evidently peripheral to the activities of these professional musicians, and best avoided. If their view of the profession is narrow, however, they are in no doubt that numbers are increasing at alarming speed. 'Think well', warns one of them, 'before adopting a profession which at present is *overcrowded*, and bids fair to be more so'.[9]

Too many musicians

It was common knowledge in late-nineteenth-century England that music had become an overcrowded occupation. Not that the number of complaints can be taken as a reliable indicator. Established practitioners have always been sensitive to intrusion, and rising indignation may simply indicate a new articulateness and the availability of means for its expression. Such facilities were expanding vigorously, in the general press and a growing number of musical and 'trade' journals, which provided unprecedented opportunities for the ventilation of grievance; but there was substantial evidence of glut. It was condemned in 1880 when a lecturer to the Royal Musical Association 'On Music as a Profession' lamented 'increased and increasing competition', concluding with an 'unsatisfactory estimate' of the profession's 'financial status' in comparison with what it had been in the recent past.[10] Some of his audience maintained their equanimity. W. H. Cummings, a singer and antiquarian who was soon to become principal of the Guildhall School of Music, thought that 'talented musicians need not despair'. If they qualified themselves thoroughly for their profession they would 'find work to do', but others expressed a degree of apprehension which was remarkable for people whose presence at that meeting probably indicated a measure of success. The chairman, W. H. Monk, editor of *Hymns, Ancient and Modern*, spoke of the cathedral organist, whose career was the 'beau ideal of a musical professor's existence . . . relieved from pecuniary anxiety by an assured stipend; a gentleman respected and admired, in and out of his profession; visiting on equal terms his most worthy neighbours'. Even this paragon now received such 'miserable payments' that it was a 'matter of astonishment that so many estimable men and first-rate musicians were willing to occupy these posts'.

A decade later there was a prevailing sense of livelihoods being threatened and incomes continually being depressed by the ceaseless inflow of players and teachers. The *British Musician* complained of 'a great congestion of orchestral players struggling for an existence'.[11] Kuhe compared conditions in 1896, when there would be fifty applicants for a position in the opera orchestra, and in 1846, when the reigning impresario, Lumley, deserted by singers, orchestra, and chorus to a rival establishment, had to scour continental cities for efficient, and expensive substitutes.[12] The *St. James's Gazette* expressed a common opinion: 'Other professions are overcrowded too; but the evil is admitted, and candidates are warned and discouraged. In music alone they are urged to come on, and their increasing numbers are proclaimed with rejoicing'.[13]

According to the same source, conditions were more satisfactory for two groups. Singers were unique in enjoying immunity from foreign competition in a substantial market: 'the English repertory'. If America and Australia sent some rivals, they also provided good pickings for English vocalists in their own concert halls. Organists were the other privileged group, their instrument offering 'the safest road to the best academical appointments in the profession', and 'many consolation prizes' to the less fortunate. Annual salaries varied from £40 to the £200 or £300 received for most cathedral posts, but these sums could be richly supplemented by a 'a ready made teaching connection . . . first claim to local conductorships and the like'. There was even a prevalent, and often misplaced, belief that organists were innately qualified to teach and practise any branch of music. The nominal stipends, £8 or £10 a year, paid in small churches and chapels, were either mere stepping-stones for young aspirants, or subsidiary to other employment. Generally 'the most solid and satisfactory branch of the profession' resided in the organ loft, its well-being 'wisely administered' by the Royal Society of Organists, which had been granted its charter in the previous year (1893). If there was truth in these remarks, the author's view of pianists was eccentrically complacent. Admitting that they were overwhelmed by foreign competition, he believed this led them not to 'cherish unreasonable expectations'. Every year a few hundred newly 'certificated pianists' emerged, expecting only to become teachers, for whom the demand appeared to be unlimited. So much time and labour in training was ill-rewarded by a career which was 'neither agreeable nor remunerative', but 'if they know that before hand no harm is done'.

If some victims of oversupply showed forbearance, others were quick to articulate complaints. Typical of such protests was a series of letters to the *Musical Opinion* on the 'decadence of the musical profession—if it is worthy of such a title'.[14] Competition, argued one correspondent, was 'more rampant, more unfair, more dishonest' in music than in any other occupation, and 'this must go on so long as no restrictions are imposed'. A small midlands town, for example, populated almost entirely by artisans, boasted some fifty music teachers whose fees ranged from 15*s*. a quarter to 2*d*. a lesson. It also had seven doctors and six lawyers, which some thought excessive; but they, like accountants and architects, were required to pass qualifying examinations, while anyone could practise as a musician. Even organists were becoming victims of an overcrowded market. One who was well educated and armed with exemplary testimonials had applied for 222 appointments, and received acknowledgements from only four. Posts worth £70 and £40 had attracted respectively 176 and ninety-seven applicants.

Apart from general lamentation over the damnable flood, there were two kinds of response: a belief that market forces would eventually establish a new equilibrium which it would be immoral or fruitless to attempt to impose by artificial restriction; and a mounting conviction that controls must be established, though there were widely different views about suitable procedures. The former belief, representative of current liberal orthodoxy, was expressed by *Musical News*, attempting to dispel fears expressed in an Italian journal. The *Gazzetta Musicale di Milano* had referred to 2,000 female students at the Guildhall School of Music, 300 studying the violin, as 'poor young girls' without prospects. Only a small proportion of them, retaliated *Musical News*, expected to become professionals, as was the case for most English colleges, except for the 'two great schools', particularly the RCM. There was indeed considerable 'pressure in the ranks', a 'natural result of the immense artistic awakening which has taken place during the past few decades', and 'a little time is required to allow the flood to settle to its rational level'. Many of the women would marry and give up work, their culture, 'if not carried beyond prudential bounds', benefiting future generations. 'Temporary inconvenience, and even great hardship' would end when 'the average paterfamilias' realized that success required exceptional ability and work. Like all professions and trades, music was 'subject to the usual laws of supply and demand'.[15] Similarly anodyne essays and letters, filled many pages of print to express the conventional wisdom of the times: an amalgam of empty rhetoric, genuine belief in free markets, rationalization of vested interests and, increasingly, attacks upon those who were determined to impose controls. That determination was expressed by a growing number of musicians who sought effective protection.

It was inevitable that established musicians should attempt to restrict the entry of newcomers, but they had long ceased to possess effective sanctions. Their predecessors had discouraged intruders by means of guilds and appeals to authority, now obsolete. The founding of various associations demonstrated and contributed to a measure of group loyalty, but none were overtly protectionist. Some, like the Muşical Association (est. 1844, later RMA), the Musical Institute of London (est. 1851), and numerous concert societies, were devoted to scholarship or the promotion of music. Others, like the Royal Society of Female Musicians (founded in 1839 and merged with the RSM in 1866) and the Glasgow Society of Musicians (est. 1884), were either charitable or friendly societies, for public benevolence or mutual insurance against distress in sickness or old age. Attempts to control supply were focused upon two new kinds of mutually antagonistic organization: professional associations and trade unions. Their fundamental incompatability may not be obvious to the modern observer. As Eliot Freidson has remarked, in a notable study of American medicine, 'so far as the terms of work go, professions differ from trade unions only in their sanctimoniousness'.[16] But in nineteenth-century Britain, when sanctimony was a way of life, that antagonism can scarcely be doubted: 'the very Victorians who condemned trade unions as vicious, restrictive, futile, and as unwarrantable interferences with individual liberty, flocked to join professional combinations'.[17]

The Incorporated Society of Musicians

The origins of the ISM were self-consciously modest and provincial, but its founders had no doubt about their protective ambitions. James Dawber, Mus.B. (Cantab.), was a blind organist from Wigan who sought better local representatives for the profession than those 'individuals quite outside the pale' who were the only speakers at a meeting which had assembled in February 1882 to discuss the proposed national conservatory.[18] His initial approach to MacFarren for support elicited no response, but he found an ally in Henry Hiles, Mus.D. (Oxon.), a Manchester lecturer. In October 1882, at a meeting in Manchester Town Hall, the 'Society of Professional Musicians' was launched from this modest base, enrolling fifty members. A note in the *Musical Times* likened the proposed society to the Musical Association, its purpose to 'read papers . . . and invite discussion',[19] but Dawber hastened to correct this misapprehension. The new society would be open only to '*bona fide* musicians', and, although intending to advance the art, its chief object was 'guarding the interests of the artists'.[20] The next few years were devoted to 'missionary work': members' names were displayed in music shops; deputations visited northern centres, establishing sections in Nottingham, Birmingham, and Leicester. In 1885 the first general council met in Blackpool, electing Edward Chadfield, an organist and teacher from Derby, as general secretary. Hiles became editor of the *Quarterly Musical Review* in the same year, and provided regular space for the Society's news.

The decision to introduce its own system of examinations in 1884 was premature and divisive. The Society denied any 'spirit of opposition to other examining bodies', and claimed to reform their alleged deficiencies by appointing examiners without local bias, and insisting that candidates be anonymous. An official history asserts that it was also an attempt to 'raise the standards of teaching qualifications and so to enhance the status of the teacher'.[21] In practice the system added to an already anarchic proliferation, and exacerbated opposition, from Trinity College of course, and more seriously, from Grove, who opposed the Society's first application for incorporation in 1886. Some other dignitaries were more accommodating, including the principals of the GSM and RAM (where Mackenzie had succeeded the uncooperative MacFarren). The Revd. Sir Frederick Arthur Gore Ouseley was even persuaded to present the first certificates.[22] Nevertheless there was considerable resentment at the presumption of a group of nondescript provincial music teachers. It was expressed, in an elaborate lampoon, by men of a similar stamp who nevertheless took pride in their metropolitan sophistication. Under the new order, jeered the Trinity men, Hiles would become musical dictator of England; the Queen and Houses of Parliament taking up residence in Manchester. Amateur music would be published only by special permission, with an attached label, 'composed by an amateur'; and non-professional performers would be similarly humiliated. London University would close and Owens College (Manchester) be declared the sole seat of learning. The Society's certificates would rank higher than any other qualifications.[23] These heavy sarcasms were penned in the hope that the Society's 'esteemed members' might abandon their 'short-sighted, localising, illiberal, popularity-seeking yet criticism-suppressing policy'. Returning to the fray a few months later, Turpin assured the Senate of TCL that the Society was merely 'a protest against the pre-eminence of London. Half a dozen gentlemen in Manchester wished it to be known that they were quite equal in status to any London men'.[24] Some members of TCL's senate feared more sinister motives: 'unless carefully watched' the Society could become 'a professional trade union, destructive to the best interests of profession and art'.[25]

These apprehensions were prompted by the Society's bold decision to hold a national conference in London, inviting metropolitan musicians to discuss its scope and purpose. Frederick Cowen presided, and a large congregation included Prout, Curwen, and even the TCL antagonists,

Hunt and Turpin. The latter grudgingly conceded a measure of success to 'a friendly invasion', adding, in his monthly editorial, customary platitudes about the 'craving for unity and organization' to 'achieve a more dignified place in our social system'.[26] The *Musical World* sat on the fence: reporting that 'most of our leading composers and conductors held aloof'; conceding the presence of 'several well known names'; but concluding that the Society was attempting too much if it sought to be 'a tribunal of musical manners and morals, and to raise social status'.[27] The *Daily Telegraph* was more caustic: 'Don't let them come before society asking to have their status improved by other means than their own professional worth'. They would do better to encourage 'brotherly feeling in a profession which, more than any other, is divided by narrow party spirit and rivalry'.[28] Such critical attention was good for morale and a sense of group identity. The Society proceeded to vindicate its claim to be representative on a national scale, by increasing the number and geographical spread of its members, and by organizing annual conferences, with as much pomp and ceremony as could be mustered, in major cities. In 1887 it met in Birmingham, and again earned useful publicity from reports and attacks in the press. The *Birmingham Daily Post* approved some of its aims, but drew blood by attributing the failure to secure registration as an incorporated society to objectives which were 'too comprehensive to entrust to so unimportant a body', particularly the award of 'musical proficiency certificates'.[29] It was good publicity: by warning readers against 'another form of trade unionism destined to result in the creation of a new privileged class like the lawyers and doctors, outside whose membership no practice is legal', the paper was putting the Society into precisely the category its members most desired.

Birmingham was followed by another conference in London, with the Lord Mayor in attendance, and by subsequent annual assemblies in Cambridge (the Master of Peterhouse acting for the Vice-Chancellor), Bristol, Liverpool, and Newcastle, all graced by the presence of local dignitaries.[30] Rousing speeches boosted self-esteem: the profession will soon be 'intellectually and socially second only to the Church', Chadfield told the Liverpool conference. In 1888 the Society began to publish a *Monthly Journal*, and claimed a membership of 'nearly five hundred eminent and esteemed professional musicians from all parts of the country'.[31] In 1892 it became the Incorporated Society of Musicians, 'the only registered body of composing, teaching, and performing musicians in this country—others exist only for education or examination'.[32] Members were assured that the omission of 'professional' from the title did *not* imply any relaxation of standards: 'we do not speak of "professional" doctors'.[33] Incorporation was played up as a momentous achievement, 'second only in prestige to a Royal Charter'.[34] Overcoming its sensitivity to metropolitan disdain and opposition, even 'persecution by vested interests', the ISM moved office from Derby to London, despite so much internal dissension that local branches were not consulted about the move. 'It does *not* mean the Society will become metropolitan', insisted Chadfield, who became full-time secretary, as the letters of complaint flowed in.[35] The appointment of HRH the Duke of Edinburgh as president was another action which had to be defended in a Society which had taken pride in its 'unostentatious' origins, 'unaided by pomp and power'. A rather shamefaced editoral proclaimed 'every difference between crippling an art by selfish patronage and giving it assistance on the broad lines of general favour'.[36] The inherent paradox was temporarily put aside without resolution. A self-consciously provincial, non-élitist body of men was making a bid for collective mobility. Claims to professional status were the keynote of the ISM's existence, by which its members meant far more than a mere separation from amateurs.

Nineteenth-century professionalism

The ISM was seeking parity with contemporary professions. 'Is it too much to ask that the profession of music should have as honourable a status and recognition on equal terms with those of Law and Medicine?'[37] pleaded the Birmingham organist, Stephen Stratton. The question was constantly reiterated, sometimes invoking less elevated professions—accountants, surveyors, and dentists—but lawyers, doctors, even, as we have seen, the Church, were favourite exemplars. It *was* too much to ask, and reiteration ultimately confirmed the question's futility. Where was the promised land, and how had others reached its shores?

Despite the generalizations of many sociologists, there is no 'ideal' (in the sense of a paradigmatic model) pattern and chronology of professionalization. Daniel Duman has demonstrated this conclusively for the bar, and historical studies of other professions lead to a similar rejection of neat generalizations.[38] Nevertheless the successful professions of Victorian Britain did share certain characteristics, in their attributes of success, and in the paths by which their coveted status was achieved. Among several traits, two were fundamental: autonomy and monopoly control. The professional man enjoyed a degree of freedom from *external* interference in his work, as distinct from regulation by his peers. His customer was a client, not a patron.[39] Entry to his profession was circumscribed, and ultimately controlled. The public's acquiescence in such powers derived, in the last analysis, from its social evaluation of the work. It was from that evaluation, rather than from the demonstrable effectiveness of specific feats of advocacy, prayer, or medical treatment, that lawyers, clergymen, and doctors derived their power and prestige.

By such evaluation music rated low, despite the temporarily buoyant market for teachers and performers. 'The difference between the profession of music and the other learned professions of law, physic and the Church', wrote F. E. Bache in 1856, 'is that the latter are necessary, whereas the former is not'.[40] Opposition to that commonsense view was essentially wishful thinking, inflated by propaganda. 'Music is as great a necessity as law and physic', claimed Stratton.[41] T. H. S. Escott was a more reliable guide: 'The ordinary Englishman has ambitions, social and professional, and he subordinates all other things to them . . . The degrees of esteem allotted to the different English professions are exactly what might be expected in a society organized upon such a basis and conscious of such aims. Roughly it may be said professions in England are valued according to their stability, their remunerativeness, their influence and their recognition by the State'.[42]

If music was 'unnecessary', what chance was there for its purveyors to achieve the status of a profession? A hierarchical pyramid of the Victorian professions would undoubtedly, as Duman asserts, have placed barristers at the top.[43] Few musicians could hope to reach its base, yet there was a loudly trumpeted desire to be accepted there, at least. Routes to that unlikely destination were well mapped. To have emulated the successful professions would have required something like the following journey. Stage one required clear emergence as a separate full-time occupation with specific, recognized skills which the public were eager to employ. Then the group needed collective organization to boost its morale, encourage mutual assistance, arrange publicity, and move towards the exclusion of the 'unqualified'. The next step might be the establishment of specialized training, assessment, and validation, to acknowledged, and eventually mandatory standards. A code of practice would require enforcement, both for self-justification and to protect the public. Recognized monopoly of title, by means of a charter, might be followed by the ultimate accolade: legal monopoly of practice as an absolute barrier to unqualified practitioners.[44] Neither the order of progression nor completion of every stage was obligatory, but there were many false paths and dead ends, and the final ascent was too steep for most climbers.

The fight for registration

We left the ISM at a satisfactory pause in its climb; incorporated, with an office in London. Several stages had been completed by advance parties, and stragglers were constantly being encouraged along the route. Regular local meetings and annual conferences, mounted with decorum, propaganda, and correspondence in the *Monthly Journal*, sometimes taken up by the national press: all had some public impact and helped to raise morale among the Society's isolated, widely-scattered members. Since most of them were private teachers, unattached to institutions and conscious of their lowly status, it was a useful contribution to their well-being. Association, however remote, with civic and musical dignitaries; a chance to don the trappings of academe, or wishfully assume the demeanour of professionalism, were deeply satisfying to the shabby genteel. There were even gestures of international solidarity. A representative of the Music Teachers National Association of America attended the 1888 conference in London, and in the following year Chadfield read a paper to that association's conference in Philadelphia, on 'National Musical Associations. Their Duties to Music, to Musicians, and to the People'.[45] The activities of a German association were reported with approval, as an 'assertion of the rights of the profession—our case is as urgent as that of our German cousins'.[46]

Attempts to establish codes of practice and protect the public from quacks were, by implication, an attack on the unqualified, again fitting a professional simulacrum. Advertisements in local newspapers were culled to deride the widespread availability of excessively cheap, presumably inferior lessons. 'Wanted, by an Experienced Person, Pupils for the Pianoforte, Terms 7s. 6d. per quarter' was a typical example, submitted by a Newcastle correspondent.[47] Neither such advertisements nor attacks upon them were new, though lessons were now cheaper than ever. In 1861 a representative notice in the *Musical Times* had advised that 'Ladies and Gentlemen desirous of learning a great deal about music in a little time should apply to Mr Charles Field, teacher of pianoforte and singing. Euston Square. 8 lessons. 1 guinea'.[48] A generation later young teachers were being urged by Fisher not to compete with 'ladies who advertise lessons at 12s. 6d. a quarter', or the man who offered '15 tunes the first three months—13s. per quarter of twelve private lessons—two pupils at one house £1. 3s.'[49] The exposure of such practices had long been a standby of musical journalism, but in the pages of the ISM's journal it was developed into a systematic and intensive campaign against 'the charlatans'.[50] The generally low level of music teaching, argued the *Journal*, was perpetuated by the public's lack of discrimination, and by an 'overgrowth of the semi-professional weed'.[51] Clerks and other incompetents took pupils in their spare time: far more than could be traced from advertisements, because many kept a low profile, lest their employers become disgruntled. Like its American counterpart, whose views were quoted with approval, the Society was anxious to eliminate those who taught for 'pin money', without knowing how. Even degrees and diplomas were admitted to be insufficient safeguards: an uncharacteristic concession. The former lacked a 'practical side'; the latter were difficult to assess. While it repudiated accusations of 'despotism', the Society offered to provide guarantees of 'education, experience and respectability' to any member of the public seeking a teacher.[52]

If such activities were primarily aimed at limiting competition and raising the general level of fees,they were also imbued with a genuine desire to raise standards. Thus the Society lent its support to the Associated Board's system of co-ordinated examinations, while continuing to run its own, and hoped that 'other systems' would collapse.[53] There was constant emphasis upon the need to prepare pupils for recognized examinations; work which, it was argued, could only be undertaken by 'bona-fide qualified' teachers—the adjectives were ceaselessly reiterated. There were times when this preoccupation with formal training, examination and diplomas approached caricature. Thus delegates at a Bristol prize-giving were assured that Schubert would have been a better composer had his works not 'betrayed want of training':[54] a common enough belief among contemporary pedants, but grotesque in that company. Metropolitan critics, accustomed to another kind of professionalism, in which paper qualifications count for nothing against the talent to compose or perform, tilted at a callow philistinism which 'merely deals in music lessons as a grocer deals in tea and sugar'. Such professionals were 'raw, unread, uncultivated', and considered 'a doctor's hood and a selection of the alphabet after their names the dizziest height of human ambition'.[55]

A fitting tribute to their accomplishments was *British Musical Biography*, compiled by James D. Brown and Stephen S. Stratton 'to record the achievements of British workers in the field of musical art'.[56] Listed in its 463 double-columned pages are 3,251 men and 316 women, approximately half of whom were born after 1760. The authors guessed that there were probably more than 40,000 currently engaged in the profession, and therefore devote most space to 'living musicians'. Analysis of this copious data might provide a collective biography, but it would make dull reading. Few of the listed individuals made any contribution to music as a communicative art; scarcely thirty would be recognized by historians and, more to the point, even fewer would have been familiar to the contemporary public. By erecting a monument to mediocrity, the authors achieved, in a sense, their intention of presenting 'the true position of the British Empire in the world of music' in 1897.[57] More significant than their obsession with dull pedantry, however, is their neglect of many men and women, equally obscure, perhaps, but at least in touch with living music. That disregard was implicit and mutual. More damaging to the ISM's hopes for a united profession than any London critic's opinion was the attitude of practising musicians, rarely expressed in print, who were unimpressed by those who sought to assess and certificate the muse. It was an issue never to be resolved.

Despite such reservations the Society had good cause to celebrate a decade of achievement. *Musical News* paid homage: 'It has gathered together the isolated units of the profession, made them mutually acquainted with each other, created an *esprit de corps* amongst them, increased their interest in the art, and by giving them broader and more harmonious views, has largely diminished the envies and jealousies which must exist in all art professions'.[58] Continuing to provide such facilities and satisfactions the ISM increased its membership and apparent influence. By 1898 there were few urban centres without a branch, and the membership of some 2,000 included many with strings of letters after their names. In 1903 the *Journal* listed them, to indicate distinctions and an ecumenical 'sinking of differences'. Seventy-three members held doctorates from Oxford, Cambridge, London, Durham, Dublin, or the Archbishop of Canterbury; 138 were bachelors of music; sixty-one fellows, members, or associates of the RAM; 192 possessed an LRAM and 101 an ARCM; 259 were fellows or Associates of the Royal Irish Academy of Music; 107 were licentiates or associates of TCL, and seventy-six held the ISM's own diploma. Twenty were professors at the Guildhall School of Music and fifty-two held diplomas from foreign conservatories. Even if some of the statistics involved double counting because of plural honours, the public could hardly fail to be impressed. But further progress towards real professional status required more than morale-building and expansion of membership.

The means by which monopoly control might be secured had been envisaged in the first year of the Society's existence, when Liverpool members demanded the lobbying of Parliament about 'legal registration'. It originated with the idea of a register for schoolteachers, equivalent to those established by the General Medical Council and the Incorporated Law Society, which was aired during the 1860s debate on secondary schools but abandoned.[59] It was revived thirty years later, and a register of schoolteachers was actually established in 1902, but soon withdrawn.[60] The belief that a similar procedure could be applied to music teachers, even to musicians, was taken up, with typical energy and self-importance, by Trinity College's Bonavia Hunt. A draft of legislation 'for the organisation and regulation of musicians', it was announced, would be submitted to Parliament; its only obstacle 'the lamentable want of unity amongst the members of an inchoate profession'.[61] In 1891, when teachers' registration was again before Parliament, the possibility of including musicians was considered and rejected. After examining twenty-seven witnesses, including Mackenzie, Cummings, and Sullivan, it was conceded that the profession was 'not within measurable distance' of establishing a register.[62] Nevertheless the Society, immediately after its incorporation, decided that registration must be its next target. A paper was prepared, making the familiar comparisons with lawyers, doctors, accountants, architects, and surveyors.[63]

The aim was to protect the public by enrolling recognized music teachers on the register. It was thought that most teachers of piano and singing would accept the need for a qualifying examination, but orchestral instrumentalists might not be convinced. Most 'public performers, and perhaps some of the composers' would probably fail to grasp the importance of registration at first. Apart from organists they took no interest in degrees since they were tested at every public appearance, and many orchestral players were 'put to an instrument by musician fathers', came from Kneller Hall, or moved imperceptibly from amateur status into theatre bands as deputies. But despite the diverse origins and attitudes of the people it had to convince, the ISM persisted in its declared belief that all musicians would benefit from registration. The register would be 'classified' in order to prevent people from 'posing as teachers of things in which they had never been examined and of which they have no experience'. There would also be an elaborate system of grading, to separate those who taught the poor, the rich, children, and professional students. Existing teachers, but not part-timers, would all be registered. This indiscriminate inclusion might be criticized as 'giving a legal status to the very class it wishes to wipe out', but doctors had been similarly inclusive, and had survived.[64] These matters were debated at a public meeting under the Society's auspices, Sir John Stainer in the chair. Support was expressed by Sullivan, opposition by Grove, Mackenzie, and Stanford.[65] Scepticism was widespread. The *Musical Times*, for example, deplored the 'cumbersome goad of an Act of Parliament', and reported fears that registration would threaten the livelihood of the omnipresent '18 year old musical governess belonging to a large and impoverished family'.[66] The Orchestral Association resented not being invited to the meeting, and claimed that it was merely a gathering of organists.[67]

During the next few years the ISM was frequently attacked for its presumption in claiming to represent the profession. A typical letter, to the Member of Parliament for Loughborough, complained that the Society's 2,000 members were an insignificant proportion of the country's 100,000 musicians (*sic*), yet they aimed to create a monopoly. The MP agreed, and promised to oppose any attempt at legislation. Correspondence in the *Loughborough Herald* elicited a feeble promise from the ISM's secretary that parents would be perfectly free to employ registered or unregistered teachers. A similar correspondence appeared in the *Dundee Advertiser*.[68] Confusion was worse confused by the equivocal status of the Society's examinations. Certificates, it insisted, were not to be used for professional purposes: 'nothing could be more unfair than to permit the holders of pupil certificates to lead the public to believe that the Society has certified them as teachers'.[69]

Clearly the campaign for registration had become a farce. Sustained for twenty years it had degenerated into a sad litany of futile aspirations, its protagonists scarcely pretending to believe their own rhetoric. A register was indeed approved by Parliament in 1912, as part of the general Teachers Registration Council. Later this became the Royal Society of Teachers, and members were allowed to add the letters MRST to their names.[70] Underlying this fiasco were conditions of supply and demand which made it impossible for musicians, as a group, to achieve parity with the great, or even the minor, Victorian professions. The Society inevitably failed to reconcile existing interests and future aspiration. Who was to be excluded from the proposed register? To include everyone would entrench the feeblest, as was sometimes acknowledged, and thus fail to protect the public, which was the alleged purpose of registration. The Society's defence of this policy was that other professions had overcome similar difficulties, registering incompetents and allowing them to die off. But among music teachers the minimum standard was so low, and numbers, both actual and potential, so large, that effective registration was a chimera.

In any case the public did not much care to be protected from bad musicians, not to the extent that it acquiesced in the monopoly practices of lawyers and doctors. Among those who did care, few were convinced by the Society's credentials for accreditation. In its need to attract support it tried to be all things to all men, even including a representative of the tonic-sol-fa movement on its registration council, to choruses of disdain from 'properly trained musicians'. Paradoxically a larger franchise might have helped if it could have embraced the orchestral world and remained united. But its attempt to represent musicians 'in the same manner as the Incorporated Law Society, the Institute of Chartered Accountants, and similar bodies represent their respective professions'[71] failed, during this period, to attract much interest from performers. As a journal representing the latter group remarked, 'the orchestral and band world [is] conspicuously absent in the list of members. The truth is that the older and successful performers do not feel the need of joining any such corporation, the unsuccessful either fear that they might not pass the necessary examination or fail to see that it would help them in any way'.[72] Practising instrumentalists and singers were indifferent, or sometimes hostile, seeking a different kind of representation. Academicians, among whom we may include the increasingly influential group of organists, apart from a few well-wishers and the occasional appearance of dignitaries at conferences, tended to hold aloof from a society which frequently betrayed its provincial, somewhat lack-lustre origins. (A. H. Mann, of King's College Cambridge, was a notable exception.)[73] They formed their own organizations. In later years the ISM was to consolidate and strengthen its membership and status, but before 1914 it was too weak to control and elevate a group of people occupying 'a no-man's land without definition or limits'.[74]

The Union of Graduates in Music

If the borders of an amorphous territory could be neither delineated nor defended, it might still be possible to protect an upland. The Union of Graduates in Music was established in 1893, and incorporated in 1898 for that single purpose. It existed, in the words of Sir John Stainer, its first president, to 'make a firm stand against the constantly increasing endeavours to undermine the value of our University Degrees, by bringing into circulation others not of the mint or coinage of our realm'.[75] In stark contrast to the ISM's Utopian aspirations, it was a narrow intention: 'concrete, and expressing precisely what we have to do', reported T. R. Southgate, the Union's secretary and most active champion.[76]

The threat came from fake, rather than foreign degrees, though the distinction was not always made clear. False qualifications had a long heritage, but their systematic marketing was a new enterprise, responding to increasing opportunities in a society easily impressed by paper titles and unprotected by appropriate laws. Stainer had been drawn to the problem in 1875 by his involvement in 'the fuss about Fowle', a vituperative correspondence in the *Musical Times* about the latter's claim to a doctorate.[77] The scandal elicited several admonitory pamphlets and guides (e.g. *Degrees and 'Degrees'*, 1875; and *Maxwell's Guide: a list of those holding British Degrees and Diplomas* 1892) which failed to stem the traffic. Degrees, including doctorates, could be purchased from local representatives of such bodies as the 'New England University', the 'University of the South, Tennessee' and the 'Musical University of England'. The trade was not confined to music degrees, and was probably most extensive and persistent where protection was weakest and the public most gullible. *Crockford's Clerical Directory* expressed concern,[78] and the *Lancet* published correspondence in 1890 about medical doctorates allegedly conferred by 'Trinity College, Toronto', whose Vice-Chancellor denied that his institution had ever conducted examinations in England, and insisted that candidates must sit in Toronto.[79]

For music the situation remained obscure, and was complicated by the fact that most British universities awarded degrees in the subject without requiring residence, which left questions of standards and validation open to varied and acrimonious interpretation. Southgate tackled the Toronto enterprise by challenging its right to operate overseas, rather than the standards of its degrees; and used his editorship of *Musical News* as a vantage-point for a successful campaign. From the committee which he formed to assist these efforts emerged the Union of Graduates in 1892. It soon had 500 members, rising to 700 by 1905.[80] Determined to protect their 'property' they acted as a pressure group, exposing individual 'sham degree men' and attacking suspect institutions. In 1896 the 'Guild of Church Musicians' which marketed 'University of Kansas' degrees, cash or hire purchase, was driven out of business. Next year the spurious 'National University of Chicago', offering degrees in a variety of subjects, was attacked with newspaper publicity, questions in Parliament, and complaints to genuine American universities. Support was enlisted from the Education Bureau in Washington, and several State legislatures; the head of one sham college was brought to trial for fraud. In England there were attempts to secure legislation: a private member's bill on university degrees was introduced in Parliament by one of the Union's council members in 1898, but failed to get a second reading.[81] Fake degrees were never entirely eliminated (they still exist), but there can be no doubt that the Union stemmed a potential flood. How should we judge its more general achievement?

Its resemblance to the established professional associations was superficial. Certainly it came closer to them than did the ISM, primarily because its degree requirement excluded the lowest and most easily recruited echelons of those who sought a living from music. Its members were therefore a comparatively homogeneous group, middle class and modestly successful. But there the resemblance ended. Most of them were only 'professional musicians' in a narrowly exclusive sense, peripheral to the practice of music as it has usually been understood in most societies.[82] None of the union's presidents, except Elgar, was universally acknowledged as a distinguished musician. Few of the degrees, in which members took such pride, were proof of musical attainment: the ability to breathe life into composition or performance; nor yet of genuine scholarship. Most universities required no demonstration of practical skills, but relied on pedantic, frequently obsolete, but easily examinable 'paper work', a tendency which was reinforced by the fact that most candidates were external, preparing by private study. The essential personal contact of master and pupil was almost totally lacking. The Royal University of Ireland was an exception, requiring performance for its Mus.B., at a very elementary level, and its Doctorate, where the repertory was rather more advanced, though the actual standard was probably mediocre. Several universities demanded a show of learning in acoustics. The London regulations had been devised by William Pole (1814–1900), professor of engineering, and therefore gave inordinate weight to this barely relevant subject.[83] All music degrees were burdened by a desire to convince supercilious university authorities that they were academically reputable, which added nothing to their acceptability in wider musical circles.

Nevertheless the Union's preoccupation with the defence of academic qualifications, and the demonstrable illegitimacy of many challenges to that position, enhanced its autonomy and status, and even provided 'monopoly of title' which, it will be recalled, was an essential attribute of the successful professions. It was a paradox, however, that the Union's strength lay precisely in those limitations which precluded it from leading the profession as a whole. These generalizations are based upon fairly comprehensive information. Every year the Union listed its members, and non-member graduates, in a 'Roll and Kalendar', prefaced by a reverential 'Brief History of degrees in Music', with such details of qualifications and career as they cared to furnish. Intended as a weapon against false credentials, and a guide for employers, it provides a useful, if occasionally euphemistic, 'data base' for prosopography.[84] The 1911 list is particularly informative. Its entries are too diverse and heterogeneous for neat tabulation: some members give scant biographical information, and plural appointments preclude analysis into rigid categories; but the general picture is clear. Membership was overwhelmingly male (47 women; 661 men), and weighted towards recent graduates: 269 had qualified during the 1890s; 277 since 1900.

There was inevitably some overlap with the ISM, including A. F. Smith, editor of its *Monthly Journal*; but many music graduates were not regarded as professional musicians by that otherwise undiscriminating association. One group was the clerics, including Bonavia Hunt and E. H. Fellows, later to become president of the Union. Both were positively rejected by the ISM; the former with rough justice for one so preoccupied with credentials and professionalism; the latter despite nomination by Elgar in 1914. Fellowes's distinguished career, described under the gently ironic title, *Memoirs of an Amateur Musician*, epitomizes the absurdities of rigid distinctions between amateur and professional. Less equivocal in status were those men of wide learning, or collectors of degrees, whose employment, if any, was outside music. J. D. McLure, for example, was headmaster of Mill Hill School, with the following credentials: B.Mus. 1903; D.Mus. 1909 (Lond.); BA 1878 (Lond.); MA 1889 (Cantab.); LL.D. 1896; Barrister, Inner Temple 1890; Cambridge University local lecturer 1885–93; prof. astronomy, Queen's college London 1888–94. He had also published songs and madrigals. A. H.

Barley, a 'registered chemist by major exam. Roy. Pharmaceutical Soc. 1893', was also Mus.B. 1898, (Lond.); ARAM, and had published songs, piano pieces, and a piano trio. Some members were so anxious to assert their amateur status that they added to their names in the list an admonitory 'not engaged in teaching'.

At the other extreme were ten holders of honorary degrees. Boito, Bruch, Hans Richter, Riemann, Saint-Saëns, and Sourindro Mohun Tagore,[85] were honorary members, as Dvořák had been before his death in 1904. Brodsky, principal of the Royal Manchester College of Music, Cowen, Elgar, Esposito, the Dublin musician, Henschel, and H. W. Parker, were 'ordinary' members. The latter had an honorary doctorate from Cambridge, and was professor of music at Yale. 'In appearance he was studiously inconspicuous. No one meeting him would have guessed he was a professional musician. He looked like a cultivated gentleman'.[86] Elgar had collected, by 1911, doctorates from Cambridge, Durham, Oxford, Yale, Leeds, Aberdeen and Pennsylvania, and an MA from Birmingham. His recently-acquired academic respectability (the first degree was awarded in 1900, when he was 43, one year after the 'Enigma' Variations) had put him in hitherto unaccustomed company. Although he was soon to become the Union's president, for an unprecedented term of two years, he despised academic musicians, and had long been neglected by them. He had considered refusing the Cambridge degree, as Brahms did.[87] The 'cathedral organists and directors of music in colleges for boys' whom his friend Jaeger had justly contrasted to his self-taught plebeian genius, were the predominant element in the Union. Its 1911 Kalendar listed seventy-nine cathedrals and 'chief college chapels' in England and Wales, most of which employed at least one music graduate. Irish and Scottish cathedrals and pro-cathedrals also employed musicians, but apparently only a few graduates, in Cork, Derry, and Dublin. Seventy-three public school chapels provided jobs for organists, twenty-one of them music graduates. There were similar positions in the 'colonies': Australia, New Zealand, Canada, South Africa, and India, for men with suitable backgrounds. When John Ivimey, whose book, *Boys and Music*, is an invaluable guide to the burgeoning, incestuous world of public-school music, was a young teacher at Harrow, he was offered the post at Calcutta cathedral by Lord Curzon, whom he met at a weekend party. He turned it down after considering 'the climate, the dwindling rupee and the isolation'.[88]

The careers of most members were more humdrum, similar to that of Stevens a century before, but some had seized new institutional opportunities. A small but growing number lectured at universities, teacher-training colleges, and polytechnics. Two examples will serve to illustrate these new variations on the old theme of piecing together a living. T. J. Hoggett, Mus.B. 1892 (Durh.); LRAM; ARCM; FRCO; LTCL, had been an organist and choirmaster in Whitby, and had taught in various girls' schools. In 1911 he was lecturer in 'music and declamation' at Leeds University and conductor of its music society, lecturer in theory and singing at the West Riding training college for women, teacher of harmony, composition, and 'the art of teaching' at Leeds City School of Music, and conductor of the Leeds Symphony society. H. D. Wetton, Mus.B. 1891; Mus.D. 1903 (Durh.); FRCO 1892, had been assistant organist at Westminster Abbey and at Wells cathedral, and organist and director of music at the Foundling Hospital. At various times between 1907 and 1911 he was a professor at the GSM and RCM, lecturer at St Gabriel's College, Camberwell, head of music at Battersea Polytechnic, and a 'recognised teacher' at London University.

Further enumeration would be tediously repetitive. Most members of the Union of graduates were men of the organ-loft and classroom, not the concert-hall, and still less the theatre. Their skills, tested and certified, were usually remote from the live world of music, and not commonly respected by men of that world, though in academic music they exerted a tyranny which became notorious. A few were good organists, albeit in a tradition which is no longer fashionable. Even fewer were true scholars, such as Fellowes and Riemann, whose musicological research still commands respect. Parry was generously described by Elgar as 'the head of our art in this country'. A gentleman by birth who, like Ouseley, had fought family opposition to his profession, he loathed opera, composed much dead music, and published books which are said to have helped restore music 'to the place in literary, university and national life that it had lost for more than two centuries'. His most stalwart advocate also attributes to him, with apt prevarication, 'the accepted but unacknowledged leadership of the musical profession'.[89] But the majority of graduates were neither scholars nor skilled musicians; their accredited knowledge of harmony, counterpoint, acoustics, 'composition' and history would be regarded, by modern standards, as narrow, arid, and doctrinaire. There were signs of improvement in university syllabuses and a desire for more practical musicianship, but this had litle effect on the existing membership, more than half of whom had graduated before 1900, mostly by private study, of laudable diligence and negligible artistic purpose.

The Union would occasionally join forces with the ISM: in the movement for Registration, and in exposing those institutions which sold false degrees *and* diplomas. But goodwill and brief alliance never descended to promiscuity. In 1898 the Union engaged in lengthy debate about the advisability of inviting 'visitors' to its annual dinners. The decision was firmly against, on the ground that it would be embarrassing for those who had not passed University examinations to dine with those who might have to examine them.[90] There were complex and changing cross-currents to this exclusiveness, which was not mere social snobbery. Since most music degrees had been earned by private study, the requisite training was not necessarily as rigidly class-based as most higher education in those days. Indeed when Cambridge began to impose nine terms of residence, the new regulations were widely attacked as socially divisive. 'Deserving students' would be excluded, it was said, and the future graduate would be 'a curious kind of dilettante, absolutely out of touch with the practical musicians of the kingdom'.[91]

In what sense, if any, could the Union of Graduates be regarded as an 'élite'? Before it was degraded by populist cant the word generally defined people who rank high in status, power, or wealth. Certainly there were some members of the Union who belonged to an élite; but, with a few obvious exceptions, that position owed little to the fact that they were musicians. Those among them who were well-born would probably have maintained or enhanced their inherited prosperity and social status more effectively by entering any other profession, or none. Others might derive a measure of social esteem from employment in public school and established Church: belatedly, in the lower ranks, and often on sufferance. The acquisition of wealth and power was, of course, denied them: the former being more easily dissipated than accumulated by the practice of music; the latter refused to artists by a philistine society. Even the narrower exercise of power in musical circles was limited, as has already been remarked, by fissures within that world. Academic distinction counted for nothing in the opera-house or concert-hall. There were, however, a handful of graduates working in theatres, with musicians whose concept of professionalism, and struggle for representative organization, were a world apart.

VII

Players

Nothing has appeared throughout the whole history of the orchestra which deals adequately with the players' point of view and their day-to-day lives.

Malcolm Tillis[1]

Orchestral players have generally been anonymous creatures. In the nineteenth century, unlike other pit workers, they were not regularly investigated by Royal Commissions, debated by politicians, and patronized or attacked by journalists. Nor, until the 1890s, were they represented by union leaders capable of voicing their needs. Information about their working lives therefore tends to be even more scant and scattered than is the case with most musicians, but some can be retrieved. In 1887, on the eve of a vast expansion in their numbers, London's players were surveyed in a new journal, *The British Bandsman*, which grouped them in four categories. First came those who would only accept engagements for opera, classical concerts and oratorio, though 'not despising to play in smaller theatres' on occasion. Supplementing their incomes by teaching, they made a 'fair living'. At the opera a fixed weekly salary replaced the traditional payment of up to 2 gns. for each performance. Such instrumentalists now earned from £3 to £6 for six or seven performances and rehearsals. It had long been customary for classical concerts to pay one guinea, including rehearsal, but managers could now command 'any number of players' for 15s. Principals got more, sometimes double.

A second category embraced those who made their living from private receptions and balls. One guinea was the normal fee, out of which the conductor or agent would pocket a commission of 3s. Good connections ensured a reasonable income, particularly for players who donned uniforms in imitation of a Hungarian band, the currently fashionable conceit. A third class worked in some forty metropolitan theatres which provided the 'foundation' of London orchestral playing, where young players acquired their first experience of ensemble work. Weekly pay was low: from 25s. to 36s. in drama, and 32s. to 42s. in 'opera bouffe or burlesque'. Day rehearsals were unpaid and obligatory, no matter how extensive and frequent: 'the least deviation from this rule is followed by dismissal'. Some conductors were lenient, but many were tyrannical, knowing that players could easily be replaced by 'hundreds of new applicants'. Short runs were a constant risk. Even a successful production might, at any stage, reduce its band; dismissed players received a week's notice, without compensation for rehearsals. Such conditions, however, were preferable to those imposed upon the lowest category of orchestral musician. Those who sweated in music halls for four hours a night, plus one rehearsal a week, rarely earned more than 30s. Generally poor circumstances, concluded the writer, were exacerbated by two deficiences. Unlike organists and teachers the orchestral player had no place to air his grievances: the *British Bandsman* would provide this. Nor had he yet made a sustained attempt to improve conditions by forming a union.[2]

Demands for higher wages and better working conditions were unlikely to get much sympathy from employers in a highly competitive, labour-intensive industry. Unlike many other workers whose productivity and earning power had enormously increased since the industrial revolution, musicians, as has already been argued, were no more 'efficient' than they had ever been. Managers had few means of reducing labour costs, except by keeping down wages and numbers. They could only attempt to raise productivity by increasing the audience, using larger theatres; or by means of extra matinées and two evening 'houses', as was becoming common in music halls, without proportionate increases in wages. Extensive use of almost unlimited supplies of cheap labour was the fundamental basis of the industry at every level of entertainment.[3] In the theatre spectacular productions reflected an obsession with stage machinery and 'realism', but they would have been inconceivable without cheap labour. Lavish spectacles satisfied 'an appetite for performers': 110 girls in ballets and processions at the Standard Theatre in the 1880s; 180 'supers' (at 1s. or 2s. 6d. a performance) for a version of *Romeo and Juliet*; a cast of 410 for the Drury Lane *Mother Goose* in 1881, plus seventy carpenters, fifty dressers, and sixty property and gasmen (the total labour force estimated at between 700 and 800). The lowest paid dancers earned between 12s. 6d. and 18s. a week; the highest £5 to £20. Novice actors in London, if they received any payment, would start at about 30s. a week. Good provincial companies paid similarly.

Most orchestral musicians were lowly placed in this labour force, their services rarely considered, by public and management, as central to the entertainment. It was a common complaint that musicians occupied 'the lowest social status' in the theatre. Their calling lacked the tawdry glamour attached to performers on the meanest stages. Managers were said to regard the orchestra as 'a necessary evil which they would entirely do without if they could', an attitude shared even by the stage hands.[4] The English theatre's general proclivity to neglect, or despise, music was reinforced by market realities. Apart from the occasional conductor or 'director', few musicians were able to emerge sufficiently from anonymity to claim higher fees as a reward for 'drawing power'. At rehearsals the orchestra was expected to be constantly available, subservient to the whims of stage performers. At performances and during intervals it was a mere background, except in the more vulgar halls, where target practice from the gallery was an occupational hazard, to be borne with good humour for miserable wages. £1 a week was common, and it was said that, in 1894, only one leader of a provincial theatre orchestra earned as much as £2. 15s. 0d.[5] Working conditions would have scandalized a hardened factory inspector. In 1862 a Liverpool newspaper, describing the appalling state of local theatres, concluded: 'that the musicians, whose wretched fate it is to sit in the orchestras, are ever free from colds and rheumatism speaks wonders for the acclimatising powers of human nature'.[6] A generation later there was little improvement in most theatres. Government intervention, preoccupied with drink, fire, and prostitution, took no account of working conditions. The theatre was a 'sweated industry', unnoticed by the Webbs and other social reformers who were much concerned with the similarly unregulated but well-publicized plight of clothing-workers and chain-makers. Inadequate lighting, cramped seating, poor ventilation, excessive heat, draughts, and disgusting back-stage 'facilities' were the common lot of pit musicians. Particularly scandalous was 'the pig sty genteely called the band room'.[7] Long 'unsocial' hours frequently subject to arbitrary change, encouraged the taking of irregular meals and, frequently, too much drink. It was a perfect environment for the spread of tuberculosis,[8] in addition to exacerbating those muscular ailments to which musicians are notoriously prone, often threatening their livelihood.

Few managers were perturbed by this state of affairs; instrumentalists were easily recruited and high standards of playing were rarely expected or appreciated. A 'travelling conductor' described provincial managers as 'perfectly indifferent to the quality of their orchestras so long as they are able to scrape along without collapsing altogether'. Their 'niggardliness and cheeseparing' led to the employment of amateurs and made it virtually impossible to give competent performances. Relentless economizing always began by cutting the size and wages of the orchestra, 'the department the public knows least about'. Therefore 'no self-respecting man of education and ability can support himself as a theatrical musician, and the places are filled by men who, having other business, are enabled to fill in their nights for a little pocket money'.[9] Another correspondent complained that provincial managers and conductors expected small theatre bands 'consisting of about a dozen working men, whose instruments usually are of the most curious combination imaginable, to give an artistic performance of musical play' which, in London, required an adequately rehearsed orchestra of 'thirty artists'. It was said that only two theatre orchestras in Great Britain boasted horns; six an oboe and bassoon; cellos were rare, violas virtually unknown. Managers were also accused of favouring 'incompetent time beaters and baton flourishers who can thump the piano and be cheap'.[10] Some improvement was acknowledged over the threadbare conventions of a previous generation—'ti-ti music' for low comedians, heroic chords, 'mangled ballads and tortured overtures'—but, in general, if the 'extraordinary ignorance and incompetence of the past' were in retreat, existing standards were still deemed 'loose and low'.[11] The morale and *esprit de corps* of players was usually poor, because few could take pride in playing the trumpery stuff which was their stock-in-trade, and because sullen acquiescence was dictated by the knowledge of easy replacement.

Conditions were evidently ripe for the formation of trade unions, if this pusillanimity could be overcome. Their origins were inevitably obscure. Participants probably kept few records, virtually none of which have survived. Newspapers and journals are silent, presumably because the general public remained unconcerned until its interests were affected, as by a strike. Probably the first organizers, in great contrast to their successors, were either indifferent to, or incapable of eliciting, publicity for their cause. In 1874 unions were started in three of the largest centres of employment: the Manchester Musical Artistes' Protective Association; a similar body in London, with which it was apparently linked; and the Birmingham Orchestral Association. Apart from the fact that the latter body appointed one Thomas Bailey as its official surgeon in 1875, nothing is known for certain about the activities and policies of these organizations. It is said that they opposed the employment of foreigners and amateurs, and that there were disagreements about the allocation of funds between London and Manchester. Both collapsed in 1876, and the Birmingham Association only survived until 1878.[12] We can merely guess at the reasons for their failure, although it should be noted that unions in many trades suffered reverses during the mid-1870s, as booming economic conditions gave way to recession.

In March 1886 there was a spectacular strike at Her Majesty's Theatre. After two acts of *Faust* the orchestra refused to continue until it was paid. A long, noisy interval was followed by another act, with half the orchestra. Then the stage carpenters joined the strike. The remaining audience, responding to pleas for assistance, showered the stage with coins. Thus ended what Klein describes as a 'night of horrors that will never be forgotten by those who witnessed it'.[13] Similar confrontations between feckless, or luckless, management and recalcitrant workers may have occurred elsewhere, in less august and therefore unrecorded circumstances; but there was no further attempt to organize labour until 1893. In that year the London Orchestral Association and the Amalgamated Musicians' Union were both established. The former was led by Fred Orcherton, a flautist in the Queen's Hall Orchestra and the Queen's private band, who recruited 'the very best instrumentalists in the concert world and West End theatres'.[14] Its activities were confined to London, its demeanour reflected genuine vocational pride, which avoided the feeble gentility of the ISM, but shrank from too close an identification with militant trade unionism. It would have no truck with amateurs and part-time professionals. The AMU could hardly have been in greater contrast. It was created by an obscure young clarinettist at the Comedy Theatre in Manchester, who recruited anyone who would join, including part-timers. Despite these unpromising origins it was the AMU which grew fast to become a national organization, its policies and style of leadership ultimately dominating industrial relations in music throughout the country.

Provincial militancy

In April 1893 some orchestral players in Manchester received a circular letter: legend has it that many found it on their music stands. A curious mixture of naïve, long-winded rhetoric and precisely formulated rules, it is a key document in the history of musicians' unions, anticipating much of their subsequent activity. It begins:

GENTLEMEN,

The phrase 'WE OUGHT TO HAVE A UNION' is often uttered by musicians, especially when they are compelled ... to rehearse without remuneration. Unfortunately with the phrase the matter drops. No one seems inclined to start a Union, and yet on all sides it is admitted that one is necessary.

A newspaper is then quoted, at length, to point the moral of a recently unsuccessful dockers' strike in Hull: it is essential to organize; workers must not allow themselves to be deluded by talk of 'free labour'. The union would afford protection from unscrupulous employers and the amateur, preventing him from undercutting; ensure payment for extra rehearsals and, in time, 'raise salaries to what they ought to be'.[15]

Recipients were asked to approve a set of proposed rules, suggest others, and attend a meeting. It was suggested that the society be called the Manchester Musicians' Union, with 3s. entrance fee and a yearly subscription of 5s. *Amateurs could become members*, paying half subscriptions.

Another important rule imposes procedures for the provision of deputy players: only members should be sent; amateurs solely if no professional member was available, and never to a regular engagement. Rehearsals for 'operas, pantomimes, etc.' must be paid at morning rates, or full salary if held in the evening. Attendance at morning performances must be paid, whether they take place or not. Any member accepting a date, or promising to deputize for another member, must attend, or give three days written notice. An optimistic scale of minimum fees for 'balls and assemblies' was set out, depending upon their distance from town: 17s. within three miles, 21s. within fifty, and 31s. 6d. at a greater distance. Concert fees would similarly be fixed at a mimimum, in town, of 21s. for principals and 17s. 6d. for 'seconds'; out of town, 31s. 6d. and 21s. respectively.

The Circular, which was signed 'Anonymous' from an address in Old Trafford, was written by Joseph Bevir Williams (1871–1929), probably with the assistance of his mother, the formidable Kate, who was to play a dominant role in the union's early years. On the paternal side, Williams came from 'good middle class stock'. His grandfather, after whom he was named, was, significantly, a lawyer. But his father, whose indentures are reproduced in the Appendix, and all three of his brothers were theatre musicians. Kate was born into the theatre. Her mother was a prominent actress; and a brother, adopting the name W. H. Denny, created several leading roles in the Gilbert and Sullivan operettas.[16]

Joe started work as a pupil-teacher, but soon began to play the clarinet. His talent for music is unknown, but as a union organizer he was to have few rivals, in an age of prominent labour leaders, despite the virtual absence of his name from their copious hagiography. Unfortunately we cannot document the early emergence of these talents during the crucial first months of the union. The rapid spread of branches suggests good communications and well-judged timing; but the essential point is that Williams never allowed initial enthusiasm to be dissipated, as had probably happened on numerous previous occasions when players, incensed by some provocation, or encouraged by some temporary opportunity of pressing a claim, would form an ephemeral alliance. The 1893 Manchester initiative was apparently sparked by such an 'incident' at the Gaiety Theatre:[17] its details are unrecorded. By calling a meeting on 7 May, of some forty musicians who had been given time to consider specific, carefully prepared, proposals, Williams prevented momentary indignation from lapsing into fruitless incoherence.[18] When a group of Birmingham musicians also decided to form a union, a few months before the Manchester meeting, but possibly after seeing one of his circulars, Williams grasped the opportunity to address them and advise against 'the mistake of splitting up

Branches, as was being suggested, instead of making one Union for the Country'.[19] Similar groups sprang up within a few weeks in Glasgow, Liverpool, Dundee, and Newcastle and were rapidly consolidated into the Amalgamated Musicians' Union, which was formally launched in November 1893, with over 1,000 members.

In the following year membership rose to 2,400, more than double the size of its London rival, with branches in Oldham, Leeds, Preston, Southport, Bradford, Edinburgh, Hull, Sheffield, Bristol, Dewsbury, Huddersfield, Middlesborough, Sunderland, and South Shields. The Union issued its first directory, and began to circulate a *Monthly Report and Journal*. One threat to unity was a widespread desire for local autonomy, a reluctance to allow Manchester to dominate. Even more difficult was the need to reconcile unavoidable conflicts of interest within the hierarchy of the profession. The first challenge came from a Manchester branch 'drawn from artiste orchestras'. It resented what was later described as the dictates of 'an executive committee composed mostly of music hall and theatre musicians' and 'a boy general secretary in an inferior orchestral position'.[20] Considering the calibre of some of the musicians Williams had to convince, and the fact that, at first, he could claim no practical success, his ability to command loyalty, or impose uniformity, depending upon one's point of view, while maintaining central control, was a remarkable personal achievement. Most original and contentious was his approach to the fundamental problem of stemming the flood of applicants for jobs. By recruiting part-time musicians into the union, rather than keeping them outside, he proposed to exert control over the labour force and eventually create closed shops. The first task was to make employers recognize the validity of collective bargaining, which was impossible without continuous demonstrations of unity. The union's rules were essentially those set out in the first circular, although a few details were changed: entrance, for example, was fixed at 7*s*. 6*d*., and subscriptions at 3*d*. a week. Above all, administrative control was firmly established, with executive power unequivocally in the Secretary's hands. After some bickering this was achieved at a conference of delegates in 1895 which gave Williams a vote of confidence and established a paramountcy which he maintained until his retirement in 1924.

Many contemporaries were outraged by these intentions. The first of a continuous barrage of attacks came even before the union was formally inaugurated. Ebeneezer Prout, most redoubtable of Victorian self-taught pedants, had been asked to become its patron. His reasons for declining were pungently and publicly expressed. Agreeing that orchestral players were subjected to increasing competition, he attributed their distress to commercial depression, for at such times the public first cut its expenditure on amusements. Presumably the burgeoning prosperity of the entertainments industry had escaped his notice; but he had found time to nurture a profound loathing for the 'organised tyranny' of trade unionism, and regarded the AMU's aims as indistinguishable from those of the London dockers. Reputable institutions and individuals—the Philharmonic Society, Richter, Henschel, and Harris (the opera impresario)—would never bow to such pressures. They would retaliate, he argued, by forming an employers' association, importing players from Germany, where wages were lower, or simply cancelling concerts. In any case the union would fail to attract the best players. 'What will you do', he asked his readers, 'if, in time to come, unionists refuse to play with you?'[21] A similar attack was launched by Southgate, secretary of the Union of Graduates, and editor of *Musical News*. Sharing Prout's antipathy to trade unions, 'the most unpleasant feature of the time', he was particularly upset by the AMU's recruitment of part-timers, which would reduce it to 'a strange collection of skilled and unskilled entities'. Readers were asked to compare his own organization, and the Incorporated Society of Musicians, which together embraced some 1,500 of the profession's 'elite ... an Upper and Lower House, possessing sufficient influence and power to do very much for music in our country'. Since 'competent' non-graduates could join the ISM, 'it would appear that musicians are now provided with all requisite means for following the fashion of the day and joining a Union'. But music, continued Southgate, with breathtaking hypocrisy, must not be grouped with other professions, for 'Art is, and must be free'. Attempts by 'some self-appointed clique' to fix wages must fail: set too low, they will force better players to 'emancipate themselves from the tyranny of the level men'; set too high, they will attract 'poor' foreign players and amateurs. Only by using force could Williams forestall these results, and that was his proclaimed intention.[22]

Despite their inconsistencies and special pleading, these early attacks have been given space because they exemplify, in tone and content, the antagonism with which Williams had to contend. They reek with the self-deception and deceit of 'professional men', who condemned non-discriminatory recruitment to a protective trade union, while indulging their own prejudices, 'ecumenical' or restrictive. They advocate 'freedom of art' with an enthusiasm which came most easily to those least dependent upon the practice of art for their livelihood. The belief that free trade in musicians, nationally and internationally, must necessarily persist, by some natural, immutable law, was already under attack in the United States, where musicians' unions had to contend with successive waves of immigration.[23] It would inevitably be similarly challenged by organized labour in England, not excluding the Incorporated Society of Musicians.

One sentiment was common to everyone who shared the prejudices of Prout and Southgate: a conviction that Williams represented a new brand of trade unionism, possibly appropriate, if reprehensible, among match-girls and dockers, but wholly unbecoming to musicians. Membership of trade unions had doubled between 1889 and 1891 and the 'new' unions were a subject of heated public debate. They were characterized, by contemporaries and later commentators, as militantly socialist organisations of low-paid, unskilled workers, quite distinct in membership and demeanour from the earlier, skilled craft unions. In fact they were neither necessarily nor continuously violent, not even in the docks. Some unions organized workers with skills, which gave them a measure of bargaining power, and wages higher than the national average of 25s. a week. But most of them were tough, particularly at the outset, not hesitating to strike, picket, and intimidate 'blacklegs'. At a later stage they tended to share two other new characteristics: a desire for government intervention to enforce minimum standards, and willingness to spend a high proportion of their 'dues' on administration.[24] We shall see to what extent Williams's union fitted this image; certainly his opponents eagerly depicted it thus, and deplored the likeness.

Support for the new union came from the *British Musician* which kept its promise to provide a sympathetic forum. The two unions also began to publish their own papers. The Orchestral Association *Gazette* started in October 1893; the AMU's *Monthly Report and Journal* began as a private circular in March 1894 and was published after 1900. Their secretiveness, 'withholding of course, such matters as is not meant for public discussion',[25] reduces their utility to historians, and their immediate readership was inevitably small, but they served to collect information and focus opinion which could be culled by wider organs of public opinion. Since Williams was an energetic and effective publicist who never let his case go by default, this extension of print contributed to his emergence as a national figure, and to the furthering of his cause. Meanwhile the *British Musician* had no difficulty in exposing the weakness of Prout's and Southgate's arguments, deriding their pretentiousness and lack of relevant experience. Reprinting its 1887 article on working conditions, the paper reported that, in the past six years, it had frequently experienced 'the cold blast of contempt that has blown from the higher professional quarter upon the deserving body of orchestral players and bandsmen'.[26]

Membership of the AMU rose to 3,000 in 1895, with branches in Bristol, Brighton, and throughout the midlands and north. Belfast and Dublin were added in the following year, making a total of thirty-eight branches. During these early years Williams's tactics were systematically aggressive. Improvements in wages and working conditions were enforced by strikes and the 'blacking' of recalcitrant theatres, as in Bradford, Leeds, and Hull during the summer of 1895. Members were warned not to play there, no matter what inducements might be offered.[27] A few examples will illustrate the numerous disputes of this period. The first to be recorded was fairly amicable, by later standards. At Liverpool's Court Theatre it as customary to close for a month or two in the summer. In June 1894 the manager offered to continue for another four weeks if the orchestra, in which Williams was playing, would agree to accept a 5s. weekly reduction in wages. The union refused, fearing that the reduction might become permanent, but accepted a compromise: all the players were paid full wages, except for two horns whose fees were contributed by the men themselves. A dispute at the Theatre Royal, Ashton-under-Lyne, could scarcely be described as successful, except in terms of recognition and publicity. Apart from the musical director's weekly 35s. and first violin's 25s., most of the players were earning 1 gn., and one second violin 10s. A branch of the union was established, demanding 25s., paid rehearsals, and the dismissal of a man who had refused to join. The demands were refused, the orchestra locked out, and handbills accusing the management of sweating, appealed to the public to boycott the theatre. The union was sued for libel and had to pay damages of £70.[28]

Clearly Williams faced an uphill struggle, with frequent appearances in court, which he evidently relished: often he would boast that he could paper his rooms with writs. His target for a minimum wage was 35s., with strikers to be paid 25s. a week out of union funds. 'Blacklegs' were kept out by a variety of devices in addition to picketing. An 'out of town' rule required members to ensure that no dispute existed at a theatre outside their home town before accepting an engagement there for more than a week. 'Flagrant breaches' of the rule were attacked in the *Journal*. Potential competitors were identified and either excluded or enrolled. The greatest attention was concentrated upon the largest single source of competition. Military bandsmen, it was argued, 'had their daily bread found for them' and therefore posed the most serious threat of undercutting. This was a persistent theme throughout Williams's career. The campaign began in September 1894, when he wrote to the commanding officer at Salford barracks to report that four regimental bandsmen were playing in Manchester with the Carl Rosa opera company for less than a quarter of the civilian fee.[29] The officer refused to prevent his men from 'playing out' but agreed that they should only work at 'the market price', and asked for a scale of fees. In this and many similar disputes Williams secured the support of local Trades Councils, exploiting the indignation of trade unionists at the idea of soldiers competing with civilians in their trade. If men who depended upon music for their livelihood were thus threatened, he argued, there was no reason why soldiers should not take up part-time tailoring and shoemaking. He wanted to prevent them not merely from undercutting, but from 'accepting engagements outside their duties at any price'.[30] Some trade unionists remained unconvinced because, as they saw it, Williams was encouraging similar activities among his own members. At the 1896 Trades Union Congress in Edinburgh his attempt to move a resolution against 'unjust competition' by Army, Navy and Police bands met considerable opposition from those who argued that civilians who worked two shifts a day were themselves blacklegs. 'You vote for an eight hour day, and then support men who work twelve at two trades' said one delegate.[31] But Williams carried his resolution, beginning a political career which was to culminate in membership and, ultimately, chairmanship of the TUC General Council.

London professionalism

While Williams was adopting the stance and tactics of militancy, London musicians cultivated an altogether different image. A typical article in their *Gazette*, under the heading 'Trade Unionism or something higher', proclaimed their status as 'men in a profession and not a trade', and deplored 'picketing and parading the streets' as activities 'undoubtedly degrading to professional men' which 'cannot fail to disgust the public'.[32] The London Orchestral Association, another writer explained, would exclude that 'class of performers, now happily diminishing, who never considered their duty to their employer, who drank deeply, and dressed badly, and who were at all times by their action and language ready to prove that they were anything but gentlemen'.[33] Gentility was a recurrent theme. The behaviour of some players had apparently not improved since Francis Fleming's day.[34] Bad language in the pit could sometimes be heard in the stalls, and the boredom of repetition was 'apt to induce a careless, free and easy demeanour'. After the AMU had moved into London in 1896, its procedures were frequently reported with distaste. An advertisement placed by Williams in the *Daily Mail* informed his members that they could see 'disengaged' and 'deputy' lists (jobs wanted and available) in a number of named pubs and in Gatti's billiard saloon. The *Gazette* deplored a return to 'the old Tottenham Court Road days, when anyone who wanted a musician was sure to find one in one of the public houses'. Metropolitan disdain for the rival union's provincial *gaucherie* was even extended to contempt for skilled men in other trades. Thus when Edinburgh members of the AMU joined a procession which included engineers, cabinet-makers, and printers, the *Gazette* listed all fifty participating trades, and sarcastically congratulated the Scottish musicians on being 'in the best of company'.[35] Such

1 (*top left*). Sir William Herschel (1738–1822)
2 (*top right*). Sir George Smart (1776–1867).
3 (*right*). Robert Lindley (1776–1855).

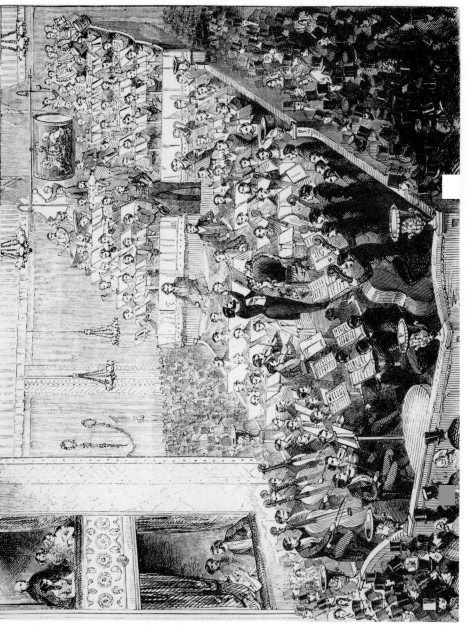

4. Jullien's Orchestra and four military bands at Covent Garden, 1846.

5. The Fair Sex-tett: Accomplishments of the rising female generation (*Punch*, 3 April 1875).

6. Competing for an RCM scholarship (*Illustrated London News*, 13 December 1884).

7. Marie Hall (1884–1956).

"TIME, GENTLEMEN, PLEASE!"

8. The American invasion (*Punch*, 9 April 1913).

9. The All-British Dance Orchestra: 'The work of dance bands has almost entirely been captured by foreigners and this is a serious attempt to prove that English musicians are at least equal to the bands from America. Every member is a British born subject and an ex-service man.' (1920)

10. Roy Fox and his band in Monseigneur's Restaurant (1931).

outbursts of prissiness were common enough, and were vigorously countered by Williams. It was unrealistic, he argued, to weaken aggressive trade unionism by sentimental talk about professional etiquette. Musicians were paid, at best, as skilled workers in a trade, and should adopt an appropriate 'tone'. Orcherton's men retaliated by exposing their rival's failures and reiterating loftier aspirations. At the Leeds Grand Theatre, they jeered, the entire 'machinery of trade unionism—boycott, picket, and blacklist'—had failed to dislodge a newly installed non-union orchestra. The Association would never support such tactics, but behaved as professional men, 'to raise our tone and the dignity of our calling', not as 'mere artisans . . . fettered by the earthbound dictates of a trade union'.[36] An advertisement in the Union of Graduates Roll and Kalendar proclaimed the eligibility of 'all professional orchestral players in the U.K. and of good character' to join the Association.[37]

Like all practised antagonists the two unions tended to polarize each other's rhetoric. But their verbal gestures, which became obligatory, tended to obscure some common interests. Beneath its mantle of professionalism, the London Orchestral Association was, in most essentials, a union of craftsmen, similar to the Amalgamated Society of Engineers. Such trade unions were primarily concerned to protect the status and wages of their members, controlling entry to the craft through elaborate procedures of apprenticeship and demarcation. Less skilled workers were regarded with suspicion as social inferiors who might become competitors and must therefore be kept down or out. Women, of course, were in the same category, the very embodiment of inferior, cheap labour. Union leaders were full-time officials who generally eschewed politics and concentrated on collective bargaining. They avoided, or at least claimed to avoid, strikes, and attempted to impose their wishes upon employers by insisting on adherence to the rule book, backed by a variety of sanctions. They also attempted to maintain the traditional functions of a friendly society, organizing pension funds for sick and funeral benefits. Partly in order to safeguard those funds, they tended to proceed cautiously, keeping industrial disputes at a distance, and allowing time to calm tempers and induce compromise.[38]

From its inception the Orchestral Association followed this pattern closely. Like the AMU, but with far more decorum, it came into existence through a circular calling recipients to a meeting, in the (highly respectable) board room of the Royal Society of Musicians, to which some fifty leading instrumentalists already belonged. About sixty attended, and appointed a provisional committee to draft a programme, which was presented in June 1893 to an enthusiastic gathering at the Royal Academy of Music, of some 500 men.[39] The new association's objectives were proclaimed as the encouragement of music; the enactment of rules and regulations, observance of which would entitle members to its support in disputes with management; the provision of legal aid, and the enlightenment of public opinion with a view to raising the status of orchestral musicians. Within three months membership had risen to 800, mostly based in London, but with a few 'engaged in country work', including some players in the Hallé, Scottish, and Carl Rosa Opera orchestras. There was a great deal of fuss about appropriate registration procedures, because trade union legislation had been designed 'for a totally different class [and] would not give orchestral players the status they were entitled to'. Finally the Association was registered as a company, to give it 'the character of a chartered society'. In addition to the objectives already outlined, it planned to establish a register of 'duly qualified' players, regulate their terms of employment, maintain high standards of 'attainment and conduct', and discipline members who offended against the code. It also proposed to set up an 'employment agency' and an 'institute', with library and meeting rooms. Members' instruments would be insured, up to £20 (an interesting indication of current costs), and it was hoped that surplus funds would provide scholarships at the RAM and RCM for their children.[40] Future relations with the rival union were also discussed. Williams had sought some form of collaboration and, with typical thoroughness, had drawn up detailed plans, which were not acceptable to the Association, but it was thought that some form of working agreement would be desirable; an aspiration which was not to be fulfilled for many years.[41]

Meanwhile the Association had to prove its worth, a challenge which became peremptory in 1896, when the AMU established a London branch. It is difficult to make a fair appraisal of the Association's activities during these testing years. We have the opinion of H. G. Farmer, a well-informed authority with personal experience, that it 'had a most salutary effect on wages, salaries, fees, contracts and conditions of employment for the professional musician'.[42] But proof is difficult for, in contrast to the AMU, it was rarely in the public eye, and therefore left scant record of its work. A preference for quiet conciliation and tact, except when confronting its rival union, is reflected in the *Gazette*, which reports activities too mundane to bear extensive recapitulation, but of undoubted benefit to the Association's members. A solicitor was engaged to draft model contracts of employment and provide general legal assistance.[43] One case concerned the theft of a violin which had been left for repair, its owner being offered an unacceptable substitute. Settlement for £10 was secured.[44] More common were disputes about claims for unpaid fees, or salary in lieu of notice, as when a play closed abruptly. The sums were typically a mere 2 or 3 gns., but such cases had to be fought almost every month. On at least one occasion the Association paid for the services of an interpreter: an interesting example of its support for foreign members.[45] Death benefits were another service. By paying 12*s*. a year for at least three years, members under the age of fifty were entitled to £10 funeral expenses.[46] Such modest activities served its members well, but the Association was unable to give effective force to its larger aspirations. Its original intention to establish a register of qualified players degenerated into the posting of 'disengaged' lists to theatres, and a jobs requirements column in its journal: a worthy service, to be sure, but far removed from professional registration. It was doing nothing to stem the flood of newcomers, and apparently little to enforce better working conditions. Indeed, there were already mutterings of dissent: a member contrasted 'the robust and stalwart brethren of the provinces' with 'our own timorous mode of procedure', and forecast a more general 'recourse to trade union tactics'.[47]

Certainly the Association was failing to keep pace with the Union in membership which, after an initial spurt, settled at about 1,000, only one-third the size of its rival by the turn of the century. Yet this was a period of rapid expansion in the number of players, particularly in London. Table IV suggests that the number of instrumentalists seeking employment in the metropolis increased fourfold between 1890 and 1900. The number of wind players was growing even more remarkably, thanks, no doubt, to Kneller Hall and the brass band movement. The table excludes pianists who were, of course, a glut on the market; nevertheless it may be thought to exaggerate the overall rate of growth. Since it is drawn from names listed in directories, it could partly reflect an increase in their coverage, rather than in the actual numbers of players, particularly for the early years when such publications were becoming more comprehensive. This is probably the case in certain instrumental categories, such as the recorded increase of clarinettists from 18 to 171 between 1890 and 1900. But scepticism about the statistics should not be pushed too far. Before telephones became common, trade directories were a sufficiently important means of communication to encourage musicians to use them. An individual's appearance in their pages also suggests that he is an active performer, and not merely a teacher; so the totals can be taken as reasonably accurate indicators of increasing competition for orchestral jobs.

There can be no doubt that opportunities were growing apace. The two decades after 1890 were a period of unprecedented expansion in the theatres and music halls of greater London. Listing only the theatres built or improved by the architect Frank Matcham between 1890 and 1912, we have a total of thirty-one completed buildings, with seating capacity well in excess of 60,000. These included 'Empire' theatres at Chiswick, Finsbury Park, Hackney, New Cross, Shepherd's Bush, Willesden, and Wood Green; the Ilford, Lewisham, and London 'Hippodromes'; the Coliseum (now the home of the English National Opera), and the Palladium.[48] A wider and more precise assessment of the market's growth would be far more difficult, although a few contemporaries attempted to measure what was happening. We have already noted that the 1911 official census made a brief foray into the entertainment industry: in itself a recognition of extraordinary developments.[49] In the same year an unofficial estimate of London's 'places of amusement' suggested that they had increased, since 1896, from seventy-two to 324. Function and location are vaguely defined, but the estimate is probably conservative.[50] In 1901 the 'city and suburbs of London' were already said to have licensed 320 such places, seating 400,000, an increase of 100,000 over the previous decade.[51] Since the 1911 reporter was solely concerned with the employment of musicians, primarily in theatres and music halls, his figures serve our purpose. He concludes that seating capacity was now 231,000, and the vast majority of houses gave two evening performances, while many were running continuously from 2 p.m. till 11 p.m. At the Coliseum, which opened on Christmas Eve, 1904, there were four performances a day—at 12 noon, 3 p.m., 6 p.m., and 9 p.m.—though the noon performance was abandoned by August 1905. Even if we allow a wide margin of error in such estimates, there can be little doubt that jobs for musicians in London increased at least fourfold during this crucial period.

Such conditions could breed complacency, in some quarters and for short periods. In February 1899, for example, at the season's peak, the Association expressed satisfaction with current employment of orchestral players in London. More than 500 were supplying accompaniments for thirty-four pantomimes. At the Empire, Alhambra, and Palace there were orchestras of some fifty players, and those at the Savoy, Daly's, Lyric, Gaiety, Shaftesbury, and Prince of Wales each averaged thirty. Several so-called 'comedy theatres' employed a dozen or so instrumentalists, and what was described as a 'large' orchestra was playing a more demanding repertory, including *Lohengrin*, for Carl Rosa Opera at the Lyceum.[52] All this activity totals at least one thousand jobs, and takes no account of diverse alternative employments. Unfortunately for the players, if not for the standards of musicianship, there were far more instrumentalists than there were jobs, and their numbers were increasing in a Malthusian progression. Many were women.

Women

Prejudice against women players was pervasive and, like most prejudices, compounded of fact and myth. They were indeed beginning to compete for jobs. Apart from the harp and piano few instruments had been 'permitted' to them in the past, and the violin had only recently become socially acceptable. In mid-Victorian times 'no young lady ever thought of learning it or carrying a violin case about in the streets'[53] and Scotswomen were said to be horrified at the idea of 'a lassie playing the fiddle'.[54] Changing attitudes, a generation later, were often attributed to the influences of Wilma Neruda, the eminent Czech violinist, from a family of musicians, who became Lady Hallé without sacrificing her career. By the 1890s Émile Sauret was presiding over a large class at the Academy where there was 'a perfect craze for learning the fiddle'.[55] It may have been rather undiscriminating—a student concert in 1893 included eighty violinists playing Handel's 'Largo' in unison—but a few of the ladies went on to better things. Marjorie Hayward, for example, later studied with the great Czech teacher, Ševčík, and became a respected chamber player. Another who went to Ševčík was Marie Hall, daughter of a penurious music-hall harpist, who emerged as England's first universally acclaimed virtuoso, ranked with Kubelik and Sarasate.[56] There were prodigious developments at the RCM. In 1883 only sixteen women, of whom one was successful, had applied for violin scholarships, as compared to 185 aspiring pianists. Ten years later the student orchestra was praised for 'the general excellence of the violin playing, and more especially the remarkable fact that for absolute purity of intonation, for finish and charm of style, the lady students are not only *facile principes*, but leave their male colleagues simply "nowhere" '.[57]

Increasing numbers of capable players and a few outstanding talents were audible proof that women could perform tasks previously considered to be the exclusive, biologically determined, province of the male; but this had little effect on ancient assumptions about the natural order. Male chauvinism was widespread, of course, far beyond the confines of music, and was underpinned by the authority of public men and the medical profession. In 1892 Asquith acknowledged 'those indelible differences of faculty and function by which Nature herself has given diversity and richness to human society'. Crass rationalizations of prejudice were common among physiologists who, in 1908, for example, wrote 'learned but strange' letters to *The Times* to explain, with pedantic and vicious condescension, the behaviour of suffragettes. One representative of the most successful and arrogant profession, the appalling Sir Almroth Wright, became a recognized authority on female 'hysteria'.[58] Since increasing numbers of women were determined to make a living in music they entered, perforce, the front line of the battle between the sexes.

The prejudices of London musicians were frequently aired by the

Gazette. One article, by a Mr Wallace Sutcliffe, begins with the question 'Should ladies be admitted into professional orchestras?' and proceeds, with a brief liberal flourish to reject 'the old idea that woman is fit for nothing more than housekeeping and dressmaking'. But the writer's endorsement of her musicianship is limited to its refinement and delicacy: 'power of tone is always lacking', as is 'firmness of attack'. In sum 'the average lady player is inferior to the average male player for all orchestral purposes', her weakness inescapable because 'according to physiologists, there is one muscle entirely absent from the female arm'. The rejection of women, ordained by scientific principle, was also desirable economically, socially, and morally. Their employment took jobs from men who had families to support. 'Rough apprenticeship' and the band room's 'unguarded language' in music halls and theatres would grievously hurt 'an educated, refined and sensitive girl'. After performances 'the undesirability of a lady having, probably without companionship, to wend her way home at such an uncanny hour need not be further commented upon'.[59]

This outburst, which was unusual only in its comprehensiveness, had been prompted by the engagement of a sixty-piece ladies' orchestra, with only two cornets, two trombones and euphonium manned by men, to play for 'Noah's Ark' at Covent Garden. A similar group had worked for eighteen weeks in 'Uncle Tom's Cabin' at the Lyric Theatre. Their leader, Ada Molteno, retaliated, point by point. She had frequently played with men, in amicable professional accord, and without moral degeneration. She had even *led* the male orchestra of a prominent touring opera company. Journeys home were not a problem, though she lived in the suburbs. In any case it had never been suggested that *actresses* should cease to work in the theatre, yet they had to leave even later, after changing and removing make-up. In her experience it was the feeblest male players who became the most vigorous critics of women's playing. Missing arm muscles were surely intended as a joke. The great majority of orchestral students at the Academy, College, and Guildhall were women, some of whom were bound to seek careers. Male professors did not refuse fees to teach them. The crux of the matter was that 'the charmed circle of orchestral players' feared competition: 'only one phase of the larger question of the employment of women generally'. Any doubts about women as professionals, she concluded, had already been resolved by their success.[60]

The unabashed Mr Sutcliffe admitted that he was mistaken about the missing muscle, but voiced what must have been a common trepidation: at present female instrumentalists were only emerging from the 'leading academies', but soon 'every girl who can fiddle a bit will think she has a perfect right to join the orchestral army'.[61] So the battle of words continued. Why were ladies barred from the Association, asked a correspondent in February 1895; and in April 1900 the question was still 'about to be considered'. Another member felt threatened primarily by the woman from 'a comfortable home who puts all she earns on her back'. Since his sartorial judgement was apparently incapable of distinguishing between affluent clothes-horses and other women, he proposed to keep them all out. And that is essentially what happened. For almost two more decades women were excluded, not merely from the Association, but, by silent discrimination, from the general run of orchestral engagements. Their main opportunities of employment continued to be in ladies' orchestras, in salon or tea-shop ensembles, where gentility was all, and, of course, in teaching.

The idea of the ladies' orchestra may have originated with the *Vienna Damen-Orchester*, which visited New York in 1871, 'a score of blushing maidens attired in purest white', playing strings, flutes, and piano, in a programme of waltzes.[62] In Britain the movement started with amateurs: the Dundee ladies' string orchestra in 1882; Lady Radner's seventy-two string players, who raised funds for the Royal College of Music; and the Revd. E. H. Moberley's 'charming white robed force' of 100 Wiltshire and Hampshire ladies.[63] Among professionals the fashion was soon exploited, both because it provided 'something different', and because the virtual exclusion of women from most conventional ensembles ensured a ready supply of cheap labour. Among the groups advertising their services in 1899 were the Anglo-Swiss Ladies Orchestra; the *Aeolian*, Miss Clay's, Miss Grave's, Mrs Hunt's, and Mme Marie Levante's ladies' orchestras; the *Blue Zouave* Orchestra; Miss Flora Handel's Ladies' *Napoleon* Band; the Ladies' Royal Hungarian Band, and the *Pompadour* Ladies' Band. There was a thirty-eight-piece orchestra at the Earl's Court Exhibition in 1901, including brass and woodwind, and smaller ensembles became a regular feature at various restaurants, including the new Lyons Corner Houses. There was even a Royal Naval Ladies' Orchestra in 1911.[64]

Such activities, and the alternative employments deemed suitable for women—'light concert work, soirées, at homes, etc.' in Mr Sutcliffe's condescending words—often insulted the musicianship of the more capable players, and usually impeded its further development. Emerging from the colleges, like their male counterparts, with minimal experience of the serious repertory, of sight-reading and ensemble work, they were then, unlike some of the best men, denied the principal means of artistic and professional advancement: the experience of playing in an opera or symphony orchestra under a competent conductor. The point was frequently made by their most formidable and articulate representative, Ethel Smyth, who deplored a segregation which cut them off from the main stream of music at precisely the moment when they were most in need of stimulus and education. That an increasing number of women were capable of advanced musicianship was demonstrated by their prominence in chamber music. Until the gramophone and the BBC began to educate a larger audience, no one could make a living by performing such repertory in Britain, though it was, in other respects, the most rewarding employment for the best musicians. Opportunities of hearing chamber music were dependent upon the enthusiasm and patronage of a few individuals, notably Walter Cobbett, and the dedication of players who could afford, or were driven by their art, to ignore the dictates of the market-place; for fees were low, and rehearsals unpaid. The increasing difficulty of contemporary compositions, and rising standards of interpretation, beyond mere reading, threw great responsibilities upon professional chamber musicians.

A number of remarkable women made their mark in this demanding work.[65] Emily Skinner (Mrs Liddle), a pupil of Joachim, who was one of the first to enter the Berlin Hochschule when it was thrown open to women in 1876, came home to lead what was probably the first successful female quartet in England, with Lucy Stone, Cecilia Gates, and Florence Hemmings. Nora Clench, another Joachim pupil, was born in Canada, studied at the Leipzig Conservatory, and received favourable notice by Shaw for a performance of the Mendelssohn concerto in 1892.[66] Her quartet, with Lucy and Cecilia Stone, and the gifted cellist, May Mukle, survived for eight years of successful touring throughout Europe, with a large repertory. They gave English premières of quartets by Wolf, Reger, and Debussy. Jessie Grimson, one of a large family of string players, studied at the RCM and established a quartet in 1901, with Frank Bridge as second violin, which kept together for ten years. The Motto, Langley-Mukle (with Marjorie Hayward), Solly, and Lucas string quartets, and the Henkel Piano Quartet, were all reputable London groups, led by women during the pre-war decade. Another outlet for their energies was the Strings Club, established in 1902 with about eighty members, which aimed to raise standards of quartet playing and provide opportunities for performance. Keeping five rooms in constant use for rehearsals, it was open to amateurs, but each quartet included at least one professional. Outside London the audience for chamber music was very sparse, despite an unsubstantiated assertion that its evolution was 'one of the outstanding features of the history of musical activities' in Britain during this period.[67] But women were prominent in the few groups to emerge. In Manchester there were two female quartets, stimulated by Brodsky's classes. Scotland's solitary professional quartet was led by Emily Buchanan.

Female orchestral instrumentalists were confined principally, but not exclusively, to the harp, violin, and, increasingly, the cello. Rosabel Watson was apparently the first woman to play the double-bass seriously, not just as a music hall turn, and by 1900 eleven female bassists were advertising their services.[68] Miss Watson was also listed as the solitary female exponent of the horn, and later conducted an orchestra for Wolfit in Shakespeare. Eight women flautists appeared in the same directory, out of a total of 146. Several of them had been playing in music halls since the 1880s, but their numbers were diminishing. There were even six female trombonists and four timpanists. Many of these women were heirs to a family tradition, like their eighteenth-century predecessors. Thus the five daughters of Leopold Mukle, manufacturer of mechanical musical instruments, were professional performers on the violin, viola, cello, double-bass, flute, trumpet, cornet, ophicleide, and timpani. Their brother played the horn. Less versatile and distinguished, but in a similar tradition, the Allen and Kent families mustered a total of eight trombonists, including the six women already mentioned. Greta Kent (*b.* 1895) later published a delightful memoir, with enchanting photographs.[69]

Such careers were a useful demonstration of feminine accomplishments, but the real threat to male dominance in London came from violinists. Between 1900 and 1910 the number of women players listed in the directory increased from 132 to 166; more than 16 per cent of the total number of violinists. Clearly the majority of them were actively seeking jobs, since 137 applied for positions in the Queen's Hall Orchestra in 1913. It was here that women achieved their first significant breakthrough: four violinists and two viola-players were appointed. This remarkable initiative by Henry Wood was prompted by Ysaye's assurance that in his Brussels orchestra they were as good as the men. Wood allowed his women equal status and pay, and provided a separate band room.[70] The importance of this advance can hardly be exaggerated. As Ethel Smyth explained in a letter to *The Times*, not only did it give them access to 'the training and stimulus of professional life', but it also enabled them to ask good fees for lessons, a principal source of income. The advance was consolidated by the exigencies of war. In 1917 one of the original six, Dora Gartland, replaced the orchestra's leader for a week of Promenade concerts, topping her success with what Wood described as 'a capital performance of Bach's Chaconne'.

Crisis in London

By the end of the nineteenth century the Malthusian conditions of supply described in Chapter IV were becoming so fertile that the flood of applicants for virtually any appointment was far greater than could possibly be absorbed. If established players, at least among the men, could retain coveted positions, even they were beginning to feel the pressure of relentless competition. In the 1840s, during Costa's regime at the Royal Italian Opera, principals had received 9 to 12 gns. a week; rank-and-file players 4 to 5 gns. Fifty years later their successors were far worse off. In 1894 London theatres were said to be paying their principals from £1. 15s. 0d. to £3. 10s. 0d. a week, the latter in very few instances, and secondary players from £1 to £1. 10s. The deputy conductor at the Crystal Palace, whose recent suicide had excited comment and elicited a few elusive facts about pay and working conditions, was found to have been earning less than £4 a week, despite his exalted position. Full-time musicians were reported as earning less than 'skilled mechanics or even coal miners, though they have to dress and keep up appearances on the money'. A few months later it was estimated that out of approximately 2,000 orchestral players in London, fewer than fifty were earning £250 a year from that employment. Many received less than £150. Although 1 gn. was still the customary fee for a single engagement (2 gns. for principals), the supply of players so exceeded demand that 'underdealing' was already common. Music-hall players were getting the lowest pay for the longest hours: typically £1. 10s. 0d. for four hours a night and a weekly rehearsal, though the best halls, such as the Empire, paid upwards of £2. 15s. 0d. But their work was at least comparatively permanent, whereas most theatres were closed for four months in the year. At a leading comic opera-house one musician's annual wages, over two successive years, had averaged £70. Dance bands could get players for 5s. a night.[71]

A decade later levels of remuneration had again deteriorated, while the cost of living increased. The best rank and file players in the principal West End theatres and music halls were earning about £2. 10s. 0d. for an eighteen-hour week.[72] The leader of a fashionable restaurant orchestra received the same wage for a seven-day week, from 6.30 p.m. till midnight;[73] and £2. 10s. 0d. was also the fee received by most members of the Queen's Hall Orchestra during the arduous eleven-week season of promenade concerts in 1904, for six concerts and three or four rehearsals a week. Such wages were tartly compared with the £3 a week regular, as distinct from occasional, pay of 'any decent mechanic'. Yet most players had to be content with much less. One small West End music-hall paid its eight-piece band from £1. 3s. 0d. (double-bass) to £1. 10s. 0d. (first violin).[74] Suburban wages were descending to derisory levels. The manager of the Shakespeare Theatre in Battersea admitted to the London County Council that he was paying 25s. a week for seven performances, to players who were 'not worth more' and were working 'simply for pocket money'.[75] The band for a ball in Balham—three violins, double-bass, flute, and cornet—received 7s.

6*d*. each for five hours on the stand.[76] The existence of this lumpenproletariat was attributed by the Association to an invading army from the provinces, which it proposed to 'take in hand'. Manifestly unfitted for that task, it could attempt to dissuade newcomers by publicizing the low wages and high cost of living in London, but its craft union tactics and gentle demeanour were wholly inappropriate to a battle for survival. The way was open to Williams, if he could adapt his strategy to the metropolis.

VIII

'War'

I've been most awfully bothered lately, what with the New Theology
and the Music Hall War and things. I simply haven't known what side
to take.

Punch, 13 February, 1907

In February 1901 John Burns, MP and London County Councillor,
made a speech in his Battersea constituency on music and musicians. It
was an unusual event, since public men in Britain never spoke about
such matters, except to say with complacent modesty, 'I know nothing
about music, but . . .'. Burns knew enough to touch upon a diversity of
subjects, ranging from the changing social status of musicians—no
longer 'half fiddler and half flunkey', but now dependent upon the
masses for popular support— to the need to raise artistic standards. In
the tradition of Victorian reform he sought 'rational recreation, instead
of vulgar satisfaction', the allocation of hard-won leisure to 'the music
that elevates and not the drink that degrades'. In place of 'mediocre
performers vulgarly playing down to the gutter', instead of 'Hungarian
Blues' and 'Bulgarian Reds', catering to 'the luxurious middle class' he
envisaged, with a nice blend of radical and patriotic sentiment, a new
breed of British musicians, called forth by the patronage of a lower-
middle and working class, 'educated to love music'. Battersea was
spending £10,000 of public money on 'municipal music'—mainly free
summer band concerts—and such activities should be greatly extended.
London should have 'a Municipal Opera House, a Municipal Academy
of Music, a Municipal Orchestra'. Since Burns was speaking at a public
meeting organized by the AMU, in support of its claim for 'a fair and
reasonable wage', he added some hackneyed themes: unfair competition
from army players, 'too many unions and not enough unionists', the
divisive 'snobbery' of classical musicians, the need to unionize part
timers.[1]

Stripped of its rhetoric, it is a curious speech, a rickety bridge to the
twentieth century, perhaps, in its loose assemblage of old and new
preoccupations. By netting a prominent politician, and jumping on the

municipal bandwagon, Williams had again demonstrated his resourceful-
ness, but the occasion had a deeper purpose. Far from being a
momentary flourish in a flamboyant career, the Battersea meeting was
part of a major reorientation of union policy. Henceforth musicians were
to be recruited to the belief that 'the vote is more potent than the strike
for improving their conditions in life'.[2] What caused him to redefine
strategy, and how were tactics subsequently modified?

New industrial relations

Once Williams began to take a serious interest in London, widening
industrial conflict was inevitable, but it soon became apparent that his
energetic policies would require substantial modification. The evolution
of a new strategy was influenced by change in the general climate of
industrial relations, and by the specific problem of adapting to
conditions of orchestral labour supply in the metropolis. Most of the
'new unions' had become more 'cautious, limited, conservative, and
sectional', and employers were reacting to trade unions by forming their
own organizations.[3] After 1901 the Taff Vale Case, which threatened
trade union funds, drove them to seek political power, but the next five
years were also a period of unemployment, stagnating union membership,
and industrial quiescence. The 1896 Conciliation Act encouraged the
settlement of industrial disputes, by allowing the Board of Trade to
conciliate, if requested by labour or management, or arbitrate, if both
parties agreed. Trades Councils were increasingly active; in the Trades
Union Congress, in municipal politics, and in the exploitation of mutual
aid among the organized workers of their districts.[4] An example of such
activities, which Williams would cleverly modify and exploit, was the
'relentless pursuit', by labour councillors, of firms employed as
contractors to local authorities. Thus, in the London County Council,
John Burns 'waged ceaseless war against those who refused to pay
adequate wages', and attempted to force them to meet union demands
for fair wages, hours, and conditions of work.[5]

Williams was quick to assess these changing circumstances. If, for
example, Burns could use local government contracts as bargaining
counters for fair wages, he could deal similarly with music hall licences,
a proposal dismissed as absurd by the Orchestral Association.[6] More
fundamentally, he had to come to terms with an unfamiliar orchestral
market, in which, for example, it was going to be far more difficult to
establish closed shops. In contrast to many provincial towns, where the
supply of local players was limited, and 'blacklegs' could usually be
imported only with difficulty, and for short periods, London employers
could dip into a bottomless pool of labour. The difference, to be sure,
was one of degree. Several big towns were almost as difficult to seal. But

London's pool of experienced players was far larger and more mobile than Manchester and Liverpool could muster. In addition there was a huge reserve army, unique to London, which could be recruited from recent graduates and students of the main colleges, women, foreign and provincial immigrants and, at the bottom, untold numbers of barely proficient part-time players, all willing to accept very low fees. By 1905 the union was frankly admitting these difficulties: 'If we were in the position in London that we occupy in several provincial towns, where we can successfully object to any non-member entering an orchestra, the whole matter would be simplified'.[7] The union's continuous expansion had ended in 1898; membership had declined from 3,600 to 3,000 in 1902,[8] and was recovering very slowly, despite a reduction in the entrance fee from what was deemed a 'prohibitive' 7s. 6d. to 2s. 6d. London enrolments crept up to about 500 by 1904, and seemed unlikely to accelerate until Williams proved capable of securing the 'improved terms' which had been widely expected on his arrival.[9] If further recruitment required successful wage negotiations, similar to those which had hitherto been dependent upon a united and constantly growing membership, it was a vicious circle which could be broken only by fresh initiatives.

The LCC elections of 1901 provided an opportunity to experiment with political tactics. Musicians were given a list of sixty-two 'approved progressive' candidates, who would attempt, if elected, to attach fair wage clauses to licences for places of amusement. Fifty-seven were successful. In Clapham, where there was 'a strong musicians' vote', one candidate was named as an enemy because, as a music-hall agent, he would represent the Music Hall Proprietors' Association.[10] The mutual-aid-via-Trades-Council gambit was played in Battersea. At the meeting addressed by John Burns, the Trades Council agreed 'not to patronise' the local Shakespeare Theatre until its management accepted minimum wage demands.[11] A small theatre in a working-class suburb, dependent upon local goodwill, was vulnerable to this form of boycott. It had difficulty in attracting distant audiences, but cheap, efficient urban transport, and plenty of competing attractions, ensured that its former patrons were not deprived of alternative amusement. Battersea also gave Williams an opportunity to forge an alliance, which was to have far-reaching consequences, with a recently established Union of Theatre and Music Hall Workers. Despite inevitable opposition from those who shrank from association with stage-hands who earned as little as 2s. a night,[12] Williams, adopting the principle that allies were indispensable, sought them high and low.[13]

After what was acknowledged as its 'first organised attempt' at political action in 1901, the union continued to exploit these new tactics, not always successfully. It failed, for example, to persuade the LCC to attach a fair wage clause when licensing the Holloway Empire music-hall, despite protests by the London Trades Council.[14] Strikes were deprecated (in the AMU journal!), but occasionally called. In two South London music halls, wages of £1. 7s. 0d. a week were thus advanced by 3s.[15] In Croydon an attempt to lower wages was defeated, again with support from the local Trades Council. That dispute was notable for the management's ruthlessness in dismissing its orchestra and attempting to recruit novices with the bait of free tuition. The replacement conductor was to have received a weekly wage of £2, his leader £1. 10s. 0d., and the pupils £1. 5s. 0d.[16] But victories of this kind were too isolated and parochial for Williams to do more than hold a ragged line of defence. To consolidate his men, and advance upon suburban and central London, he needed a major victory, with its attendant publicity. The opportunity came in 1907 with the music-hall strike, an event which inevitably attracted public attention and, because of its timing, mobilization of loyalties, and subsequent arbitration, marked a turning-point for everyone in the industry.

Its timing could scarcely have been more propitious. In 1906 the Liberals won a huge majority, Burns entered the cabinet, and the Trades Disputes Act legalized peaceful picketing.[17] Williams brilliantly exploited these opportunities, latching the grievances of his musicians and stage-hands on to those of the variety artists, in a concerted attack. If they shared a common adversary, their grievances were poles apart.[18] Indeed the arbitrator, whose taciturnity was a prime qualification for the job, could scarcely conceal his irritation with the manner in which Williams hogged the stage. In a lack-lustre account, published in 1920, Lord Askwith never mentions him by name, but complains that 'difficulties were much increased by the long time taken by the preliminary cases of the musicians and stage-hands, which were more or less the usual trade cases. The artistes' case was on quite a different footing'.[19] The latter's origins lay in the transformation of music-hall into big business, under its new sobriquet, 'Theatre of Varieties', and in the long-delayed creation of protective associations by both capital and labour.

The scale of theatrical entrepreneurship and investment had greatly increased by the 1890s. Private ownership of individual theatres was ceasing to be the norm, and was being replaced by limited liability companies, capable of financing larger, more comfortable theatres, with elaborate equipment and adequate safety precautions to satisfy licensing authorities. Initially the typical company was small, controlling a single theatre; but inevitably, in an expanding market, some of the more successful entrepreneurs began to extend their businesses, by means of loose association with other firms, amalgamation, or the floating of new companies. Such activities could be highly profitable, and attracted widespread investment. Economies of scale were their principal *raison d'être*, including the strengthening of bargaining power in the labour market. Hence their unpopularity among performers, who feared eventual domination by 'monopoly trusts'. Two men emerged as the acknowledged leaders of this encroaching movement.[20] Both began in the provinces. Edward Moss (1852–1912) was born in Manchester, the son of a theatre manager, and, by the age of seventeen, was running a small travelling company which presented 'dioramas', a modest precursor of *son et lumière*. Entering the music-hall business with his father, under the flag of 'artistic and respectable entertainment' for the family market, he opened a theatre in 1877, and then proceeded to build a chain of establishments, including Matcham's brilliantly successful Empire Palace in Edinburgh which opened in 1892. Oswald Stoll (1866–1942) was born in Melbourne and raised in Liverpool, where his mother owned the little Parthenon music-hall, in which he was working by the age of fourteen. He managed a theatrical agency, and allegedly wrote songs. In 1889 he acquired Leveno's music hall in Cardiff, renamed it the Empire, and introduced twice-nightly programmes. Undeterred by rowdy audiences who merely strengthened his resolve to 'raise the status of music halls and make them places of family entertainment', he conquered new empires, eventually controlling eight theatres.

During the 1890s Moss formed an alliance with other managers, including Frank Allen and Richard Thornton, and 'in or about 1898' they were joined by Stoll. In December 1899 Moss Empires Ltd. was registered in Edinburgh, with £1m. capital, which was increased by a further £60,000 in 1903. By then the company controlled seventeen theatres, accommodating some 50,000 people, though double houses brought in a much larger audience to 'entertainment suitable for all classes of the people . . . free from all vulgarity'. Four houses were in London: three suburban Empires, with over 9,000 seats; and the spectacular Hippodrome, which had opened in 1900 as a 3,000 seat circus, and would switch to 'variety' in 1909. The company also had substantial interests in other theatres and concert halls, including facilities for booking performers to appear as far afield as Dublin. Moss and Stoll were the most prominent examples of a new breed of theatre entrepreneur, capable of exerting monopoly pressure in wage-bargaining. Since the industry was labour-intensive, there was every incentive to drive hard bargains, encouraging firms to form loosely co-operative organizations, which culminated in the London Entertainments Protection Association. Although they naturally attempted to keep all wages down, their primary concern was not with orchestras, which were generally easy to reduce or replace; and less still with stage-hands. More intractable were the 'turns', particularly those stars whose drawing power, enabling them to command high fees, was enhanced by the 'turn system', which facilitated brief appearances at several theatres in a single evening. Managements sought to curb such activities by various means, including the 'barring' contracts which would become central to the 1907 strike and arbitration.

The performers' response to managerial encroachments was to attempt to form protective associations. There had long been antagonism between management and performers, of course, not least about contractual ambiguities. Doubtless there were several attempts to establish unions, such as the Anti-Agency Society, the Peculiar Order of Muff's Society, and the Music Hall Artists' Association of 1885, in which Charles Coborn ('the man who broke the bank') played a leading role.[21] Most significant, however, was the Music Hall Artists Railway Association, which began by organizing reduced fares for groups of travelling performers. It soon acquired 5,000 members, and an energetic committee which turned to the investigation of grievances about contracts. Conditions had improved in some respects, as the managers' arbitrary powers were constrained, and some uncertainties eliminated, by test cases in the courts; but the desire for 'equitable and universal contracts' was not yet appeased. In 1903 a meeting of the MHARA at the London Pavilion demanded fair contracts, and Coborn made another fruitless attempt to form a union. At last, in 1906, the Association and three other friendly societies joined forces to form the Variety Artists' Federation, which submitted a 'Memorial' to theatre proprietors and managers, outlining their grievances. It claimed to represent nearly 10,000 performers, and laid particular emphasis upon the 'barring' clause in contracts. This prevented an artist from appearing anywhere within a named distance from the specified theatre, before or after a specified time.

The Memorial 'respectfully' asked that barring be confined to five miles and six months in provincial contracts; one mile and three months in London and its suburbs. Stoll was the only prominent manager to answer, claiming that the proposed reform would merely 'provide more engagements for the few and fewer engagements for the many'. Further correspondence left the matter unresolved, but meanwhile a dispute, which appeared to be trivial and easily resolved, precipitated the 'music hall war'. Walter Gibbons, owner of several halls, was refused a licence for the Brixton Hippodrome, which he proposed to convert to twice nightly music-hall. His attempt to defeat the LCC by transferring contracted artists to an adjacent theatre was challenged by the Variety

Artists' Federation. Pickets were posted outside both theatres, and the local Trades Council organized a boycott. The strike lasted two weeks, and the Hippodrome remained closed, but an amiable agreement was sealed by a 'peace luncheon' attended by numerous 'stars'.

War

The truce was short-lived, and, in the few remaining weeks of industrial peace, the unions representing 'artists', musicians, and stage-hands drafted a 'Charter' which was addressed to all proprietors and managers. This was a far more comprehensive and forceful document than the *Memorial*; essentially a form of contract which, if signed, would endorse minutely specified fees and conditions for all three groups of workers. In addition to limitation of barring and abolition of enforced transfer between theatres, the VAF listed various claims for matinée fees, control of agents' commissions, procedures for arbitration in future disputes, and indemnity from recrimination. Williams was even more ambitious, for, as well as enumerating detailed minimum rates of pay (36s. a week for London instrumentalists), he demanded, with cool effrontery, a closed shop. The relevant musicians' clause reads: 'All the musicians engaged at all the halls under the control of . . . shall be members of the Amalgamated Musicians' Union'.[22] At that moment he controlled fewer than 20 per cent of London's orchestral players. There was no reply, so the Alliance attempted to enforce its Charter, calling for support, by boycott, from organized workers in all trades throughout the United Kingdom. Gibbons, whose signature was the first to be demanded, objected specifically to the closed-shop clause and immediately had all six of his suburban theatres shut down by strikes, on 21 January, 1907. Next day *The Times* reported that the audience at the Tivoli had to be 'dismissed' because the 'syndicate' which controlled it, the Oxford, and several other halls, had refused to recognize the Alliance. Before its dismissal the audience was told that the Tivoli's staff had long been happily employed, and that several performers were paid more than Cabinet ministers. Some theatres attempted to gain temporary respite by engaging 'scratch companies', bioscopes, performing elephants, and other diverse entertainments.[23] A distinct group of entertainers, the 'Concert Artistes', whose genteel orthography betrays their provenance, were particularly useful blacklegs. The chairman of their benevolent association, responding to an appeal from the Alliance, urged them to resist 'glorious offers' and join the fight against 'managerial trusts', the common enemy. Despite his claim of '99 per cent support' for the strike, he was forced to resign. 'Music hall stars advertise for *concert* engagements. Why shouldn't we retaliate now', said the artistes.[24]

The proprietors reinforced their position by extending membership of

the London Entertainments Protection Association to provincial establishments, and were joined by the Variety Agents Association. Forty-two
representatives of the various bodies, including Stoll, agreed to desist
from individual treaties of peace. Their opponents also carried the war
to the provinces, with numerous public meetings. Within a few days
fourteen London theatres were affected, most of the stars were on
strike, and the dispute was front page news: 'the most sensational
"show" ever', said the *Daily Express*.[25]

The *Morning Post* asked if the public might discover that 'constant
music halls' were not indispensable, and turn instead to extension
lectures and ethical societies.[26] *Punch* reported the activities of Little
Tich, Gus Ellen, and Victoria Monks, and claimed that Marie Lloyd was
'ready to start at any moment on a tour throughout the country in a
motor car of a vivid red colour. Her purpose is to address roadside
meetings from her car, in the hope of arousing the people of the country
to a sense of their duty in this great struggle. (Costumes by Worth, wigs
by Clarkson. Parish and Borough Councils interested should apply to
Miss Lloyd's manager.)'[27] *The Times*, alleging that Arthur Roberts was
getting £160 a week, and Marie Lloyd £115, argued that the genuine
grievances of orchestral musicians and stage-hands could only be
rectified at the cost of such 'improvidence'.[28] Letters to the press
rehearsed grievances and demands, and explained away high fees. Joe
Elvin, for example, famous for the sketch 'Appy Ampstead' and
generous philanthropy, earned an acknowledged £175 a week; but he
worked in three theatres, in each of which he had to pay five or six
supporting players.[29]

The campaign continued with support from the Parliamentary
Committee of the TUC and the General Federation of Trade Unions.
Labour leaders, including Ben Tillett, spoke on Alliance platforms, and
Williams was never far from the front. A large assembly at the Surrey
Theatre, with many stars in attendance and a fifty-piece orchestra, sang
'Rule Britannia, Britannia rules the waves, Two shows every night, and
six matinées'. The Scala Theatre was used for mass meetings and public
performances to raise funds, including 'A Night with the Stars'. A few
performers reneged: a pantomime comedian announced his resignation
from the VAF because it was 'on a par with the socialists'; another
denounced the stars for tyrannically 'inciting the stage-hands'. But there
was no general breaking of ranks. Five more halls were called out
because their manager refused to sign the Charter, and twenty picketed
to deter audiences and artists. Elvin was involved in an 'angry scene'
outside the Chelsea Palace, and had to be moved on by the police.[30]
Employers kept halls open by organizing the 'lending' of artists, staff,
and musicians, but it was already becoming apparent that 'tolerable

entertainments' left audiences only 'moderately content', sitting 'uncomfortably in halls, wishing to be friends with their old favourites'.[31] Ultimately profit-seeking showmen could not dispense with the 'bright particular stars' who had 'thrown in their lot so unreservedly with their weaker and less dazzling colleagues'.[32] It was this which forced the proprietors to sue for peace. Despite the scale of operations—at its height the dispute affected twenty-two theatres, and pickets numbered 2,500—they could probably have continued to resist attack by the Alliance's rank and file. Boycotts by audiences inflicted small damage, outside a few working-class suburbs, and probably none in the West End. Pickets were rarely more than a nuisance, and possibly sometimes an extra attraction. Staff and minor performers, including musicians, could be reshuffled from vulnerable to immune theatres. But 'the supply of real genius', as a contemporary newspaper observed, was 'as rare on the variety stage' as anywhere else; and London audiences would 'soon miss and then clamour' for its return.[33] At current levels of musical taste it was inconceivable that any musician could have commanded such allegiance, and therefore exerted such bargaining strength; but those who sheltered behind that power, and urged it on, were set to prosper.

After several fruitless attempts to make peace, a conciliation board was set up, with four representatives from each side, not including Williams, which eventually agreed to ask for an arbitrator. On 25 February a banner outside the Vaudeville Club declared 'Peace. All the old favourites will appear at the music halls tonight', and many theatres carried lavish displays of flags and bunting.[34]

Inquest

As President of the Board of Trade, it was Lloyd George's task to appoint an arbitrator. His first choice was the suitably flamboyant T. P. O'Connor, whose attempts to deal with Williams would certainly have enlivened the proceedings.[35] His refusal led to the appointment of G. R. Askwith, who began a series of twenty-three formal meetings and innumerable conferences. More than 100 witnesses were heard and cross-examined, sixty-seven of them produced by Williams. He wished to prove, of course, that despite the greater expense of living in London, wages and conditions were more wretched there than in the provinces, where the AMU had forced improvement. Orchestral leaders, for example, commonly received £2 a week or less, as against the £2. 10s. 0d. paid at the Edinburgh, Glasgow, Manchester and Liverpool Empires. For rank-and-file players, he alleged, the Orchestral Association's 'rule' of 6s. minimum for each performance, was generally ignored.[36] Only four theatres paid a minimum rate of £1. 16s. 0d. a week. Against customary usage Stoll refused to pay for matinées, and was extending this practice to his provincial theatres. There were few opportunities to supplement these earnings by teaching. The national colleges got the best pupils, and institutions like the College of Violinists provided instruments and lessons for an enrolment fee of 3s. and 1s. a week. Alternative daytime employment was restricted, he argued, because musicians needed time to practise, were at the beck and call of management, and dared not be tired by the evening. There had been few complaints because the men were 'bullied and intimidated into expressing satisfaction with anything'.[37]

The lawyer appearing for the London Entertainments Protection Association argued that music-halls had greatly extended opportunities for musicians by offering regular, almost permanent employment. Low wages should be regarded as adequate recompense for unskilled labour, and essentially part-time earnings, supplementing income from other sources. Moreover the widespread use of deputies enabled players to take advantage of occasionally remunerative engagements, without sacrificing their regular music-hall employment. Except in a few theatres, perhaps only the Empire, Alhambra, Palace, and Hippodrome, 'there never has been any demand for high class music, or for musicians of high character, or for people possessing a high degree of efficiency, or a large amount of technical skill'. The entire programme in cheaper halls, and much of it in the better ones, only required music which was generally 'trashy kind of stuff . . . the road sweepings of the profession'.[38] Playing it was 'mechanical or hackneyed' work, demanding a minimum of skill and no practising at home. Most players were low-class men of poor education. Commenting on one of Williams's witnesses, he said 'a man who has any ability at all is not likely to be out of employment for seven months, and have to depend on his wife doing casual jobs to keep him. He is not the class of man, the type of man, who really can be called a musician in the best sense of the word.' Such people could not get pupils, simply because they were too poorly qualified.[39]

Both sides produced carefully selected witnesses to substantiate their claims, all of whom were asked where, and for how long they had been employed; their wages, rent, cost of instrument and travel to work; and their experience in attempting to get outside jobs. By parading numerous cases of hardship, Williams inevitably revealed their generally low calibre. A double-bass player with twenty years' experience, including three years in an African music-hall (sic), earned £1. 12s. 0d. at the Walthamstow Palace, plus another 10s. as an insurance agent, which left no time to practise and improve. Travelling expenses from Balham were 8s., and his £10 instrument was half the usual cost. His father had been an organist, encouraged him to be a chorister and, unfortunately, refused to put him to a trade.[40] A violinist at the Euston earned £1. 7s.

6*d*., paid 13*s*. 6*d*. rent, and travelled from Camberwell for 2*s*. His violin cost £15, bow 10*s*. 6*d*., and case £2. 15*s*. 0*d*.; repairs averaged 1*s*. a week. 'Unfortunate enough to be in a musical family', he had started eight years before as a deputy, at the age of seventeen. Since others were giving lessons for as little as threepence, he did not seek pupils. In any case people in a working-class district only wanted lessons at night.[41]

Another violinist had worked at the Oxford for ten years, receiving £1. 10*s*. 0*d*., plus 7*s*. for a matinée. Sometimes he could earn 10*s*. 6*d*. at a 'cinderella' dance (finishing at midnight), but would then have to pay 7*s*. 6*d*. to a deputy. Although he had been good enough to play in the Queen's Hall promenade concerts, he now performed 'ordinary music hall trashy songs'. He still thought it necessary to practise, to prevent fingers stiffening, and because occasionally he had to be able to play *Home Sweet Home* and *The Lost Chord*.[42] A second violinist at the Metropolitan earned £1. 12*s*. 0*d*., after ten years; taught four pupils for 1*s*. each a week; and tried to sell jewellery on commission because his doctor would not allow him to take 'ball jobs'. He supported a wife and six children, and paid 7*s*. 6*d*. rent and 4*s*. for travelling.[43]

Some were even worse placed. A 50-year-old drummer had worked at the Star in Bermondsey for seven years. Previously he had been a hospital porter (16*s*. a week plus meals and uniform) and had served twenty-one years in the army, starting as a 'band rat' at the age of twelve.[44] Now he earned £1 a week, plus 1*s*. 8*d*. for a matinée, and drew a pension of 10*s*. 9*d*. His instrument cost £12, rent 6*s*. 6*d*., and he paid £1. 12*s*. 6*d*. a quarter for the education of a son, who aspired to a civil service clerkship. At the Star, where gallery tickets cost 3*d*., the orchestra was not required to wear evening dress: some theatres paid 'white tie' money, typically 4*d*. a week. But he took pride in his work: 'Oh yes, I am a proper professional musician; I can always do my business when I am there'.[45] Such 'business' was crucial to music-hall entertainment: rolls and crashes for pratfalls and the like. A 25-year-old trombonist in the same band earned 28*s*. a week, but also worked as a clerk from 10.30 a.m. to 5.30 p.m. for 14*s*. Accused of taking someone else's job and being tired at night, he protested that he was primarily a musician. After eighteen months as an army bandsman he had left for deputy work and secured this, his first permanent engagement, seven years ago. His instrument cost 3 gns., rent 8*s*.; he supported a wife and two children.[46]

And so the doleful procession continued, its dispiriting testimony giving a rare glimpse into undocumented lives. There was a Croydon drummer who supplemented his £1. 10*s*. 0*d*. wage by summer earnings of £2. 15*s*. 0*d*. a week in the Blue Viennese Band at Folkestone, sending £1. 5*s*. 0*d*. home. Normally he would pawn his Sunday clothes every

Monday, to pay the 7s. rent, but it was also necessary to 'get a new suit on tick and pay a bob a week for to keep up appearances'.[47] Debt was a constant theme: at the Clapham Grand somebody in the band always had to borrow 6d. or 1s. every week; and a double-bass player at the Oxford regularly charged interest of 1d. a week on 5s. loans.[48] There was a violinist earning £1. 6s. 0d. a week in Walthamstow, and supporting a wife and two children in Mile End, without additional income. The 13s. 6d. left out of his wages was insufficient, he considered, for food and clothing. He had been taught the violin by his brother, and had tried unsuccessfully to get a daytime job, 'clerking'.

Apart from those who had been Army bandsmen, few appear to have had any formal musical training: at best they had 'picked up' an instrument within the family. An exceptional witness who had spent three years at the Academy, was earning £2 a week as second viola at the Palace Theatre, which took pride in its orchestra, under the well known Herman Finck. He was also paid the full rate of 6s. 8d. for matinées, or 8s. 4d. when he moved up to the principal's seat. Since there was only one show a night, and the orchestra was large enough for players to alternate, it was possible to get a break of twenty minutes to an hour. Such privileges were inconceivable in the suburban halls, where little bands had to 'slog' at a consistent *forte* throughout the evening. He also secured about half-a-dozen oratorio engagements each year, at 1 gn.; and taught seven pupils, who brought in a total of 8 gns. a quarter. he had occasionally deputized in a suburban music hall, but there were 'not many Academicians burning to go' to such places. Conflicting deductions were drawn from this information: that suburban and West End players were breeds apart or, as Williams argued and Askwith appeared to concur, that good players were sometimes driven into cheap halls by necessity.[49] The final witness to appear for Williams had also worked at the Palace Theatre, and was a member of the recently established London Symphony Orchestra, a co-operative of players who had broken away from the Queen's Hall Orchestra when Henry Wood attempted to stop excessive deputizing.[50] One of the new radicals in the Orchestral Association, he intended, in Williams's words, to 'turn it into a trade union . . . a fighting organisation', and had written a 'manifesto' on the subject. Living in Battersea, he paid 10s. rent, supported a wife and child, and spent 2s. 4d. a week on transport. He was capable of earning five guineas a week with 'the German opera', and one guinea for concert or ball engagements; 18s. as an absolute minimum. He would never accept 'laborious and undignified' deputizing jobs in suburban music halls, which paid a 'ridiculous' 6s.[51] Working in such places was bad for one's playing, yet he thought it required a kind of expertise; a remark which reopened arguments about prevailing standards: an earlier deponent had emphasized the need to read manuscript parts at sight, only to be told that, in music halls, it was routine stuff, easily read.[52] The LSO man, attempting to reassert the need for skill, was asked if Shakespeare required more reading ability than 'Comic Cuts'.

The employers produced two kinds of witness: players, whose task was to express satisfaction with prevailing conditions, and apprehension about the influence of union agitators; and managers, whose expert testimony was intended to explore more subtle themes. Among the former group were two members of the Chelsea Palace orchestra: a violinist who supplemented his wage of £2 by collecting debts; and a £1. 12s. 0d. flautist, formerly an articled pupil at Norwich Cathedral, who ran a 'teaching academy' in Regent Street, where the fees paid to his assistants were too confidential for disclosure to Williams.[53] Light entertainment was provided by a garrulous £1. 17s. 0d. pianist, forty-five years at the Metropolitan, and crestfallen that his evidence would not be published, for he wanted 'all Kilburn to see it'. By day he made doors, but, 'in deshabille' could 'play Chopin splendidly after sawing . . . twelve feet of oak, two inches thick'.[54] Thus real work by day was proved compatible with a remunerative hobby at night. A few humbler citizens described their tranquil lives before the union had 'fomented discontent' A viola-player at the Hackney Empire, with ten children, one serving the King in India, had been satisfied with £1. 8s. 6d. a week. A trombonist at the Metropolitan was happy with £1. 12s. 0d. to supplement his army pension of 8s. 5½d. He also made considerable use of deputies, spending up to three months away with Lt. Charles Godfrey's private band. This allowed Williams to argue, uncharacteristically, against the deputy system, on the ground that it lowered wages. All of these witnesses expressed their pride in avoiding the union, and fear of its future activities.[55]

The managers' attack was launched on two fronts: a challenge to the representative credentials of Williams and his witnesses; and an attempt to prove that music-hall was too risky an enterprise to survive the imposition of minimum wages. The manager of the London Pavilion brought long experience of the industry to the first of these tasks. Six years in his present post, he had previously devoted seven years to the administration of provincial theatres, and fifteen years as a 'professor of music and conductor'. He could therefore confirm that most provincial and suburban players were merely part-time musicians, and could easily be engaged at current rates of pay. Recently in East Ham, for example, there had been 200 applicants for a few jobs. At the Brighton Empire the conductor had been a lithographer, the pianist a tailor, and other players included a carpet-layer and lodging-house-keeper. Since the repertory was easy, such men required no time for practice, except, perhaps, the oboist, who constantly had to prepare new reeds. It was his information about the union affiliation of London players, however, which was intended to deliver the *coup de grâce*. He wished to distinguish between membership of the Orchestral Association, recogized as 'a sort of hallmark', and of the AMU, which was negligible in those places requiring 'music of a first class character'. The Adelphi, Daly's, Prince of Wales, Savoy, and Vaudeville theatres, he claimed in a useful survey of top jobs, employed no one who had joined the AMU. Membership was less than 25 per cent at the Alhambra, Apollo, Empire, Gaiety, Haymarket, London Pavillion, and Lyric theatres; in the Criterion and Holborn restaurants; and in the LSO, Queen's Hall Orchestra, and New Symphony Orchestra.[56] Among the few who had recently joined, most were activated by fear that the *Memorial's* insistance upon membership might be accepted by the arbitrator.[57]

These allegations were intended, of course, to confirm the employers' case against the 'impertinence' of Williams's demands, but, despite their semblance of authority, they were too poorly documented to survive his counter-attack. In contrast to broad opinions and vague percentages, he recited an appropriate selection of figures and names from AMU records. Among the 'fine players' who had joined the union were the *leaders* (with all the prestige and influence that implied) at Drury Lane, the Royal Italian Opera, Daly's, the Empire, the Aldwych, Apollo, Criterion, Gaiety, Seymour Hicks, and His Majesty's theatre; the Hotel Provence and Trocadero. All the Drury Lane players, most of the New Symphony Orchestra, and many of the Queen's Hall Orchestra were also members.[58]

The managers were equally maladroit in making their submission that high costs and risks would prevent them from paying the requested minimum wages. Elaborate figures and labyrinthine arguments were produced to demonstrate that the business was 'subject to the widest fluctuations', with falling profits in recent years; that there was no syndicate (a semantic digression); and that minimum wages would merely act as thresholds for an inflated scale (from drummer to violinist), and increase costs by 25 per cent. The proprietor of the Star music hall[59] gave a demonstration of rock-bottom economics, implicitly conceding that larger halls could afford to pay more. Ticket prices ranged from 2*d.* to 9*d.* The band of nine, whose leader-conductor earned £2, rehearsed only on Mondays at six, to suit the majority of the players, who had daytime jobs. To impose the proposed minimum rates would cost, by some strange feat of mensuration, more than £150 a week, and would force the hall to close.[60]

Simple arithmetic, and a few references to recent dividends and glowing company prospectuses, were sufficient for Williams to dispose of many of these arguments. He had long been monitoring the industry's profits, noting, for example, that Moss Empires Ltd. had paid over 37 per cent in its first three years.[61] His final speech summarized the evidence as justification for a strike which had been due, not to his personal efforts as a virtuoso pied piper, but to years of neglect and exploitation. Work loads had steadily increased while wages remained at traditionally low levels. The employers' praise for the Orchestral Association was merely intended to denigrate the AMU; in practice they preferred non-union men. Therefore the arbitrator's award should recognize both organizations. For the majority of orchestral musicians, he concluded, a theatre or music-hall wage was 'the chief, if not the sole, source of income. We ask that our profession shall be recognised as a profession; that the musicians shall be paid a fair rate; that the commercial spirit shall not predominate to the extent of debasing our art into a sort of casual employment.'[62]

Neither the opposition's incompetence, nor his own verbal dexterity, were entirely sufficient to carry the burden of Williams's case, but he had achieved a primary objective. By joining ranks with stage-hands and stars he had staked a claim for his London men. How profitable was the outcome?

Before examining Askwith's first award (there was a second in 1912) and its subsequent history, it is worth asking what the sums of money being discussed were worth. Was £1. 10s. 0d. a week, for example, a 'fair and reasonable' wage? There can be no simple answer. In 1906 the national average annual wage of skilled men was £96 a year; and of semi-skilled urban workers, £71. To take a few representative cases, railway guards earned £80, London postmen £81, cabinet-makers £85, bus-drivers £93, and engine-drivers £119. These were all full-time jobs, comparatively secure and unaffected by seasonal change. To compare the orchestral player's £1. 10s. 0d. a week we would have to add an estimate of his supplementary earnings, subtract for seasonal unemployment, and allow for the element of risk. Music-hall proprietors argued, with some justice, that they offered more regular and reliable employment than had generally been available to musicians in the past. The balancing of these various factors is an unavoidably subjective exercise. The musician who could net the equivalent of a weekly £1. 10s. 0d. throughout the year would have earned slightly more than the average semi-skilled man. If, like some of the employers' witnesses and possibly the LSO freelance, he was sufficiently talented and industrious to double that income from various sources, he would still have been earning less than the lowest-paid solicitors and dentists (lower quartile £185 and £155 respectively).[63]

One must also take account of a significant change in the cost of living, which had fallen considerably during the last quarter of the nineteenth century, but was now rising steeply. Index numbers are unreliable measurements of such movements, so there is no point in attempting to calculate 'real' wages. But in this case we are dealing with the earnings of a relatively homogeneous group of urban workers, over a reasonably short period of time, so approximate orders of magnitude are acceptable, provided they are not taken too literally. Broadly speaking, living costs fell by over 20 per cent between 1880 and 1900, then began to rise by a few points each year, fast between 1914 and 1918.[64] The implications of these changes were particularly serious, of course, for people dependent upon fixed money incomes. Musicians who continued to receive 'traditional' rates of pay had made real gains during the late nineteenth century, but stood to lose rapidly after 1900 unless they could raise their fees. The benefits to be won from fixed minimum or 'fair' wages were greatly at risk. Contemporaries, including employers, arbitrators, and union officials, were generally unaware of these facts, in 'an age of statistical darkness',[65] but they are crucial to an adequate appraisal of wage levels in the decade after arbitration.

Arbitration

Askwith's award dealt at length with the variety artists' grievances, specifying forms of contract, intricate limitations of barring, and procedures for dealing with disputes.[66] His code for musicians and stage hands appeared to be much simpler, establishing arrangements for a return to work, and minimum wages. The latter were fixed at £1. 10s. for those London players who had been earning less, except for drummers, who were to get £1. 8s. 0d. Minimum wages of £1. 12s. 0d. and £1. 10s. 0d. respectively, were awarded to the better-paid men, and for new contracts. Askwith explicitly ignored all 'other claims on behalf of musicians'.[67] At first glance, Williams seems to have gained very little. There is no mention of closed shops, and the minimum rates are lower than were demanded. Yet he proclaimed a victory and promised more. 'We are going to give the award a fair trial', he told a large and enthusiastic audience, 'and then kick up a row for more'.[68] This prediction of continuing belligerence, which was amply fulfilled, scarcely accords with Askwith's retrospective vision of peaceful progress. An industry, he tells us, which developed 'without guidance or cohesion on any suitable relations between employer and employed', subject to low wages and constant litigation, was transformed into 'one of the most law-abiding, organised and progressive industries in the United Kingdom'.[69] The learned Henry Farmer, a staunch union man, took a similar view: 'The chaos in the music profession gave place to an elaborate process of negotiation, first by secretaries of branches and paid

Union officials, who dealt directly with local theatre managers and directors, and then through Conciliation Boards which worked reasonably well and produced agreements which were respected by both sides with a remarkable degree of consistency'.[70]

Neither man is a reliable guide to the actual course of events after 1907, which was far from peaceful, or to the alleged benefits of the system. Both are unduly impressed by administrative tidiness, and too ready to equate the increased activity and enhanced status of union officials with the well-being, as distinct from growing numbers, of people in their charge. The procedures laid down for future negotiations gave unprecedented recognition to union officials. 'Authorised representatives' and, if necessary, the General Federation of Trades Unions, were always to be consulted.[71] There can be no doubt of the benefits to Williams's career, and to AMU enrolments. The former blossomed in trade union politics and at international conferences; the latter increased steadily between 1907 and 1910, and dramatically after 1912. The unions' newly-sanctioned powers were arguably more formidable to musicians than to employers. This was obviously so with regard to existing jobs. Union men would be represented, and non-union men not, in complex bureaucratic procedures, requiring the frequent attention of full-time officials. Equally important, but more obscure, was the function of placing men in new jobs; a continuous process for the overwhelming majority of players who were, of course, constantly seeking appointments.

Locating jobs had always been difficult for rank-and-file players, who could not afford to employ agents. They and their prospective employers could scan the trade press and lists in selcted public houses, or meet at such places as 'Poverty Corner' in York Road, as Coburn recalls, and outside union offices.[72] They might also depend, as many do today, upon 'fixers': players or ex-players with an intimate knowledge of the market's requirements and of available musicians. The modern fixer, whose services are indispensable to London's concert-life, works by telephone. In 1907 there were only 41,000 telephones in the metropolitan area, and few musicians could have afforded one. In Smart's day, when only a few players had to be directed into well-defined channels, the task was easily accomplished, but as the market grew and diversified it became increasingly complex, particularly for employers unaccustomed to hiring musicians, which provided new opportunities for intermediaries. Fixers have generally been shadowy figures, except when their activities blossomed into a fully-fledged agency, abandoning the rank and file. One such man was Henry Jarrett, a horn-player who, after touring with Jullien, began to provide him with players. He also supplied Hallé in 1848, and Berlioz on his London visit in 1862; dabbled in opera for the

1869 season, and was accused of collusion with a critic, to praise or damn singers according to their levels of commission. He died in Buenos Aires in 1886.[73]

By the early twentieth century there were, no doubt, many fixers operating in the main centres of orchestral employment. Their activities were unpopular among unionists who, believing that middlemen were parasitic, accused them of squeezing undeserved income from the provision of an unnecessary service. Attempts to recruit and allocate players on a large scale were taken as a direct challenge, at least to the union's privileges, and possibly to its very existence. Two such initiatives deserve notice, the first naïve and vainglorious, the second more serious. In 1911 William Benson, a Manchester 'professor of music' who had anticipated modern technology by inventing a 'resonator' to make a small orchestra sould like a large one, attempted to raise £2,500 for The United Orchestras Ltd. Its prospectus claimed that most employers in the entertainments industry experienced most 'trouble, worry, expense and dissatisfaction' with the band. The selection of players was expansive and undiscriminating, increasingly constrained, as was their subsequent weeding out, by a 'coercive and socialistic' union. The new company would, in return for a small fee, take over all of these responsibilities, and eventually destroy the deputy system and end strikes: the Musicians' Union would 'cease to exist'.[74]

The National Federation of Professional Musicians addressed itself, more plausibly, to a similar range of tasks. Its prospectus announced that, unlike the AMU which it dubbed the 'Amateur Musicians Union', it would accept only 'competent musicians of good moral character who practise the art of music as a means to subsistence'. A board of examiners would debar ineligible amateurs and the '*two-job monopolising undercutter*'.[75] In contrast to the Orchestral Association, however, the Federation registered as a trade union, and attempted to establish credentials by applying for affiliation to the GFTU and various trades councils. The latter initiative won a measure of success, in Glasgow, for example, but the GFTU manœuvre was easily blocked by Williams, now strategically placed on the TUC parliamentary committee, who branded the newcomers as 'blacklegs, excluded and seceded members' of his own union.[76] This could not prevent the Federation from acting as an employment agency in Manchester. It ran a column for 'Wants and Wanted among the disengaged' and boasted of supplying musicians for engagements ranging from the Carl Rosa and Moody-Manners Opera Companies, to diverse seaside employments, and leading skating-rinks (wind players were preferred for the latter).

Meanwhile the Orchestral Association, which had been quiet during the music-hall war, and was even accused of organizing the supply of blacklegs, was struggling to maintain a separate existence. Resisting the radical blandishments of 1907, it still claimed to represent only the best, fully professional players, and retained a respectable image; earning a place, for example, among the 'chief musical institutions' listed by *Who's Who in Music* (1913). Twenty-two pages of the latter compilation also included the NFPM, and even the Piano Manufacturers' Association,[77] but excluded the AMU. Some musicians were probably insuring against the new industrial climate by belonging to two, or possibly all three organizations, a manœuvre which was strenuously opposed by Williams, who was determined to exploit the system by driving on to a 'complete membership'. In 1911, after a summer of unprecedented industrial disruption and violence, he was urging musicians to 'emulate the solidarity' of railwaymen and dockers, by expelling members of the Association and the Federation, and restricting deputy work to their fellow unionists. Thus job-placement and wage negotiations would be integrated into an impregnable collective. These ideas were reinforced by lessons drawn from foreign visits. The American Federation of Musicians, he reported, charged a high entrance fee, organized *'all competitors'*, not just the 'bona-fide' men who were in a minority, and heavily fined those who played with non-members. They 'made trouble' if outsiders secured engagements, and paid their officials well. The French were even tougher: having decided that enough musicians were working in Paris, they were refusing to accept new members, or those attempting to transfer from outer branches. Similarly Williams intended to 'draw the Unionist net around London'. The 'highly respectable element in the profession' would object to these abrasive tactics, but eventually they would 'have to fall in line'.[78]

Askwith again proved to be an effective recruiting sergeant in 1912, when his second award extended the system to provincial music halls. It did not impose minimum wages, but allocated rates for overtime, additional rehearsals and matinées, and recommended a quarter-hour interval between performances.[79] AMU membership increased by 2,000 in the following year, and conflict between the players' organizations reached new levels of intensity. The Orchestral Association, which had hitherto generally stayed in London, while supporting the Federation's provincial ventures, now reversed all of its former policies. Changing its name to National Orchestral Association, it announced its intention of becoming a trade union, welcomed the 'inferior strata' of part-time players as members and, at a meeting in Manchester, called for the formation of 'one society for all throughout Great Britain'. Williams attended the meeting, which collapsed into an inconsequential sequence of recrimination and calls for unity. For the AMU there was only one road to unity. Its London branch resolved to enforce closed shops by 'sudden strikes', expelling 'the camp follower ... a kind of parasite whose courage few respect, but whose cowardice and snobbery all despise'. A target of 10,000 members was set, to be achieved by the union's twenty-first birthday in May 1914. Laggards were addressed in an open letter which appealed to the '25,000 individuals who live almost entirely by playing a musical instrument' of whom 'we have only 8,000 organised'. Many who had benefited from the union's efforts continued to offer excuses for not joining. 'We are tired', continued the diatribe, with a long list of remonstrances; its provenance and tone suggesting less concern to win support from the hesitant, than to upbraid them, and whip up fervour among the faithful.[80]

Two conflicts dominated AMU activities during these stormy years; the Dallimore–Williams case, and an interminable dispute with Stoll. The former began in October 1911, with disagreements about fees for a National Sunday League concert, and allegations of slander; but it developed into litigation of great complexity which entailed differing interpretations of the notoriously controversial Trades Disputes Act. The case went to the Court of Appeal, lasted until March 1914, and earned Williams the plaudits of the TUC Parliamentary Committee; but it cost the AMU over £2,000.[81] An additional £3,000 was spent on other legal actions. With an entrance fee of 2s. 6d. and monthly subscription of 1s. 6d. the union's annual income was approximately £8,000 by 1913. Doubtless it was this taste for litigation—Williams boasted of having appeared before six judges—which led the NFPM to promise prospective members that their fees would not 'line lawyers' gowns'.[82] The Stoll dispute began in December 1912 when, after ten months of acrimonious negotiation, the union decided to 'withdraw from the award' and demand a minimum wage of £2. 2s. 0d., only to find that there were plenty of players, including members of the Association, still willing to play for £1. 16s. 0d., and some expressing satisfaction with less. Theatres in six towns, including London, Manchester and Bristol, were plagued by what was variously described as a strike or lockout, dragging on until August 1914. Williams accused the management of 'apathy, delay and indifference' in its approach to arbitration, and complained that his members were being 'ousted in favour of Association men, unless they desert their union'. Stoll claimed that the dispute was not about wages and hours, but concerned broken contracts and an attempt to impose a closed shop.

The conflict was resolved after the personal intervention of Ramsay MacDonald. Stoll withdrew his claims for damages against contract breakers, and Williams announced an 'honourable' peace, after 'the biggest fight the AMU has ever entered into'. It had cost 'thousands of pounds' but 'our reputation as a fighting organisation has been enhanced, and our position as a union rendered stronger than ever', he told his followers.[83] Presumably the martial strain was intended to appease the young turks among them, who accused him of appeasement. Meanwhile Orcherton was reporting a different outcome: that the union's London branch was 'hopelessly broken up, and a large number of its best members have become members of this Association'. Williams rejected the accusation, of course, and with it, all overtures for peace.

On the eve of a real Armageddon these incessant bickerings cannot but appear tedious and absurd, yet they merit passing attention. Orcherton's depiction of a defeated enemy was *parti pris* and overdrawn, but it contained an element of truth which must be acknowledged if the extent of the AMU's subsequent recovery is to be understood. It was on the brink of a period of massive expansion which would double its membership in five years, destroy the Federation and absorb the Orchestral Association; yet, just before this success it was all but consumed by a sense of disappointment and apprehension. The pages of its journal are weighed down with expressions of grievance and frustration, alternately whining and belligerent, seeking excuses and scapegoats for a series of defeats which were attributed to a variety of malefactors. Uncompromising employers were blamed; as were blacklegs, who secured benefits in 1907, joined the union and then deserted, joined again for the 1912 agitation, bringing London membership up to nearly 2,500, and were now ratting again, simply because the Association's subscription was cheaper.[84] Variety artists had also become culprits, their 'exorbitant salaries' making it impossible for managers to pay decent wages, and their Federation reneging on its commitments.[85]

If the chorus of lamentation was, in large part, an articulation of wounded *amour propre*, it also voiced a genuine distress. The immediate cause was a recession in the industry which prompted managers to cut bands and resist wage demands, followed by the bleak early months of the war, when citizens were urged to forsake entertainment as a patriotic duty. But these were merely temporary setbacks, not to be confused with a fundamental disequilibrium between supply and demand. For stage artists the market, reflecting public taste, exerted some control over quality; and therefore, given a limited supply of talent, over numbers and remuneration. But it rarely exercised a similar discernment in the pit. Far from stemming the flood of barely competent musicians, trade unions and the machinery of arbitration probably encouraged its continuance, by easing recruitment and guaranteeing wages—at near subsistence levels.

The acceptance of such conditions is adequate proof of a glut which could not be contained. It could, however, be absorbed, for a time, by a new form of entertainment which promised employment to practically anyone who could play an instrument, even, *mirabile dictu*, certificated pianists.

IX

New Directions

No one can say that ours is an overcrowded profession.

F. Corder, 1922[1]

The cinema is at present the most important musical institution in the country.

Edwin Evans, January 1929[2]

Between about 1910 and the autumn of 1929 the flood of musicians appeared to subside, and in some quarters there was even talk of shortage. This extraordinary reversal of previous conditions owed little to the protective efforts of unions and professional associations, but was largely due to war and technological innovation. The former reduced the supply of musicians, particularly of skilled performers, and may have increased the demand for their services; but its effects, though immediate and spectacular, were neither profound nor long-lasting. The latter—gramophone, cinema, and radio—began to transform the musician's world. Until 1929 their influence on employment was benign, creating new, but not yet destroying old, forms of employment.

Armageddon

Many kinds of entertainment, particularly sport, were disrupted by the war; but those which employed musicians soon resumed activity, after a few months of uncertainty, despite frequent remonstrance from outraged patriots. Indeed the war economy brought positive benefits to those musicians who could avoid the slaughter. Full employment, including unprecedented opportunities for women, generated increased incomes. Shortages of goods left more cash to be spent on pleasure, and audiences were augmented by soldiers on leave. Native musicians at every level found it easier to get jobs: leading players because there was less competition from foreigners; part-timers because the trenches emptied the pits, and because the widespread availability of 'war work' eased the piecing together of a living. Even the humblest piano teachers acquired new pupils among children whose parents were buying the 'munitions workers' pianos' which symbolized a new working-class prosperity.[3]

The most immediate and obvious change was the departure of German musicians, leaving many positions vacant, some of which were highly coveted. British players 'found themselves with increased work and considerably improved chances of livelihood'.[4] A few began to establish careers as soloists, such as Myra Hess, Irene Scharrer, and Solomon, who was eleven when he made his debut at the Proms in August 1914. But if wartime conditions encouraged the emergence of native talent, there were still many barriers to be overcome: of personal diffidence, national 'temperament', real or imagined, and the prejudices of agents and audiences. An interesting case was Albert Sammons (1886–1957), the prodigiously gifted son of an obscure violinist, who was largely self-taught, and had no formal education or training after the age of 12. Playing in the theatre and restaurant bands, he was discovered at the Waldorf Hotel in 1908 by Beecham, who immediately appointed him to lead his orchestra. He was taken up by Monteux in France, and made occasional solo appearances in England, and even in Germany.[5] Yet Henry Wood failed, despite the wartime absence of foreign virtuosi, to persuade an impresario to 'push an *English* violinist'.[6]

The exodus of foreign musicians was inevitably accompanied by displays of xenophobia; and internment and deportation procedures were arbitrary and indiscriminate. Even Brodsky, principal of the Manchester college, and a Russian subject, was incarcerated for nearly a year. Hun-baiting was seldom practised with the dedication of devotees in other walks of life, perhaps because the cosmopolitanism of musicians, in origins and working environment, induced tolerance. Nevertheless there was sufficient expression of that mean and philistine parochialism which afflicts nations at war to indicate a change in attitudes which would survive the peace, and be codified by the Aliens Order of 1920. Resentment of foreigners was as old as the profession of music, but in Britain it had rarely had much practical effect. Henceforth it was freely expressed and reinforced by nationalist sentiment, benign and malevolent, disinterested and self-seeking, absurd and sinister. It forced musicians to Anglicize their names, in striking contrast to the long-standing tradition of cultivating exoticism. Thus Basil Cameron (1884–1975) who had adopted the name Hindenburg in 1912, as conductor of the Torquay Municipal Orchestra, was born again as Cameron two years later. Thus Brother Scholz informed fellow unionists that, as a British subject, born in Shorncliffe camp, honourably discharged from the Durham Light Infantry, and a member of the National Reserve, he would henceforth be known as Gus. Barret.[7] Imagining the dread return of alien musicians, a union hack declaimed

'Can we agree to sit with them in the same orchestra? Shall we be able to stifle the thought that the German or Austrian is an embryo spy gathering details for the renewal of an attempt to impose German "Kultur" on us?'[8]

All foreigners were competitors, and therefore enemies. In the first few months of the war there was even a brief, but vociferous, outcry against the employment of Belgian and French refugees. Williams, who had been a leading advocate of international co-operation among musicians, providing they were male and unionized, displayed considerable skill and strength of purpose in resisting these extremes of chauvinism. Proudly acknowledging that he had 'placed' Belgian refugees in music-hall jobs, he demanded sympathy for suffering allies: the Colonne and other orchestras had lost most of their players to the armed forces, and 'in Belgium, the musicians who are not fighting are homeless. Just think of it'.[9] But vituperation increased as the war's appetite for men was recorded each month in the 'Rolls of Honour' exhibited by colleges and musicians' organizations. It was alleged that 'Dutchmen, Russians, and Belgians (or shall we say foreign musicians posing as such) are being engaged in preference to Britishers'. Italian and Jewish players were subjected to particularly vicious obloquy.[10] In 1916 a union branch in Burnley resolved that 'no foreign musician, of whatever nationality, should be admitted to the AMU'; but musicians in Bath were prepared to discriminate between allied and enemy aliens.[11]

If antipathy to foreigners continued to be voiced by the union's rank and file, its leadership was generally more concerned with other forms of competition: military, female, and 'amateur'. The depredations of army and navy bands were a nagging theme. In September 1914, for example, the TUC Parliamentary Committee protested that marine bandsmen were allowed to take evening engagements while union members were confined to barracks; and in March 1915, that guardsmen were allowed to participate in recruiting bands(!).[12] In November 1917 the War Office and Admiralty were nagged about the employment of service bands by 'private speculators at a time when every available man is required at the front, while civilian musicians, called from their musical employment, are sacrificing their lives in the trenches'.[13] Women were a threat because the progress of female players was being accelerated by the war, which hastened feminine emancipation from personal and vocational constraints.[14] Although there was no attempt to revive the legend of the missing muscle,[15] antagonists continued to rehearse ancient prejudices. Women were accused of lowering wages, which was arguable, and standards, which was absurd. A typical editorial attack in the union's journal deplored their lack of 'vim ... particularly in the climaxes and anti-climaxes necessary to a proper performance'.[16] The reply of a 'Lady Instrumentalist, AMU', displaying a firmer grip of language and events, gives an illuminating description of conditions in 1916. Current problems, she explained, were not a result of feminine ineptitude, but arose from changes in supply and demand. 'Continuous picture shows, and the two houses in other places of entertainment, combined with the scarcity of properly trained musicians' had unleashed 'a perfect deluge of incompetent amateur musicians of both sexes who, with no further qualifications than a few hurried lessons on some sort of instrument, have the impertinence to undertake important engagements, accepting disgraceful lowering terms, and impossibly long hours of work'.[17]

Yet many people continued to argue that musicians were in short supply; including bellicose trade unionists who were not concerned with questions of competence. 'Owing to the great shortage of musicians at present we have the very finest opportunity of getting what we want', declared a professed Marxist, with quotations from the Master.[18] Another militant announced that 'circumstances today give the musician the opportunity of betterment, and he should seek now . . . to entrench himself in his better position'.[19] Williams agreed, but attempted to identify real enemies. Musicians from France, Belgium, and Italy would return home after the war. Women and amateurs would remain, and 'when the boys come home . . . reinstatement and the maintenance of terms' would be immensely difficult.[20] Primarily a decent attempt to subdue xenophobic excess, this statement might also suggest that Williams was at last beginning to reconsider the fundamental principle on which he had built the AMU: the acceptance of all comers.

Meanwhile, however, union membership was continuing to grow rapidly and, despite the alleged shortage, players could still be found to work for a pittance. At Coventry's 'Opera House' in August 1915, non-union instrumentalists were accepting one pound a week.[21] A year later, when it might be assumed that players were getting scarce, the members of a Cheltenham orchestra, who earned £1. 5s. 0d., were subject to a strict code of discipline which, in addition to requiring a complete wardrobe (black and white ties), enforced an appropriate gentility by forbidding the wearing of caps when travelling to and from work.[22] A typical provincial contract in 1917, conforming to Askwith's 1912 award, was signed by a flautist at Moss Empire's Grand Theatre in Birmingham. For £1. 16s. 0d. a week he had to wear evening dress (white tie) and was not allowed to leave the pit without the director's permission. Absence required a doctor's certificate and a paid and proficient deputy. Departure necessitated two week's notice, except in case of indiscipline, which brought instant dismissal.[23] Even the Hallé orchestra's rank-and-file players were paid only £4 a week during

Beecham's winter season in 1917. Despite AMU boasts[24] that these were higher rates than the Orchestral Association had secured for Queen's Hall players, in real terms they were actually lower than those prevailing in 1907, because the cost of living had doubled.

Throughout the war it appears that musicians could be procured for very low *rates* of pay. Their incomes may have improved, in return for very long hours, because more work was available throughout the week and year. A hundred or so outstanding players, mainly in London, probably did exceptionally well; because of the German exodus, and in new forms of employment. Gramophone companies were turning to the orchestral repertory, recording truncated classics and endless light music.[25] Such jobs could often be fitted into the mornings, without affecting other engagements. The cinema was a far more potent influence, throughout the country, in a manner, and for reasons, which will shortly be explained. In addition to such conspicuous changes there was, or so it was said, a profound change in the public's attitude towards music, rooted in the 'keener psychosis' of a nation at war.[26] The critic Ernest Newman observed a larger audience for serious music; and Beecham, whose inspiring performances both created and satisfied a substantial part of that audience, was similarly impressed: 'In wartime the temper of a section of the people for a while becomes graver, simpler and more concentrated ... thoughtful intelligence craves and seeks these antidotes to a troubled conscience of which great music is perhaps the most potent'.[27]

Business as usual

After the war most people were anxious to get back to normal life as soon as possible. Few did so more rapidly and successfully than the musicians. For many players the post-war decade was a time of seemingly limitless opportunities. For most teachers the prospects were less clear, but that did not deter aspirants to the profession, few of whom deliberately intended to teach. Students therefore flocked into the eagerly welcoming colleges, which imposed few barriers except an ability to pay fees. Some ex-servicemen were even encouraged by grants from 'a well intentioned but muddle-headed government'.[28] Enrolments at the Royal College of Music doubled within a year of the Armistice, and approached 600 by 1920. At the Guildhall School of Music they increased from 1,400 to 2,800 in 1921. Manchester College, where there were 153 women and thirty-four men in 1917, was teaching 350 students by 1920. Trinity College celebrated its fiftieth anniversary in 1922, with 700 students in attendance, and 50,000 candidates for its local examinations at centres all over the world.[29] Vigorous expansion was unaffected by radically changing market requirements. The innate conservatism of several institutions was reinforced by ageing, inbred leadership. At Trinity College the septuagenarian J. C. Bridge succeeded his brother as principal. At the RAM McEwan (1868–1948), who had taught there since 1898, took over from Mackenzie. Too many students at most of the colleges were acquiring a smattering of obsolete 'theory', or acquaintance with a few concertos which they would never perform professionally; too few were receiving a thorough training, including ensemble work, knowledge of the repertory, and ability to read at sight. None were encouraged to pursue the new vital, and remunerative American styles of popular music.

The fake diploma mills continued to grind mercilessly and find customers. There was a 'National Academy', 'National College', 'National Conservatory', and 'Victoria College' of music. The latter boasted a staff which included an individual claiming to be 'sometime Professor of Elocution in the Universities of Oxford and Cambridge', and several 'Professors of Intoning'. In advertisements announcing that it had awarded 60,000 certificates and diplomas, a variety of academic robes were on offer, but proper uniformity was also ensured: 'all hoods Oxford shape'. Such trappings were still able to promote images of authority and distinction. Notices for a concert at a Primitive Methodist Church in 1921, for example, promised that 'Mr L. Crapper, FVCM, will appear in his robes.' On another occasion a fifteen-year-old 'professor of music', LVCM, gold medallist, complete with brass door-plate and visiting cards, demonstrated her skill at the pianoforte with a rendition of Wyman's 'Silvery Waves', foot firmly clamped to pedal. She had paid 3 gns. for her examination, 3 gns. for her medal, and 10 gns. for a resplendent cap and gown. She now charged one guinea a term for lessons.[30] The colonies could enjoy identical cultural facilities. In 1916 Charles Emmanuel Graves Esq., FVCM (born Kwamina Abayie, of the Anona clan) established at Cape Coast the West African College of Music and Commerce (which ultimately collapsed 'through lack of support') and represented the Victoria College of Music. Photographed in his robes, he appears in *Gold Coast Men of Affairs Past and Present*.[31]

The battle against these activities was now taken up by Percy Scholes, in his journal, the *Music Student*, and in a pamphlet, *Musical Examinations, Dubious*. In 1922 he persuaded a number of editors to refuse advertising space to 'unauthorised examining bodies'.[32] The Incorporated Society of Musicians also reiterated old protests; calling for the establishment of a Ministry of Fine Arts to prevent the distribution of 'spurious diplomas and caps and gowns to children',[33] but the trade persisted. In 1930 a girl who had been judged incapable of taking the lowest grade of Associated Board examination (intended for 8-year-old children), was reported to possess 'letters' which the public could easily confuse with an ARCM.[34] Scholes also provided guidance through the morass of 'reputable' diplomas and degrees. The former were listed, with examination costs, and a few cautious remarks about 'relative difficulty and standing . . . the ATCL is the easiest, with the ARCO coming next'. He also published the syllabuses of twenty-one university degrees, adding the quaintly-worded, but illuminating, observation that a younger generation of examiners now required 'more *musical* work, and strict counterpoint seems likely to diminish in favour, as it has at Oxford'. Some candidates could now be 'examined in PLAYING SOME INSTRUMENT in lieu of the more extended composition formerly demanded'.[35]

A more critical assessment of the nation's education and training facilities appeared in a substantial League of Nations report, *Les conditions de Vie et de Travail des Musiciens* in eighteen European countries. Britain's national colleges were described as only remotely linked with the state, and uncommitted to the diffusion of music among the people. Their high costs were said to deter working class students, particularly from the provinces, many of whom therefore sought a cheaper training abroad, especially in Brussels. Scholarships were awarded for merit, not need; but there was no lack of enrolments, not least by young women, even of modest means, who had accumulated savings during the war to pay for a musical training. Private teaching was omnipresent: 99 per cent of unionized musicians had received no other form of training. It was accompanied ('chose singulière') by a unique proliferation of diplomas, examined externally and therefore impersonally, by professors from the national colleges, which were dependent on this source of income. The system debased the value of all paper qualifications and, by extending competition, forced the cost of lessons down to 'un prix dérisoire'. It benefited neither public nor profession, but the ISM's attempts at reform had produced no tangible result. The deleterious effects of these abuses were currently offset by favourable conditions, economic and cultural, for British music and public taste had greatly advanced. At the highest levels the training of musicians had also improved—it was no longer obligatory for talented students to complete their studies abroad—but more generally musical education continued to be dominated by obsolete practice.[36]

The report was ignored by government, profession, and public, but there were atttempts to prune excrescent diplomas. In 1921 the Burnham committee, which recommended scales of payment for schoolteachers, allowed only a few such certificates to qualify for graduate increments;[37] and in 1929, after much internal dissension, the ISM ceased to conduct examinations. The latter reform has been depicted as a fundamental change, establishing 'a Professional Association in the truest sense'.[38] It is an exaggerated claim. With some 2,000 members, fewer than 10 per cent of practising music teachers, and a minute proportion of the total profession, the Society still exerted no real powers of autonomy and control.[39] But dropping examinations was indeed an important change of direction: a temporary defeat, not yet decisive, for the old guard, represented by Hugo Chadfield, who had succeeded his father as secretary in 1906. This advance was consolidated by constitutional reorganization, including the establishment of a solo-performers' section, and the election as president of such men as Landon Ronald, Donald Tovey, and Adrian Boult, interspersed with, and later succeeded by, the more familiar men of the organ-loft. The Society continued primarily to represent teachers, a thankless task, in an increasingly harsh environment.

According to the 1921 census there were approximately 21,000 music teachers in England and Wales, and 2,000 in Scotland; 76 per cent were women, mostly working on their own account. By 1931 the total number had risen by more than 1,000, and the female percentage by about 2 per cent. It is impossible to be precise about their levels of remuneration, but few were likely to have earned more than £100 a year: below the wage of a domestic servant, above that of a shop assistant.[40] Some evidence emerged in 1920 from a newspaper discussion of the 'New Poor'. One holder of an LRAM, for example, was earning barely £2 a week. Most piano teachers held lesser credentials, and many lacked any paper qualification.[41] In the same year a short-lived union of music teachers conducted a survey of fees in Liverpool. They ranged from 1s. to £1. 5s. 0d. a lesson. Of the respondents 40 per cent were receiving 1 gn. or less for ten lessons; 35 per cent between one and 2 gns.[42] Average fees probably fell during the 1920s; certainly after 1930, when 1s. lessons were the norm in working-class districts. Since most pupils had to be taught outside school hours, it was difficult for many teachers to cram forty lessons into a week and earn £2.

If teachers were incapable of creating a large, united, and powerful association, players appeared to be more successful. Union membership was practically equivalent to the 1921 official census of all players (which was, as always, an underestimate). In July of that year, after decades of bickering, the AMU and its rival, currently dubbed the National Orchestral Union of Professional Musicians, finally agreed to join forces, creating the Musicians' Union. Fewer than half of the 2,700 members of the smaller society bothered to vote, and only twenty were opposed to joining forces with the 20,000 strong AMU.[43] A similar indifference was displayed by press and public, perhaps because the betrothal had been prematurely announced on so many previous occasions. It was 'astonishing', complained the *Musical Mail*, that 'an occurance of such infinite importance should be allowed to pass with such scant notice'.[44] In truth the event's significance was primarily symbolic, for the two unions had long ceased to represent separate and distinct groups of musicians, though there had been recent complaints that the NOUPM was 'a brigade of foreigners'.[45] More serious was a perceptible weakening in the new union's leadership.

Although he was to enjoy a few more years of politics, becoming chairman of the TUC General Council in 1922, Williams was already a sick man. In 1925 he relinquished his leadership of the Musicians' Union, and retired to France, where he died in obscurity four years later. His successor, E. S. Teale, was ten years older, and also suffered from ill-health, until his death in 1931. After an undistinguished career as cellist in a Liverpool theatre orchestra, he had joined Williams in the earliest days of the AMU and became assistant secretary in 1896. Even Henry Farmer's generous obituary admits that for the next eighteen years Teale merely 'took instructions from Williams, with little opportunity of exercising his own will or individuality'. Perhaps, as Farmer argues, there could be no adequate successor to 'a subtle genius and dominating personality like J. B. Williams',[46] but an image of gerontocracy was reinforced by the election of Fred Orcherton (1858–1929) as president of the Union's London branch. Perhaps creative leadership was unnecessary; for competent players could easily find jobs, and talented musicians were enjoying unwonted prosperity. Unaffected by the economic difficulties which began in 1921 with the end of the post-war boom, they were attached, temporarily, to a flourishing new industry.

Cinemas

Silent films functioned as if they had been designed to create jobs for musicians. Far from being silent the cinema required a ceaseless flow of music which it could not yet provide by mechanical means. In every other respect it was a highly productive, and therefore hugely profitable industry since, encountering no language barriers, it could tap an international market. Exhibitors made easy profits from these economies of scale, with minimal costs and inconvenience. In stark contrast to the necessarily inefficient, labour-intensive business of theatre and music-hall, they required only a projectionist, simple equipment, and a few house staff, to display rented films which were rich in drawing power. Not only could they dispense with a costly stage and back-stage army of semi-skilled and unskilled labour; it was no longer necessary to employ directly those stars whose unique and brilliantly promoted talents made the whole enterprise possible. Show business had at last caught up with the industrial revolution: as with the best factory products, excellence became cheaply available, thanks to mass production and technology. When Chaplin (1889–1977) was 19 he played three music-halls a day, beginning with a matinée at the half-empty Streatham Empire, and proceeding to the Canterbury and Tivoli; entertaining a few hundred people for a pittance.[47] Ten years later he was rather better placed, playing to a world audience of millions.

In Britain it was, furthermore, predominantly a *new* audience: an additional market, not merely a diversion of purchasing power away from other forms of entertainment. Apart from the obvious attractions of new visual excitements, there were locational and social reasons for this remarkable fact. The early cinema was a uniquely flexible enterprise. In addition to supplementing existing theatre schedules, as part of a mixed programme, or as an occasional show in conventional premises, films were profitably exhibited in a wide variety of locations: shops, town halls, skating-rinks; and eventually in custom-built cinemas, the first of which is said to have been at Colne, Lancashire, in 1908.[48] Even scattered populations in remote areas could be tapped. Previous forms of commercial entertainment had depended upon concentrated urban populations to provide audiences large enough to make them remunerative. The location of the largest and most comfortable cinemas continued to be so determined, of course, but whereas village theatres and music-halls were inconceivable, village cinemas became commonplace.

The social composition of British cinema audiences underwent a rapid transformation which also helps to explain their phenomenal growth. Initially regarded as fit only for ill-bred children and servant-girls, films rapidly became popular in working-class districts, and then extended their appeal, particularly to young people, not least courting couples; to a hitherto neglected 'women's audience' and ultimately to a classless family market. When the self-appointed 'National Council of Public Morals' investigated the cinema in 1917, it estimated that half of the country's population was going to the 'pictures' once a week. A few years later the attendance rate was doubled, and most of the audience was said to attend no other form of theatrical entertainment. Precise statistics are unavailable for the early period, but in 1914 there were at least 3,500 halls showing films. By 1926 the total number had probably not changed, but their average size had certainly increased and many were purpose-built cinemas.[49]

The importance of these developments for the employment of musicians can scarcely be exaggerated. They were the only group of people employed as professional entertainers whose services remained unmechanized but indispensable to a new industry whose extraordinary mass appeal ensured its continuous expansion. Since their own productivity was quite unchanged, every step in that growth occasioned an increase in the demand for musicians without, as yet, destroying existing jobs. At every level of size and quality, from 'fleapit' pianist to quasi-symphony orchestra, there were unprecedented opportunities of full-time continuous employment.

Generalizations about the origins of cinema music are often mere surmise, masquerading as documented fact. Its principal purpose may originally have been to drown noise from projectors, before they were separately housed.[50] Less plausible is the supercilious suggestion that it was intended to mask the sound of audiences 'coughing, spitting, or reading the sub-titles aloud'.[51] A contemporary participant explains it as simply an additional inducement: patrons had originally been wooed by diverse means, including tea and cake; later it became 'common practice to supply music'.[52] Imperceptibly music came to be regarded as indispensable; even on set, where it apparently encouraged (silent) actors to emote, and universally, in cinemas, as a continuous background to films and filler of intervals. Usually it was supplied by a piano or a small combination. In 1915, for example, a 300-seat cinema in a Leeds suburb employed a string quartet, flute, and piano. One of the players was an ex-RAM 'professor', ruined by whisky; the pianist was a competent, deaf lady, with a time-keeping sniff; the flautist Gerald Jackson, 15 years old and destined to play under Toscanini.[53] The self-taught percussionist, James Blades, began a similarly distinguished career by leaving his first job, with a circus, to join an orchestra at the Wisbech Hippodrome, which consisted of two violins, cello, double-bass, trumpet, piano, and drums.[54] Managers, inexperienced in such matters, needed guidance about musicians and music, but encountered few practical difficulties: pianos and tuning were cheap, and pianists readily available. Halls with more than 500 seats were recommended to raise the volume level by adding a harmonium and cornet, the latter also useful for currently fashionable military subjects. Percussionists could provide various effects; comedies were said to benefit from an intrinsically comic double-bass; and a trombone was required for drunken knockabout.[55]

Pianists were everywhere in demand, particularly if they had stamina and could improvise. There began an unprecedented, and never-to-be-repeated, two decades of job opportunities for a sizeable proportion of the largest single group of instrumentalists; most of whom, without the cinema, would scarcely have found employment, except as progenitors of their kind. Their wages and working conditions in the smaller places were inevitably poor; from all over the country there were reports of women playing the piano for £1 a week or less. Some were prepared to work for nothing, to get experience.[56] In 1918 a 17-year-old girl was paid £1. 10s. 0d. for attending a London suburban cinema from 4.30

p.m. until 10.30 p.m. on weekdays, and 6 p.m. until 10.30 p.m. on Sundays. Another was engaged from 2 p.m. until 10.30 p.m., but was allowed rest intervals.[57] In the smallest halls men sometimes worked as manager-pianists. Larger cinemas would often engage two players, one to perform with the orchestra, and a 'relief pianist' to accompany the 'second feature'. Full orchestras were uncommon enough at first to excite comment. Thus the 'Grand Symphony Orchestra' employed by a Manchester cinema in 1916, was reported as 'quite unnecessary except for such films as a life of Wagner' and thought 'unlikely to survive because of the salary list'.[58] A dozen players became the normal complement in most urban establishments; far more in 'super-cinemas', the first of which opened at Dalston in 1920.[59] Large orchestras were also needed for special features, such as Griffith's 'Birth of a Nation' which required excerpts from the symphonic repertory. At Covent Garden in 1922 Eugene Goossens conducted sixty-five members of the London Symphony Orchestra, accompanying *The Three Musketeers*.[60] In 1926 Richard Strauss conducted a cramped 'augmented' orchestra—there were no singers—in a single performance of *Der Rosenkavalier* at the Tivoli Cinema. In contrast to normal procedures, film was made to follow music, frequently getting ahead and having to wait for the composer's 'electronic button'.[61]

An arbitrary selection of music was probably common in the early days. Jackson's employer 'just bought stacks of music (the choice of film didn't seem to matter), and we played for his pleasure—and perhaps that of the audiences'. Blades's director followed a similar policy.[62] Pianists contributed their distinctive repertory, ranging from 'The Maiden's Prayer' and 'The Robin's Return' to Beethoven's 'Moonlight' and 'Pathétique' Sonatas. A tremolo 'Hearts and Flowers' became inextricably associated with pathos, and an urgent 'Hall of the Mountain King' with menace. In instrumental ensembles the pianist was an essential link, binding the 'hotch-potch of music together with his rapid modulations and improvised chords'.[63]

There was an enormous increase in the demand for sheet music, because everyone was playing simultaneously, in cinemas all over the country, with programme changes at least once a week. Publishers benefited, and the lending libraries which catered for music halls were greatly extended. A typical provincial library, in Stockton-on-Tees, advertised over 4,000 pieces 'selected to suit all films, to give true atmosphere, which is quite essential in the art of playing to pictures'.[64] Distributors began to issue 'cue sheets', giving timings and suggestions for appropriate music. It was an ancient device. A theatre musician recalled 'the old stock company days, when the Musical Director had a set of books with little bits of music to fit all situations . . . enter villain, number 48 . . . enter heroine, number 6 slow, then segue to 15, when struggle commences. She dies, chord'. The reinstatement of this 'scrappy system', he concluded, 'will destroy the individuality of the orchestras . . . The only logical and satisfactory method will be to have music arranged for each picture as it is produced'.[65] Meanwhile publishers were responding to the new market with music appropriately arranged, or at least titled, and sometimes specifically composed: affording new opportunities of employment to hack writers. Catalogues listed titles by mood: 'agitatos, church, sad, sinister, happy, chase, furious, majestic'. A Bach chorale would thus appear as 'Adagio lamentoso for sad scenes'.[66] Such products reflected the needs of musical directors with insufficient time or, perhaps, ability to make their own arrangements, but they also helped managers to avoid the risk of infringing copyright, which was important after 1906, and performing right, after the establishment of the Performing Right Society in 1914. Publishers were urged to produce 'easy, convenient arrangements of non-copyright pieces'.[67]

The business of commissioning background music was most highly developed in New York, where Max Winkler's 'sprawling empire of Dawns, Dusks, and Furiosos' spawned a new, evanescent repertory.[68] It culminated in 1925 with the publication of Erno Rapee's *Encyclopaedia of Music for Pictures*, which listed some 20,000 pieces, with advice on the proper synchronization of mood. British activities were less extensive, but included the publication of 'photo-play' compositions, and such collections as Paxton's *Music for all occasions*. Cheap editions of classical symphonies, such as Curwen's, for salon orchestra, and the *Star Folio* of seven symphonies, arranged for piano (3s.), violin and cello (2s. 6d.) were much in demand.[69] In addition to backing films, musicians would provide 'interludes', which were singled out for praise by the National Council, both because they relieved 'the tendency to ocular strain' and because they elevated public taste: 'the supreme pages of musical literature, such as the Overture of the "Magic Flute" and B minor Symphony of Schubert, are frequently to be heard at the best houses'.[70] Other tastes were served by Miss Cynthia Bishop's 'Picture Palace Sketches'. Miss Bishop's credentials were advanced by her publishers. A drawing-room entertainer at the age of fifteen, she had led a juvenile company of performers in character songs and solos on the ocarina, performed piano duets with the Princess Pachnanye in society, and exchanged letters of mutual admiration with the novelist Elinor Glyn. Her compositions included *Love's Anthem*, and *Bees and Clover*, which had been well received by the *Daily Mail*'s reviewer. The *Sketches* were infantile piano pieces, said to be much played at 'some of the best London cinemas'.[71]

Cinema music could be educational for both players and audiences. Jackson acknowledges his indebtedness to a cinema in Headingley which, although it was not the largest and most modern in the district, gave him a 'substantial introduction to the concert repertoire'. Only 'snippets' were performed, but they provided an 'excellent groundwork' for his subsequent career; perhaps better than he could have obtained at one of the colleges. In addition he played Gershwin and Kern, imported by a ship's musician on the Atlantic run, who were certainly forbidden fruit in the garden of academe.[72] Contemporary opinion about the effect on audiences alternated between accusations of a 'debasement of taste' and extravagant claims to cultural enlightenment. The most knowledgeable commentators tended to be commendatory. After a typically balanced and informative discussion Dan Godfrey concluded, in 1924, that cinema '*is* playing, and in the future will play, a great part in the growth of musical appreciation'.[73] Five years later, on the eve of the demise of silent cinema, the critic Edwina Evans argued that it was 'the sole, or at any rate the chief, venue by which music reaches three-quarters of the potential audience in the population. For about fifty-nine hours weekly, music is being performed in upwards of three thousand cinemas, and for shorter periods in perhaps a thousand isolated halls'.[74] His conclusion, which is quoted at the head of this chapter, has several implications. There can be no doubt that cinemas immensely increased the British public's exposure to music, some of it good, more widely and cheaply than the pre-electric gramophone, and before broadcasting. Since taste always grows, and sometimes improves, by mere listening, the experience, which was new to many cinema-goers, must have converted some of them to its pleasures: more, perhaps, than any previous attempts to win an audience.

How much work did silent films create for musicians? In 1924 cinemas were said to be employing half of the union's members;[75] and by 1928 to be providing between 75 and 80 per cent of 'paid musical employment'.[76] Since membership of the union exceeded 20,000, more than double the pre-war figure, and some cinemas employed non-union players, these are astonishingly high proportions of a greatly expanded labour force. The 80 per cent estimate is vaguely expressed, and derived from statistics which are probably no longer available; but it does not conflict with other evidence. Equivalent to at least 16,000 full-time jobs, or four to five players per cinema, it is clearly a modest approximation; for some, like the Piccadilly Plaza, had fifty; many employed a dozen, and few less than four. In March 1929 it was reported that nearly 4,000 cinema musicians were working in greater London, and at least 20,000 'in the whole country'.[77] Employers had few means of cutting the costs of this enormous labour force. Neither their association nor the formation of 'trust circuits'—the Gaumont British company controlled 300 cinemas by 1929—reduced wages much below minimum levels negotiated with the union. Despite occasional clashes, the industry was probably too competitive and anxious to maintain good public relations, in a time of industrial unrest, to risk a repetition of the 1907 'war'. Nor could the larger urban cinemas afford to reduce the size of their orchestras, previously a common practice in the slack summer months, without damaging a sedulously cultivated image of luxury in a highly competitive environment.[78]

The obvious alternative was to replace musicians with machines. Cinema organs were already proving effective in America, enabling a single player both to accompany a film and to exhibit a wholly modern, chromium-plated technology and trans-Atlantic showmanship. But in Britain their widespread use was constrained by lack of suitable performers. There was no shortage of men accustomed to keyboard and pedals: in 1920 the National Union of Organists' Association had 2,500 members, perhaps one-tenth of its potential membership, many of whom would have welcomed the chance of earning some cash.[79] Unfortunately, in the words of a tutor which set out to repair the deficiency, 'the ecclesiastical style' did not 'constitute the right type of photo playing'.[80] In 1927 the Royal College of Organists invited Reginald Foort to demonstrate a Wurlitzer, but that 'ponderously dignified and supremely conservative' body of men probably agreed with the chairman's opinion that it was like an 'ice cream stall'.[81] In 1928 the *Kinematograph Weekly* reported that there were 'now more organs in Kinemas than capable men to fill the seats', and advised 'straight organists' to undergo conversion by attending the British School of Cinema Organists, promoted by Gaumont British and several organ-builders.[82]

Could live musicians be entirely displaced? Trade journals offered advertisements and advice. Cinema managers were urged to 'cut running costs: instal the J.S. Orchestral Gramophone Electrical Reproducer'. In the manner of gramophone advertising since its inception, such equipment was said to make it 'practically impossible to distinguish any material difference between the machine and the real orchestra, artiste, organ or other instrument'. The four-minute limitation of 78 r.p.m. records was overcome by using two turntables. An acknowledged limitation was the machine's tendency 'to break down—but musicians can be ill or on strike'. A pianist should be employed to operate the controls, or play, as required. Subtle advertisements could announce 'Paul Whiteman' and, in small print, 'on the electrical reproducer'.[83] But mechanized music was still a mere auxiliary; inevitably perhaps, so long as actors could only mime on screen.

Hot music

Second only to the cinema as a new source of employment was a craze for dancing to 'American' music which was sweeping the country, at every social level. Fashionable hotels, restaurants and night clubs reordered the social season, with immaculately clad, highly rewarded band-leaders as its new arbiters. For ordinary people the Hammersmith Palais de Dance spawned imitations in every large town, which were cheap to enter and profitable to run. Even before electrical amplification the music, with prominent saxophones and brass, was loud enough for prevailing levels of expectation and endurance. Smaller halls also required bands, for tea dances and Saturday hops.[84] Provincial dancing-teachers were reported to be visiting London during the summer months to acquire the latest steps, foxtrot, black-bottom, or Yale blues. Seaside entertainments had to keep in step. In 1924 Bournemouth's town council, worried by a £6,000 deficit in its symphony orchestra's budget, reported that 4,000 people were at dances on the same night as a concert attended by only 100, and that every alternative form of amusement was losing trade.[85] Music-halls, now dubbed 'variety theatres' fought back with 'show bands'—the Savoy Havana, Ambrose, Jack Hylton, Debroy Somers—each displaying 'syncopated rhythms'.[86] By 1927 there were forty-two 'revues' on tour, with such titles as *Hello Charleston* and *Still Jazzing*.[87]

The gramophone and radio provided further stimulus. Two of the most popular bands made over 300 records between 1922 and 1927.[88] Broadcasts began in 1923, and by 1926 over 2m. licence-holders could hear the London Radio Dance Band twice a week.[89] In the following year dance music was filling 16 per cent of a typical BBC weekly schedule, exceeded only by the 29 per cent devoted to the somewhat arbitrarily separated category of 'light music'.[90] Experts debated 'Hot Music versus Melody' at tedious length, and usually concluded that decent British folk preferred the latter. The violinist, De Groot, whose respectability was vouchsafed by twelve years residence at the Piccadilly Grill Room, possession of a Stradivarius, and a son at public school, swore fealty to melody.[91]

Opponents of the 'American invasion' suggested that the musicians who supplied these needs were an entirely new breed, their demeanour crass, their training inadequate or non-existent, their music 'execrable, profitless, deplorable, freakish and degenerate'. Pronouncements about what was indiscriminately termed 'jazz' were, to be sure, no sillier than contemporary comments on Bartok, Stravinsky, or even Bruckner, proudly displaying an ethnocentric parochialism, so shaming in retrospect as to deter later music critics from reacting honestly to any provocation. A representative view was that 'low negro plantation music', hitherto 'taboo amongst the whites', had suddenly, but only temporarily, emerged, solely because of its advocacy by 'rich American decadents'. It had a 'debasing effect upon the subconscious mind' and a 'far more serious effect upon the prestige of the white races'.[92] Such outbursts, frequently tinged with a racist invective which was excessive even by pre-Holocaust standards of public discourse, were not confined to musicians. Their articulation by churchmen, ex-colonial governors, and other guardians of public taste, was widespread, and remarkable in a society which had previously been largely indifferent to the changing language of music. Most jeremiads utterly failed to distinguish between great jazz players, sophisticated exponents of American popular music, and feeble purveyors of dance tunes and 'novelty numbers'.[93] Indeed the records of many English bands, which demonstrate, incidentally, the unreliability of written evidence about performing practice, make it difficult to comprehend the antagonism generated by their pallid efforts. In practice, as enthusiasts frequently complained,[94] there were very few opportunities to hear live performances of authentic American music in Britain. The Original Dixieland Jazz Band appeared at the London Hippodrome in 1919 (only once, because the comedian George Robey objected) and played for several months at the Hammersmith Palais. Paul Whiteman displayed his 'symphonic jazz' on two occasions, and a few London bands employed individual Americans. But generally the market was sufficiently protected for British players to be free from competition.

Despite the wide range of alternative musical employment there was no general shortage of candidates, though good players of some instruments might temporarily be scarce. the factors which determined this response were much the same as those which had released a flood of musicians after 1870; particularly the ease of movement from amateur to professional. But recruitment into dance bands was even faster and more widespread for several new reasons. Some popular instruments were easily picked up, by old hands doubling (clarinet and saxophone, for example) or newcomers plucking, blowing, banging, and squeezing (piano accordians were a new importation). Since jazz was an aural tradition, favouring spontaneity and impromptu performance, the ability to *read* music was no longer indispensible to artistry or professional status. Self-tuition was immensely stimulated by the gramophone, for people from the most diverse backgrounds. Blades transcribed xylophone solos from this source.[95] Spike Hughes, who was the son of a composer, and had studied composition in Vienna with Egon Wellesz, picked out the bass notes of the basic chord sequences as accompaniment to 'hot records', and within two years was voted Britain's Best Bassist in the *Melody Maker*.[96] Humphrey Lyttelton, son of an Eton master, whose temperament and upper-class upbringing protected him from a conventional musical education, was tutored, apart from one trumpet lesson, by the gramophone.[97]

Lesser talents followed similar paths. They were further assisted by the diversity of acceptable groupings: practically any combination of instruments could form a dance band. Additional encouragement came from the *Melody Maker* which, starting publication in 1926, offered 'hints for semi-pro bands', 'simple hot choruses', and 'new rhythms' and organized contests throughout the country.[98] Bert Ambrose, who had returned from America at the Prince of Wales's behest, to furnish appropriate music to English high society, later blamed the journal for flooding the market; inciting 'bank clerks and mechanics', anyone who could 'blow a few tunes on a saxophone or play a few wrong chords on a banjo' to follow 'an imagined El Dorado'.[99] But some of the gold was real enough, and not all prospectors were newcomers. Many were familiar figures in changed costume, their Hungarian gypsy outfits discarded in favour of tuxedos and horn-rimmed spectacles. There were temporary shortages of good trumpet and trombone players, some of whom were said to be earning ten times their previous theatre fees.[100] But violinists were not yet redundant in a world of popular music inhabited by a motley collection of individuals and groups. Many pretended to play 'straight or jazz', and successful bands were a curious amalgam of old and new. Debroy Somers, for example, fielded a team led by Jean Pougnet, who later became a serious violinist, and made up as follows: two violins, three saxophones, two pianos, oboe (doubling cor anglais), bassoon (doubling harp), two trumpets, trombone, tuba, and drums.[101] Pianos and pianists were so abundant and cheap that they were limited only by space: at least one band featured five players on three instruments.[102] Weaning to new styles was assisted by such tutors as 'Secrets of Dance Playing' by Billy Thorburn, pianist of the Savoy Orpheans, and the 'Billy Mayerl School of Modern Syncopation', available by correspondence;[103] but above all by listening to records and the wireless.

Dance-band players were therefore not exclusively a new breed. Indeed, a decade later their 'commercial' music was ridiculed by the self-consciously amateur New Orleans revivalists who claimed to be playing 'the real authentic jazz for the first time in England'.[104] But in the 1920s there were already sufficient men of a new type to excite intense antagonism from established musicians. Pedants, accustomed to the manipulation of inanimate notes, and players for whom the ability to read all 'dots' at sight was the *sine qua non* of professional status, were equally outraged. Their distress was compounded by diverse prejudices and fears: moral disapproval, distaste for undignified cavorting, and apprehension at encroachment upon hard-won skills. Nothing could be more alien to their conception of music as written, studied, and instructed than the seemingly anarchic and untutored raw vitality of the new noise.[105]

Good Times

The 1920s were a golden age for orchestral players, if not for orchestral playing. Their situation was described by the League of Nations Report as 'splendide', with improved working conditions, good wages, and a near immunity to the unemployment which was ravaging musicians in some countries and many other occupations in Britain. This good fortune was obviously attributable to cinemas and immigration barriers which the Government, in consultation with the union, had made 'pratiquement prohibitive'.[106] Dan Godfrey reached the same conclusions, and was perturbed by the effects of such prosperity on playing standards. Applauding the ban on foreigners, he argued that high salaries and the unprecedented offer of '*permanent* engagements' (his italics) in cinemas, were tempting young instrumentalists to abandon their studies and 'lapse into a state of mediocrity'.[107]

A remarkable expression of the new optimism is 'Music as a Profession', published in 1925. Writing in an Americanized idiom of breezy commercialism, its author, Basil Hogarth, departs from a shelf of predecessors by radiating enthusiasm. Acknowledging that Victorian parents had been wise to protect children from a career in music, he asserts that times have changed and 'a decidedly reasonable living' can now be assured.[108] From £10 to £40 a week is a common salary; and a 'cute artist' can earn between £350 and £450 a year; £200 or £300 in the cinema, £30 in concert work, £20 from 'sidelines' like journalism, and £100 from pupils. Since the musician's income was now 'as good and as secure as that of an established medical practitioner', his profession would soon be 'acclaimed as safe for the newcomer as the law or medicine', accountancy, pharmacy, or banking.[109] Although these assessments of income and status were sanguine, and irresponsible in so far as they promoted recruitment, their lower estimates were not wholly misleading. Cinema wages, by far the most important component, varied widely, but were probably close, on average, to Hogarth's minimum figure of £4 a week. In the early 1920s they were subject to cuts during the summer, at least in smaller provincial and suburban houses, but the circuits soon began to stabilize employment, and raise wages, to attract and retain better players.

Despite necessary reservations as to the reliability of published information about musicians' fees, and particularly their incomes, it is possible to make a few tentative generalizations about levels of remuneration. We have one dependable source: a union 'price list' for London in 1926. Recommended fees for orchestral rank and file ranged from a minimum of 12s. 6d. a night in West End theatres and cinemas, to £1. 5s. 0d. for symphony concerts and recording sessions. Principals received a few shillings more, and leaders approximately twice the standard rate. Sunday and overtime work, after 11.30 p.m., was also paid double.[110] Fees in London were usually somewhat higher than in the provinces; a few individuals could negotiate better terms; and doubtless some players, particularly in small dance bands and 'fleapit' cinemas accepted lower rates. But since the majority of players were members of the union these figures probably give a fair approximation of the general level of payments. Another union document indicates that additional fees of 5s. (7s. 6d. for principals) were asked for provincial 'broadcast relays'.[111] London broadcasts were more lucrative. If the majority of players earned no more than £200 a year, this represented an improvement over pre-war conditions, both in real income, and in comparison with other occupations. Between 1906 and 1924 rank-and-file wages probably doubled, keeping well ahead of living costs, and became less susceptible to seasonal fluctuations and the whims of employers. In 1924 a musician earning £200 was above the average level of semi-skilled (£158) and skilled (£182) workers, or the London postman's £160; and was, in that sense, better off than his predecessors.[112]

One can distinguish three fairly distinct groups, separated by income and primarily, though not consistently, by marketable skills (which were not always commensurate with training or musicianship). By far the largest category consisted mainly of older and weaker players, working in small provincial cinemas, declining music-halls and theatres, with insufficient technique, flair, or ambition to occupy better positions. Their ranks were constantly being replenished by amateurs and part-timers, primarily in cinema and dance bands, but also in response to new opportunities, such as a skating boom, which temporarily increased the demand for wind players.[113] Some of these newcomers were familiar with new instruments and styles, but their skills were easily acquired, and therefore vulnerable. The whole group was enjoying tolerably full employment because practically every form of entertainment still required 'live' music. By the late 1920s it probably numbered some 20,000 players.

A second group of no more than 3,000 musicians were better equipped, with conventional or newly fashionable skills, which earned them between £200 and £500 a year. Organists who could 'avoid a churchy style' were earning between £6 and £8 a week;[114] and considerably more in super cinemas. Competent orchestral players did traditional jobs in Manchester and, particularly, in London's West End, but many were also eagerly sought by the super cinemas, better dance bands, and as principals and leaders in theatres, music-halls, and cinemas throughout the land. Some were accomplished musicians. The Lyons chain of restaurants, for example, which spent £150,000 a year on music,[115] engaged Margaret Holloway, a pupil of Auer, to lead its ladies orchestra at the Oxford Street 'corner house'.[116] Gerald Jackson played in one of their teashops. Henry Farmer (1882–1965), the leading authority on military music, orientalist, polymath, and union official, directed the orchestra at the Empire Theatre, Glasgow. Louis Levy, who was soon to dominate music in British film studios, presided over twenty instrumentalists and two organists at the 'vast new super cinema' in Shepherds Bush.[117] Spike Hughes earned £10 with his bass for a six-day week in the relief band at the Café de Paris; and considered it preferable drudgery to that of a previous generation, when Gustav Holst had played the trombone in music halls and a 'White Viennese' band.[118] James Blades earned £10 a week in the Claribel Band, performing at *three* cinemas; and £8 during the summer in the Isle of Man. Such musicians had little in common, except marketable skills.

A few hundred musicians of diverse but scarce talent formed an élite, in economic, if not always strictly musical terms. Highest paid were the fashionable band-leaders, led by Ambrose, who allegedly received £10,000 a year for presiding at the Mayfair Hotel and guiding the future Monarch's faltering dance steps.[119] Even the dozen or so serious conductors and established soloists could not aspire to that income and life-style: Beecham, of course, was *sui generis*; and McCormack, whose fabulous income was greatly enriched by recordings, had become an American citizen. British artists earned much less. During the Hallé Orchestra's 1929–30 season in London, for example, Jelly D'Aranyi and Moiseiwitsch each received fees of £52. 10s. 0d., and Suggia £42.[120] It is unlikely that these outstandingly popular artists secured 200 similar engagements in a year: the biographer of Myra Hess cites 100 concerts as evidence of exceptional activity.[121] The American market could be far more remunerative, but only a few British musicians were, as yet, in regular demand; and, like Hess, they tended to accept low fees.

Far below these levels were the leading orchestral instrumentalists, who accumulated an adequate income from long hours of hectic sight-reading and untrammelled exploitation of the deputy system. To maximize financial benefits they had to be based in London. Their traditional chores in theatre and concert hall were now supplemented by recording the classical repertory for HMV and Columbia, occasional broadcasts, and brief forays, for special occasions, into the cinema. Most of them took turns to attend 'an occasional afternoon's or evening's engagement' with Goossens and Douglas Fairbanks, and no doubt the pick of them were available for the voiceless *Rosenkavalier*.[122] From these exhausting routines they may have accumulated incomes equivalent to that of an average doctor (£723); but it was generally acknowledged that none earned £1,000 a year, the salary of a principal in the civil service, and considerably less than the earnings of successful men in those professions with which Hogarth had made glib comparisons.[123]

Serious music did not prosper among all this activity. Symphony concerts and opera were worst affected because their costs were unavoidably high. In 1926 orchestras in Manchester, Bournemouth, Birmingham, Eastbourne, Hastings, Glasgow, and Edinburgh all reported substantial losses.[124] The Albert Hall's shareholders faced a deficit of nearly £2,000, and considered alternative uses for a 'faded relic of a bygone age'.[125] Even the Queen's Hall was threatened with conversion to cinema. The BBC's rescue of the Proms was a portent of future progress, but inadequate, as yet, to finance properly rehearsed concerts. Apart from a few weeks at Covent Garden, and the Old Vic's frugal glories, where Lilian Baylis was uniquely capable of applying shoe-string economics, opera was notable for projects rather than achievements. The 'National Opera Trust' was attempting to raise £500,000. There were rumours of a Beecham opera company. Isidore de Lara planned a national opera house, to be large enough for cheap seats. Ethel Smyth contemplated a London Repertory Opera. The general public was said to be confused by such a multiplicity of schemes, but was probably indifferent. The British National Opera Company was still touring, but had to appeal for £25,000 to cover losses from a season which had shrunk from forty weeks to twenty-six.[126]

Financial insecurity was accompanied by artistic enfeeblement. In 1927 a visit by the Berlin Philharmonic under Furtwängler demonstrated the inadequacy of customary London makeshifts. A few patriots attributed the audience's enthusiasm to snobbery, or declared a belief that too much discipline was bad for music,[127] but the truth, as Francis Toye indicated, was less comfortable. Without a permanent orchestra the public normally had to make do with the impromptu efforts of 'a pool of players from which . . . some three orchestras can be formed, at a pinch'.[128] It was an accurate, but superficial explanation. A ludicrously overworked deputy system was undoubtedly responsible for slovenly, ill-prepared concerts, and for a general inducement to mediocrity. But at root the problem was economic, as Beecham and Wood, accustomed to extracting music from refractory material, were quick to point out. Sir Thomas declared, with customary acerbity, that the typical London concert was a disgrace simply because the available cash was sufficient only for 'prodigious sight reading'.[129] Sir Henry, recently returned from the cultural delights of Los Angeles, complained that too much money was spent on training musicians and too little on employing them; and explained that 'rich Americans pay for orchestras; rich Englishmen don't'.[130] Without public or private patronage no orchestra could achieve stability and distinction.

In addition to providing inadequate support for concerts and opera, market forces, assisted by current levels of taste, led to a curiously inept distribution of orchestral resources. While managements imposed Draconian reductions in the opera house (a band of eighteen for the Old Vic *Tristan*),[131] 'full' orchestras were *de rigeur* in the concert hall, without regard to repertory. Edward Clark's experiments in 1921 with a 'small' orchestra of fifty players, were therefore welcomed by some reformers as a possible solution to the crisis.[132] Others suggested that audiences should be attracted by more comfortable accommodation, as in better cinemas. Radicals advocated a retreat from 'the blasé upper and middle classes', taking music to the common people. During the General Strike d'Aranyi played to 2,000 allegedly enthusiastic dockers; and soon afterwards the Brosa Quartet were observed dispensing Mozart and Beethoven at twopenny concerts in the People's Palace, Mile End.[133] Optimists expressed confidence in the 'innate musical capacity of the nation' which, educated by the necessary repetition of gramophone, cinema, and wireless, would soon 'fill the concert halls'.[134] Pessimists were content to declare London 'the most unmusical city in the world'[135] and Britain still 'the land without music'.[136] No one made sufficient allowance for the time which was necessary for adjustment between musicians and audiences in these watershed years. New influences were slowly beginning to educate a wider audience. 'Musical appreciation is the latest craze', wrote a contributor to the *Gramophone* magazine in 1925; 'nowadays you don't let your children learn to play the piano and inflict themselves . . . you buy a gramophone and let them listen to good music till they appreciate it'.[137] The message was biased and premature, but not wholly misleading. Above all the BBC was beginning its great cultural mission. 'In five years time', wrote Percy Scholes in 1923, 'the general musical public of these islands will treble or quadruple its present size'.[138] It took longer, and met countervailing forces.

Meanwhile gifted musicians frequently had to quell their sense of vocation. Singers were particularly vulnerable, faced by the decline of oratorio and ballad (Chappell's series ended in 1926), and negligible opportunities in opera. Even the exquisite Maggie Teyte was forced into musical comedy, and 'variety' at the Victoria Palace.[139] But the bulk of practitioners were unconcerned with these niceties. Their market was undiscriminating and shifts in direction always led to more jobs.

X

Technology Takes Command

You ain't heard nothing yet.

Al Jolson, 1929

Music demands more from a listener than simply the possession of a tape machine or a transistor radio . . . some preparation, some effort.[1]

Benjamin Britten, 1964

The early 1930s were watershed years for professional musicians. Three influences coalesced to transform their world: technology, patronage, and the collapse of domestic music-making. Only the latter was gradual and slow in effect, an inheritance from the twenties, eroding the demand for traditional forms of low-level teaching. If the origins of technology and patronage could also be traced to the recent past, their impact was sudden and dramatic, displacing cinema orchestras and establishing the BBC as central to the distribution of music. The effects of all three determining factors, interconnected and cumulative, were peculiarly difficult for contemporaries to comprehend and assimilate. They coincided, first with the onset of economic depression, and then with the exodus of Jewish musicians. In the long run they had to be absorbed in the context of fundamental changes in western music: serious composers failing to communicate with the public; popular entertainers ceasing to require formal training. All of this challenged traditional values and institutions, destroying entrenched interests, and offered fresh opportunities. In times of flux it was inevitable that people should attribute misfortune to temporary events, rather than root causes. Thus the recession was customarily blamed for causing, as distinct from exacerbating, distress; and remedies were sought by appeals to Government for assistance and protection. In fact large numbers of musicians would have suffered almost as badly in a buoyant economy, because their rejection was the result of a collapse in demand, rather than a temporary shortage of purchasing power.

Some of these changes can be illustrated by statistics. The effect on total numbers during the next twenty years was unequivocal. Between

1931 and 1951 (there was no census in 1941) the number of musicians recorded in the census fell from approximately 26,000 to 15,000; of music teachers, from 21,000 to 11,000. Like all such figures they are underestimates, but there is no reason to believe that they exaggerate the decline. In proportion to total population it was even more precipitous.[2] There are other simple indicators. The number of musicians listed in trade directories, for example, fell sharply in practically every town. Statistics of unemployment are more complex, and require some interpretation.

Widespread adoption of a new technology had usually been a slow process in Britain, delayed by problems of assimilation, real or imagined, and effective opposition from vested interests, including trade unions. The application of sound to film was an extraordinary exception to this general pattern. *The Jazz Singer* was first shown in New York in October 1927; and within two years over 9,000 American cinemas were wired for sound. In Britain the transformation was almost as rapid, after an initial delay. By the summer of 1932 more than 4,000 cinemas were devoted to 'talkies' and only 900 small and remote houses remained silent. The effect on musicians' employment was catastrophic. According to the 1931 census 7,458 male and 2,013 female musicians were out of work: 38 per cent and 32 per cent of their respective totals. At a time when the general level of unemployment was unprecedented, these proportions were much higher than in most occupations; more than double the average, and from nine to twenty times worse than in the professions. Only among actors was the incidence of unemployment comparable.[3]

Even these appalling figures understate the musicians' plight, for several reasons. They were collected before the final annihilation of silent films in 1932, by which time some 12,000 to 15,000 may have lost their jobs. Many displaced players could not draw the dole because they were assumed to have been earning more than the limit of £250, which excluded them from national insurance.[4] Most grievous was the fact that, unlike other unemployed workers at that time, cinema players were victims of technological, not cyclical, unemployment, and could therefore expect no reinstatement when business improved. Perhaps the majority would never again find adequate alternative employment as musicians. Drawn predominantly from the poorest group of players, described on p. 205, they were accustomed to the anonymity and simple, old-fashioned routines of provincial music-halls and darkened cinemas. Few were capable of more demanding work, for recording and radio, or suited to the highly visible antics of dance and show bands. Finally there was a regional aspect to their misfortune, a cruel juxtaposition of time and place; for most of them were trapped in the old northern industrial districts, where the general economic depression was far more serious and persistent than in the south.[5] Only younger, better, or more enterprising players, like Jackson and Blades, escaped to London, which had become the undisputed centre of a new entertainment industry, flourishing despite the slump, but highly selective in its recruitment of musicians.

Unemployment among music teachers did not appear in the census, but this was merely a statistical anomaly. Since most of them were self-employed, enforced idleness took the form of 'underemployment', a slower, equally painful atttrition, not recorded by the enumerators. The demand for teachers was falling, for reasons less immediate and obvious than the impact of talkies on cinema orchestras, reflecting new patterns of leisure, consumption, and social emulation. The great majority of lessons had been connected with the ownership of pianos: having prospered together for a century, they were now jointly in decline.[6] As instrumental study became increasingly an expression of musical, rather than social, aspirations, standards of elementary instruction may have improved, assisted by the rising expectations of a public educated by records and radio, and by reforms within the profession, but numbers of lessons fell. As with orchestral players, it was the bulk of mediocre practitioners who became casualties, trying to hold on in grinding, unprotected poverty. In 1934 a representative music teacher complained to the *Observer* that her pupils had been reduced in six years from thirty to three. In 'starvation and hopelessness' she appealed for 'work, not charity'.[7] Neither was forthcoming.

The economics of technological innovation and patronage profoundly changed the relationship between musicians and their audiences. The crucial effect of technology was to break that firm link which had always existed between a demand for music and the simultaneous employment of musicians. Those who found work in recording, broadcasting, and film studios were singularly favoured, not merely because their efforts were indispensable to the productive process, at least until the arrival of synthesizers, but also because their productivity was enormously increased, belatedly enabling them to bid for remuneration comparable with workers elsewhere. Those outside fell victim to 'Baumol's Disease', except where they could be assisted by subsidies from private or public patrons.[8] The economics of their live performances retained the characteristics of pre-industrial work, low in productivity and therefore increasingly difficult to finance by sales of tickets, if the players were to be adequately rehearsed and paid. It still took four musicians an expensive half hour to play a Haydn quartet to a small audience; but eventually, thanks to technology and economics of scale, *recordings* of a lavish opera could be profitably sold, and repeatedly enjoyed, for less than the unsubsidized cost of a ticket to a single live performance.

Except in cinemas, where expensive equipment and appropriate acoustics rapidly established the new medium, technology did not take command overnight. Its use in public places was limited by the deficiences, inconvenience, and high cost of 78 r.p.m. records, and primitive relay systems. But there were some experiments. In 1930 dancers at the Tottenham Palais were offered food, a floor, and blaring loudspeakers, which were reported to have reduced them to 'a contingent of miserable soulless automatons':[9] a condition then regarded as unsuitable for humanity. The age of discos and inescapable background noise was still a generation away. Neither juke-boxes nor 'wired music', which flooded America during the 1930s, were common in Britain.[10] Musicians therefore continued to be employed, in hotels, restaurants,[11] dance halls, and on passenger ships (the latter, too, destined for oblivion), in concert halls, and the dwindling theatre.

While domestic muisic-making all but perished, music flooded into people's homes, the number of radio licences increasing to 9m. by 1939, seventy-three out of every 100 households in the United Kingdom.[12] Revenue from licence fees enabled the BBC to introduce patronage as a major determinant of the country's musical life. It rapidly became the largest employer of musicians. For composers it provided 35 per cent of the Performing Right Society's revenue in 1930, rising to 50 per cent by 1945.[13] Competent performers enjoyed a wide range of opportunities. By 1939 the Corporation was employing some 400 orchestral musicians on regular contracts, and offering several thousand occasional engagements. This patronage could have been allocated, with 'fair shares for all' in passive response to the lobbying of professional and commercial pressure groups. Instead it was distributed with the deliberate intention of moulding public taste, in an attempt to reverse centuries of philistinism and neglect. Like the Victorian reformers,[14] Reith wanted to raise standards. Unlike them, argues an American historian, 'he had the means to do so . . . It was in large part owing to the work of the BBC that Great Britain began to gain that reputation as a land of cultural distinction that would have amazed most Englishmen half a century before'.[15] This generous verdict, tending perhaps to equate aspirations with achievements, is nevertheless a refreshing antidote to conventional sneers at Reith's Calvinistic authoritarianism.

Conflict and adjustment

The Union's unavoidable but useless attempt to defeat sound films deserves close study because it was the first major conflict with technology. Ineptly fought against overwhelming odds, the battle almost destroyed a union which was singularly unprepared for battle. Its membership and income were mainly drawn from the most vulnerable group of players. Its leaders were elderly and unaccustomed to command. Indifferent or even antagonistic to the industry's new developments, their remoteness was symbolized, and given practical effect, by retaining headquarters in Manchester. For an account of the struggle we are largely dependent upon the voluminous writing of one of them, Henry Farmer, who began to edit the union's journal in 1929, and filled its columns, under a multitude of pseudonyms. His chronicle of defeat begins with attempts to dismiss sound films as a temporary aberration from the great silent tradition: reasonable at first, because silent films commanded loyal audiences, and early experiments with sound were often crude and unconvincing. But prejudiced reports continued to be circulated long after the public had been won over by the new medium; they ceased to make sense, except as an increasingly unconvincing attempt to raise morale.

Appeals were addressed to the government, and to the public's innate good taste and (anti-American) patriotism. The former was asked, and refused, to limit either the importation or the exhibiting of films, so that only half would contain 'mechanised music'. Cinemas were urged to advertise that 'Silent pictures are best, with the best music from professional musicians'.[16] Magistrates were asked to refuse licences to managers who failed to employ 'a human orchestra', and the public to boycott them. Some 600,000 handbills, leaflets, and posters were distributed. Members of Parliament, trade union secretaries, and journalists were lobbied, allegedly with great effect: 'By propaganda, the Americans have forced the Talkies down the throat of the public, and by *our* propaganda—which we might call an emetic—we have forced them to throw them back again'.[17] The Irish government was praised for imposing a tax on sound films which was expected to conjure 'the general return of kinema orchestras'. In June 1930 Union members were assured that 'the Atlantic deluge has spent its force and has failed to submerge the art of real music and those dependent on it'.[18] In October 1931 they were told that talkies were 'losing their hold'and future cinemas would depend upon 'variety and bands'.[19]

The demonstrable absurdity of these claims led Farmer to vent his spleen on 'the immodesty, nay immorality, aye—even the filth of the modern film'.[20] The *Daily Telegraph* was quoted with warm approval: 'Americans have everything for the making of good films except decent minds'.[21] The *Methodist Times* was applauded for condemning the cinema as 'a den of vice and iniquity'.[22] Musicians were assured that 'sooner or later human music will prevail' but meanwhile they should economize by drinking water, a 'far more substantial beverage than the expensive drinks that only Ministers in the Labour Government can afford'.[23] Frustration had engendered a self-defeating petulance and prissiness, curiously inappropriate for men whose livelihood depended upon entertainment. More positive, but equally fruitless, was an attempt to prohibit members of the Union from recording music for films by creating a 'Musical Performers' Protection Association Ltd'.[24] It aimed to control the production and use of records and sound films; grant licences and conduct legal proceedings. Here was a key to future tactics, but its initial design was ill-considered and grandiloquent, requiring no subscription or meaningful commitment, and therefore attracting vociferous support from those least able to enforce its uncompromising demands. The Association made a single, unsuccessful appearance in court, attempting to restrain use of the soundtrack from Hitchcock's film *Blackmail*,[25] and then petered out. By 1932 it was admitting that 'the avalanche of mechanical music ... has been too much for us'.[26] Discussion with the International Confederation of Musicians was equally futile: a typical recommendation was that restaurant musicians should avoid playing music from *The Jazz Singer* and *The Love Parade* because it encouraged people to attend cinemas.[27]

Attempts to enlist support at the 1929 Trades Union Congress in Belfast were a fiasco. Instead of concentrating upon the main issue of 'mechanical music and unemployment', in which the musicians were joined by the theatrical employees, time was wasted and tempers frayed by preliminary resolutions about competition from police and army bands; a 'hardy annual' so boring to delegates that it had to be 'shouted out amidst a general hubbub'.[28] The main resolution was opposed, as a useless attempt to impede progress, and because it might embarrass the Labour Government. Old prejudices were reawakened at a time of universal distress in the labour movement: distrust of 'two jobbers' and the deep-rooted belief that musicians are not real workers. In 1906 an American economist had noted the 'long struggle of the musicians to get themselves looked upon as workers instead of players'.[29] Hanns Eisler describes a universal tendency: the musician has created 'the illusion that he does it for fun, that he earns his living without honest labour, and this very illusion is easily exploited'.[30] Thus it was in Belfast that the goodwill and influence in the labour movement, which Williams had done so much to create, was dissipated in mutual recrimination. The *Daily Herald* was 'amused' and the musicians' representatives 'disgusted'.[31] At the next year's Congress, protests against 'the wiping out of an entire branch of the profession by this Americanised mechanical monstrosity' received some sympathy, but were swept aside by the powerful president of the Amalgamated Engineers Union, who explained that talkies had *created* jobs for his men.[32]

In 1931, wrote a Birmingham contributor to the *Sackbut*, professional musicians faced 'the most distressing and critical period ever known'.[33]

The state of the Union's finances was revealed in a desperate appeal. Despite reductions in the number and salaries of officials, expenditure was exceeding income, which had declined from £18,000 to £13,000 in two years, and was continuing to fall as members were forced out. The pamphlet's exhortations to 'avoid pessimists and disloyalists, scaremongers and mischief-makers', and 'beware of disruption and the hidden hand', were still larded with forecasts of doom for the talkies: 'There is reliable information that in the U.S.A. the reaction has set in'.[34] Meanwhile the union's ability to adapt to radical change was stifled by its loyalty to a majority of members who were unable to keep up their contributions or render practical support. This commitment was reinforced by the election for General Secretary which had to follow Teale's death. The victor, Frederic Dambman, was a long-serving official whose background and support were overwhelmingly provincial. Out of 3,198 votes he collected only seventy-eight in London; his nearest rival polled a total of 1,482 votes, 1,017 from the metropolis.[35]

The rift could scarcely have been more complete. Born in the provinces, the Union seemed likely to die there. Some musicians would continue to make a living in the provinces, but the real opportunities, as never before, were in London, where many were learning to survive and even prosper in the new environment. A revitalized union would have to base itself there; or stay 'altogether out of touch'[36] and perish. Two groups of London musicians were of paramount importance: the best orchestral players, who were about to enjoy the linked benefits of improved job security and artistic discipline; and dance band performers, who were working in a protected 'infant industry'. As employer, and creator of reputations and standards, the BBC was in a commanding position. In 1930 it created, for the first time in Britain, a permanent symphony orchestra, with full-time contracts. The significance of this event can hardly be exaggerated; it receives only brief notice in these pages because it has been fully documented in an indispensable book, which requires no further gloss.[37]

Orchestral reform was not confined to the BBC, though it was undoubtedly precipitated by the Corporation's initiatives, in the teeth of opposition from men like Beecham and Harty,[38] who had done much to build orchestras in impossible conditions, and many others who had done nothing. In 1932 Beecham established the London Philharmonic, a blend of experienced and young freelance instrumentalists, with contracts less exclusive than the BBC's, but sufficiently permanent to ensure stability and ensemble for a few years, until his wealthy friends withdrew their support, illustrating the limitations of private patronage.[39] Thus within five years London's orchestral life was transformed from fustian mediocrity to undoubted excellence, as the superb HMV and

Columbia recordings of the 1930s bear witness. It was achieved without need of foreign musicians, apart from visiting conductors and soloists. Inevitably it aroused provincial enmities, particularly in Manchester, where Harty had presided over the country's best orchestra, and naturally resented 'poaching' of his principal instrumentalists. The Hallé steadily declined until it began to revive under Barbirolli in 1943. Meanwhile some of its players were assisted by employment in the BBC Northern Orchestra after 1934.[40] There were similar arrangements in Birmingham, Cardiff, Edinburgh, and Belfast.

Although the Union was involved in negotiating these new symphony orchestra contracts, its principal concern continued to be with 'popular' musicians; yet it was in this area that headquarters was most out of touch. Far from representing dance band performers, the *Journal* alternated between indifference and open disdain. One particularly supercilious essay earned a rebuke in the *Melody Maker* which demanded that 'the Diehards' be restrained.[41] Farmer was at the centre of this controversy. Probably the most able official, after Williams's departure, certainly the most educated and articulate, he devoted prodigious energy to the Union but, like most of his provincial colleagues, remained profoundly unsympathetic to the new generation of popular musicians. Wounds had recently been salted when the *Melody Maker* challenged his competence to judge a band contest, and had to settle out of court for 50 gns.[42]

In August 1930 some 500 players met to establish a Dance Band Section of the Union.[43] Several were prominently successful men. Jack Payne was already a seasoned and popular broadcaster, director of the BBC Dance Orchestra.[44] Jack Hylton was a pioneer of on-stage showbands, with wide experience. Ambrose, 'holiday-making on the Continent', sent his manager. Their attitudes and demeanour were remote from lost battles, but conditioned by harsh experience. In 1928, when the BBC appointed Jack Payne, there had been a dearth of suitable groups. By 1937 its Director of Variety would be able to report 'an ample supply of dance bands and the facility to create as many as we like'.[45] In the interim players sought to protect their livelihood by similar procedures to those which had been perfected by Williams, but adapted to new conditions and couched in a new language. They wanted to secure minimum wages by 'complete unionisation', including the 'semi-pros' who, as they acknowledged, could not be prevented from taking 'gigs'. Their strongest card, which they were determined to preserve, was the exclusion of 'aliens', which in this case meant Americans.[46]

Foreign bands and rank-and-file players, classical or popular, were already effectively prevented from working in Britain, but soloists were more of a problem. Hylton, himself a recent victim of union intransigence in New York,[47] sounded a warning note. A few 'star foreigners', he argued, could raise a band's musical standard, and perhaps its remuneration, not least by securing recording contracts.[48] This practice, which had become common among the finest jazz musicians, doubtless continued. It was described by Farmer, without conscious irony, as 'dilution' of labour.[49] A few artists of genius, including Louis Armstrong and Sidney Bechet, were briefly heard; and one American, who had entered music via a Salvation Army band, became one of London's most fashionable band leaders.[50] But generally the union succeeded in persuading employers, sometimes reluctant, and officials, usually complaisant, to seal hatches which were already tight. A few months after the dance band section was formed an 'extremely friendly meeting' took place between representatives of the Ministry of Labour, the union, and leading hotels and restaurants. Procedures were agreed for preliminary consultation before the award of labour permits.[51] Prevailing attitudes were so restrictive that even exchange visits were frowned upon. Thus a 'Negro band from Paris' was refused permission to 'change places with the English band at a prominent West End club'.[52]

In 1931 the 'diehards' bowed to the inevitable and shifted the union's headquarters to London. Old loyalties had delayed, but could not prevent, realignment and the acceptance of new realities. Unable to defeat the first onslaught of technology, the union had to learn how to tame its later manifestations and, in the process, abandon those who could no longer be defended. Once the move had been accomplished, new attitudes could soon be discerned, in hesitant acknowledgement that 'mechanical devices have come to stay'[53] and even that 'the more skilled performer is finding no difficulty in getting placed'.[54] In 1932 the painful but inescapable process of casting off began with a refusal to continue granting exemptions from payment of subscriptions.[55] The fall in membership, already serious, inevitably accelerated. A total of 20,000 in 1929 was reduced to 16,000 in 1930, 13,000 in 1931, 10,000 in 1933, and less than 8,000 in the following year.[56] Then our records cease for several years. Disillusioned with labour politics,[57] the leaders no longer attended TUC conferences, whose reports give figures for participating unions. Copies of the *Musicians' Journal and Report*, if they exist, are also unprocurable. Even Farmer was silent, occupied with further research in Oriental music.

The union's subsequent history can only be sketched. Membership recovered so vigorously that by 1950 it had risen to 27,000 of whom about 1,500 were women.[58] There is an enormous discrepancy between these figures and the census returns, presumably because part-timers had again become a large part of the labour force. The union succeeded

in recruiting enough of them to reassert its bargaining power. Evidently
Dambman became an effective leader, despite his initial association with
the old guard. He was joined by Hardie Ratcliffe, who took over as
general secretary in 1948: 'a doughty fighter for the view that musicians'
jobs—and indeed live music itself—were endangered by modern
technology'.[59] Their militancy reflected the bitterness of the early
thirties, but it was mild in comparison with their flamboyant American
contemporary, who fought similar battles in a blaze of publicity. James
Caesar Petrillo had risen to power by organizing musicians in Chicago,
where 2,000 cinema players had been reduced to 125 by talkies; and
bomb attacks and bullet-proof cars accompanied the job.[60] Becoming
the highest-paid labour leader in the United States, and a 'national
symbol of union intransigence',[61] he imposed, in 1942, a ban on
recording which lasted for more than two years, undeterred by President
Roosevelt, and resulted in contracts which were 'a milestone in labour
relations'.[62]

The British musicians frequently supported Petrillo's actions,[63] and
devised similar policies in a gentler environment. Unlike many
American radio stations, for example, the BBC did not play recordings
'with the specific intention of misleading the public into the belief that a
live rendition was taking place'.[64] Any likelihood of their indiscriminate
use was prevented by a series of 'needle-time' agreements, which
restricted the broadcasting of commercial records; not merely in return
for specific payments, but as continuing protection for live performers.[65]
The repetition of recordings made during broadcasts was also rigorously
controlled.[66] Such safeguards became all the more important with the
introduction of tape-recording and long-playing discs. Wherever
musicians were employed, wage rates, hours, and conditions of work
were enforced in closed shops, backed, if necessary, by 'blunt strike
threats'.[67] These actions were often criticized by 'those who think music
and trade unionism fit ill together'.[68] As in the past, the Union was
frequently condemned for philistine indifference to artistic standards. A
seminal book on the professions suggests that, like the National Union
of Journalists, the Musicians' Union was narrowly protectionist: 'In the
typical "professional" association, though disciplinary action may be
employed for protective purposes, these are never the sole or even the
chief uses to which it is put'.[69] The observation refers to conditions in
the late twenties but, so far as musicians were concerned, it was no less
true after the toughening experiences of the subsequent decade. Yet it is
arguably misplaced because, as our study has shown, the Musicians'
Union never pretended to be a professional association. Protection of
members was its sole purpose, and in that single-mindedness lay its
strength, sometimes inducing unpalatable rigidities: non-members, for

example, were allowed to conduct, but not play: a rule which did not fit the revival of baroque performing practices.[70] Insecurity does not beget liberalism.

Defending a heritage

If a powerful trade union had difficulty in adjusting to new conditions, a feeble professional association was hard put to it to justify its continued existence. Like the Union, the ISM was unable to protect the most vulnerable of its members, and was forced to voice their frustration, while attempting to recruit from a new generation of musicians, with different expectations. It managed to retain between 3,000 and 4,000 members, probably because the new sectional organization imposed some coherence. Nearly 500 music masters and mistresses were drawn from grammar and public schools. A cinema organists' group survived until 1938. More important was the soloists' section, with over 500 members by the late thirties, including some who achieved, and many who aspired to that status. Morale was boosted, and music occasionally served: by a campaign, for example, against the imposition of entertainment tax on non-profit-making music societies.[71]

Unlike the Union, however, the ISM allowed its own breed of 'diehard' to remain in place, assuming the right to speak, not merely for 'the profession', but for the nation's music. These presumptions were couched in language which impeded perceptions of reality, perpetuating a brand of that mythology with which institutions are prone to clothe an undistinguished heritage. Pronouncements were delivered *de haut en bas*, with a confidence in society's acquiescence which was sorely misplaced. There was indeed a new militancy during the early thirties,[72] but it was difficult to reconcile with continuing postures of high-minded professionalism; and nothing could be more futile than abrasive gestures in defence of an obsolete pedantry which had rarely impinged upon the living world of music, and was fast losing any vestige of public support.

The Society's sole objectives, claimed its president in 1930, were to preserve the dignity of the profession and the musical well-being of the community. A few months later his successor was declaring: 'I am a Trade Unionist and regard the ISM as being a Trade Union before anything'.[73] No disagreement was intended, as an editorial in the Society's journal explained, attempting, with learned references to Francis Bacon, to elucidate the impenetrable. Tired images of 'professionalism' were resurrected to revive the dying tradition of Chadfield and Southgate.[74] A lecturer at the 1936 conference reached new depths of obscurantism with four incantations in a single sentence: original aims had been 'very largely achieved' since 'the profession of music is recognised by every other professional body as a "profession", and it is in a real sense a "quantified" profession'.[75]

Practical efforts were largely confined to lobbying Government and the BBC, the former to exclude foreigners, the latter on a wider front. As a 'manifesto', signed by the directors of the RAM and RCM, made clear, the 1931 crisis was conceived solely in xenophobic terms. The *Musical Times* agreed, arguing that, in the absence of an informed public opinion, 'both educated and patriotic', the Ministry of Labour should 'act in regard to concert artists as it does in dealing with dance bands and other forms of imported labour'.[76] Leaving American popular musicians to the Union, except for an occasional cinema organist, the ISM concentrated its fire on classical soloists and chamber groups, precipitating a public outcry, and the resignation of some distinguished members.

Open debate began with the publication of a letter from an archdeacon, protesting against the exclusion of an eminent foreign quintet from a Newcastle's society's season. This 'singular manifestation of the "buy British" policy' offended the 'comity of art', revived wartime prejudices, and would excite reprisals.[77] The ISM's secretary retorted that Newcastle had booked only one English artist, out of eight recitals; that times were hard, and that it was practically impossible for Englishmen to get foreign engagements.[78] The acerbic tenor, Stewart Wilson, pointed to protectionism in France, and suggested that foreign competition did not threaten the livelihood of the established clergy.[79] Several music lovers supported the archdeacon and cited further examples of 'narrow nationalism . . . a retrograde step in European civilization'.[80] Samuel Courtauld, whose rare and munificent patronage entitled him to a voice, advised that it would be foolish to 'advertise an inferiority complex'.[81] Harold Samuel, the great pianist, and Tovey resigned in protest, the former on general principle, the latter incensed by shabby treatment of a pupil.[82]

The essential questions were about artistic status and drawing-power. Government policy decreed that 'artists of clearly international standing will be admitted without conditions'; others required labour permits, which could be challenged.[83] But who should be the arbiter—the ISM, an official, or concert organizers, including the BBC, which was attempting to satisfy and extend audiences now becoming more discriminating, largely through the activities of the latter organization? Established stars presented no difficulty—few patriots advocated the exclusion of Kreisler or Schnabel—but how should younger or less renowned artistes be treated? An example was Simon Barere, a formidable Russian pianist[84] who was prevented from playing at the Queen's Hall in 1932. Farmer applauded a decision in defiance of 'drawing-room tittle tattle in the West End' and hoped for a general ban on 'foreign artists of no reputation and of mediocre attainments'. He also welcomed 'a glorious opportunity for the ISM to join forces with the Musicians' Union'.[85] Neither event took place.

A new and tragic turn of events came with the Holocaust: an agonizing problem, since people were attempting to flee for their lives, and their escape to Britain might represent, not a few concert engagements, but permanent residence and competition. Nor, it must be said, could the Society's representatives be expected to have a firmer grasp of events in Germany than the majority of their countrymen. There was also truth in a remark by Beecham, who had become the Society's atypical President in 1939. The Government, he complained, was posing as a champion of human rights, while expecting a small section of the community to assume a disproportionate share of the burden.[86] It is in this context that one must read the Society's various pronouncements about Jewish refugees. In 1935 it claimed credit for saving the country from being 'overrun with every class of foreign musician', aggravating 'an already difficult economic situation . . . quite apart from the enervating influence such foreigners would have exerted upon native musical Art'.[87] In 1938 it viewed 'with much concern the admission of large numbers of alien refugee musicians' and requested the Home Secretary to make 'a closer scrutiny of professional attainments'.[88] Perhaps the most original proposal came from a member who suggested that, as in Russia, where musicians could be sent anywhere, refugees might be invited to develop music in 'remote parts of the Empire'.[89]

The Society's most strenuous efforts were directed against the BBC. In 1936, when the Corporation's charter was due to expire, and the Ullswater Committee was considering future arrangements, a triumvirate of past, present, and future ISM presidents signed a letter to *The Times*, reporting 'the almost universal dissatisfaction now felt throughout the musical profession'. Broadcasting had 'profoundly disorganised the whole musical life of the country'. It was too centralized in London; its selection of performers and modern music reflected 'an anti-national bias'; and its choice of light music was crass. A 'Statutory Advisory Council' of professionals should be given real powers. The letter also refers to a 'reasoned and temperate memorandum' to the Ullswater Committee, which Reith accurately described in his diary as 'a monstrous document'. As Briggs observes, the 'tacit assumption that all had been well with music before the advent of the BBC' was 'a parody of the truth', and 'other remarks about music were plain nonsense'. The testimony of Adrian Boult, himself a past president of the ISM, with some claim to speak for British musicians, was dignified and crushing. In response to complaints about employment he explained that the BBC was 'the greatest employer of musicians that this country has ever known';

that it overwhelmingly favoured British solo performers; and that any substantial increase would undoubtedly lower standards.[90]

If the Society's complaints were preposterous and rightly ignored, they nevertheless reflected widespread resentments which continued to fester. In an otherwise balanced and sensible book on 'Music as a Career', published in 1939 by the editor of the *Musical Times*, condemnation of the BBC was repeated *in toto*. Its sole benefit to the profession, he argues, had been the provision of work for orchestral players. Consistently ignoring professional advice, it had managed music by 'amateur muddling', and was still allowed to do so. 'We get the BBC we deserve. We shall get a better one when we have made England a more truly musical country'.[91]

Even if one prefers overt self-interest to sciolism and cant, it would be inconsistent to condemn the Society for activities which were often similar to those of the Union, particularly since they tended to receive more publicity, and are therefore easily documented. British musicians had to assert their independence from foreign influence, and sometimes deserved preferential treatment, to encourage fresh talent and counter-balance ancient prejudices in favour of the exotic. But the ISM was unfortunate, or careless, in becoming, for a time, the principal soundboard for conservative and discredited residual elements. Its case was weakened by extravagant claims to be 'undoubtedly representative of the musical profession'[92] and able to provide sufficient native artists of high calibre. Both arguments would have some validity a generation later, but during the thirties they lacked credibility and were, on balance, ignored.

Few institutions were less capable of adjusting to the new environment than the colleges of music. Henceforth, and with increasing force, the market required fewer and better musicians. While a drastic reduction of numbers was the immediate necessity, there were new opportunities for skilled performers. Experienced orchestral instrumentalists, particularly string players; and, above all, soloists of international calibre, faced a future which, if it could never be free of hazards, was more protected than ever before. The colleges' ability to meet these requirements was limited by familiar constraints.[93] With Government grants to the RAM and RCM still a derisory £500, poverty continued to impose dependence upon student fees and ill-paid, part-time staff.

The RCM's jubilee in 1933 provided a focus for criticism, which could have been addressed, with equal force, elsewhere. Noting the 'prolonged orgy of self-congratulation', one writer acknowledged the presence of some 'splendid teaching', but deplored the influence of dillettante pupils, enjoying 'a few terms of idle music-making after leaving their high school'. A national conservatory should be prosperous enough to accept only students of 'uncommon standard'.[94]

Since there was no national conservatory, and most of the competing institutions survived the slump, inherent weaknesses were reinforced by a beleaguered parochialism; which may explain a reluctance to profit from Hitler's gifts. A committee including Michael Tippett later deplored the failure 'to secure the services of the few great Continental teachers who found in this country temporary refuge from political persecution. Several would have stayed but for the general indifference shown to their unique qualifications, and because of the active opposition organised by a number of leading musicians in the teaching profession'.[95] An exception was Max Rostal, formerly assistant to Flesch and professor at the Berlin Hochschule, who was allowed to teach at the Guildhall School of Music. His influence on the next generation of string players was later widely acknowledged; among his pupils were three members of the Amadeus Quartet.[96]

The employment of an eminent refugee was not the GSM's sole departure from current practice. Other colleges, as Thomas Russell observed, continued to be directed by latter-day Victorians, 'organists, composers of choral and religious works', who were anachronistically endowed 'with the greatest power in moulding the shape of future generations of our musicians'.[97] In contrast, the GSM appointed an unorthodox successor to Landon Ronald. Edric Cundell had played the horn at Covent Garden, and worked as a repetiteur under Fritz Busch at Glyndebourne. In place of the customary Gilbert and Sullivan, his first student production, in February 1939, was *Così Fan Tutte*. *Don Giovanni* was planned for the following year, but abandoned for obvious reasons.[98]

In a witty and perceptive essay, too idiosyncratic and tight-knit to summarize adequately, Sydney Harrison, then teaching at the GSM, anatomized the profession on the eve of the World War II. Its representative types range from the 1s.-a-lesson piano-teacher to Dr Brown, the conservatory dignitary, dispensing medals and certificates throughout the provinces, and occasionally the Empire, with a house in Hampstead, boys at a good school, and £1,000 a year in good years. There is also young Robinson (Mus.B.) teaching in a London secondary school, on an assured salary of £400, with prospects; and Sammy Katz, intended to follow an illustrious relative as a concert pianist, but content with a precarious £12 a week in a hotel dance band. Future changes, concluded Harrison, would require so many adjustments that a university should encourage social research, to chart dangerous waters.[99]

Point of change?

World War II is commonly depicted as a decisive 'point of change' for music and musicians in Britain.[100] As in 1914 an initial period of disruption was followed by a boom in leisure spending which stimulated 'phenomenal demand for all kinds of musical enterprise', in traditional centres and scattered camps.[101] In addition to extensive popular entertainment, there was a resurgence of cultural euphoria, celebrating that 'keener psychosis' which had been detected by a previous generation in similar circumstances. The prevailing images were of Myra Hess playing Mozart to uniformed audiences in the National Gallery, and common men uplifted by Beethoven's 'Victory' Symphony. Belief in the potency of 'musical appreciation' to extend and consolidate the influence of gramophone and radio, building a large and faithful audience for serious music, reached its height.

Dissenters were unconvinced by a plethora of concerts which usually consisted of the same handful of hackneyed works and fabricated film 'concertos' perfunctorily read through by scratch orchestras. The most pessimistic articulation of these doubts came from one of the country's most innovative performers. Boyd Neel was a naval officer who turned to medicine and then to music, forming in 1932 a seventeen-piece orchestra whose modest forces and lithe style anticipated a late-twentieth-century trend. Its performance of Britten's Frank Bridge Variations at the 1937 Salzburg Festival established an international reputation for both composer and orchestra. Neel's experience of wartime and immediate post-war Britain led him to distinguish between the undoubted 'great renaissance of English music' and what he regarded as dubious celebrations of cultural enlightenment. Most large audiences, he claimed, were simply exhibiting temporary bouts of 'mass hysteria ... usually connected with a stunt artist or film star'. One should not confuse great music and big music, said Britten, in a foreword to Neel's book. His scepticism was partly induced by difficulties which were soon to be overcome: inadequate concert halls, and the public's antipathy, outside London, towards such then unfamiliar works as the Brandenburg Concertos. But his forecast for the future was not so easily dismissed: 'a morass of musical inflation'.[102] It was an apt phrase, in so far as it envisaged, not merely '1812 with full cannon effects', but a continuing tendency for too many musicians to pursue too few paying customers.

In the festive climate of 'Musical Britain 1951' it was more common to believe that serious music would become an appurtenance of the welfare state, with deficiencies in market demand offset by official patronage. Not only was the BBC reaching a peak in influence and commitment to high culture, but local authorities and the newly established Arts Council appeared to promise generous disbursements of public funds. There were also indications that the Government was prepared, at last, to give adequate support to training. So far as the future of the profession was concerned, the important question was whether these new initiatives would, on balance, reduce or worsen the inescapable tendency for supply to outrun demand. While any form of public funding would help to bridge the 'Baumol gap', discriminating patronage, along lines initiated by Reith, could concentrate demand upon good music and skilled players, while selective expenditure on training could similarly restrict and focus supply.

None of this came about. On the demand side enlightened patronage was deterred by entrenched interests and, more insidiously, by a steady erosion of confidence in the nature of cultural improvement and desire for its propagation. Even the BBC eventually abandoned its proselytizing mission, and there were many who argued that the very conception of a hierarchy of taste was absurd. This was a paradigmatic change in the nation's cultural history, for whereas authority in the past had paid at least lip-service to enlightenment, and common people eagerly sought its rewards, such concern could now be deprecated as 'élitist'.[103] Qualitative aspects of this revolution were everywhere apparent, not least in music. Quantitatively it reinforced the tendency to distribute public funds like prizes for the Caucus Race. Before assessing the effects of Alice's comfits on musicians in the market-place, we must briefly survey the post-war history of its commercial, as distinct from public sector, an arbitrary procedure, of course, because they were inextricably combined.

Omnipotent technology

The most remarkable development was a long boom in the recording industry, after the innovation of long-playing, followed by stereo, discs, which lasted until the early 1970s, with London as a world centre. British pop groups became the principal exploiters of an enormous new market created by the manipulation of adolescent purchasing power. The industry's cosily monopolistic structure was transformed by a new mobile technology. British orchestras and instrumentalists were employed to record a huge repertory of serious music. One of the best orchestras ever to be assembled in Britain was financed, for a time, by recording-contracts—with assistance from a Maharaja.[104] Highly skilled musicians worked as 'backing' for pop, their traditional sight-reading ability a major asset, because it minimized time spent in studios. These new sources of income were additionally opportune, since film-studio work declined, as people stopped going to the cinema, and directors of new films no longer insisted on a ceaseless background of 'big music'.

The boom ended when 'Beatle-mania' spent its force, British groups ceased to dominate the 'charts', and classical catalogues were full. While demand for pop continued to be buoyant, because the product was ephemeral, serious music, which never accounted for more than about 6 per cent of total sales, was constrained by limited outlets for alternative versions of the same works, negligible interest in new music, and the increasingly satisfactory 'remastering' of previously recorded performances. A more damaging threat to the livelihood of every musician was the introduction of cheap cassette recorders, which allowed copying from a greatly expanded broadcasting service, and record libraries, without payments to the original artists or effective legal redress. By the 1980s between 50m. and 60m. blank cassettes were sold every year. Similar domestic 'piracy' with rented video machines had the same implications for television performers.

The recording industry was of paramount importance because its products now dominated the consumption of music: as a background to every sort of private and public activity—only silence was rare—or for intensive listening in conditions which were increasingly preferred to attending a live performance. A myriad of opportunities for the continuous employment of musicians, which had emerged during the nineteenth century, was therefore disappearing. Moreover unlimited exposure to artificial sound began to change people's perception of music. Even its basic constituents were experienced largely through the distortions of existing technology. At home the 'mellow-toned' wireless and radiogram, which used to eliminate high frequencies, were replaced by transistor radios and television sets with tiny speakers and no bass. In public, volume levels, discreet or overwhelming, bore no semblance to reality. Even 'audiophiles', who took pride in the fidelity of their reproducing systems, usually judged them without reference to live music. The typical recording became a total artefact, spliced together from bits of tape, manipulated by engineers, and often remote from the efforts and capabilities of the original performers. An extreme case was the grotesque spectacle of pop groups miming to 'their' records; but even serious musicians had to pit their live performances against the audience's expectations, which had been engendered by the impossible 'perfection' of manufactured sound. Technology had indeed taken command, and was threatening to complete the rout which had begun in 1929.

There were pockets of resistance to these trends, not merely by traditionalists and the Union, but by strangely assorted groups of predominantly young people, who had little in common except a wish to keep music live and preferably simple. Skiffle groups, folk-singers, punk rockers, and early-music enthusiasts (in their simpler manifestations) were all revolting against complexity, manipulation, and impersonal technology. Far from increasing the demand for conventionally skilled and trained musicians, their influence tended to be either neutral, creating closed circles of participation; antagonistic, in a desire to 'deprofessionalize' music; or even competitive; since many who entered with guitars or recorders, as their predecessors had begun with pianos and cornets, went on to become self-taught professionals. In this volatile environment official paymasters allocated funds to musicians already in the market place, and towards the training of their successors.

Patronage

The dealings of successive post-war governments with the arts have been the subject of continuous and inconclusive debate, which concerns us here only in so far as it affected musicians. Expenditure increased considerably, though it was never generous in comparison with other European countries.[105] Opera took a large proportion, to choruses of outrage from populists, and mild protests by composers.[106] The resulting efflorescence was astonishing. As late as 1954 George Dyson, director of the RCM, was voicing ancient prejudices about opera's being fundamentally alien to the British temperament: perhaps we were too musical to accept its 'posturings and mouthings'.[107] Within a few years regular companies were mounting excellent productions, not only in London and Wales, where they could be expected, given a modicum of support, but even in Scotland. Singers and conductors were at last allowed opportunities to learn their craft which no academy could match; sixty years after Stanford's wise comments and,[108] ironically, at a time when opera, apart from a few, mainly British, exceptions, had become a museum art.

In other branches of music, pittances were distributed among numerous supplicants. A notorious example of this 'fair shares' procedure was the London orchestras, which collectively received far less than the individual grant of any major foreign orchestra. In 1970 the Peacock Report recommended that subsidies should be confined to fewer orchestras;[109] and there were later proposals for even greater concentration: the creation of a single orchestra from the best players, drawing regular salaries instead of session fees, and properly rehearsed in an enterprising repertoire. Nothing was done, and orchestral conditions in London began to revert to those of the 1920s, larger in scale, and often on a higher plane because individual standards of playing had improved, though great conductors were a rarer breed. Too many concerts were routine demonstrations of virtuoso sight-reading by tired, overworked players. Provincial orchestras were usually fresher, more stable, and better rehearsed, but their predominantly youthful players had few opportunities of supplementing low incomes. At the BBC an attempt to 'rationalize' a structure of twelve orchestras, employing 589 instrumentalists, was countered by a spectacular and largely successful strike.[110]

Training

The Government's first serious attempt to accept some responsibility for the training of civilian musicians came in 1944, as a result of an initiative by Keynes.[111] The RAM, RCM, and RMCM received grants of £10,000, £8,500, and £4,000 respectively, which were increased in subsequent years. No attempt was made to reform the system, which was given a new lease of life, as in 1918, when students flocked back after the war; many of them, according to Dyson, with 'little more than a school-child's accomplishment and a natural desire to follow an attractive and favourite hobby'.[112] Sparse resources continued to be thinly spread. A dispassionate, carefully researched book, published in 1959, attempted to be generous—'the strength of the system lies in its lack of system'—but found little to commend. Students were without guidance; directors preoccupied with 'ceremonial and public duties'. The only full-time staff were administrators who, like Harrison's 'Dr. Brown', were much concerned with external examining. Some good part-time instructors were able to establish 'a sort of apprentice-master relationship', but even this valuable work was uncoordinated. Far too much routine teaching was undertaken by poorly paid 'professors who have no independent reputation in the musical world'. Accommodation was so bad—'inferior to many an ordinary grammar school in the provision of elementary amenities'—that students were 'effectively debarred from spending time usefully'. Radical reform was essential 'if an obsolete tradition of training is to be effectively converted into a musical education appropriate to the needs of the present day'.[113]

Six years later a group of distinguished musicians, under the chairmanship of Sir Gilmour Jenkins, and commissioned by the Gulbenkian Foundation, was equally critical, and more explicit about the need for active intervention, rather than mere subsidy.[114] By 1964 grants had been increased until they covered about 14 per cent of expenditure. While this was paltry in comparison with needs, or expenditure on other branches of higher education, disparities were due, at least in part, to the conservatories' 'traditional reluctance' to surrender any particle of independence. The Jenkins report did not delve into history; but readers will appreciate that zeal for autonomy had been largely responsible for proliferation and inadequacy. If it was based on concern for academic or artistic freedom, Jenkins continued, this could not be sustained by the experience of universities. Having failed to secure adequate private patronage, the conservatories were reinforcing 'the English habit' of failing to distinguish between amateurs and professionals. Instead of training gifted students in a professional discipline, they were forced to depend on income from tuition fees and a 'prolixity' of external examinations and diplomas. No other important sector of higher education was so placed. Proper financial and administrative arrangements were now indispensible.

Drastic reforms were proposed. Sufficient funds should be provided to enable the colleges to raise standards and reduce intake, intensify tuition and supervision, greatly extend practice accommodation, improve the status and remuneration of staff, and design a curriculum for advanced studies. Instead of reducing overcrowding by removing teacher-trainees to a separate institution, which some reformers would have preferred, the report suggested that their numbers should be decreased. Finally, for the first time since the botched attempt of the 1860s, it grasped the nettles of proliferation and autonomy. In the longer term, it advised, the RAM, RCM, and TCL should be amalgamated into a 'National Conservatoire' with a staff whose status and remuneration should be comparable to that of a university. The GSM would remain independent, as the City of London's own school, providing 'a valuable spur to excellence'. Special provision could be made for regional needs.[115]

Nothing came of these recommendations. Greeted with a resounding silence, the report was ignored rather than shelved, for copies are now hard to find, even in major libraries. A later Gulbenkian committee, under the chairmanship of Lord Vaizey, attributed this neglect to three factors: a financial crisis, the colleges' entrenched independence, and the prevailing fashion for greater regional diversification.[116] The first argument is not convincing, for thoroughgoing reform would have cost little in comparison with other expenditures on higher education, which was still expanding vigorously. Regional interests were indeed a problem. But this had been anticipated by the Jenkins report, which had noted the obvious cultural advantages of London to a selected group requiring advanced training for a profession 'where competition at the highest levels is international and is based entirely on quality and not at all on numbers'.[117]

That was probably the last chance for Government to impose greater rationality and selectivity. By the time that the second Gulbenkian report appeared, with much wider terms of reference, and plans for improvement, the economic situation had deteriorated, vested interests were more deeply entrenched, and ideas about the nature and purpose of musical education were in great flux.[118] Vaizey argued that training 'had not changed to meet employers' needs', and that *malaise* was profound, just when 'the reputation of British music has never stood higher'.[119] One source of discontent, a sad but inevitable legacy of the past, was at last being publicized, after years of genteel reticence. It was even rumoured that the London colleges were facing 'serious disruption because of the scandalously low fees paid to their professors'.[120] Most were employed as casual labour, without holiday or sickness payments, their total incomes unpredictably dependent upon the number of pupils, and rarely equivalent to the lowest salaries available elsewhere in education. They were 'nervous of making a fuss', but their plight was described in a letter to *The Times* as threatening 'the very basis of our profession. It is a shame to a civilised community that it has been tolerated for so long'.[121] The letter was signed by ten of the most distinguished figures in British music, including Clifford Curzon, Colin Davis, Geraint Evans, Jacqueline du Pré, and Michael Tippett.

If accelerated growth without fundamental change was the general pattern of expansion, there were at least two important exceptions. Youth orchestras flourished, many of them providing incentives and training for future professionals, though their long-term influence on the supply and demand for musicians is unclear. The National Youth Orchestra was in a separate category. Established by Ruth Railton in 1947, and subsequently nurtured by the indefatigable Ivey Dickson, it became a focal point for exceptional talent, throughout the country. Its rigorous procedures of audition, instruction, rehearsal, and discipline, and its relentless pursuit of excellence, enabled schoolchildren aged between thirteen and nineteen, working in their vacations under first-class tutors and conductors, to gain experience which was nowhere else available, and achieve incredibly high standards.[122] So many became successful professionals that the NYO has some claim to be regarded as the most 'cost effective' musical institution to have emerged since the war.

The other significant advance was in the universities. Expansion took place as a by-product of the Robbins revolution; so rapidly that by the late seventies there were nearly 2,000 students in thirty-two departments. Working conditions were generally superior to those available in the conservatories; but far more important were changes in curricula and intellectual climate. A retreat from the organ-loft had been noted in 1952 by Russell, who applauded a movement towards 'the tradition of research which has distinguished other branches of study'.[123] It was confirmed by Dyson's fulminations against new-fangled 'musicological degrees' which could not be 'safely accepted as exemptions from the more practical and professional diplomas'. Such graduates might 'write plausible essays on historical byways of music, but they could not harmonise a simple hymn tune grammatically'.[124]

The transformation of university music had several effects. Study of composition became more eclectic, and esoteric. The advance of musicology can be readily discerned by comparing the fifth and sixth editions of Grove's *Dictionary*; the latter representing current trends in Britain and in the USA, where a similar, but more extensive revolution was taking place. The employment prospects of graduates were problematical, unless they could live by scholarship and teaching, or secure jobs to which their knowledge was relevant. It was commonly assumed within the university that studying music was a liberal education, neither more nor less appropriate to the market-place than history or philosophy. Most university departments stimulated musical activity, on campus and in neighbouring communities. This development, again, was less extensive here than it was in the USA, where the 'campus circuit' is an essential part of concert life, and distinguished performers are commonly members of staff. But some British universities appointed 'artists in residence', particularly important in the case of string quartets, which need ample time for (unpaid) rehearsals. A final benefit was the opportunity for students, often NYO 'graduates', many of whom were reading other subjects, to gain practical experience. Several successful musicians have taken that route.

Conclusion

By the early 1980s the number of musicians in Britain could be estimated by their affiliation, though this involved some double counting. The Union had some 40,000 members, of whom 5,000 were women. At least half of the total membership were part-timers, mostly in pop, dance, and club bands. Three-quarters of the musicians in the ISM were teachers. A few thousand singers belonged to the British Actors' Equity Association; a few hundred serious composers to the impoverished Composers' Guild, and several thousand pop and 'light' composers and lyricists to the Song Writers' Guild. The majority of performers worked, or sought engagements, in the following combinations: 115 symphony and chamber orchestras, 85 dance and jazz bands, 536 ensembles, 111 early music groups, and 79 choruses.[125] Apart from early music specialists, who were a recent and fairly exclusive category, there was considerable overlap: several 'orchestras' met infrequently to sail under flags of convenience, and some ensembles derived from larger combinations. But no allowance for double counting can alter the fact of proliferation. Many new achievements are interred in these statistics: a number of brilliant young cellists, inspired by Pleeth and du Pré; several chamber orchestras of international repute, and many good string quartets, performing regularly, rather than briefly assembled for an occasional appearance. Some performers found employment abroad, on tour or even permanently; for Britain's international trade in musicians was no longer a one-way movement. Perhaps this was the most remarkable change. Did it signify a change in national temperament, away from the characteristic phlegm and reticence which had seemingly limited the careers of even gifted musicians in the past? Or was it simply that potential talent was now less subdued by neglect and disapproval, particularly among middle-class boys, and more systematically tapped and exploited? A new means of doing so was the gladiatorial competition, prestigious or crass, which focused public attention, at least momentarily, and sometimes assisted careers.

But most British musicians were still primarily dependent upon the home market, which gave few indications that it could absorb such profusion. Only a small proportion of the population were regular concert- or opera-goers; and no form of live professional music-making rated high among the interests of an increasingly prosperous and leisured society.[126] The typical musician, unless he could find a regular, pensioned job, still pieced together a modest and precarious income. If his working and living conditions were better than those of his predecessors, this tended to reflect changes in society, rather than in his professional status. Like the rest of western mankind, he no longer succumbed to tuberculosis which, according to Williams, had accounted for 40 per cent of musicians' deaths in 1912.[127] In sickness, unemployment, and old age, he enjoyed the minimum benefits of the welfare state, supplemented, perhaps, by the Royal Society of Musicians, or Musicians' Benevolent Fund. Few occupations offered fewer material rewards to skill and hard work, yet nothing could stem the tide of aspirants.

The persistence of glut is due to the cumulative effects of the supply factors described in this book, many of which are inescapable. Young people with 'an itch of music' find teachers, or teach themselves; and many attempt to live by it, through family tradition, a sense of vocation, or ignorance of prospects. An ideal system of training would make some attempt to stem the tide, channelling talent wisely and flexibly in accordance with society's needs. In practice it is an impossible task in a liberal democracy, but few systems could be devised which are less appropriate than what has evolved in Britain. Since career guides have been quoted throughout this book, it is fitting to end with a 1984 version.[128] It concentrates upon the needs of the 'aspiring professional' and selects only those 'relatively few colleges', from many alternatives, which are 'first choice'. Aspirants are warned that a career in music will entail much travel and long, unsocial hours of work; but assured that, in addition to performing and teaching, there is a wide range of possible careers. Thirteen institutions are listed, currently teaching 4,235 full-time students, and many part-timers. In addition it names sixty universities and colleges which award first degrees, twenty-one with post-graduate courses leading to certificates of education in music, and two which provide 'advanced courses' for orchestral players.

TABLES

TABLE I

Musicians in England and Wales 1794–1951 (thousands)

	(1794)	1841	1851	1861	1871	1881	1891	1901	1911	1921	1931	1951
Musicians and Teachers		6.6	11.2	15.0	18.6	25.5	38.6	39.3	47.1	43.9	48.5	26.3
Male		5.6	8.1	10.3	11.6	14.2	19.5	20.6	22.8	20.6	24.5	13.7
Female		0.9	3.1	4.7	7.0	11.4	19.1	18.7	24.3	23.4	24.0	12.5
Musicians	(1.5)	3.6	6.1	9.5						22.6	25.9	14.8
Male		3.3	5.2	7.8						15.6	19.6	11.0
Female		0.3	0.5	0.6						6.9	6.3	3.7
Music Teachers		3.0	5.1	5.5						21.4	22.6	11.5
Male		2.3	2.8	2.4						4.9	4.9	2.7
Female		0.7	2.3	3.1						16.4	17.7	8.8

TABLE II

Musicians and music teachers in England and Wales 1841–1951

	Musicians and Music Teachers (thousands)	Total Population (millions)	Conurbations*	Musicians and Music Teachers per 10,000 population	Musicians and Music Teachers per 10,000 conurbation population
1841	6.6	15.9		4.4	
1851	11.2	17.9		6.2	
1861	15.0	20.1		7.5	
1871	18.6	22.7	8.3	8.2	22
1881	25.5	25.9	10.1	9.8	25
1891	38.6	29.0	11.7	13.3	33
1901	39.3	32.5	13.4	12.1	29
1911	47.1	36.1	14.7	13.0	32
1921	43.9	37.9	15.3	11.6	29
1931	48.5	39.9	16.4	12.1	29
1951	26.3	47.7	16.9	5.5	15

* Greater London, South East Lancashire, West Midlands, West Yorkshire, Merseyside, Tyneside.

TABLE III

Musicians in some regional centres

	1890	1900	1910	1920	1931
Manchester	123	315	299	567	291
Liverpool	133	318	405	312	160
Birmingham	95	273	246	201	197
Glasgow	67	127	166	137	127
Leeds	45	74	94	129	87
Edinburgh	133	124	112	85	68
Bournemouth		37	37	38	41
(population ['000s])		(38)	(63)	(79)	(92)

TABLE IV

Musicians in London

	1890	1900	1910	1920	1931
Teachers	1,993	4,823	4,908	5,546	3,650
Instrumentalists (excluding piano)	633	2,533	2,704	3,155	1,264
Violin/Viola	255	929	1,017	1,319	529
Cello	45	188	245	340	174
Double-bass	43	178	187	235	87
Flute	31	146	153	140	72
Clarinet	18	171	179	153	46
Cornet	45	171	185	175	52

TABLE V

Musicians employed in theatres, music halls and picture theatres. England and Wales 1911

	Men	Women	Total
Theatres	2,219	201	2,420
Music Halls	1,194	182	1,376
Picture Theatres	319	141	460
Total	3,732	524	4,256*

* We assume that this figure is part of the total of 47,116 'musicians, music masters and singers' recorded in the 1911 census, *not* an additional number. The source, noted below, is obscurely phrased, and can be differently interpreted. See H. J. Harris, 'The Occupation of Musicians in the United States', the *Musical Quarterly*, Vol. 1, No. 2 (April 1915), p. 300

Source: Census of England and Wales, 1911, vol. X, part I, p. xxiv.

TABLE VI

Some music colleges

1823	Royal Academy of Music
1857	Military School of Music (Kneller Hall)
1861	London Academy of Music
1864	College of Organists
1865	London Organ School (later London Music School)
1873	The Royal Normal College and Academy of Music for the Blind
1874	Trinity College of Music
1876	National Training School
1878	Cork Municipal School of Music
1880	Guildhall School of Music (Landon Ronald, 1910; Cundell 1938)
1881	Blackheath Conservatoire of Music
1883	Royal College of Music
	Croydon Conservatoire of Music (Carrodus, Col. Taylor)
1885	Forest Gate School of Music (later Metropolitan Academy)
	Hampstead Conservatoire
1886	Birmingham and Midland Institute School of Music
1887	London College of Music
	Huddersfield College of Music
1889	College of Violinists
1890	(Glasgow) Athenaeum School of Music (1929 Scottish National Academy)
1893	Manchester College of Music
1898	City of Leeds School of Music

Articles of Apprenticeship, 1860

ARTICLES OF AGREEMENT had made and fully agreed upon this eighth day of November in the year of our Lord One thousand eight hundred and sixty BETWEEN Mary Williams of No 37 Southampton Buildings in the County of Middlesex Widow Grandmother and Guardian of Edward Williams next hereinafter named and the said Edward Williams Grandson of the said Mary Williams of the one part and Ferdinand Wallerstein of 24 College Place Camden Town in the said County of Middlesex, Musician, Professor of Music and Musical Composer of the other part.

WITNESS that the said Edward Williams of his own free will and choice and with the consent and approbation of his Grandmother and Guardian testified by his execution of these Present Doth put and place himself to and with the said Ferdinand Wallerstein as his Apprentice to be taught and instructed in the Arts or Businesses of playing on the Violin, Pianoforte and of Musical Composition which he the said Ferdinand Wallerstein now follloweth from the date hereof for the term of Four years thence ensuing AND the said Mary Williams doth hereby for herself her executors and administrators covenant promise and agree with and to the said Ferdinand Wallerstein in manner following that is to say That he the said Edward Williams shall and will diligently and faithfully serve him the said Ferdinand Wallerstein as his Apprentice during the said term of Four years in his aforesaid Arts and Businesses and shall and will perform and obey all the lawful and reasonable instructions orders and directions of the said Ferdinand Wallerstein And shall not nor will absent himself from the service of the said Ferdinand Wallerstein without his consent during the said term nor wilfully spend waste or destroy any of the monies goods or effects of the said Ferdinand Wallerstein or the monies goods or effects of any of his Employers which shall come to the hands or possession of or be entrusted to him the said Edward Williams by the said Ferdinand Wallerstein during the said term but shall and will at all times during the continuance thereof well and truly account for pay and deliver to the said Ferdinand Wallerstein all and every the sum and sums of money and other things which he the said Edward Williams shall have take or receive of from or be entrusted with for or on account of the said Ferdinand Wallerstein or any of his Employers as aforesaid. And further that she the said Mary Williams her executors and administrators shall and will at their own costs and charges find and provide the said Edward Williams with food lodging apparel and all other necessary things during the said term AND the said Edward Williams doth consent and agree to serve the said Ferdinand Wallerstein in manner and for the term hereinbefore specified AND these Presents further WITNESS that in consideration of such service so to be performed as aforesaid HE the said Ferdinand Wallerstein Doth accept and take the said Edward Williams as his Apprentice for the said term of four years and doth hereby for himself his executors administrators and assigns covenant promise and agree with and to the said Mary Williams her executors and administrators That he the said Ferdinand Wallerstein shall and will according to the utmost of his skill and knowledge teach and instruct the said Edward Williams or cause him to be taught and instructed in the Arts or businesses of playing on the Violin, Pianoforte and of Musical Composition which he the said Ferdinand Wallerstein now useth And further shall not nor will during the said term assign over the said Edward Williams or these Presents to any person or persons whomsoever without the consent in writing of the said Mary Williams her executors or administrators for that purpose first had and obtained Provided always And it is hereby agreed and declared by and between the said parties hereto respectively That the said Ferdinand Wallerstein shall be at liberty at any time or times during the said term without the consent of the said Mary Williams her executors or administrators or any other person or persons to engage and take the said Edward Williams to play on the Violin or Pianoforte at any private or public Theatre, place of resort or amusement either in Town or Country or enter into and make such Contract, engagement or agreement as he the said Ferdinand Wallerstein shall think fit and proper for the said Edward Williams to play or perform on the Violin and Pianoforte at any private or public place of assembly or amusement or at or in any private house or public Company upon such terms or for such sum or sums of money or other emoluments as he the said Ferdinand Wallerstein shall think fit just and reasonable And that the said Ferdinand Wallerstein shall and will bear pay and sustain all travelling and other charges and expenses which shall or may be incurred in or occasioned by such Contracts, engagements or agreements as aforesaid or any or either of them And that the clear residue or remainder of the profits gains or emoluments to arise or be received therefrom or made thereby after payment and deduction thereout by the said Ferdinand Wallerstein of all such Travelling expenses and charges as aforesaid shall be shared and divided by and between the said Ferdinand Wallerstein and the said Mary Williams in equal moieties shares and proportions And that the said Mary Williams her executors or administrators or any other person or persons whomsoever by her or their procurement shall not nor will intermeddle with or obstruct the performance of any such Contract or engagement or agreement so to be made by the said Ferdinand Wallerstein as aforesaid or the making thereof IN WITNESS whereof the said parties to these Presents have hereunto set their hands and seals the day and year first above written.

(Signed). MARY WILLIAMS
(Signed). EDWARD WILLIAMS
(Signed). FERDINAND WALLERSTEIN

Signed sealed and delivered in the presence of
Joseph Bevir Williams,
37, Southampton Buildings,
Middlesex.

Notes

Chapter I

1. Mortimer.
2. Doane.
3. Highfill. Except where otherwise indicated, these volumes are the principal source for biographical information in this chapter.
4. *DNB*.
5. Landon, 293–304.
6. Stone, 57.
7. George, 313.
8. Mozart's is the obvious case. See Einstein, 55–60.
9. Hughes, C. W., 103.
10. McVeigh.
11. Baker, 129–34.
12. Holmes, 31.
13. Baker, 130.
14. Johnson, 40–1.
15. McKendrick, Brewer, and Plumb, Ch. VI.
16. Humphries and Smith, 17.
17. Wilson, 302.
18. Wilson, 303.
19. Harley, 170.
20. Hawkins, 700, 788–9.
21. Mackerness, 103–4. Cf. Sadie, and Milligan, Ch. 1.
22. *London Stage*, 4. ii. 815.
23. Burney, *Memoirs*, i. 135.
24. Rosenfield, 131.
25. Gardiner, i. 24.
26. Woodfill, 129.
27. Temperley, in Grove VI.
28. Piggot. Cf. Temperley, in Grove VI.
29. Woodfill, 122.
30. Anon, *General Description of Trades*, 152–3.
31. Campbell, R., *London Tradesman*, 91–3. Cf. Kassler, i. 164–5.
32. Collyer, 198–9.
33. Trowell, *Defoe*, 403–27. Cf. Kassler, i. 270–1.
34. Potter, 100.
35. McClure, 230–3.
36. Burney, *Memoirs*, 234.
37. Galton, 230.
38. *DNB*.
39. Archenholtz, 109.
40. George, 132–3.
41. Fiske, 368.
42. Boase.
43. Greer, 12.
44. Fiske, 492.
45. Ibid. 623.
46. Ibid. 622.
47. Burney, *An Account*, 19.
48. Cohen, 502.
49. Ibid. 94.
50. Ibid. 462.
51. Ibid. 368.
52. Anderson, 198.
53. Burney, *General History*, 879.
54. *DNB*.
55. Family tree in Fiske, 131.
56. *Annual Register*, 1775, 71–2.
57. *London Stage*, 2. i. 137.
58. Quantz, *Autobiography*, quoted Carse, *Orchestra*, 78.
59. Lang, 458–9.
60. Farmer, *Artillery Band*, 8–37.
61. Wright, *Sancho*.
62. Colman, *The Musical Lady*, quoted Nicholl, iii. 196.
63. Archenholtz, 112.
64. Wendeborn, ii. 237.
65. Parke, ii. 213.
66. Ibid. 330–3.
67. Ibid. 213.
68. Landon, 248.
69. Cf. Milligan, 19.
70. Wendeborn, ii. 238–9.
71. Petty, 12–17.
72. Landon, 281.
73. Dibdin, *Professional Life*, iv. 157.
74. Sadie, 26.
75. Gardiner, i. 67.

76. Ibid. 110.
77. Wilkinson, 267.
78. Porter, 241–68. Cf. Fawcett, *Provincial Art*.
79. Woodfill, 119.
80. Mann papers; F.2.2. Court book 130. 27 Aug. 1672.
81. Fawcett, *Music*, 1–4.
82. Corfield, 21–3.
83. Fawcett, *Music*, 6–32.
84. Ibid. 35.
85. Hargrave. On Herschel see Turner, 24–5.
86. Dibdin, *Tour*, 196.
87. Hargrave, 337.
88. Money, 82–3.
89. Sutcliffe Smith, *Birmingham*, 12.
90. Goldsmith, 34.
91. Green, 5.
92. Hugh Walpole, quoted Bor and Clelland, 66.
93. Bor and Clelland.
94. Holmes, *Mozart*, 54. Anderson, 160–1.
95. Fiske, 413.
96. Woodfield, 14.
97. R. Landon, 266.
98. Gye.
99. Plumb, *Persons*, 106. Cf. Phillips, 88–91.
100. Boydell, *Dublin*.
101. Boydell, *Four Centuries*, 34.
102. Johnson, 199.
103. Ibid. 38.
104. Edinburgh Musical Society minute books 27 Feb. 1759, quoted Johnson, 39.
105. Johnson, 59.
106. Porter, 91.
107. Crewdson, 56.
108. Hawkins, 481.
109. Burney, *General History*, 286.
110. Crewdson, 55–6.
111. R. Landon, 106.
112. Drummond.
113. Lasocki, 139.
114. Drummond.
115. Loft, 269–70.
116. Miller, quoted Dibdin, *Musical Tour*.
117. Dibdin, *Musical Tour*, 165–9. Cf. *QMMR*, iii (1821), 328–35.

Chapter II

1. Quoted in Turner, 24.
2. Hawkins, 896–7.
3. Dawe, 18–20.
4. Fleming.
5. M. Weber, *Protestant Ethic*, 76.
6. Stevens papers. All quotations of Stevens are from this source. See also Temperley on Stevens in Grove VI; Trend; and Cudworth.
7. Cudworth, *RJS*, 834.
8. *QMMR*, iii. 1821, 275.
9. W. MacFarren, 73.
10. Crotch papers. All quotations of Crotch are from this source. See also Temperley on Crotch in Grove VI; and Rennert.
11. Rennert, 90–2.
12. Fétis, 'On Music in London', *Harmonicon*, 1829.
13. Cox, *Leaves*. Young, *Beethoven*, x.
14. Smart papers, Add. 41771–9, 4222, 42251. All quotations of Smart are from this source, except where otherwise indicated.
15. Young, *Beethoven*, ix.
16. *MW* quoted in Renert, 81.
17. Mount-Edgcumbe, 232.
18. Temperley, 'Sir George Smart', in Grove VI.
19. Smart papers, Add. 41772, 5.
20. Young, *Beethoven*, 3.
21. Sainsbury, i. 287.
22. J. Warrack, 317–18.
23. M. Cooper, 71–2. Hamburger, 238–40.
24. Ehrlich, *Piano*, 104–5.
25. *Monthly Mirror*, quoted in Highfill, i. 173.
26. Smart papers, Add. 42225.
27. Ibid., letter 177, n.d., probably Apr. 1867.
28. Phil. Soc. Arch., Loan 48/13/7, 8 Feb. 1821. Cf. Ehrlich, 'Economic History', 198–9.

29. Phillips, i. 213.
30. Lonsdale, viii.
31. *MT*, May 1868.
32. Maurice.
33. H. B. Thomson.
34. Ibid. 308–9.
35. Ibid. 317–19.
36. See pp. 8–9.
37. Gardiner, i. 341–3.
38. Pleasants, 216.
39. Bushnell, 150.
40. Bunn, i. 242–4.
41. Troubridge.
42. Phil. Soc. Arch.
43. Pleasants, 208–9.
44. Phil. Soc. Arch. Directors' Meetings, 23 Mar. 1823.
45. See p. 84.
46. Walker, 107–8.
47. Phil. Soc. Arch. Directors' Meetings, 29 Apr. 1827.
48. *Harmonicon*, Dec. 1831.
49. Schwarz on Paganini in Grove VI.
50. *Harmonicon*, Jan. 1832.
51. de Courcy, i. 251.
52. Ibid. ii. 101.
53. Schwarz.
54. Parke.
55. Phillips, i. 131.
56. Ibid. i. 127.
57. Ibid. i. 234.
58. Slatford on Dragonetti in Grove VI.
59. Phil. Soc. Arch. 13/10. 21 Jan. 1825.
60. J. E. Cox, i. 29–33.
61. *Felix Farley's Bristol Journal*, 20 Oct. 1821.
62. Phil. Soc. Arch. 5/1. 19 Mar. 1819.
63. Autobiography in Farmer papers. Cf. Sainsbury, i. 34–6; and Grove I.
64. Sainsbury, ii. 64–5; and Grove I.
65. Phil. Soc. Arch. 13/21. 21 Nov. 1822.
66. Ibid., 1 Dec. 1834.
67. *Harmonicon*, 1828, 217.
68. Phil. Soc. Arch. 12 and 19 Dec. 1824; 4 Feb. 1827; 28 Nov. 1831.
69. Weston, 105.
70. Ella, 338.
71. Sands.

Chapter III

1. *MT*, Apr. 1868.
2. *MT*, Jan. 1887.
3. Baines, 153.
4. Ware and Lockard, 184–5.
5. See Briggs, *Mass Entertainment*.
6. Dyos, 72.
7. Ehrlich and Walker, 21.
8. Maynard, 109.
9. *Mapleson*, 61.
10. Ibid. 93.
11. Ibid. 120.
12. 'Ideal Tours arranged by Mr E. Lockwood', *Dramatic and Musical Directory* (1893).
13. Parke, i. 319.
14. Kuhe, 99–100.
15. See Young.
16. Spark, 287–300.
17. *Rept. . . . Theatres* (1892), 79.
18. Ibid. 57.
19. Bailey, *Leisure*, 147–9.
20. See Ch. VIII.
21. Vicinus. Bailey, *Leisure*, particularly ch. 7. Stedman Jones, 'Working class culture'.
22. Runciman, in *MMR*, 1 Aug., 1895.
23. *Rept. . . . Theatres* (1892), 349, 450–1, 490–1. Lamb, 98–9, 105.
24. See Ch. VII.
25. Weber, W., *Music and the Middle Classes*, tables 1, 4.
26. Cox, 43–4.
27. Young, 208.
28. Berlioz, letter to Joseph d'Ortigne, 30 Apr. 1852.
29. Davison.
30. *Preston Guardian* 18 Jan. 1848, quoted in Smith, M. B., 117.
31. Berlioz, letter to Auguste Morel, 12 Feb. 1848.
32. Carse, Jullien.
33. Benas, cf. Klein, and Kuhe.
34. Shaw, *London Music*, 59.
35. Jevons, 18.
36. Hallé, 107.
37. Ibid. 116.

38. Ibid. 111.
39. Ibid. 129–32.
40. *MW*, 14 Jan. 1860 quoted in Young, *Concert tradition*, 225.
41. Quoted in Taylor, S. de B., 17. Cf. Nettel, *Orchestra in England*, 262.
42. Royal Liverpool Philharmonic Society 125th Anniversary Concert Programme, 12 Mar. 1965. 'Historical Essay' by A. K. Holland.
43. Liverpool Philharmonic Society archives. 1 Dec. 1849.
44. Ibid., 20 Jan. 1850.
45. Ibid., 18 Apr. 1872.
46. Taylor, op. cit. 39.
47. Ibid. 41–2.
48. Nettel, *Orchestra in England*, 234–7. Anderton, 44–6. Taylor, *Two Centuries*, 119–22.
49. Godfrey, 72–4.
50. Miller, 103.
51. Godfrey, 177.
52. See Chapter VIII.
53. *MRJ*, Feb. 1913.
54. Ingall papers.
55. See Ure, A., *The Philosophy of Manufactures* (1833).
56. Heap, M., 'My life and times' quoted in Elbourne, 41.
57. S. Greg, quoted C. Waters.
58. See Cunningham.
59. *Preston Chronicle*, 7 Nov. 1835, quoted in Elbourne, 64.
60. 'Music in Human Life', *Household Words* (1850), 161.
61. Jevons, 5, 9, 11.
62. Haweis, 84–5.
63. Zeldin, Chapter VII.
64. Cf. Ehrlich, *The Victorian Piano*.
65. Schmitz, O. A. H., *The Land Without Music*.
66. Shaw, London Music, 95.
67. Dean, 146–7. Cf. Kuhe, 124–5 on the *Traviata* scandal.
68. Pritchard, 339.
69. First Glasgow Musical Festival, Jan.

1860: Prospectus, in Farmer Papers, 17/52.
70. Morris, 218.
71. Spark and Bennett.
72. Morris, 217–18.
73. *The Times*, 15/28 Oct. 1878.
74. See Scholes, *Mirror*, 618–19. Cf. Rainbow.
75. Correspondence in *The Times*, 15/17/18/22/25/26/28 Oct. 1878.
76. MacFarren, W., 45.
77. MT, May 1861.
78. Ibid., Sept. 1883.
79. Ibid., Jan. 1883.
80. Ibid., June 1887.
81. Thackeray, W. M., *The Book of Snobs*, 110–12.
82. Ehrlich, *The Piano*.
83. Fellowes, 9.
84. Ibid. 9–13.
85. Fuller-Maitland, 39.
86. Rainbow, 'Music in Education', in Temperley (ed.), *The Romantic Age*, 43. Scholes, *Mirror*, 627.
87. Barnby in *MOJ*, 1 Feb. 1894. Cf. Hullah's remarks on p. 149.
88. Ivimey.
89. Union of Graduates.
90. Cf. Edwards, 'Social Aspects of Creativity' in *Encyclopedia of the Social Sciences*.
91. Cf. Haskell, Ch I.
92. Ella, 133.
93. Chissel, 167.
94. Peacock and Weir, 38–40.
95. Havergal Brian, in *OAG* Aug. 1909; Cf. *The Referee*, 4 July 1909.
96. MS, Sept. 1912. Cf. Scholes, *Mirror*, 662–3.
97. Gane.
98. See Chs. VII and VIII.
99. Cf. Howes.
100. Cf. Banfield, 'The Artist and Society' in Temperley (ed.), *Romantic Age*, Ch. I.
101. Camden, 75.

Chapter IV

1. Kuhe, 154.
2. Galton, 230–1.
3. Brown and Stratton, 4.
4. Ella, 142.

5. Soc. of Arts Report.
6. *The Athenaeum*, 10 Feb. 1866, 212.
7. Cf. ibid., 3 Mar. 1866, 309.
8. See Chapter I.
9. Foster, 53.
10. W. MacFarren, 46–7.
11. G. A. MacFarren, 149.
12. Corder, *Souvenir*.
13. 'State of Music in London', *Harmonicon*, 1829.
14. Corder, *History*, 63.
15. *Harmonicon*, Aug. 1826.
16. Temperley on Bochsa, in Grove VI.
17. *QMMR*, 1822, 516–26.
18. *Harmonicon*, Dec. 1825; Jan. 1826; 1827, 141; 1828, 113.
19. G. A. MacFarren, 152–3.
20. Phillips, ii. 179–80.
21. Crotch papers, iii. 187A.
22. Walker, 112–13.
23. *Harmonicon*, 1829.
24. Gerig, 130.
25. Boyden on violin technique, in Grove VI.
26. A. M. Taylor, 34.
27. Pierre, 273–4, 873.
28. L. M. Phillips, *Leipzig*, 25.
29. Ibid. 146–7.
30. G. A. MacFarren, 168.
31. Berlioz, *Memoirs*, 60–1, 401–3.
32. Gardiner.
33. Burney, *France and Italy*, 184–5.
34. G. A. MacFarren, 155.
35. Burney, loc.cit.
36. Brown and Stratton, 50. Temperley on Blagrove, in Grove VI.
37. Burghersh, 260.
38. 'Royal Academy of Music' in Grove I.
39. Hullah, evidence to Soc. of Arts, 7 Feb. 1866.
40. Corder, *History*, 57–9. Corder believed that this reply should be

'painted up in the hall in letters of gold'.
41. Ibid. 60–1.
42. G. A. MacFarren, 167.
43. Bacon, 'On the character of Musicians', *QMMR*, 1818–19, i, 284–94. Cf. Kassler, i. 39–42.
44. W. MacFarren, 75–6.
45. Corder, *History*, 69–72.
46. 'Royal Academy of Music' in Grove IV.
47. Minihan, Ch. 4. Bonython.
48. Corder, *History*, 72.
49. Lucas, evidence to Soc. of Arts. All further quotations in this chapter are from the same source, except where otherwise indicated.
50. Kuhe, 57.
51. J. E. Cox, i. 176. Cf. Horner on Costa, in Grove VI.
52. Brown and Stratton, 245. Scholes, *Mirror*, 695. Mackerness on Leslie, In Grove VI.
53. See Temperley on Bennett, in Grove VI.
54. See Duckles, in Temperley, *Romantic Age*, 491–2.
55. Ouseley, in Howson, 210–34.
56. Brown and Stratton, 318.
57. Binns, 61.
58. Marr, 23, Rogan, 'Military Bands and Military Music', *MRJ*, Feb. 1901.
59. See p. 17.
60. Reeve's Musical Directory.
61. *Athenaeum*, 14 July 1866.
62. Letter to *The Times*, 20 June 1868.
63. Corder, *History*, 74.
64. *MT*, June 1868.
65. Perkin, 295.
66. Best, 156–7.
67. Perkin, 302.

Chapter V

1. Mapleson, 297.
2. Fisher, 1.
3. See Tables I and II.
4. Buxton, i. 201.
5. Advertisements in *Musical Directory*.

6. Article on violin in Grove I. Cf. *Monthly Musical World*, April 1871, 43–4.
7. Advertisement in Union of Graduates Roll and Kalendar, 1904.

8. Auer, xi.
9. Ehrlich, *Piano*.
10. Camden.
11. Krummel, 'Music Publishing' in Temperley, *Romantic Age*, 49–50.
12. Hurd. Grove, *Cheap music*.
13. Peacock and Weir, 41–2.
14. Hurd, 85–7.
15. Temperley, *Romantic Age*, 129–30.
16. Ehrlich, *Piano*, 95–6.
17. Peacock and Weir, 33–5.
18. Ehrlich, *Piano*, 97.
19. Volti, 29.
20. Nettel, *Brian*, 15.
21. Volti, 40.
22. Fisher, 2.
23. *Musical Directory*, 1880 *et seq.*
24. Kennedy, RMCM.
25. *Who's Who in Music*, 1915, 360.
26. Advertisement in MS, 1914.
27. Robert-Blunn.
28. *Who's Who in Music*, 1913.
29. Ibid., 1915, 355–6.
30. Ibid. 356.
31. Colles and Cruft, 3.
32. Fuller Maitland, 91–2. Schonberg, 294.
33. Corder, *History*, 78–9.
34. Colles and Cruft, 6–7.
35. Scholes, *Mirror*, 699.
36. Stanford, 216.
37. Duke of Edinburgh, in *Music in England*, 30.
38. *The Times*, 8 May 1883.
39. P. Young, *George Grove*, 167.
40. *MT*, June 1883.
41. *Punch*, 30 June 1883.
42. Stanford, 138–9.
43. *MT*, May 1883.
44. Stanford, 216.
45. Jenny Lind's letter to Grove, Aug. 1882, is reproduced in *MT*, Nov. 1920.
46. Stanford, 217.
47. Pirie, 37–9.

48. Godfrey, 42.
49. Stanford, 220.
50. Ganz, 153.
51. Marr, xxiii–xxv.
52. G. Warrack.
53. But see Goossens, 252, for a critical view of Arbos's playing.
54. Shaw, *Our Theatres*, ii. 247.
55. Stanford, *Pages*, 213–14. 'The case for a national opera' in *Studies*.
56. Colles, 467.
57. Article on RCM in Grove IV.
58. Cf. article on Grove in Grove VI.
59. Robinson, 137.
60. Gulbenkian 1978, 62.
61. *BBM*, Jan. 1896.
62. Barty-King, 59.
63. Ehrlich, *Piano*, 152.
64. Barty-King, 70.
65. Kennedy.
66. *TCAG*, June 1892.
67. Temperley, *Romantic Age*, 200.
68. *TCAG*, Jan. 1885.
69. TCL Local Examination Register, 1882.
70. *TCAG*, June 1892.
71. Ibid., July 1883.
72. Ibid., Oct. 1897.
73. Ibid., Oct. 1897.
74. Ibid., Dec. 1885.
75. Ibid., Feb. 1886.
76. *MT*, June 1913.
77. *TCAG*, Mar. 1916.
78. Ibid., June 1885.
79. *MT*, Apr. 1894.
80. *MT*, Oct. 1905.
81. TCL Calendar, 1910.
82. *TCAG*, Mar. 1895.
83. Ibid., Oct. 1897.
84. Gane, 86.
85. *MT*, June 1913.
86. Quoted in the *Saturday Review*, 14 Oct. 1899.
87. Ibid.
88. Ehrlich, *Piano*, 91.

Chapter VI

1. Brown and Stratton, 145–6.
2. Fisher, 5.
3. Ibid. 110.
4. Ibid. 117.
5. Ibid. 122.
6. Ibid. 127.

7. Ibid. 83.
8. Ibid. 86.
9. Ibid. 9.
10. Salaman.
11. *BBM*, July 1896.
12. Kuhe, 309–10.
13. *St. James's Gazette*, reprinted in *MO*, Dec. 1894.
14. *MO*, Nov. 1893.
15. *Musical News*, 27 Apr. 1895.
16. Freidson, 367.
17. Thompson, 149.
18. See Ch. V, 108.
19. *MT*, July 1882.
20. *MT*, Aug. 1882.
21. Bohan, 16.
22. *MT*, Dec. 1884.
23. TC*AG*, Mar. 1885.
24. Ibid., Aug. 1885.
25. Ibid., Feb. 1886.
26. Ibid.
27. *MW*, quoted in TC*AG*, Feb. 1886.
28. *Daily Telegraph*, quoted in TC*AG*, Feb. 1886.
29. *Birmingham Daily Post*, quoted in TC*AG*, Feb. 1887.
30. *MOJ*, Jan. 1891.
31. Ibid., Oct. 1888.
32. Ibid., July 1892.
33. Ibid., Nov. 1892.
34. Ibid., July 1892.
35. Ibid., Mar., Apr. 1893.
36. Ibid., July, Aug. 1893.
37. Ibid., Dec. 1888.
38. Duman. Cf. Carr-Saunders.
39. Freidson, Ch. 4. Duman. On limitations of autonomy, see Peterson, 112–14.
40. F. E. Bache, in C. Bache, 119.
41. *MOJ*, Dec. 1888.
42. Escott, ii. 38–9.
43. Duman, 49.
44. Perkin, *Professions*.
45. Chadfield.
46. *MOJ*, Jan. 1889.
47. Ibid., Mar. 1890.
48. *MT*, Dec. 1861.
49. Fisher, 13–14.
50. See, *inter alia*, *MOJ*, Oct. 1888 and Jan. 1889.
51. *MOJ*, Sept. 1889.

52. Ibid., Jan. 1889.
53. Ibid., Jan. 1890.
54. Ibid., Dec. 1889.
55. Runciman, in *Saturday Review*, 22 Jan. 1898.
56. Brown and Stratton, ii.
57. Ibid., i.
58. *MNH*, 1892.
59. See p. 98.
60. Archer, 173, 324–5.
61. TC*AG*, July 1884.
62. *MOJ*, June 1892.
63. Ibid., Feb. 1893.
64. Ibid., June 1894.
65. Ibid., May 1894.
66. *MT*, Apr. 1894.
67. *OAG*, June 1894.
68. Loughborough and Dundee correspondence reported in *MOJ*, Mar., Apr. 1901.
69. ISM Local Examination Syllabus and Regulations, 1911.
70. Scholes, *Mirror*, 724. Cf. Anderson, *Music*, 110–11.
71. ISM Register of Members, 1898.
72. *BBM*, June 1896.
73. See 'The necessity for a strong central society for the musical profession': paper read at various ISM conferences. Mann papers.
74. ISM Register, 1898.
75. Union of graduates, *Roll*, 1903, 80.
76. Ibid. 92.
77. Scholes, *Mirror*, 685–7.
78. TC*AG*, Feb. 1890.
79. *Lancet*, 15 Mar. 1890, 631, and 19 Apr. 1890, 887.
80. Union of Graduates, *Roll*, 1906, 3.
81. Ibid., 1903, 82–90.
82. Blacking. Cf. Ringer, 3–6.
83. Fisher, 237–41. Cf. article on 'Degrees in Music' in Grove IV.
84. Cf. Ch. I, pp. 2–3, 132.
85. See article on Tagore in Grove VI.
86. Parker Semler, 95.
87. Kennedy, *Elgar*, 120. Cf. Norris.
88. Ivimey, 37.
89. F. Howes, in Grove VI.
90. Union of Graduates, *Roll*, 1903, 84.
91. *Chord*, quoted in *MNH*, 28 Apr. 1900. Cf. *MOJ*, Aug. 1893.

Chapter VII

1. Tillis, 2.
2. *BBM*, Oct. 1887.
3. Booth. Cf. Baker, *Victorian Actor*, 109–38.
4. *OAG*, Oct. 1896.
5. *St James's Gazette*, quoted in *MO*, Dec. 1894.
6. *The Porcupine*, quoted in *Liverpool Daily Post* Centenary Number, 1955.
7. *OAG*, Feb. 1895.
8. Cf. Hunter, D., *The diseases of occupations* (1962), 685.
9. Letter to *Stage*, quoted in *OAG*, Dec. 1897.
10. *BBM*, Dec. 1897.
11. Articles from *Stage*, quoted in *OAG*, Dec. 1897.
12. See Farmer's article on the Musicians' Union in Grove V; and Teale in *MRJ*, Apr. 1929.
13. Klein, 185.
14. Farmer, in Grove V.
15. The letter is reproduced in *MRJ*, Apr. 1929.
16. 'The Williams Family' by 'Antiquary' (Farmer), *MRJ*, 1932.
17. *MRJ*, Apr. 1929.
18. *MRJ*, May 1914 (celebrating 21st birthday of AMU).
19. Williams, quoted in *MRJ*, July 1929.
20. *MRJ*, Apr. 1929.
21. *MMR*, July 1893.
22. *MN*, 4 Nov. 1893.
23. Loft.
24. Brown, *English Labour Movement*, 169–76.
25. *OAG*, Aug. 1900.
26. *BBM*, Dec. 1893.
27. *OAG*, July 1895.
28. *OAG*, June 1897.
29. *BBM*, Dec. 1894.
30. Ibid.
31. *OAG*, Oct. 1896.
32. *OAG*, Mar. 1896.
33. *BBM*, Mar. 1895.
34. See p. 31.
35. *OAG*, Nov. 1897.
36. *OAG*, Apr. 1896.
37. Union of Graduates, *Roll*, 1902.
38. Hunt, 259–64. Brown, *English Labour Movement*, 138–47.
39. *OAG*, Oct. 1893.
40. *OAG*, May 1894. Public Records Office, BT 31/6018/42504.
41. *OAG*, May 1894.
42. Farmer on 'Musicians' Union', in Grove V.
43. *OAG*, Feb. 1895.
44. *OAG*, Feb. 1896.
45. *OAG*, Aug. 1894.
46. *OAG*, Jan. 1896.
47. *OAG*, Apr. 1896.
48. Walker, *Matcham*, 166–73.
49. See pp. 59, 237.
50. *MRJ*, Oct. 1911.
51. *MRJ*, Mar. 1901.
52. *OAG*, Feb. 1899.
53. Ganz, 11.
54. Volti, 43.
55. Corder, *History*, 82–90.
56. Fellowes, 79–81, 183–5.
57. Scholes, *Mirror*, 732.
58. Harrison, B., 57, 67, 193–4.
59. *OAG*, Feb. 1894.
60. *OAG*, Mar. 1894.
61. *OAG*, Apr. 1894.
62. *New York Times*, 13 Sept. 1871, quoted in Neuls-Bates, 193.
63. Scholes, *Mirror*, 731–2.
64. Kent.
65. See supplement to the *Music Student* June and Oct. 1913; Nov. 1914 (an account of women musicians at the Leipzig Exhibition); and May 1918.
66. Shaw, *Music*, ii. 132.
67. Scholes, *Mirror*, 207.
68. *Musical Directory*, 1900.
69. Kent.
70. Wood, 286, 303.
71. *OAG*, July 1895.
72. *MRJ*, May 1902.
73. *OAG*, Oct. 1904.
74. *MRJ*, May 1904.
75. *MRJ*, Mar. 1901.
76. *OAG*, Feb. 1900.

Chapter VIII

1. *MRJ*, Mar. 1901.
2. *MRJ*, Apr. 1901.
3. Hobsbawm, Ch. 10 Wrigley, 106–8.
4. Hunt, 263–4.
5. Brown, *London*, 229–30.
6. *OAG*, Oct. 1900.
7. *MRJ*, Jan. 1905.
8. *Farmer papers* 67/29. Labour Party Annual Conference Reports give 3,600 for 1901 and 4,000 for 1902. Presumably these are over-estimates. The 1903 figure drops to 3,247.
9. *MRJ*, Aug. 1914.
10. *MRJ*, Apr. 1901.
11. *MRJ*, May 1901.
12. *Theatrical Employees' Journal*, Jan. 1905.
13. *MRJ*, Apr. 1901.
14. *MRJ*, Dec. 1901.
15. *MRJ*, Aug. 1901.
16. *MRJ*, Mar. 1903.
17. Brown, 'Trade Unions and the Law', in Wrigley, 126–31.
18. Askwith, 106.
19. Askwith, 105–6.
20. There are no adequate biographies. See *DNB*; obituaries in *The Times*, 26 Nov. 1912 (Moss) and 10 Jan. 1942 (Stoll); and 'A Napoleon of Entertainers' in *Daily Mail*, 5 July 1902.
21. Coburn, 157–73.
22. 'The History of the Music-Hall War', *The Stage Year Book*, 1908, 57.
23. Press Association Report, *Belfast News Letter*, 23 Jan. 1907.
24. *Concert Artistes' Journal*, Feb. and Mar. 1907.
25. *Daily Express*, 23 Jan. 1907.
26. *Morning Post*, 23 Jan. 1907.
27. *Punch*, 30 Jan. 1907.
28. *The Times*, 25 Jan. 1907.
29. Ibid., 26 Jan. 1907.
30. Ibid., 28 and 29 Jan.; 1, 2 and 4 Jan. 1907.
31. *Daily Telegraph*, 25 Jan. 1907.
32. *Daily Express*, 31 Jan. 1907.
33. *Daily Telegraph*, 25 Jan. 1907.
34. *Stage Year Book*, 1908, 61.
35. Halévy, 106–7.

36. *Arbitration*, 45.
37. Ibid. 38.
38. Ibid. 223.
39. Ibid. 218.
40. Ibid. 62.
41. Ibid. 90–1.
42. Ibid. 72–83.
43. Ibid. 106–7.
44. Mays.
45. *Arbitration*, 111–13.
46. Ibid. 114–15.
47. Ibid. 150.
48. Ibid. 227.
49. Ibid. 185–90.
50. Nettel, *Orchestra*, 252–3.
51. *Arbitration*, 191–2.
52. Ibid. 132.
53. Ibid. 271–3.
54. Ibid. 263–4.
55. Ibid. 257–63.
56. The New Symphony Orchestra, like the LSO, was a players' co-operative, established in 1905.
57. *Arbitration*, 234–40.
58. Ibid. 246–8.
59. See p. 174.
60. *Arbitration*, 353.
61. *MRJ*, Mar. 1903.
62. *Arbitration*, 353.
63. For comparative incomes see Routh, 60, 99–112.
64. Routh, 134–5; Stedman Jones, 326; Mitchell and Deane, 344–5.
65. Phelps Brown, 336.
66. *Stage Year Book*, 1908, 60–8.
67. Ibid. 66.
68. *MRJ*, Aug. 1907.
69. Askwith, 103–4.
70. 'Sixty Years in Brief' (n.d. *c.*1953) *Farmer Papers*, 67/33.
71. 'Arbitrator's Award: Musicians and Employees', *The Era, Supplement*, 15 June 1907.
72. Coburn, 120.
73. Davison, 56, 241, 331, 336.
74. *MRJ*, Aug. 1911.
75. Prospectus in *Farmer Papers*, 79/1 (n.d. *c.*1910). Cf. *Who's Who in Music* (1915) 366.
76. *TUC Parliamentary Committee Reports* 16 Aug. 1911.

77. Ehrlich, *Piano*, 170.
78. *MRJ*, Sept. and Oct. 1911.
79. *MRJ*, Mar. 1912.
80. *MRJ*, June, Nov., Dec. 1913, and Aug. 1914.
81. *TUC Parliamentary Committee Reports*, 14 Apr. and 20 Nov. 1912; *Minutes*, 7 Apr. and 14 May 1914. *MRJ*, Apr., May, June 1914. Cf. Webb, 606.
82. *Farmer Papers*, 79/1.
83. Correspondence of Askwith, Williams, Orcherton, and Stoll, in *MRJ*, Aug. 1914.
84. *MRJ*, June, July 1914.
85. *MRJ*, July 1915.

Chapter IX

1. Corder, *History*, 6.
2. Evans.
3. Ehrlich, *The Piano*, 171–3.
4. Goossens, 110.
5. *MRJ*, Nov. 1913. *Who's Who in Music* (1915), 245.
6. Wood, 294.
7. *MRJ*, July 1915.
8. *MRJ*, Oct. 1915.
9. *MRJ*, Nov. 1914.
10. *MRJ*, Dec. 1915.
11. *MRJ*, Apr. 1916.
12. *TUC Parliamentary Committee Reports*, *2 Sept. 1914, 10 Mar. 1915.*
13. *MRJ*, Jan. 1918.
14. See Marwick, *Deluge*, Ch. III.
15. See p. 158.
16. *MRJ*, June 1916.
17. *MRJ*, Aug. 1916.
18. *MRJ*, Jan. 1916.
19. *MRJ*, May 1916.
20. *MRJ*, Dec. 1916.
21. *MRJ*, Aug. 1915.
22. *MRJ*, Apr. 1916.
23. Agreement: Moss Empires and Frederick Lees (Archives: Birmingham).
24. *MRJ*, Oct. 1917.
25. Gelatt, 196.
26. Quoted in Marwick, *Deluge*, 154.
27. Beecham, 152.
28. Warrack, 282.
29. *MT*, 1 June 1922.

30. *MS*, Oct. 1921.
31. Sampson, M. J., *Gold Coast Men of Affairs Past and Present* (1937).
32. Scholes, *Mirror*, 724–6.
33. *ISMR*, Feb. 1925.
34. *MT*, Feb. 1930. Scholes, *Mirror*, 725.
35. *MS*, Jan. 1921, Apr. 1921.
36. League of Nations, *Les Conditions*, ii. 21–2.
37. *MS*, Apr. 1921. Cf. Proctor, Appendix B, 'Diplomas'.
38. Bohan, 21.
39. See p. 129.
40. Routh, 111.
41. *MS*, July 1920.
42. *MS*, May 1921. *MNH*, 4 Feb. 1922.
43. *MRJ*, Aug. 1921.
44. Quoted in *MRJ*.
45. *MRJ*, Nov. 1920.
46. *MRJ*, Apr. 1931.
47. Chaplin, 105.
48. PEP, *Film*, 25.
49. Ibid. 33–4.
50. London, 27. Cf. Palmer on 'Film Music' in *Grove VI*.
51. Wenden, 39.
52. Jackson, 13.
53. Ibid. 13–14.
54. Blades, 75–6.
55. *TC*, 31 Dec. 1914; *Bioscope*, 13 Jan. 1916.
56. *MRJ*, Sept. 1913, July 1914.
57. *TC*, 3 Jan., 31 Jan. 1918.
58. *Bioscope*, 13 Jan. 1916.
59. PEP, 38.
60. Goossens.
61. *MMM*, May 1926.
62. Jackson, 13. Blades, 75–6.
63. William Alwyn, quoted Manvell and Huntley, 23.
64. *MRJ*, Aug. 1921.
65. *MRJ*, May 1918.
66. Winkler.
67. *Cinema News*, 24 Sept. 1914.
68. Heinsheimer, 192–6.
69. *MMM*, Aug. 1924.
70. National Council, lxx, lxxi.
71. *Music Trade*, Apr. 1918.
72. Jackson, 28–9.
73. Godfrey, 235.
74. Evans.

75. League of Nations, ii. 24.
76. Evans.
77. *MM*, March 1929.
78. *MMM*, Oct. 1922, Sept. 1923, Apr. 1924.
79. *MS*, Oct. 1920.
80. Tootell, 5.
81. *MMM*, Jan. 1927.
82. *KW*, 5 Apr. 1928.
83. Ibid., 26 Apr. 1928.
84. *MB*, July 1920.
85. *MMM*, Feb., May 1924.
86. *MB*, July 1920.
87. *MB*, June 1927.
88. McCarthy, 44.
89. Briggs, *Broadcasting*, i. 278–89.
90. Briggs, *Broadcasting*, ii. 35.
91. *MB*, July 1920.
92. Dr Henry Coward, in *MMR*, Apr. 1926.
93. For contrasting interpretations of the American invasion, see Scholes, *Mirror*, 518–20 and Whitcomb, 79–141.
94. e.g. *MM*, Mar. 1929.
95. Blades, 95.
96. Hughes, 13.
97. Lyttelton.
98. *MM*, Jan. 1929 and subsequent months.
99. Ibid., July 1931.
100. *MB*, June 1927.
101. Ibid.
102. *MB*, Aug. 1927.
103. Advertisements in *MMR*, Mar. 1927.
104. Lyttelton, 118–21.
105. Cf. the supercilious Irving, Ch. xix.
106. League of Nations Report, ii. 24–5, 58.
107. Godfrey, 234–5.
108. Hogarth, 6–7.
109. Ibid. 9, 17–18.

110. Musicians Union, London district branch. *Directory of Members and Price List 1926.*
111. Musicians Union, Manchester, Relaying Rates, 14 Feb. 1927.
112. See p. 178.
113. Farmer papers, 67/124.
114. *MMM*, Oct. 1927.
115. Godfrey, 235.
116. *MMM*, Feb. 1922.
117. *MMM*, Oct. 1923. Cf. Levy.
118. Blades, 120–6.
119. McCarthy, 76.
120. Hamilton Harty Orchestral Concerts, Cash Book and Ledger, 1929–30, Harty Archives.
121. McKenna, 78–90.
122. Goossens, 184.
123. Routh, 60.
124. *MMM*, Oct. 1926.
125. *MMM*, Mar. 1926.
126. *MMM*, Jan. and Feb. 1926.
127. *MMM*, Jan. and Dec. 1928. MO, Jan. 1930.
128. *Morning Post*, quoted in MTR, 15 Dec. 1927.
129. *MB*, June 1927.
130. *MMM*, Sept. 1925 and Apr. 1926.
131. Findlater, Ch. 7.
132. *MMM*, July 1921.
133. *MMM*, Mar. 1921.
134. *Board of Education*, 'Report on the development of adult education through music', quoted in *MMM*, Mar. 1924.
135. Elgar, speech at the London Press Club, quoted in *MMM*, Apr. 1926.
136. Schmitz.
137. *Gramophone*, July 1925.
138. Briggs, *Broadcasting*, i. 244.
139. Teyte.

Chapter X

1. Britten.
2. See Tables I–IV.
3. Routh, 151.
4. Branson and Heinemann, 21.
5. Richardson, 272.
6. Ehrlich, *Piano*, 184–7.

7. *Observer*, 25 Nov. 1934.
8. Baumol, 3–11; Blaug, 13–22.
9. *MM*, Dec. 1930.
10. Leiter, 70–4.
11. See twenty articles on 'Famous Restaurant Players' in *The Strad* (1929–30).

12. Briggs, *Broadcasting*, ii. 253.
13. Peacock and Weir, 81.
14. See p. 67.
15. Minihan, 207.
16. *MRJ*, Oct. 1929; July 1930.
17. *MRJ*, Jan. 1930.
18. *MRJ*, June 1930.
19. *MRJ*, Oct. 1931.
20. 'Stan Brunton' (Farmer), in *MRJ*, Jan. 1932.
21. *MRJ*, Apr. 1931.
22. *MRJ*, July 1932.
23. *MRJ*, July 1931.
24. *MRJ*, Jan. 1929; *MRJ*, Oct. 1929.
25. *MRJ*, July 1930.
26. *MRJ*, July 1932.
27. *MRJ*, Apr. 1931.
28. *MRJ*, Oct. 1929.
29. Commons.
30. Eisler, 46–7.
31. *MRJ*, Oct. 1929.
32. *MRJ*, July 1930.
33. *Sackbut*, xi, 1930–1.
34. *Musicians Union* 'Reorganization: Facts and figures that every member should know' (*c*.Apr. 1931) *Farmer Papers* 67/27.
35. *Farmer Papers*, 67/28. Teale's obituary is in *MRJ*, Apr. 1931.
36. *MM*, Feb. 1931.
37. Kenyon.
38. Ibid. 41–52; Greer, D. *Harty*.
39. Elkin, 117–21; Nettel, *Orchestra*, 281–4. Russell, *Decade*.
40. Kenyon, 102–3.
41. *MM*, June 1929.
42. *Farmer Papers*, 68/35.
43. *MM*, Sept. 1930.
44. Payne, 34–50.
45. Maschwitz, quoted in Briggs, *Broadcasting*, ii. 114.
46. *MM*, Sept. 1930.
47. *MM*, Nov. 1929.
48. Hylton, in *MM*, Sept. 1930.
49. *MRJ*, Jan. 1931.
50. Fox.
51. *MM*, Dec. 1930.
52. *MM*, Nov. 1930.
53. *MRJ*, July 1931.
54. *MRJ*, Apr. 1931.
55. *MRJ*, Jan. 1932.

56. TUC Annual Reports, (1929–34). Its low tide was probably 7,000. See PEP, *Arts*, 199.
57. See critical remarks in *MRJ*, Oct. 1929; Feb. and Mar. 1930; July 1931.
58. *TUC Annual Report*, 1950.
59. *The Times*, 28 May 1975.
60. Hart, 565.
61. Leiter, 52.
62. Ibid., 132–41.
63. Ibid., 146.
64. Ibid., 67.
65. Peacock and Weir, 116, 135, 156; Kenyon, 321.
66. See agreement between BBC and MU, 27 May 1946, in Birmingham Public Library.
67. *The Times*, 28 May 1975. Cf. Dambman's notes on rates, agreements, etc. (1939 and 1943) in Birmingham Public Library.
68. *The Times*, 28 May 1975.
69. Carr Saunders, 402.
70. See correspondence in *The Times*, 15 Nov.; and *Spectator*, Nov. and Dec. 1979.
71. *AMJ*, Nov. 1935.
72. Bohan, 22.
73. *AMJ*, Jan. and Feb. 1931.
74. *AMJ*, Feb. 1931.
75. *AMJ*, Feb. 1936.
76. 'Musicians and the Crisis', MT, Dec. 1931.
77. *The Times*, 16 Dec. 1931.
78. Ibid., 18 Dec. 1931.
79. Ibid., 19 Dec. 1931.
80. Ibid., 21, 23 Dec. 1931; and 5, 15, 21 Jan. 1932.
81. Ibid., 4 Jan. 1932.
82. Samuel, in *The Times*, 31 Dec. 1931; Tovey, in Grierson, 265–7.
83. Public Records Office. *Lab 2.* 1189, ETAR 9494, 1931 (International Artists).
84. Schonberg, 336, 381.
85. *MRJ*, Jan. 1932.
86. *AMJ*, May 1939.
87. *AMJ*, Nov. 1935. Cf. Dec. 1937; Feb., May 1938; and various references in PRO *Lab 2.* 1188–9.

88. *AMJ*, Nov. 1938.
89. *AMJ*, Feb. 1939.
90. Briggs, *Broadcasting*, ii. 490–2; Kenyon, 110–15.
91. Anderson, *Music*, 157–63.
92. Dyson, in *AMJ*, Nov. 1933.
93. See pp. 108–9.
94. *Musical Mirror and Fanfare*, June 1933.
95. PEP, *Arts*, 192.
96. Tillis, 8–10, 18. Snowman, 28–30.
97. Russell, *Project*, 147.
98. Barty King, 39, 97.
99. 'Music as a Profession', in *MB*, 111–23.
100. Marwick, *British Society*, 86.
101. Mackerness, 267.
102. Neel, 50–2.
103. Cf. Taylor, 'Self-help', and Small.
104. Schwarzkopf, 90–106.
105. Nissel, 47. Peacock, 'Public Patronage'.
106. Examples of the former are too common to need citation; for the latter, see Rump, particularly 126–33.
107. Dyson, 85–7.
108. See p. 113.

109. Peacock, *Orchestral Resources*.
110. Kenyon, 431–4.
111. PEP, *Arts*, 182.
112. Dyson, 73.
113. Long, 148–58.
114. Gulbenkian, *Making*.
115. Ibid.
116. Gulbenkian, *Training*, 7–8.
117. Gulbenkian, *Making*, 45.
118. Vulliamy in Shepherd, 179–232. Small, particularly chapters 8 and 9.
119. Gulbenkian, *Training*, 7.
120. *Sunday Times*, 2 Oct. 1977. Letter from Sybil Merrick about her distinguished husband's lifetime emoluments: *Sunday Times*, 9 Oct. 1977.
121. *The Times*, 19 Sept. 1977.
122. Cf. recordings under Boulez of *La Mer* and *The Rite of Spring*.
123. Russell, *Project*, 147.
124. Dyson, 64–5.
125. Nissel, 49–57, 91. On composers see Rump, 234–58.
126. Nissel, 126.
127. *MRJ*, Nov. 1912.
128. UK Council.

Bibliography

All titles listed were published in London except where otherwise stated.

ABBREVIATIONS

AMJ	*A Music Journal* (Incorporated Society of Musicians)
BBM	*British Bandsman* (later *British Musician*)
ISMR	*Periodical Report* (later *Monthly Report*) (Incorporated Society of Musicians)
KW	*Kinematograph Weekly*
MB	*Music Box*
MM	*Melody Maker*
MMM	*Monthly Musical Mirror*
MMR	*Monthly Musical Record*
MNH	*Musical News (and Herald)*
MO	*Musical Opinion*
MOJ	*Monthly Journal* (Incorporated Society of Musicians)
MRJ	*Monthly Report and Journal* (later *Musicians' Journal*) (Amalgamated Musicians' Union)
MS	*Music Student*
MT	*Musical Times*
MTR	*London and Provincial Music Trades' Review*
MW	*Musical World*
OAG	*Orchestral Association Gazette*
QMMR	*Quarterly Musical Magazine and Review*
TC	*The Cinema*
TCAG	*Academic Gazette* (Trinity College, London)

ARCHIVES

Agreement, Moss Empires and Frederick Lees (n.d.).

Arbitration in Regard to the Music Hall Dispute: Minutes of Proceedings (1907): Birmingham Public Library.

Crotch papers, in A. H. Mann Collections: Norfolk Record Office.

Farmer Papers: Glasgow University.

Harty Archives: Queen's University, Belfast.

W. M. Ingall papers (1895): see May and May catalogue 117, Nov., 1983.

Liverpool Philharmonic Society Archives: Liverpool Public Library.

A. H. Mann Papers: King's College, Cambridge.

Philharmonic Society Archives.

Sir George Smart papers: British Library.

R. J. S. Stevens papers: Pendlebury Library, Cambridge University.

BOOKS, ARTICLES, REPORTS, AND PAMPHLETS

Anderson, E. (ed.), *The Letters of Mozart and his Family*, 2nd edn. (1976).
Anderson, W. R., *Music as a Career* (1939).
Anderton, H. O., *Granville Bantock* (1915).
Anon, *A General Description of the Trades . . . by which Parents . . . may with greater Ease and Certainty, make choice of Trades* (1747).
Archenholtz, J. von, *A Picture of England* (Dublin, 1791).
Archer, R. L. *Secondary Education in the Nineteenth Century* (1966).
Askwith, Lord, *Industrial Problems and Disputes* (1920).
Auer, L., *Violin playing as I teach it* (1921).
Bache, C., *Brother Musicians: Reminiscences of Edward and Walter Bache* (1901).
Bailey, P., *Leisure and Class in Victorian England* (1978).
Baines, D., 'Labour Supply and the Labour Market', in Floyd, R. C., and McClosky, D. N., *The Economic History of Britain*, vol. ii (1981).
Baker, C. H. C., and M. I., *The Life and Circumstances of James Brydges First Duke of Chandos, Patron of the Liberal Arts* (1949).
Baker, M., *The Rise of the Victorian Actor* (1978).
Barty-King, H., *G.S.M.D.: A Hundred Years' Performance* (1980).
Baumol, W. J., and Bowen, W. G., *Performing Arts: The Economic Dilemma* (1966).
Beecham, T., *A Mingled Chime* (1944).
Benas, B. J., 'Merseyside Orchestras', in *Transactions of the Historical Society of Lancashire and Cheshire*, 95 (1942).
Berlioz, H., *A Selection from his Letters* (ed. and tr. Searle, H., 1966).
—— (tr. Cairns), *Memoirs* (1969).
Best, G., *Mid-Victorian Britain* (1971).
Binns, P. L., *A Hundred Years of Military Music* (1959).
Blacking, J., *How Musical is Man?* (1973).
Blades, J., *Drum Roll* (1977).
Blaug, M. (ed.), *The Economics of the Arts* (1976).
Boase, F., *Modern English Biography* (1965).
Bohan, E., *The Incorporated Society of Musicians: The First Hundred Years* (1982).
Bonython, F., *King Cole: A Picture Portrait of Sir Henry Cole, KCB, 1808–1882* (1982).
Booth, M. R., 'Spectacle as Production Style on the Victorian Stage', *Theatre Quarterly*, viii. 32 (1979).
Bor, M., and Clelland, L., *Still the Lark: A Biography of Elizabeth Linley* (1962).
Boydell, B., 'The Dublin Musical Scene 1749–50 and its Background', *Proceedings of the Royal Musical Association*. 105 (1978–9), 77–83.
—— (ed.), *Four Centuries of Music in Ireland* (1979).
Branson, N. and Heinemann, M., *Britain in the 1930s* (1971).
Briggs, A., *The History of Broadcasting in the United Kingdom*, vol. i. *The Birth of Broadcasting* (1961); vol. ii. *The Golden Age of Wireless* (1965).
—— *Mass Entertainment: The Origins of a Modern Industry* (Adelaide, 1960).
Britten, B., *On receiving the First Aspen Award* (1964).
Brown, J. D., and Stratton, S. S., *British National Biography: A Dictionary of*

Musical Artists, Authors and Composers born in Britain and its Colonies (1897).

Brown, K. D., *The English Labour Movement* (Dublin, 1982).

—— 'London and the Historical Reputation of John Burns', *London Journal*, Nov. 1976.

Bunn, A., *The Stage: Both before and behind the Curtain* (1840).

Burghersh, Lord, *Correspondence 1808–40* (1840).

Burney, C., *An Account of the Musical Performances in Westminster Abbey and the Pantheon . . . 1784 in Commemoration of Handel* (1785).

—— *A General History of Music* (1935).

—— *Music, Men and Manners in France and Italy 1770* (1974).

Burney, F., *Memoirs of Dr. Burney, by his Daughter Madame D'Arblay* (1832).

Bushnell, H., *Maria Malibran* (Pennsylvania, 1979).

Camden, A., *Blow by Blow: The Memoirs of a Musical Rogue and Vagabond* (1982).

Campbell, R., *The London Tradesman, being a compendious view of All the Trades . . . calculated for the information of PARENTS and instruction of YOUTH in their choice of Business* (1747).

'Carl Volti', *Reminiscences and Verses* (Glasgow, *c.* 1910).

Carr-Saunders, A. M., and Wilson, P. A., *The Professions* (1933).

Carse, A., *The life of Jullien* (1951).

—— *The Orchestra in the Eighteenth Century* (Cambridge, 1940).

Chadfield, E., *National Musical Associations* (Derby, 1890).

Chaplin, C., *My Autobiography* (1964).

Chissell, J., *Clara Schumann* (1983).

Coborn, C., *The Man who Broke the Bank: Memoirs of the Stage and Music Hall* (1929).

Cohen, A. I., *International Encyclopaedia of Women Composers* (New York, 1981).

Colles, H. C., *Oxford History of Music*, vol, vii (Oxford, 1934).

—— and Cruft, J., *The Royal College of Music: A Centenary Record 1883–1983* (1982).

Collyer, J., *The Parent's and Guardian's Directory and the Youth's Guide in the Choice of a Profession or Trade (1761)*.

Commons, J. R., *Types of 'American Labor Unions'*, *Quarterly Journal of Economics*, 20 (1906).

Cooper, M., *Beethoven: The Last Decade, 1817–1827* (Oxford, 1970).

Corder, F., *A History of the Royal Academy of Music from 1822 to 1922* (1922).

—— *Royal Academy of Music Centenary Souvenir* (1922).

Corfield, P. J., *Towns, Trade, Religion and Radicalism: The Norwich Perspective on English History* (Norwich, 1980).

Courcy, G. I. C. de, *Paganini the Genoese* (Oklahoma, 1957).

Cox, H. B., and C. L. E., *Leaves from the Journals of Sir George Smart* (1907).

Cox, J. E., *Musical Recollections of the Last Half Century* (1872).

Crewdson, H. A. F., *The Worshipful Company of Musicians: A Short History* (1971)

Cudworth, C., 'An Eighteenth-Century Musical Apprenticeship', *Musical Times*, 108 (1967), 602.

—— 'R. J. S. Stevens 1757–1837' *Musical Times*, 103 (1962), 754, 834.

Cunningham, Hugh, *Leisure in the Industrial Revolution,* (1980).

Davidson, H., *From Mendelssohn to Wagner: The Memoirs of J. W. Davison, compiled by his son* (1912).

Dawe, D., *Organists of the City of London, 1666–1850* (1983).

Dean, Winton, *Handel's Dramatic Oratorios and Masques* (1959).

Dibdin, C., *The Musical Tour of Mr Dibdin* (Sheffield, 1788).

—— *The Professional Life of Mr Dibdin* (1803).

Dictionary of National Biography.

Doane, J., *A Musical Directory for the Year 1794.*

Drummond, P., 'The Royal Society of Musicians in the Eighteenth Century', *Music and Letters*, July 1978.

Duman, D., *The English and Colonial Bars in the Nineteenth Century* (1983).

Dyos, H. J., *Victorian Suburb* (1973).

Dyson, G., *Fiddling While Rome Burns: A Musician's Apology* (1954).

Ehrlich, C., 'Economic History and Music', *Proceedings of the Royal Musical Association*, 103 (1976–7), 188–99.

—— *The Piano: A History* (1976).

—— *Social Emulation and Industrial Progress:—The Victorian Piano* (Belfast, 1975).

Einstein, A., *Mozart: His Character, His Work* (1946).

Eisler, H., *Composing for the Films* (1947).

Elbourne, R., *Music and Tradition in Early Industrial Lancashire, 1780–1840* (Woodbridge, Suffolk, 1980).

Elkin, R., *Royal Philharmonic* (1947).

Ella, J., *Musical Sketches, Abroad and at Home* (3rd edn., 1878).

Escott, T. H., *England: Its People, Polity and Pursuits* (1885).

Evans, E., 'Music and the Cinema', *Music and Letters*, Jan. 1929.

Farmer, H. G., *History of the Royal Artillery Band 1762–1953* (1954).

Fawcett, T., *Music in Eighteenth-Century Norwich and Norfolk* (Norwich, 1979).

—— *The Rise of English Provincial Art* (Oxford, 1974).

Fellowes, E. H., *Memoirs Of An Amateur Musician* (1946).

Findlater, R., *Lilian Baylis, The Lady of the Old Vic* (1975).

Fisher, H., *The Musical Profession* (1888).

Fiske, R., *English Theatre Music in the Eighteenth Century* (1973).

Fleming, F., *The Life and Extraordinary Adventures, The Perils and Critical Escapes of Timothy Ginnadrake, That Child of Chequer'd Fortune* (Bath, 1771).

Foster, M. B., *The History of the Philharmonic Society of London, 1813–1912* (1912).

Fox, R., *Hollywood, Mayfair, and all that Jazz* (1975).

Freidson, E., *The Profession of Medicine* (New York, 1975).

Fuller-Maitland, J. A., *A Door-Keeper of Music* (1929).

Galton, F., *Hereditary Genius: An Inquiry into its Causes and Consequences* (1914).

Gane, M. J., 'Social changes in English Music and Music Making 1800–1870, with Special Reference to the Symphony Orchestra' (London Ph.D., 1972).

Ganz, W., *Memories of a Musician* (1913).

Gardiner, W., *Music and Friends* (1838).

Gelatt, R., *The Fabulous Phonograph 1877–1977* (1977).

George, M. D., *London Life in the Eighteenth Century* (1925).

Gerig, R. R., *Famous Pianists and their Technique* (1976).

Godfrey, D., *Memories and Music: Thirty-five Years of Conducting* (1924).

Goldsmith, O., *The Life of Richard Nash of Bath* (1762).

Goossens, E., *Overture and Beginners* (1951).

Green, E., *Thomas Linley: His Connection with Bath* (Bath, 1903).

Greer, D. (ed.), *Hamilton Harty* (Belfast, 1978).

Greer, G., *The Obstacle Race* (1979).

Grierson, M., *Donald Francis Tovey* (1952).

Grove, G., *A Short History of Cheap Music* (1887).

Grove's Dictionary of Music and Musicians. The following editions have been used: 'Grove I' (1879–89); 'Grove IV' (1940); 'Grove V' (1954); 'Grove VI' (The New Grove, 1980).

Gulbenkian Foundation, *Making Musicians* (1965).

—— *Training Musicians* (1978).

Gye's Bath Dictionary (1819/1826).

Halévy, E., *History of the English People in the Nineteenth Century*, vol. vi. *The Rule of Democracy, 1905–1914* (1934).

Hallé, C., *The Life and Letters of Sir Charles Hallé* (1896).

Hamburger, M. (ed.), *Beethoven: Letters, Journals and Conversations* (1957).

Hargrave, E., 'Musical Leeds in the Eighteenth Century', *Thoresby Society*, 28 (1928), 320–55.

Harley, J., *Music in Purcell's London* (1968).

Harrison, B., *Separate Spheres: The Opposition to Women's Suffrage in Britain* (1978).

Harrison, S., *Musical Box* (1940).

Hart, P., *Orpheus in the New World* (New York, 1973).

Haskell, F., *Patrons and Painters* (1980).

Haweis, H. R., *Music and Morals* (twentieth impression, 1903).

Hawkins, J. A., *A General History of the Science and Practice of Music* (1776).

Heinsheimer, H. W., *Menagerie in F sharp* (1949).

Highfill, P. H., Burnim, K. A., and Langhans, E. A., *A Biographical Dictionary of Actors, Actresses, Musicians . . . in London, 1660–1800*, 8 vols. (Carbondale, 1973–82.)

Hobsbawm, E. J., *Labouring Men* (1964).

Hogarth, B., *Music as a Profession* (Manchester, 1925).

Holmes, E., *The Life of Mozart* (1845).

Holmes, G., *Augustan England: Professions, State and Society, 1680–1730* (1982).

Howes, F., *The English Musical Renaissance* (1966).

Howson, J. S. (ed.), *Essays on Cathedrals* (1872).

Hughes, C. W., *The Human Side of Music* (New York, 1948).

Hughes, S., *Second Movement* (1951).

Humphries, C., and Smith, W. C., *Music Publishing in the British Isles* (Oxford, 1970).

Hunt, E. H., *British Labour History 1815–1914* (1981).

Hurd, M., *Vincent Novello and Company* (1981).

Irving, E., *Cue for Music* (1959).

Ivimey, J. W., *Boys and Music* (1936).

Jackson, G. (ed. Simmons, D.), *First Flute* (1968).

Jevons, W. S., *Amusements of the People* (1878).
—— *Methods of Social Reform* (1883).
Johnson, D., *Music and Society in Lowland Scotland in the Eighteenth Century* (1972).
Kassler, J. C., *The Science of Music in Britain, 1714–1830* (1979).
Kennedy, M., *The History of the Royal Manchester College of Music* (Manchester, 1971).
—— *Portrait of Elgar* (1968).
Kent, G., *A View from the Bandstand* (1983).
Kenyon, N., *The BBC Symphony Orchestra: The First Fifty Years 1930–1980* (1981).
Klein, H., *Thirty Years of Musical Life in London, 1870–1900* (1903).
Kuhe, W., *My Musical Recollections* (1896).
Lamb, Andrew, 'Music of the Romantic Theatre', in Temperley, N. (ed.), *The Athlone History of Music in Britain: The Romantic Age 1800–1914* (1981).
Landon, H. C. Robbins, *Haydn in England 1791–1795* (1976).
Lang, P. H., *Music in Western Civilization* (1942).
Lasocki, D., 'Professional Recorder Playing in England During the Baroque Era' (typescript, 1979).
League of Nations, *Les Conditions de vie et de travail des musiciens* (William Martin, Geneva, 1923).
Leiter, R. D., *The Musicians and Petrillo* (New York, 1953).
Levy, L., *Music for the Movies* (1948).
Limbaches, J., *Film Music: From Violins to Video* (N. Jersey, 1974).
Loft, A., 'Musicians' Guild and Union: A Consideration of the Evolution of Protective Organization Among Musicians' (Columbia Ph.D., 1950).
London, K., *Film Music* (1936).
Long, N., *Music in English Education* (1959).
Lonsdale, R., *Dr. Charles Burney: A Literary Biography* (Oxford, 1965).
Lyttelton, H., *I Play as I Please* (1954).
McCarthy, A., *The Dance Band Era* (1971).
McClure, J., *Coram's Children: The London Foundling Hospital in the Eighteenth Century* (Yale, 1981).
MacFarren, G. A., *Addresses and Lectures* (1888).
MacFarren, W., *Memories: An Autobiography* (1905).
McKendrick, N., Brewer, J., and Plumb, J. H., *The Birth of a Consumer Society* (1982).
McKenna, M., *Myra Hess: A Portrait* (1976).
Mackerness, E. D., *A Social History of English Music* (1964).
McVeigh, S., 'Felice Giardini: A violinist in Late Eighteenth Century London' *Music and Letters*, Oct. 1983.
Manvell, R., and Huntley, J., *The Technique of Film Music* (1975).
Mapleson, J. H. (ed. Rosenthal), *The Mapleson Memoirs, 1858–1888* (1966).
Marr, R. A., *Music and Musicians at the Edinburgh International Exhibition, 1886* (Edinburgh, 1887).
Marwick, A., *British Society since 1945* (1982).
—— *The Deluge* (1965).

Maurice, P., *What Shall we Do with Music? A letter to the Rt. Hon. Earl of Derby, Chancellor of the University of Oxford* (Oxford, 1856).

Maynard, W., *The Enterprising Impresario* (1867).

Mays, S., *The Band Rats* (1975).

Miller, Geoffrey, *The Bournemouth Symphony Orchestra* (Sherbourne, Dorset, 1970).

Milligan, T. B., *The Concerto and London's Musical Culture in the late eighteenth Century* (Ann Arbor, 1983).

Minihan, J., *The Nationalization of Culture* (1977).

Mitchell, B. R., and Deane, P., *Abstract of British Historical Statistics* (Cambridge, 1962).

Money, J., *Experience and Identity: Birmingham and the West Midlands, 1760–1800* (Manchester, 1977).

Morris, R. J., 'Middle Class Culture, 1700–1914' in D. Fraser (ed.), *History of Modern Leeds*.

Mortimer, *The Universal Director; or the Nobleman and Gentleman's True Guide to the Masters and Professors of the Liberal and Polite Arts and Sciences . . . by Mr Mortimer* (1763).

Mount-Edgcumbe, R., 2nd Earl of, *Musical Reminiscences* (1834).

Music in England. The Proposed Royal College of Music: Three Addresses at the Free Trade Hall, Manchester (1882).

Musical Directory (Reeves/Rudall Carte) (1880–   ).

National Council of Public Morals, *The Cinema: Its Present Position and Future Possibilities* (1917)

Neel, B., *The Story of an Orchestra* (1950).

Nettel, R., *Havergal Brian: The Man and his Music* (1976).

—— *The Orchestra in England* (1946).

Neuls-Bates, C., *Women in Music* (New York, 1982).

Nicoll, J. R. A., *A History of Late Eighteenth Century Drama 1750–1800* (Cambridge, 1927).

Nissel, M. (ed.), *Facts About The Arts: A Summary of Available Statistics* (1983).

Norris, G., *Stanford, the Cambridge Jubilee and Tchaikovsky* (1980).

Parke, W. T., *Musical Memoirs: An account of the General State of Music in England from the First Commemoration of Handel in 1784, to the Year 1830* (1830).

Parker, S. I., *Horatio Parker: A Memoir* (New York, 1942).

Payne, J., *Signature Tune* (1947).

Peacock, A., *Orchestral Resources in Great Britain* (Arts Council, 1970).

—— 'Public Patronage and Music: An Economist's View', *Three Banks Review*, 77, (Mar. 1968).

—— and Weir, R., *The Composer in the Market Place* (1975).

Perkin, H., *The Origins of Modern English Society 1780–1880* (1969).

—— 'The Professions in History', *Social History Society Newsletter*, 3. 1 (1978).

PEP, *The Arts Enquiry: Music* (1949).

—— *The British Film Industry* (1932).

—— *Sponsorship of Music: The Role of Local Authorities* (n.d., c.1965).

Peterson, M. J., *The Medical Profession in Mid-Victorian London* (Berkeley, 1978).

Petty, F. C., *Italian Opera in London 1760–1800* (Michigan, 1980).

Phelps Brown, H., *The Growth of British Industrial Relations* (1959).

Phillips, H., *Musical and Personal Recollections during Half a Century* (1864).

Phillips, L. M., 'The Leipzig Conservatory 1843–1881' (Indiana Ph.D., 1979).

Pierre, C., *Le Conservatoire National de Musique* (Paris, 1900).

Piggott, P., *The Life and Music of John Field* (1973).

Pirie, P., *The English Musical Renaissance* (1979).

Pleasants, H. (ed.), *The Musical Journeys of Louis Spohr* (Oklahoma, 1961).

Porter, R., *English Society in the Eighteenth Century* (1982).

Potter, J., *Observations on the Present State of Music and Musicians* (1762).

Pritchard, B. W., 'The Musical Festival and the Choral Society in England in the Eighteenth and Nineteenth Centuries: A Social History' (Birmingham Ph.D., 1968).

Proctor, C., *To Be A Professional Musician* (1951).

Rainbow, B., *The Land Without Music* (1967).

Rennert, J., *William Crotch 1775–1847* (1975).

Report of the Select Committee on Theatres and Places of Entertainment, *Accounts and Committees*, vol. xviii. 1 (1892).

Richardson, H. W., *Economic Recovery in Britain 1932–39* (1967).

Ringer, A. L. (ed.), *Yearbook of the International Folk Music Council* (Illinois, 1971)

Robert-Blunn, J., *Northern Accent: The Life Story of the Northern School of Music* (1972).

Robinson, K. (ed.), *The Arts and Higher Education* (1982).

Rosenfield, S., *The Theatre of the London Fairs in the Eighteenth Century* (1960).

Routh, G., *Occupation and Pay in Great Britain 1906–79* (1980).

Rump, A., *How We Treat Our Composers* (Arts Council, 1979).

Russell, T., *Philharmonic Decade* (1944).

—— *Philharmonic Project* (1952).

Sadie, S., 'Concert Life in Eighteenth Century England', *Proceedings of the Royal Musical Association*, 85 (1958–9).

Sainsbury, J. S., *A Dictionary of Musicians* (1825).

Salaman, C. K., 'On Music as a Profession in England', *Proceedings of the Royal Musical Association*, 6 (1880).

Sands, M., 'Music as a Profession in Eighteenth Century England', *Music and Letters*, 24 (1943).

Schmitz, O. A. H., *The Land Without Music* (tr. Herzl, H., 1925).

Scholes, P., *The Mirror of Music 1844–1944* (1947).

Schonberg, H. C., *The Great Pianists* (1964).

Schwarzkopf, E., *On and Off the Record: A Memoir of Walter Legge* (1982).

Shaw, G. B., *London Music in 1888–9* (1937).

—— *Music in London 1890–94*, 3 vols. (1932).

—— *Our Theatres in the Nineties* (3 vols., 1932).

Shepherd, J., Virden, P., Vulliamy, G., Wishart, T., *Whose Music? A Sociology of Musical Languages* (1977).

Small, C., *Music—Society—Education* (1977).

Smith, M. B., 'The Growth and Development of Popular Entertainment and Pastimes in the Lancashire Cotton Towns 1830–70' (Lancaster M.Litt., 1970).

Snowman, D., *The Amadeus Quartet: The Men and the Music* (1981).

Society for the Encouragement of Arts, Manufacturers, and Commerce, *First Report of the Committee . . . on the State of Musical Education at Home and Abroad* (1866).

Spark, F. R., and Bennett, J., *History of the Leeds Musical Festivals* (1892).

Spark, W., *Musical Reminiscences: Past and Present* (1892).

Stanford, C. V., *Studies and Memories* (1908).

—— *Pages from an Unwritten Diary* (1914).

Stedman Jones, G., *Outcast London* (1971).

—— 'Working-class Culture and Working-class Politics in London, 1870–1900', *Journal of Social History*, 7 (1974).

Stone, L., *The Past and The Present* (1981).

Sutcliffe Smith, J., *The Story of Music in Birmingham* (Birmingham, 1945).

Taylor, A. M., *Labour and Love: An Oral History of the Brass Band Movement* (1983).

Taylor, J., 'From Self-help to Glamour: The Working Man's Club 1860–1972' (History Workshop Pamphlet, 1972).

Taylor, Stainton de B., *Two Centuries of Music in Liverpool* (Liverpool, 1976).

Temperley, N. (ed.), *The Romantic Age 1800–1914 (Athlone History of Music in Britain*, vol. v, 1981).

Teyte, M., *Star on the Door* (1958).

Thompson, F. M. L., *Chartered Surveyors: The Growth of a Profession* (1968).

Thomson, H. B., *The Choice of a Profession: A Concise Account and Comparative Review of the English Professions* (1857).

Tillis, M., *Chords and Discords: The Life of an Orchestral Musician* (1960).

Tootel, G., *How to Play the Cinema Organ* (1928).

Trend, J. B., 'R. J. Stevens and his Contemporaries', *Music and Letters*, 14 (1933).

Troubridge, St V., *The Benefit System in the British Theatre* (1967).

Trowell, B., 'Daniel Defoe's Plan for an Academy of Music at Christ's Hospital, with some Notes on his Attitude to Music', in I. Bent (ed.), *Source Materials and the Interpretation of Music* (1981).

TUC, *Annual Reports*.

—— *Parliamentary Committee Reports*.

Turner, A. J., *Science and Music in Eighteenth Century Bath* (Bath, 1977).

UK Council for Music Education and Training, *Choosing Your Music Course* (1984).

Union of Graduates in Music: *Roll and Kalendar: The Organists, Precentors, Succentors, Chanters and Choirs at the Cathedrals, Chief College Chapels, Collegiate Foundations and Great Public Schools* (1904).

Vicinus, M., *The Industrial Muse* (1974).

Walker, A., *Franz Liszt: The Virtuoso Years 1811–1847* (1983).

Walker, B. (ed.), *Frank Matcham, Theatre Architect* (Belfast, 1980).

Ware, W. P. and Lockard, T. C., *R. T. Barnum presents Jenny Lind: The American Tour of the Swedish Nightingale* (Louisiana, 1980).

Warrack, G., 'Royal College of Music: The First Eighty-five Years' (typescript in British Library, *c.*1977).

Warrack, J., *Carl Maria von Weber* (1976).

Webb, S. and B., *The History of Trade Unionism* (1920).

Weber, M., *The Protestant Ethic and the Spirit of Capitalism*, tr. T. Parsons (New York, 1958).

Weber, W., *Music and the Middle Classes* (1975).

Wendeborn, G. F. A., *A View of England* (Dublin, 1791).

Wenden, D. J., *The Birth of the Movies* (1974).

Weston, P., *Clarinet Virtuosi of the Past* (1971).

Whitcomb, I., *After the Ball* (1972).

Who's Who in Music ed. Wyndham, H. S., and L'Epine, G. (1913/1915).

Who's Who in Music, ed. Ronald, L. (1935).

Wilkinson, T., *Memoirs of his Own Life* (York, 1790).

Wilson, J. (ed.), *Roger North on Music* (1959).

Winkler, M., 'The Origin of Film Music', in Limbacher, J., *Film Music: From Violins to Video* (New Jersey, 1974).

Wood, H. J., *My Life of Music* (1938).

Woodfield, I., *The Celebrated Quarrel Between Thomas Linley (senior) and William Herschel: An Episode in the Musical Life of Eighteenth Century Bath* (Bath, 1977).

Woodfill, W. L., *Musicians in English Society from Elizabeth to Charles I* (Princeton, 1953).

Wright, J. R. B., *Ignatius Sancho (1729–1780): An Early African Composer in England* (1981).

Wrigley, C. J. (ed.), *A History of British Industrial Relations 1875–1914* (1982).

Young, K., *Music's Great Days in the Spas and Watering-places* (1968).

Young, P. M., *Beethoven: A Victorian Tribute* (1976).

—— *The Concert Tradition* (1965).

—— *George Grove 1820–1900: A Biography* (1980).

Zeldin, T., *France 1848–1945: Ambition and Love* (1979).

Index